To David - one [illegible]!
Our best wishes - Betty + Ed Charr
June, 1979

# THE WRITINGS OF WILL ROGERS

## III-1

SPONSORED BY

The Will Rogers Memorial Commission
and Oklahoma State University

THE WRITINGS OF WILL ROGERS

SERIES I: *Books of Will Rogers*
1 *Ether and Me, or "Just Relax"*
2 *There's Not a Bathing Suit in Russia & Other Bare Facts*
3 *The Illiterate Digest*
4 *The Cowboy Philosopher on The Peace Conference*
5 *The Cowboy Philosopher on Prohibition*
6 *Letters of a Self-Made Diplomat to His President*

SERIES II: *Convention Articles of Will Rogers* (in one volume)

SERIES III: *Daily Telegrams of Will Rogers*
**1 Coolidge Years 1926-1929**
2 *Hoover Years 1929-1931*
3 *Hoover Years 1931-1933*
4 *Roosevelt Years 1933-1935*

SERIES IV: *Weekly Articles of Will Rogers* (in four volumes)

SERIES V: *The Worst Story I've Heard Today* (in one volume)

OTHER VOLUMES TO BE ANNOUNCED

*Will Rogers in newspaper room at Beverly Hills.*

# *Will Rogers'* DAILY TELEGRAMS

JAMES M. SMALLWOOD, *EDITOR*

STEVEN K. GRAGERT, *Assistant Editor*

## *Volume 1*

## *THE COOLIDGE YEARS: 1926-1929*

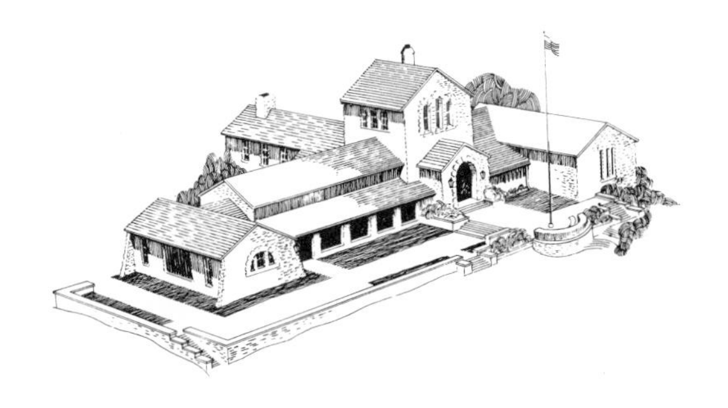

OKLAHOMA STATE UNIVERSITY PRESS
Stillwater, Oklahoma
1978

Appreciation is expressed to Theodore L. Agnew, former editor, for research conducted under his supervision which facilitated the completion of this volume.

Printed in the United States of America
Library of Congress Catalog Card Number 77-091791
International Standard Book Number 0-914956010-8

# CONTENTS



Frontispiece and illustrations
courtesy Will Rogers Memorial,
Claremore, Oklahoma

# INTRODUCTION

From 1926 until his death in 1935, Will Rogers wrote a widely syndicated, daily column which became synonymous with Rogers in the eyes of the American reading public. When he began his "Daily Telegrams," as the articles were known, he had been writing for several years a weekly column for the McNaught Newspaper Syndicate which appeared in such newspapers as the *New York Times, Chicago News, Boston Globe, Kansas City Star, Fort Worth Star-Telegram,* and many others. In 1926 he planned a tour of Europe, but before he left the States he had a chance meeting with Adolph S. Ochs, publisher of the *New York Times.* As the two men talked, Rogers told of his upcoming trip, and Ochs casually said, "If you run across anything worthwhile, cable it to us. We'll pay the tolls."

Rogers and Ochs had met after a banquet, and the publisher's remarks had been brief, almost flippant, but Rogers remembered the conversation when he was in England being entertained by Lady Astor. He sent Ochs a cable which the publisher printed on the front page of the *Times* on July 29, 1926. Other cables were forthcoming, and they immediately captured the attention of the reading public in New York. The stories also impressed Lawrence Winship, feature editor of the *Boston Globe.* When he saw Rogers' first dispatch, Winship telephoned Ochs to ask whether the *Globe* could print the column. The *Times* refused, holding the short cables to be its own, exclusively, despite the fact that Rogers received no money and had no written contract to produce the column.

Will originally had no thought of continuing the telegrams after he returned to the States, but public interest and entreaties from Ochs convinced him to begin a new series. Although he missed a few days in September and October, he continued to write for the *Times.* Meanwhile, Frank Murphy, the treasurer of the McNaught Syndicate, contacted V. V. McNitt, founder of the syndicate, who in turn convinced Rogers to permit them to handle his daily feature through the syndicate. Thus all the papers in the United States could publish the column.

Ninety-two newspapers originally purchased rights to print the Daily Telegrams which began appearing in syndication on October 10, 1926. Soon a host of smaller papers subscribed, bringing the total outlets to approximately 600. Will's royalties rose as more customers subscribed to his series. In 1926 he received a weekly guarantee of $1,700 for his daily and weekly columns. By mid-1930 a new contract guaranteed $2,500 per week.

The logistics of getting Rogers' dispatches to client newspapers proved to be no easy task. Because Will Rogers wrote on contemporary events, speed was of the essence in getting copy to editors and the public. There was little time to devote to polishing his prose. Although the McNaught Syndicate usually edited copy for its writers, Will's editors agreed that they should not tamper with his personal style. "That's the way I write it," Rogers once said, "and that's the way I want it to lay."

After Will wrote his articles, he used the telegraph for delivery because the mail was too slow. Operating without an editor, he sent his dispatches directly to the branch office of Western Union which was located in the *Times* building in New York City. The branch maintained a list of newspapers which should be supplied, and copies of the dispatches quickly were sent around the country. Normally, the process of getting the telegrams to the syndicate was hectic. Will's dispatches had to be filed by 4:00 P.M., California time. He frequently waited until the last moment and grabbed his typewriter to hammer out a story. Despite ever-pressing deadlines, Rogers seldom missed a day in preparing the telegrams. Once, while in a hospital bed awaiting a gallstone operation, he dictated three stories for his column before being carried away. When he was revived after surgery, he immediately penned yet another telegram. Writing from a hospital bed was unusual for Will, but he jotted down his telegrams anytime, anywhere—on an airplane, at a baseball game, at a restaurant, or on a table at a telegraph office.

Although Will occasionally felt the pressure of deadlines, especially while he was touring, his travels help explain the success of the Daily Telegrams. He was a hard working, investigative journalist who posted datelines across the country from Beverly Hills to New York, from Portland to Miami, and around the world. He reported on the news as he saw it happen; well could he comment on famous personalities of his era—he had met, entertained, and interviewed most of them.

Will's personality was another key to his success as a writer. He was a gregarious, friendly man who was at ease in most situations. His easygoing nature emerged on the printed page and helped enliven it. In fact, when he had no current material, he sometimes simply described his day's activities—his travels, friends whom he met, food that he ate—and did so with verve.

The importance of Rogers' daily columns cannot be overemphasized. In an era when radio news coverage was rudimentary and television news unknown, the masses depended almost exclusively on newspapers for information and upon columnists for insight and interpretation. So anxious were people to have information that many publishers found that regular editions did not always satisfy the public's desire to know and know now. Frequently "extras" were released to satisfy this demand. With his timely articles appearing on the front page of most of the major dailies, Will had the power to mold public opinion; he had more power than most other columnists who had to prepare copy two weeks in advance of their publication date and had to use the post for delivery. Yet Rogers never abused his power. His telegrams showed no malice but indicated instead his desire to be fair. Will supported Herbert Hoover early in his presidency, for example, but became more critical after the depression began. However, when several other critics became bitter and vituperative, Rogers gently reminded his readers that the depression was not Hoover's fault and that no one man could cause a national economic catastrophe.

On occasion the McNaught Syndicate became afraid that Rogers' telegrams would be received critically by the public. Once he jibed the United States government for lending the Allies tremendously large amounts of money during World War I. Because it was flooded with protest letters, the *New York Times* editorially apologized for Rogers and disclaimed any responsibility for the opinions expressed in the telegrams. His "feathers" ruffled, Will wrote,

> I would like to state to the readers of the New York Times that I am in no way responsible for the editorial policy of this paper. I allow them free reign as to their opinion, so long as its within the bounds of good subscription gathering. But I want it distinctly understood that their policy may be in direct contrast to mine. Their editorials may be put in purely for humor, or just to fill space. Every paper must have its various entertaining features and not always to be taken seriously, and never to be construed as my policy.

Although Will occasionally might have offended his critics, his work was accepted by most editors with little revision of the original drafts. Yet, a selected textual analysis reveals that slight variations appeared. When some editors saw certain phrases of which they disapproved, they deleted them; others edited references to politics or political personalities; still others "blue-penciled" lines simply for brevity. Because Rogers' work was in some cases slightly altered, our editorial task became more difficult—original copies of the telegrams do not survive. Consequently, we have chosen the best available source for presentation here. In some cases we have followed the *New York Times,* the newspaper which ran most of the articles and which is the most convenient for the use of future researchers. Other newspapers were consulted, however. When textual differences appeared, we attempted to show at least one major variation, selected from among the *Los Angeles Times,* the *Boston Globe,* and the *Kansas City Times,* other newspapers which carried most of the telegrams.

Much of Rogers' humor was of a topical nature, geared to the happenings of his day. He sometimes referred to people and events which are not common knowledge to the present generation. Consequently, endnotes have been used to identify people or explain events which would no longer be widely known. The editors, together with the editorial board and advisory committee of the Will Rogers Project, have decided to delete footnote numbers in the text to avoid needless distractions to the reader. Endnotes to the volume are "keyed" to the numbers of the telegrams and to the dates of their appearance.

This first volume of the Daily Telegrams spans the last years of the administration of Calvin Coolidge from July of 1926, when Rogers first began writing the articles, to March 4, 1929, the inauguration of Herbert Hoover. Following volumes will present the telegrams written during the administrations of Hoover and Franklin D. Roosevelt.

This volume, the first in Series III of *The Writings of Will Rogers,* has required considerable effort on the part of many people. Reba Neighbors Collins, Curator of the Will Rogers Memorial, read the manuscript carefully and offered valuable advice for the notes and introduction. Glenn D. Shirley's designs for the book continue to be a great asset. Will Rogers, Jr., has offered constant encouragement and practical suggestions. Oklahoma State University President Lawrence L. Boger and Robert B. Kamm, immediate past president, have supported the Project and provided encouragement to the editors. Special appreciation also is expressed for the continued support of the Will Rogers Memorial Commission, the Oklahoma State University Regents, administration, and advisory committee, the Oklahoma Historical Society, and the Oklahoma Legislature. The Project also has profited from the work of Dr. Theodore L. Agnew and Dr. Joseph A. Stout, Jr. Professor Agnew, first director of the Project, supervised the original research which enabled the present staff to proceed more rapidly in the editing of this first volume of the Daily Telegrams. Professor Stout served as the second director of the Project and edited the first seven volumes of *The Writings of Will Rogers.* Earlier in the project Kerr-McGee Foundation, Phillips Petroleum Corporation, Mr. and Mrs. Robert W. Love, Mrs. T. S. Loffland, and Mr. Sylvan N. Goldman provided assistance.

THE EDITORS

# PREFACE

As General James "Jimmy" Doolittle tells the story, he was visiting Will Rogers at Twentieth Century Fox Studio. The day's shooting was over, and they were preparing to leave. Rogers said, "Wait a minute. I've got to write my telegram." He went over to a typewriter and in his hunt-and-peck method quickly pounded one out. He gave it to an assistant. He and Doolittle drove off.

As they went through the studio gate headed for the Santa Monica ranch, Doolittle said, "But Will, what if there comes a day when you have no joke or simply nothing to say. What do you do then?"

Doolittle says Rogers looked at him quizzically and replied, "Did you ever read my column?"

Like all writing done against a daily deadline, some of the telegrams in this book are good, some bad, some indifferent, as Will Rogers well knew. Most were written, just as General Doolittle described, right up against the deadline.

The telegrams had to be in New York by 7:00 P.M., which meant 4:00 o'clock in California. I well remember waiting around while Dad struggled over his wire. When done, he would hand it to me, and I would dash for the Santa Monica Western Union office. The staff would be waiting for it, and it was immediately sent to New York.

However, I don't think Will Rogers was ever seriously faced with the problem of having nothing to say. When he had no particular comment on the news of the day, he could always fall back to describing what he was doing. In fact his own activities make up a good part of the columns. Will Rogers was incredibly active. Being able to write about himself relieved him of the pressure of always having to come up with a topical joke.

After Dad's death, several well known humorists tried to write a similar daily column. They were not successful. When I was reading them at the time, I could see why. Except for wisecracks, and often quite good ones, they had nothing to say. A column of just jokes is deadly. Reading these attempts by other hands, I began to realize, for the first time, what made the Will Rogers column so popular and why it was followed, day after day. He, Will Rogers, was the column. People might quote a topical joke, but it was Will Rogers, his active life, his constant travels, his meetings and his humorous descriptions of them, that carried the daily continuity and, in their own time, made these columns required reading.

This is the first of what will be several volumes of the daily telegrams. They are not his best. In these early years he was still unsure of his format. In my view, his columns got better and better as they went along. Also, as with anything tied to the news, his most memorable remarks came out of the most active time. Will Rogers was at his best in the crisis periods of the depression and the intense conflicts of the New Deal. The Coolidge years were comparatively tranquil. Will Rogers had a good summation of it, which might set the tone of this first volume. "It wasn't that Coolidge done nothin'. It was that he did it better than anyone else."

The best things Will Rogers wrote are in these daily wires. While they have always been available at the Will Rogers Memorial Museum at Claremore, they have never before been put in easy-to-use book form. It is my hope that historians, in preparing studies of the 1920s and 1930s, will use the index of these books. If they do they will discover, time and again, just what they need—a penetrating comment, an exact description, precisely pinpointing an event in their specialty. Few people writing in that period had as keen an eye as Will Rogers. Historians will find many a quotable remark that will give salt and flavor to their research.

This is not a book to be read straight through. It is to be skipped about in, picked up from time to time, and, above all, to be used for historical reference.

Will Rogers, Jr.

Beverly Hills, California
November 27, 1977

# DAILY TELEGRAMS

*1926-1929*

# DAILY TELEGRAMS — 1926

## 1 WILL ROGERS, ABROAD, BESPEAKS A WELCOME FOR LADY ASTOR

LONDON, July 29. — Nancy Astor, which is the nom de plume of Lady Astor, is arriving on your side about now. She is the best friend America has here. Please ask my friend, Jimmy Walker, to have New York take good care of her. She is the only one over here that don't throw rocks at American tourists.

Yours respectfully,
*Will Rogers.*

## 2 WILL ROGERS FORWARDS A TIP ON THE MOVEMENTS OF MELLON

LONDON, July 30. — Mellon is escaping through France, trying to reach the Italian border to go under the protection of Mussolini.

Yours,
*Will Rogers.*

## 3 WILL ROGERS SAYS ONLY IRELAND WELCOMES AMERICAN TOURISTS

LONDON, Aug. 1. — I have been in twenty countries and the only one where American tourists are welcomed wholeheartedly by everyone is in Ireland. And the funny part about it is, there is more to see there than in all the others put together. They don't owe us and they don't hate us.

The Lakes of Killarney is where Switzerland got their idea of lakes. Americans, go where you are welcome! Ireland is a friend to everybody, even England.

This endorsement is on the level and calls for no appointment from Tammany Hall whatever.

Yours imploringly,
*Will Rogers.*

## 4 Stones Thrown After Buying, Will Rogers Finds Abroad

LONDON, Aug. 2. – A bunch of American tourists were hissed and stoned yesterday in France, but not until they had finished buying.

Yours,
*Will Rogers.*

## 5 Borah, Lenglen And Shaw Draw Will Rogers's Comment

LONDON, Aug. 3. – When Borah asked England and France what had become of that 400,000,000 acres of land they divided up after the war, that stopped all debt arguments over here. He is always thinking up some question nobody can answer. He even sticks Coolidge.

Suzanne Lenglen has been landed by Pyle. He is now here in London trying to get Bernard Shaw to turn professional and write for money.

Regards to "cuckooland."

*Will Rogers.*

## 6 Why Commons Adjourned, As Will Rogers Sees It

LONDON, Aug. 4. – England's House of Parliament, or Commons rather (I have seen it and prefer calling it the Commons), closed today to give some of the lady members a chance to try and swim the English Channel.

I wanted to have my wife try it, but the Channel is all booked up for the next month.

Churchill, in his closing remarks, still says we borrowed the money, but we doubt it.

Yours aquatically,
*Will Rogers.*

## 7 Will Rogers Warns Democrats About Coolidge And Wheat

LONDON, Aug. 5. – Don't put too much faith, you Democrats, in rumor that peasants of Middle West will defeat Coolidge.

They change with the wheat crops, and he has two to go.

Everybody still hates us.

Yours politically,
*Will Rogers.*

## 8 Will Rogers Gives His View Of Gen. Andrews's Mission

LONDON, Aug. 6. – General Andrews, our prohibition director, is here and has just held a meeting with the British shippers to eliminate any delay in getting it in.

Yours,
*Will Rogers.*

## 9 Will Rogers Offers A Reason For Mellon's Trip Abroad

LONDON, Aug. 7. – Mr. Coolidge has just sent Mr. Mellon over to Italy to find out for him how Mussolini stands in with everybody.

Yours respectfully,
*Will Rogers.*

## 10 Will Rogers Commends Work To Other Channel Swimmers

LONDON, Aug. 8. – Hordes of other Channel swimmers are leaving for their respective homes. If they will only go to work when they get there Gertrude Ederle will have accomplished much more than her original feat.

England is trying to get in on the credit of it. They claim they furnished the land for her to land on, otherwise she would never have made it. France can't get any ad out of it at all, outside of being a good place to start somewhere from.

Yours truly,
*Will Rogers.*

11

## Will Rogers Gives His Idea Of Clemenceau's Appeal

LONDON, Aug. 9. — I had this debt thing about quieted down when this old fellow Clemenceau broke out. I can't be everywhere.

I think any man over eighty or under sixty should be barred from expressing an opinion on debts.

Yours,
*Will Rogers.*

12

## Will Rogers Says Europe Has Opened Game Season

LONDON, Aug. 10. — It is the open season now in Europe for grouse and Americans.

They shoot the grouse and put them out of their misery.

Yours truly,
*Will Rogers.*

13

## Will Rogers Has New Idea About The Tourist Problem

LONDON, Aug. 11. — I told you how bad it's getting with the tourists over here.

Some of them are getting almost what they deserve.

Yours informally,
*Will Rogers.*

14

## Will Rogers Speculates On Clemenceau Note Source

LONDON, Aug. 12. — I had a long talk with friend Barney Baruch. He did not dictate that letter Clemenceau wrote; he only gave him the idea of it.

Baruch has gone to shoot grouse.

He names them after the Republicans and has never missed one.

Yours for information,
*Will Rogers.*

## 15 Will Rogers Thinks British Uneducated in Earthquakes

LONDON, Aug. 16. – England had an earthquake yesterday and their newspapers didn't know enough to call it a fire. What are you going to do with people with no education like that?

P. S. – There is a cricket match going on here that has been on for three months–one game. The earthquake didn't even wake up the spectators.

Yours observingly,
*Will Rogers.*

## 16 Will Rogers Still Watching Cricket Match In England

LONDON, Aug. 17. – The King is in Scotland, and it certainly is lonesome here.

The same cricket game that I told you about before is still going on. One man has been batting three days.

The score is now 800 runs to 500, and Australia has only been to bat once.

Come over and see it. If the tea holds out, it will run till Winter.

I have been thrown out of the grounds twice for applauding. They contend I was a boisterous element.

Yours for long, lingering sportsmanship,
*Will Rogers.*

## 17 Kellogg's Disarmament Talk Reminds Rogers of Geneva

LONDON, Aug. 18. – Secretary of State Kellogg spoke last night in Plattsburg on disarmament. It is a good idea for Plattsburg and even Chicago and New York, but our delegation starved to death trying to get somebody interested in it at Geneva this Summer.

Yours for preparedness,
*Will Rogers.*

## 18 Will Rogers Says He Can Pick American Bootleggers Abroad

LONDON, Aug. 19. – You can pick an American bootlegger out of a crowd of Americans every time. He will be the one that is sober.

Yours temperately,
*Will Rogers.*

## 19 Will Rogers Backs Coolidge On The Philippines Issue

LONDON, Aug. 20. – President Coolidge refuses to give the Philippines their complete independence. I am with Mr. Coolidge. Why should the Philippines have more than we do?

Yours for 100 per cent. freedom for everybody, including Ireland,

*Will Rogers.*

## 20 Why Germany "Quietly" Pays, As Viewed By Will Rogers

LONDON, Aug. 21. – Germany keeps on paying her reparations and never saying a word.

You can afford to do that when you have lost a war and don't have any army and navy to support.

Yours for relief of the Oklahoma farmers, particularly,
*Will Rogers.*

## 21 Will Rogers Gives His Idea Of A Quiet Week In Europe

LONDON, Aug. 22. – One of the quietest weeks over here in months–nobody wrote an open letter to Coolidge, nobody swam the Channel; in fact, not even a single European dictator was shot at. Can it be the League is working?

Yours for truth, even if it interferes with news,
*Will Rogers.*

## 22 Dictators And Baby Hippos Compared By Will Rogers

LONDON, Aug. 23. – Biggest news over the week-end was an amateur dictator found escaping by wireless in Greece, and a baby hippopotamus was born at the London zoo. Of the two events the last was the biggest and of more interest to humanity. Baby hippos are rare, but alleged dictators are lurking in every cafe in Europe. Mussolini has had more bad imitators of him than even Georgie Cohan.

Yours for a better class of dictators,

*Will Rogers.*

## 23 Will Rogers On Legislators, Both English And American

LONDON, Aug. 24. – Parliament, which had adjourned, has just today called a special session within a few days. If we ever did a thing like that in the Summer we would have to hold it in Europe or out on a Chautauqua circuit, so we could get a few members present. Queer people, these English legislators. They are satisfied to stay in their own country; in fact, they rather like it.

Yours for constant public service,

*Will Rogers.*

## 24 Will Rogers Discusses Deer, Debts, Dictators And Taxes

LONDON, Aug. 25. – France is very quiet. The rise in taxes was only proposed. Deer season opened in Scotland for all those who can't hit grouse. Debts and dictators quiet today.

Yours editorially,

*Will Rogers.*

## 25 Will Rogers On Dressmakers And Bootleggers Abroad

LONDON, Aug. 26. – American dressmakers are making sketches of foreign dresses. American bootleggers are making sketches of foreign labels.

Yours for better labels,

*Will Rogers.*

## 26 Will Rogers Would Reform American Visitors Abroad

LONDON, Aug. 27. – American tourists are still coming by the thousands and bragging about where they come from. Sometimes you think France really has been too lenient with them.

Yours for quieter visitors,

*Will Rogers.*

## 27 Will Rogers Reflects On 'The Weaker Sex'

LONDON, Aug. 28. – Another American woman just now swam in from France. Her husband was carried from the boat suffering from cold and exposure. She has two children, the smallest a girl, who is swimming over tomorrow.

Yours for a revised edition of the Dictionary explaining which is the weaker sex,

*Will Rogers.*

## 28 Will Rogers 'Humilated' By Our Women Swimmers

LONDON, Aug. 29. – A man came within thirty yards of swimming the Thames River here today. He was dragged out when overcome. It's the nearest any man has come to swimming the river since 1889.

Immigration authorities are barring any woman that comes from America if she is found to have a bathing suit. Is there any way I can change my sex? I am becoming humiliated.

Yours weakly,
*Will Rogers.*

## 29 Will Rogers Sees Commons; Reminds Him Of Congress

LONDON, Aug. 30. – Parliament met today. One member was thrown out. It seemed like Washington.

Every foreigner is tickled over Newt Baker's cancelling of all debt.

Hobbs, the English cricket champion, hits 316 runs and still is not out. Wake up, "Babe."

Daily Channel catastrophe: A German swam in here today from Germany, got one look at England, turned around and is swimming back.

Yours for the latest Channel news,

*Will Rogers.*

## 30 WILL ROGERS OFFERS PRIZES FOR MALE PARENT SWIMMERS

LONDON, Aug. 31. – Since a mother swam the Channel there has been no living with my wife over here. Will you please find out for me if this German who swam it is a father? If he was not I will give $500 to the first father that swims it and $1,000 to the first grandfather.

Yours for equality in sex,

*Will Rogers.*

## 31 WILL ROGERS SEES AN ENTRY FOR THE DEMOCRATIC FOLLIES

LONDON, Sept. 1. – Former Secretary of State Hughes had an interview with former Premier Briand of France, but nothing official transpired, as neither carried an employee's card.

Russia wants to discuss debt payments with us. If you promise to pay America, it will loan you twice as much as you promise to pay. Wise guys, those Russians. I see Newt is entered for the 1928 Democratic Follies.

Yours in exile,

*Will Rogers.*

## 32 WILL ROGERS WARNS WARRING ATLANTIC FLIERS

LONDON, Sept. 2. – Say, what is all this argument about who is to fly over here and who ain't? If they don't hurry up some American woman of European nationality will swim the thing. What difference does it make? Somebody will break their record the next week anyway. Throw 'em all out and send Colonel Mitchell.

Yours for congenial aviation,

*Will Rogers.*

## 33 PEACE WITHOUT POLITICS IS WILL ROGERS'S SLOGAN

LONDON, Sept. 3. — The League of Nations to perpetuate peace is in session. On account of Spain not being in the last war, they won't let her in. If you want to help make peace you have to fight for it.

Yours for peace without politics,

*Will Rogers.*

## 34 WILL ROGERS WANTS AMERICA A NATION OF HIGH FLIERS

LONDON, Sept. 5. — I see where Mr. Coolidge says if Europe doesn't disarm he will build another airship. Just as well as start it as soon as labor gets rested up from their holiday, for nobody here is going to do any disarming.

The way to make them disarm is to start building and quit begging them to disarm.

Them game fish up there in that lake has giv Cal some new backbone.

Yours for a nation of high fliers,

*Will Rogers.*

## 35 WILL ROGERS TO GIVE BENEFIT FOR IRISH MOVIE FIRE VICTIMS

LONDON, Sept. 6. — I see by the Paris papers that Harry and Evelyn are going back together again. Well, everybody wishes them lots of happiness.

That brings up a mighty good idea. Let everybody go back and start in with the original. In nine cases out of ten it will be found they were the best after all.

*Will Rogers and Colonel Billy Mitchell.*

Can you imagine the scramble in Hollywood trying to locate the original?

Yours for originality,

*Will Rogers.*

P. S. — I know you all read of the terrible movie disaster in Ireland yesterday. Well, I am going to Dublin on Wednesday to give a benefit for them. Cable over what you can, either to me at the Hotel Shelbourne or to President Cosgrave. It's a real cause. Thanks.

## 36 Will Rogers Finds The Irish Are Getting Used To Peace

DUBLIN, Sept. 8. — It is so peaceful and quiet here in Dublin that it is almost disappointing.

Even the Irish themselves are beginning to get used to it and like it. They even have a representative at the Peace Conference.

Ireland treats you more like a friend than a tourist.

President Cosgrave sends regards to prospective President Smith.

Yours without blarney,

*Will Rogers.*

## 37 Mr. Rogers Reports The Result Of A Brief Visit To Ireland

DUBLIN, Sept. 9. — Am bringing family greetings from Dublin to every man on the force.

*Will Rogers.*

## 38 Will Rogers Plans To Return In 1928 To See Coolidge Run

BERLIN, Sept. 11. — I flew here from Dublin—looked over the edge of the plane and saw a Frenchman breaking the record swimming the English Channel.

Arrived in Berlin this afternoon in time to see Dr. Peltzer beat Nurmi and his record.

Will arrive home in November, 1928, and see just how fast Cal is.

Yours,
*Will Rogers.*

## 39 Will Rogers Says Germany Has Had Three Great Days

BERLIN, Sept. 12. — I saw a German outrun the great Finnish runner Nurmi yesterday and a Swede do it this afternoon. If a different nationality is going to beat him every day, I'm taking him on Wednesday.

This has been great three days for Germany; they won a foot race and got into the League of Nations. They feel that these two events will just set them in right for the next war.

All Channel swimming was called off today on account of rain and a wet track.

Yours for ein dunkle and ein heller,

*Will Rogers.*

## 40 Will Rogers Threatens To Fly Over Atlantic If Fonck Delays

PARIS, Sept. 17. — I've been away up in the mountains of Switzerland and couldn't get any word to you for a few days. If you didn't yodle it they wouldn't read it.

France said at the League the other day that her and Germany were old pals again. I guess they are; I floated down the Rhine in Germany all day yesterday and there was so many French soldiers in the way I couldn't see the castles.

Just flew in here this afternoon from Cologne. If Fonck don't hurry up and start, I will fly over from this end. We will fly that far over here every day.

Yours for timely and accurate news anywhere but in the Alps.

*Will Rogers.*

## 41 Will Rogers Finds Paris Meal Limit Is Not Such A Trial After All

PARIS, Sept. 18. — They limit you here in Paris to a two-course dinner. Meats, vegetables, soups, fish and dessert are not counted in either course.

It's two courses outside of any of these, so it's really not such a hardship on the ravenous Americans as was at first expected.

P. S. — Have stood all day at the airdrome looking for Fonck. If he don't start tomorrow, send Ederle and Corson.

Yours for Parisian news and fashions,

*Will Rogers.*

42

## Rogers Relays Advice To Fonck To Jump Across If He Can't Fly

PARIS, Sept. 19. — We are still setting here, looking up, waiting for that Frenchman to come by air.

These Frenchmen over here are advising him to jump if he don't get any further than Sandy Hook.

They can stand him lighting in the water, but they can't stand this delay.

Yours for a man that don't stand with his knees bent so long.

*Will Rogers.*

43

## Will Rogers Warns Gov. Smith To Steer Clear Of The Senate

PARIS, Sept. 20. — I've been reading about the primary elections over home. Looks like everybody that remains honest is getting beat.

We all used to tell a lot of jokes about Florida, mostly because we were jealous of her wonderful possibilities, and then we knew she was able to stand it, but now that she is in real trouble, she will find everybody has always loved her and admired her at heart.

What's the matter with Al Smith's plans? He is as long making up his mind to jump as Rene Fonck is. Being Governor of even New York beats nothing until a little later on when something better might show up.

Don't run for that Senate. You would be sunk in there. They wouldn't listen to Abraham Lincoln his first ten years in there if he was to come back and be elected to it.

Yours,

*Will Rogers.*

## 44 WILL ROGERS ON LEVIATHAN SPEAKS FOR HOMING TOURISTS

ABOARD S. S. LEVIATHAN, Sept. 22. – On board the Leviathan with twenty-five hundred last surviving American tourists. Have all their friends meet them at boat with tip and taxi fare. Most of them have drank up their baggage already.

Yours for deep sea news,

*Will Rogers.*

## 45 ROGERS DISCUSSES AMERICANS WHO TRAVEL INCOGNITO ABROAD

ABOARD S. S. LEVIATHAN, Sept. 23. – Some Americans in Europe are traveling incognito. They are not bragging on where they come from, and nobody knows they are Americans.

Yours for maritime news,

*Will Rogers.*

## 46 BENEFIT ON THE LEVIATHAN RAISES $30,000 FOR FLORIDA

ABOARD THE S. S. LEVIATHAN, Sept. 25. – With ex-Secretary Hughes to work with, raised $30,000 tonight for Florida.

We will have their clothes before we land.

*Will Rogers.*

P. S. – Glad to hear Kearns won the big fight.

## 47 HUGHES-ROGERS BENEFIT TEAM GETS MORE AID FOR FLORIDA

ON BOARD THE LEVIATHAN, Sept. 26. – Everybody on the boat is having a hard time packing, trying to make bottles look like soiled clothing.

Secretary Hughes and I are coming into New York with one of the best benefit acts in the show business. I hate to see the team break up. Mr. Hershey of Hershey, Pa., gave us $8,000 more this afternoon for Florida for repeating the act.

Hope my wife gets her Irish table linens in free. Back home and broke,

*Will Rogers.*

48 WILL ROGERS GOES A-SHOPPING

TORONTO, Ont., Oct. 10. — Had just arrived home after fixing everything up in Europe, when White House spokesman dispatched me to look over Canada and make England following offer for it. One doubtful World Court seat. Prohibition, including enforcement officers. "Peaches." Hayti. All States south of Dixon Line. And throw in Al Smith. Deal pending. Will wire tomorrow.

*Will Rogers.*

49 WILL ROGERS REPORTS:

OTTAWA, Ont., Oct. 11. — Arrived Canada capital today. More sentiment here to be annexed by Mexico than by America. They know us too well. If we get any nation to join us it will have to be some stranger. We only have one reason for wanting Canada and a modification of the Volstead Act will eliminate. Waiting instructions.

*Will Rogers.*

50 WILL ROGERS'S DAILY REPORT

MONTREAL, Que., Oct. 13. — All my work gone for nothing. Just received following wire from White House spokesman:

"Let Canada deal go having enough trouble with American farmers without annexing any more."

Called to Buffalo for conference with Democratic leaders.

*Will Rogers.*

51 WILL ROGERS REPORTS:

CINCINNATI, Ohio, Oct. 14. — Centering all prominent political speakers in Ohio I opened it up here last night in favor of Nick Longworth, the only short-haired violin player in politics. We are the first to open the campaign of November, 1928, for position including house rent and detectives free.

Dempsey and Wills both made big mistake by not fighting each other. If they had fought each other we would have still thought they both were good.

Yours for latest news,

*Will Rogers.*

## 52 Mr. Rogers Finds Queen's Visit Is Affecting Nashville, Tenn.

NASHVILLE, Tenn., Oct. 14. – The visit of Queen Marie, the roving Rumanian, is causing much excitement here in Nashville. They claim her journey encourages imperialism on impressionable minds, and all references to Queens has been stricken from school books.

I opened campaign here last night and gave physical demonstration that Darwin was right.

Yours for science and more Queens,

*Will Rogers.*

## 53 Mr. Rogers Reports A Mission To Save Birmingham, Ala.

BIRMINGHAM, Ala., Oct. 15. – My opposition tonight was to be Judda Krishnamurti, the amateur messiah from India. The modern savior got in here this morning, took one look at Birmingham and said it was a No. 2 Sodom and Gomorrah, and left them bogged down in their sin. So Judge Gary's Youngstown of the South's salvation is entirely in my hands. I will rescue these heathen single handed, but it will cost them $3 a head.

Yours for reasonable salvation,

*Will Rogers.*

## 54 Mr. Rogers Studies Prohibition In The South; Decides It's Not An Issue There, But A Privilege.

MACON, Ga., Oct. 16. – I thought I would hear a lot of election excitement on account of being down here just two weeks before it comes off, but their elections were all held last August at the primaries.

Republicans sometimes enter the race down here, as they are generously allowed to do so by a law, but of course they just go for the ride. Well, the same thing happens in New York State. They sometimes put up a man against Al Smith, which is also permissible by law.

Prohibition is never an issue in the South, their habits and their votes have nothing in common. They feel they are the originators of the still, and any legislation to permit large breweries would be unfair competition and would perhaps destroy the entire revenue of hundreds of thousands of small still owners, who have no other visible means of support. Corn likker is their product, and I can't blame them for voting to protect its life.

You see, you must not condemn a people until you have been among them and can see and know their angle. I don't blame them for not wanting big corporation breweries to be allowed by law to try and change their tastes. We would be a fine liberty-loving country if we allowed a few Yankees to dictate to us what we could make and what we could drink.

Prohibition isn't an issue down here; it's a privilege.

Yours,

*Will Rogers.*

## 55 Will Rogers Offers His Aid To Queen In Seeing America

ATLANTA, Ga., Oct. 17. — Let Queen Marie, the rambling Rumanian, join me in my campaign for farmers' relief, and I will show her more of America than Rand McNally. Lois Fuller didn't lay out my route, but one of the round-the-world fliers did. We could help each other on our weekly articles and endorsements.

Yours, for hospitality to Queen or peasant,

*Will Rogers.*

## 56 Mr. Rogers Welcomes Queen And Tells Why He Is Grateful

SPARTANBURG, S. C., Oct. 18. — Welcome to Queen Marie. Bless her heart! America will always owe her a debt of gratitude for running Peaches and Aimee McPherson back among the want ads.

Yours for credit where credit is due,

*Will Rogers.*

P. S. — This is Spartanburg, a real town where the Twenty-seventh New York Division trained for Democracy!

## 57 Mr. Rogers Wants A Divorce From The Browning Case

ATLANTA, Ga., Oct. 19. – Browning and Peaches are suing for divorce. We hope they will be happy. Now, if the newspapers will just get a divorce from both of them the whole of America will be happy.

Yours for new cases,

*Will Rogers.*

## 58 Queen's Visit Moves Rogers To Remarks On Americanism

MONTGOMERY, Ala., Oct. 20. – It took two weeks to coach New York politicans how to dress and act to meet the Queen so they all looked like twins and spoke the same little piece. Americans are getting like a Ford car—they all have the same parts, the same upholstering and all make exactly the same noises.

Yours for Pat Harrison for President—Pat is at home with anybody without being coached.

*Will Rogers.*

## 59 Will Rogers Is Moved To Cover The News In Verse

MEMPHIS, Tenn., Oct. 21. – Here is all the news there is today in the Memphis papers:

Peaches lost her Papa;
Ford's curtailing toil;
Marie is selling her dairy,
And Aimee's got a boil.

Yours, the poet of Claremore, Okla.,

*Will Rogers.*

## 60 Mr. Rogers Reports Progress From A Tour Of Oklahoma

ADA, Okla., Oct. 22. – Queen Marie, the ballyhooing Balkan, had nothing on me for a turnout when I hit Oklahoma today. It looked like Alexander returning from the series to Nebraska.

Did you read about the fellow yesterday in Los Angeles remembering seeing Aimee change clothes in her car? No wonder he remembers.

This Ada sounds like a girl, but it's not. And it's not a town; it's a city. This is the only authentic and authorized daily diary of my American trip. It's a wonderful country.

*Will Rogers.*

61

## WILL ROGERS SUGGESTS A USE FOR SOUTH'S BIG COTTON CROP

MUSKOGEE, Okla., Oct. 23. – Just arrived back home in Oklahoma in time to solve the problem of too much cotton in the South. Let everybody put it in their ears to keep from hearing campaign speeches.

Still running neck and neck with Marie. The Banker's Club of Claremore are going to give me a lunch, more exclusive than her bankers lunch. Just he and I alone.

Yours for an American diary,

*Will Rogers.*

62

## WILL ROGERS FINDS ODD PEOPLE AND A WONDERFUL COUNTRY

JOPLIN, Mo., Oct. 24. – You meet the oddest people on your travels. I met a fellow who did not claim to be in Lovers' Lane the night of the Hall-Mills murder. If they had charged admission to that they would have made more than the Dempsey-Tunney fight. You people certainly have a wonderful country in this America, and I am thoroughly enjoying my trip.

A leaf from my official diary.

*Will Rogers.*

63

## MR. ROGERS ANTICIPATES THE QUEEN'S RANCH VISIT

PONCA CITY, Okla., Oct. 25. – Am at Miller Brothers' 101 Ranch just ahead of the Queen's visit here. She will love it. It's just the size of Rumania, only more conveniences. There is a bathroom here to every revolution there. Cowboys sleep in silk pajamas, round-up in Rolls-Royces and dress for dinner. If I were the King I wouldn't trust her with this outfit.

These open faces out here are marvelous.

Today's travel diary.

*Will Rogers.*

## 64 POLITICAL NOTE BY MR. ROGERS ON THE SITUATION IN OKLAHOMA

OKMULGEE, Okla., Oct. 26. – Oklahoma is a doubtful State, and after hearing all the candidates on both sides, it's still doubtful what good any of them will be to it.

Mine is the only authentic tour of America that is getting anywhere. All others are balking.

*Will.*

## 65 MR. ROGERS MAKES A DISCOVERY ON HORSEBACK TOUR OF RANCH

TULSA, Okla., Oct. 27. – Been riding horseback over my ranch and old birthplace today, and found two stills. That's some stuff I haven't been getting rent on. If I can show 'em how to make that Russian vodka that made Mary Garden kiss me I will have the best paying ranch in the West.

Yours,
*Will Rogers.*

POSTSCRIPT.

TULSA, Okla., Oct. 27.

Will Rogers held one of his characteristic Democratic rallies in Tulsa tonight. Everybody having $3 attended.

*AN ADMIRER.*

## 66 WILL ROGERS LEAVING OKLAHOMA, OUT OF TOUCH WITH THE NEWS

OKLAHOMA CITY, Okla., Oct. 28. – Leaving the glorious State of Oklahoma tonight by popular demand.

The South is dry and will vote dry. That is, everybody that is sober enough to stagger to the polls will.

P. S. – Where is Marie? We have lost track of her. Did Peaches can her papa? How is Aimee and Al Smith making out, and Pomerene?

Yours,

*Will Rogers.*

## 67 WILL ROGERS' DISPATCH

FORT WORTH, Tex., Oct. 29. – That famous murder case, where the big preacher shot a fellow opens here tomorrow.

The preacher had his own broadcasting station and the man murdered kicked on the amount of static. The preacher shot him to keep him from listening to it.

The defense will be that he was putting the man out of his misery and they are trying to get men on the jury that own radio sets.

Yours for news the world over,

*Will Rogers.*

## 68 ROGERS REPORTS HE'S PULLING FOR A TIE IN THE NEXT SENATE

SAN ANTONIO, Tex., Oct. 30. – Well, the candidates have only got one day more to wish.

Tonight they will be setting like a condemned man, waiting for a last minute word that they are needed to carry out the President's policies. Calvin is a pretty wise guy that way. He remembers what happened to the candidates, one time, when President Wilson went out and endorsed them all in a bunch. This year there will be many a one that will die waiting in vain. We only have a couple of more days and then we will know who is to handicap us for the next four years. If the Democrats can gain nine in the Senate they will split the front page news for the next few years, but if they don't gain any, and maybe lose some, why the only way you can read about one, will be to look in the "to lets." I am pulling for a tie between the Democrats and Republicans in the next Senate, and then we will have some excitement in there.

*Will.*

## 69 Will Rogers Gives Advice Receiving Election Returns

SAN ANTONIO, Tex., Oct. 31. – Don't be too enthusiastic Tuesday night over the election returns. They won't mean a thing. Many will be elected, but few will be seated.

Yours,
*Will Rogers.*

## 70 Will Rogers Sees Some Hope Of Another Election In 1928

SAN ANTONIO, Tex., Nov. 1. – If the Democrats make a good showing tomorrow it will encourage them, maybe, to have another election in 1928. If not, this will perhaps be the last election day you will ever witness.

Yours,
*Will Rogers.*

## 71 Will Rogers Remarks:

AUSTIN, Tex., Nov. 2. – Had dinner in the Governor's mansion tonight with Ma and Jim. Got just as much to eat as I did at Calvin's. There are two Senate jobs in '28. Jim and Ma are going to run for both of them so they won't have one salary between them. Had lunch with Dan Moody, and have date for dinner with him at mansion next year. This is the town Col. House first gave his advice in. More men will be elected tonight through good counting than were elected today through voting.

Yours for reasonable honesty in politics,
*Will Rogers.*

## 72 As Mr. Rogers Sees Election On The Morning Afterward

DALLAS, Tex., Nov. 3. – Butler of Massachusetts got his Presidential indorsement, but there is no salary connected with it. Poor Jim Wadsworth said, "Why did the voters pick on me? He didn't indorse me."

I got just what I was praying for—a tie in the Senate. Now it will be worth listening to.

Dollars may be corrupt, but they beat indorsements in this or any other election.

Yours for high-price votes,

*Will Rogers.*

73

## Bought Vote, Mr. Rogers Says Is Better Than No Vote At All

LUBBOCK, Tex., Nov. 4. — They say it's wrong to buy votes, but you notice from the election returns that the fellows in Pennsylvania, and Illinois that bought the most, got elected. A bought vote is better than no votes at all. The counters can't tell whether they are bought or just bargained for.

I told you I could shake Oklahoma out of the cuckoo's nest. It wasn't doubtful all this time; it was just demented.

*Will Rogers.*

74

## Rogers Finds A Republican Doing Well Down In Texas

SAN ANGELO, Tex., Nov. 5. — I found quite a novelty down here in this Texas town. It was a Republican and the funny part about it is he is doing well and has every Democrat in town patronizing him.

It's remarkable what one lone man of a party can do when he sets his mind to it. He has got him a little postoffice here and has worked himself up into a nice little business. It pays to pioneer.

Yours,

*Will Rogers.*

75

## Thoughts From Mr. Rogers; He Likes His News Assorted

WACO, Tex., Nov. 6. — Marie, the meandering monarch, will be swinging back into the States from Canada now that the election is over and the front pages are as vacant as a movie fan's mind. The Government has sent a new referee on her train.

*Will Rogers with Miriam A. "Ma" and James E. "Pa" Ferguson at Governor's Mansion, Austin, Texas.*

Ma Ferguson told me she tried to land Marie for Austin, the capital of Texas, but when she couldn't get her she got the preacher Norris trial and is to follow that with the Tunney-Sharkey fight.

Today is "romance and knighthood news." Tomorrow we get back to politics and comedy.

Yours for an assortment,

*Will Rogers.*

## 76 WILL ROGERS SEES PRESIDENT IN THE BIG GAME OF 1928

FORT WORTH, Tex., Nov. 7. – It looks like a cinch now that Calvin Coolidge will hear the referee's whistle in the big kick-off of 1928. He has already engaged his old coach, Butler. Coaches should always coach and never play themselves. He has two years to perfect a signal system with him. They have gone into a huddle already.

Yours for accurate weather, scandal and political predictions,

*Will Rogers.*

## 77 MR. ROGERS REPORTS DISCORD ON HIS OWN SPECIAL TRAIN

AMARILLO, Tex., Nov. 8. (On Board My Special Train at Amarillo, Texas, Where the Biggest Oil Fields in the World Are) – There has been some dissension on my train. We put a man off that claimed he was furnishing all the gum for my American tour. Everything is now serene and I will go through with the tour as originally planned, putting out articles daily.

Yours,

*Will Rogers.*

## 78 MR. ROGERS, IN THE SOUTH, DEFINES A REPUBLICAN

WICHITA FALLS, Tex., Nov. 9. – Lots of people can't tell the difference between a Democrat and a Republican. After making a sort of a small time Queen Marie tour through the South I can tell you. A Republican is the fellow that knows enough to stop planting cotton.

Yours,

*Will Rogers.*

## 79 Will Rogers' Dispatch

ABILENE, Tex., Nov. 10. – Mr. Coolidge is to be in Kansas City tomorrow to dedicate their monument that resembles a silo. First appearance in West since November catastrophe. He will speak on war relief and not farmers' relief.

Marie follows him in there Friday.

I follow 'em both in next Tuesday, when I will launch Jim Reed for President, talk of farmers' relief, monuments, Balkans, absent queens and seat Vare and Smith, so if you miss them you have something to look forward to.

Yours, not afraid to come out on any question,

*Will Rogers.*

## 80 Will Rogers Remarks:

TEXARKANA, Ark., Nov. 11. – Today was Armistice Day, celebrated to commemorate the end of slaughter. There were more casualties in football games celebrating the Armistice than there were before the Armistice was declared. We got enough people for another war but not enough to stand another Armistice Day. But football is not nearly so devastating as the Armistice Day oratory. If we fought like we declaimed we would be paying reparations.

Yours,

*Will Rogers.*

## 81 Will Rogers Nominates Reed As One Of Missouri's Bravest

CORSICANA, Tex., Nov. 12. – President Coolidge, in his speech lauding the names and bravery of Missouri and Kansas fighters, left out the bravest ones of all, the James Boys and Jim Reed. All three of them were raised under the very shadow of the monument. Whoever compiled his local data was either ignorant or a Republican, perhaps both. Jim Reed has fought the Republicans single handed for fifteen years and never even asked for an armistice.

Yours for more accurate Armistice speeches,

*Will Rogers.*

## 82 MR. ROGERS MUSES ON CONSCRIPTION OF WEALTH AND FINDS IT TOO GOOD TO COME TRUE

LITTLE ROCK, Ark., Nov. 13. – I been reading and studying over President Coolidge's message to Kansas and Missouri. He brought out Mr. Harding's idea (he didn't say it was, but it was) about the conscription of all wealth in case of war.

That sounds fine after the war is over. Funny nobody thought of it before the last war started, and I doubt if you hear anything of it just before the start of the next one. If they did do it, it would be a great enlistment boost for war, as we all know thousands that would go themselves just to see some of the money taken away from the ones that copped it during the last war.

It would be a very interesting experiment and would add novelty to the next war, as we have lots more fellows ready and willing to give lives than we have ones that would give their fortunes. You would have more suicides and heart failures on your hands than you would have shot by bullets.

It was a great idea even when Mr. Harding recommended it, but it's like a campaign promise; it's too good to ever come true. It would be worth a war just to try it out.

Yours for serious consideration of promises,

*Will Rogers.*

## 83 WILL ROGERS SUGGESTS ROCKNE AS COACH FOR ARMY IN NEXT WAR

FORT GIBSON, Okla., Nov. 14. – The Harvard Lampoon must have written an exceedingly humorous article about Brown to get beat Saturday, 21-0. It's a compliment to Harvard to say they broke off athletic relations. They haven't shown any athletics in years.

Why not get Rockne to coach the United States Army in the next war?

Yours,

*Will Rogers.*

## 84 ROYAL TRAIN AND ROGERS TRAIN MOVE MR. ROGERS TO COMPARISON

INDEPENDENCE, Kan., Nov. 15. – I see where Ferdinand, the Acting King of Rumania, is trying again to get Marie to come home. He wants her out of the banquet halls by Christmas.

The Ford car guy is back in good standing with his upper berth on the royal train again. He tried to make the jumps in one of their products and missed seven receptions.

All serene on my Proletariat Special. Arrive at the Kansas City monument tomorrow.

*Will Rogers.*

## 85 Will Rogers Continues His Western Travelogue

KANSAS CITY, Mo., Nov. 16. – Arrived in Kansas City, following in wake of Cal and Marie. Town sore on receptions. All that met me was a Red Cap. Saw the much discussed monument. It was to commemorate peace, but has caused war.

Chevrolet dealer has again been allowed to join our train. Only had two punctures on way to Grand Royal Bull judging contest, the only thing put on in my honor.

My wife wants me to quit this banqueting around and sail for California before Christmas present buying time; but the more traveling the more articles.

Yours,
*Will Rogers.*

## 86 Suggestions From Mr. Rogers On War And Conscription

TOPEKA, Kan., Nov. 17. – Mr. Coolidge said in the next war we would draft wealth as well as men. Now everybody is arguing if it's practical. Why not postpone having the next war till the cause for it is so popular that you won't have to conscript either of them? If you will wait till we are invaded and everybody knows what they are fighting for, you won't need conscription.

Yours from Kansas, the comedy relief of the United States,
*Will Rogers.*

## 87 Mr. Rogers Is For Fewer Cults And For More Cultivation

WICHITA, Kan., Nov. 18. – I see where they captured old King Ben, the perpetual sheik of Michigan. They have been looking for him for four years, everywhere but in the harem where he has been for twenty years.

Ben is head of a cult. Their side line is to cult-tie-vate whiskers. What we need is less cults and more cultivation.

Yours,
*Will Rogers.*

## 88 FARMERS AND FILLING STATIONS DRAW WILL ROGERS'S COMMENT

DENVER, Col., Nov. 19. – Hit Denver and ran into another farmers' conference, passing resolutions for relief. What the farmers need to pass is filling stations and they won't need to pass resolutions. Colorado voted dry and now they are blaming it onto the altitude.

Yours,
*Will Rogers.*

## 89 WILL ROGERS GIVES A BOOST TO WESTERN FOOTBALL TEAMS

WRAY, Col., Nov. 21. – Harvard and Yale played Saturday, as usual, to decide which was the worst team in America. Harvard students have completed more English courses and less forward passes than any school in this generation. They got correspondence school teams out West here that they have to handcuff to keep them from going and beating Harvard and Yale.

Yours for new touchdown talent,
*Will Rogers.*

## 90 WILL ROGERS ENTERS CHICAGO WITH CERTAIN MISGIVINGS

ST. JOSEPH, Mo., Nov. 22. – Playing Chicago tomorrow night, perhaps. Hope I reach the stage before the machine gun bullets lay me low. I want to go with by chaps on. Everybody in America has been good to me and I love you all, even critics and Congressmen.

*Will Rogers.*

P. S. – Don't try to find who did it. I don't want any exception made in my case.

*W. R.*

## 91 Will Rogers Safe In Chicago And Hopeful At Last Bulletin

CHICAGO, Ill., Nov. 23. – It's 9 o'clock now and I am still alive. There is one chance in a million. If I make it through the night I'll be a second Mussolini. Hoping against hope,

*Will Rogers.*

P. S. – Box score for today: Died by gunshot and other natural Chicago causes, 13; wounded, 23. Bad weather kept outdoor shooting down to a minimum.

*W. R.*

## 92 Will Rogers Gives Advice About Thanksgiving Dinner

LIMA, Ohio, Nov. 24. – Tomorrow is Thanksgiving, for no reason at all. The more turkey you eat at dinner the less hash you will be bothered with the rest of the month.

This is the biggest bean town in the world. They don't make 'em any bigger than Lima's.

Ain't it lonesome since the Queen left?

*Will Rogers.*

## 93 Will Rogers Finds Himself The Sole Touring Celebrity

PITTSBURGH, Pa., Nov. 25. – Marie, the migrating monarch, has walked out on us. That leaves nobody touring America but me.

I get over pretty big in little towns like this, where they never saw a queen. Most days here they can't even see each other.

Ford's man and Sam Hill are trying to get on my train now, but I don't want to ride from the depot in one of those. America's sole tourist.

*Will Rogers.*

P. S. – Say, what do you know about my old friend Governor Brandon of Alabama? Alabama votes twenty-four quarts for Haig and Haig.

*Will Rogers.*

## 94 ROGERS FINDS A VOTING PRICE FOR FOOTBALL TICKETS

SPRINGFIELD, Ill., Nov. 26. – All tickets for Army-Navy game tomorrow in Chicago were taken by Congressmen and Senators. They are getting as high as 100 votes a seat for them. Football is in the pork barrel, too.

Yours for the lowdown on public servants,

*Will.*

## 95 INDIANA WON'T EVER BE THE SAME, ROGERS SAYS AFTER WHAT CARNEGIE TECH DID TO NOTRE DAME

INDIANAPOLIS, Ind., Nov. 27. – Carnegie Tech and I both hit Indiana today and she will never be the same old State again.

She was just beginning to pull herself back together and get the last of her Florida stragglers back and everything was going fine when Notre Dame, the State's one best ad, went back to Pittsburgh and "Andy's Boys" jumped on 'em in the first period and did the black bottom on them the rest of the afternoon.

Say, I wish you could see the old State tonight. It hasn't been as blue since the night Jim Watson was elected. Old Abe Martin (Kin Hubbard), who is sitting here by me, can't even think of a "saying," and George Ade's golf course is "to let." It's the worst thing that has hit Indiana since the Klansmen run out of sheets.

The Army and Navy got a draw in their civil war. Chicago was so busy looking at the uniforms of the cadets and middies that they didn't see the game at all. They played a tie and if Dawes hadn't gone to sleep he could have cast the deciding vote.

Longworth, Ritchie, Lowden and Dawes represented the next President. Mayor Walker came to the Far West for the first time to see the cowboys and Indians.

Yours from the sandbanks of the Wabash,

*Will Rogers.*

## 96 WILL ROGERS MAKES COMMENT ON OUR SLOWNESS IN AVIATION

LOUISVILLE, Ky., Nov. 28. – Our army played our navy Saturday and the game was refereed by our aviation students, both good men. We will have a football team from our aviation school as soon as our far-sighted statesmen appropriate enough to have eleven students. They are just waiting for two more wars to see if flying machines are practical. Yours,

*Will Rogers.*

## 97 WILL ROGERS FEELS AT HOME WHEN HE REACHES SOUTH BEND

SOUTH BEND, Ind., Nov. 29. – I always wanted to see this town. I was born in a Studebaker wagon, awakened every morning by a Big Ben clock, grew up walking between the handles of an Oliver chilled plow, wore home made shirts made by Singer sewing machines and read all my life of Notre Dame, whose scholastic standing is one touchdown and a field goal higher than any other modern educational hindrance.

Yours for narrower minds and broader stadiums,

*Will Rogers.*

## 98 REFLECTIONS BY WILL ROGERS ON SPIRITISM AND POLITICS

KALAMAZOO, Mich., Nov. 30. – Poor Valentino! They won't even let him alone after he is dead. They got him conversing with women in spirit that he wouldn't even speak to in life.

Yours, *Will.*

P. S. – The Democrats lost in Maine yesterday. They only had one chance and that was to get Coolidge to endorse the Republican candidate, and he was too smart for 'em.

## 99 MR. ROGERS ASKS WHICH COUNTRY WANTS TO BE REGULATED NEXT

TOLEDO, Ohio, Dec. 1. – Our gunboats are all in the Chinese war, our marines have all landed in Nicaragua, Kellogg is sending daily ultimatums to Mexico and Coolidge is dedicating memorials to eternal peace.

Who is the next country wants their affairs regulated? Look what we did for Tacna-Arica.

Yours,

*Bill.*

## 100 Mr. Rogers's Idea Of The Truth On Some Current Topics

CLEVELAND, Ohio, Dec. 2. – The truth is finally coming out. Jack Dempsey was poisoned, Harvard was lampooned, Rockne forgot to bless the future Cardinals, the Army and the Navy were overcome by stockyard fumes, Hall-Mills committed suicide on account of no privacy in the lane, Peaches was canned, Aimee blames the static, Ma Ferguson says it took a man to do it and seven Republican Senators have just discovered that they were running on the wrong ticket.

The only one with no alibi was Queen Marie. She said, "I come to sell you Rumania." I think a three hundred million loan will get it–revolutions and all.

Yours for latest alibi news,

*Will.*

## 101 Will Rogers' Dispatch

FORT WAYNE, Ind., Dec. 3. – The Hall-Mills jurymen turned in the verdict they had 25 days ago. For economy's sake, if for nothing else, why don't we let the jurymen render their verdict when they are sworn in instead of when they are sworn out. Yours for economic justice,

*Will Rogers.*

P. S. – Of course we would miss the pictures of the trials, and I doubt if Americans would stand for that.

*Will.*

## 102 Rogers Sees Trouble Ahead As Congress Meets Today

CHICAGO, Ill., Dec. 5. – Congress meets tomorrow morning. Let us all pray, Oh, Lord, give us strength to bear that which is about to be inflicted upon us. Be merciful with them, Oh Lord, for they know not what they are doing. Amen.

*Will Rogers.*

103 **Mr. Rogers Calls Session Of Congress Just A Day Lost**

YOUNGSTOWN, Ohio, Dec. 6. – Congress met and adjourned right away. One more day's salary for six hundred went up the taxpayers' flue. When do the taxpayers adjourn on pay?

The President's message comes tomorrow. That's another day lost.

Yours,
*Will.*

P. S. – The farmers will get no relief before Wednesday—maybe late Wednesday.

104 **Rogers Sees Rumanian Crisis As A Good Joke On The Family**

UTICA, N. Y., Dec. 7. – Last week everybody was worrying about who would be King of Rumania. Good joke old Nick played on the whole family; he is just going to succeed himself.

Babblings from the Balkins.

*Will.*

105 **Will Rogers Analyzes A Difference In Viewpoints**

NEW YORK, N. Y., Dec. 8. – Did you ever see a man as tickled with the way a country is running as Mr. Coolidge is? Makes a lot of difference from where you are sitting.

From an agrarian—when I can afford it.

*Will.*

106 **Will Rogers Finds A Flaw In High Standard Of Living Talk**

NEW YORK, N. Y., Dec. 9. – Every official in the Government and every prominent manufacturer is forever bragging about our "high standard of living." Why, we could always have lived this high if we had wanted to live on the instalment plan. Yours,

*Will.*

## 107 Will Rogers Has Dinner With 'The Wet Nurse For Maryland'

BALTIMORE, Md., Dec. 10. – Just had dinner tonight with a guy that has every earmark of the next renter for the White House in case Cal don't renew his lease. There ain't but one thing will hold this fellow back and that ain't much, but you know how voters are. He is a Democrat. He is now the wet nurse for Maryland.

Yours for likely prospects.

*Will.*

## 108 Will Rogers Finds Congress Interested In That Surplus

WASHINGTON, D. C., Dec. 1. – Have spent the entire day watching our two great lawmaking bodies in action. The Senate debated all day on whether to have the bridge that they are building between Oregon and Washington white or orange colored. Dawes sat there so bored he looked like he could have murdered the ones that gave him his job.

Congress is just sitting around waiting with suggestions as to how to divide up the $350,000,000 surplus. Coolidge made a big mistake by ever telling them he had it at all. They won't get a thing done till they get that split up some way among their voters.

Sol Bloom and Copeland are looking after New York's interest.

Yours for the common people's share,

*Will.*

## 109 Will Rogers Advocates Single Standard Of Alimony

WASHINGTON, D. C., Dec. 12. – Say, it looks like this Count Slam-Von-Hogsa-Trottin is going to get his alimony. If he does it will be encouragement for home talent husbands to be allowed something.

Yours for single standard of alimony,

*Will.*

P. S. – It's late Sunday night here. Farmers have received no more relief than the cotton stocking manufacturers.

## 110 Will Rogers Offers Advice To The Girl Bank Robber

SCRANTON, Pa., Dec. 13. – See where the female secretary of my friend, Dan Moody, Governor-elect of Texas, has traded her typewriter for an automatic and been doing a little trick and fancy bank robbing in between dictations. If she will plead guilty and can get in jail before Ma Ferguson's time expires on January first, Ma will pardon her.

Hurray for Dan Moody, A. and M. and West Texas. Yours,

*Will.*

## 111 Mr. Rogers Suggests How A Fortune Can Be Made

JAMESTOWN, N. Y., Dec. 14. – A fortune is in store in this country for the person that can make something out of slightly used Rumanian flags.

Yours for a universal visiting flag.

*Will Rogers.*

## 112 Rogers 'Working Reasonable,' Compared With The Chorus

PITTSBURGH, Pa., Dec. 15. – Miss Marion Talley wouldn't sing 'cause she didn't get her three thousand. That just reminds me, Pittsburgh hasn't handed me my one-hundred-dollar bill for tonight yet, and there won't be a Vare vote-buying joke told till I get the hundred in my paws. If New Rochelle wants opera for the first time and Pittsburgh wants high-brow humor for the first time, let 'em dig up for it.

Yours for a mixture of commerce and art,

*Will Rogers.*

P. S. – One of our Follies chorus girls got $50,000 out of Pittsburgh last week. I think Marion and I are working reasonable.

## 113 Mr. Rogers's Idea Of The Senate Seems In Line With Gov. Small's

WILKES-BARRE, Pa., Dec. 16. – I see where Governor Hard Surface Road Len Small appointed this fellow Smith to go up to the

Senate now. He was not supposed to be thrown out of there till next session. It looks like a wise move to get the verdict six months in advance and put everybody out of their misery. Seat 'em! Cheap Senators never got a country anywhere.

*Will Rogers.*

## 114 Mr. Rogers Suggests A Deal To End Ford's Latest Crusade

DETROIT, Mich., Dec. 17. — I am in Detroit in connection with trouble between Henry Ford and Jewish people. Think if every one of them will agree to buy one of those things at cost plus 10 per cent, trouble will be patched up all around.

Yours for good feeling even among rich people,

*Will Rogers.*

## 115 Will Rogers Does His Bit For Chicago's Canal Project

CHICAGO, Ill., Dec. 18. — Am here in Chicago on way to California.

Poor Chicago! They are having a pretty tough break. They have a Senator elected that it looks like the poor devil is going to have to stand up during his term and they got them a canal all dug and they can't find any adjoining country to loan them water to put into it. It's an awful nice canal. If you hear of anybody that has any water they want to loan them for it—you see they just need enough water to get them to the Mississippi River. That's all they want.

Five bandits came clear here yesterday but I guess that wouldn't come under the heading of news.

Yours for water in every canal we build,

*Will.*

## 116 Will Rogers Visits Kansas And Lists Its Noted Men

DODGE CITY, Kan., Dec. 19. — Speeding across Kansas, noted for three Senators: Capper, who holds the rainbow sent up for the farmers; Curtis, who walks in front of the Republican Senators holding out a stick of Coolidge candy, which they never reach, and William Randolph White, home talent critic.

This is Dodge City, which used to be bad till the East made it ashamed of itself. The last murder here was in 1917. The man was fiendishly attacked by an infuriated Ford.

Tomorrow Arizona, if we are not late; if so, New Mexico.

The Rambling Mayor of Beverly Hills,

*Will Rogers.*

## 117 'Hon. Will Rogers,' He Signs It, Being The Mayor Of Beverly

WINSLOW, Ariz., Dec. 20. – Los Angeles wants to dam the Colorado River. They are short of water for booster speakers at banquets. Arizona here says: "Get it from your advertisements. You advertise you have everything."

Beverly Hills don't ask the world for a thing. We got water, even if we don't use it, and an after dinner speaker for a Mayor, like New York. Beverly's Mayor has refused more free meals than Jimmy Walker ever spoke for. Hold 'em, Doug, till I come.

A moving Mayor of a fast moving town,

*Hon. Will Rogers.*

## 118 Mayor Rogers Of Beverly Hills Records A Welcome To Town

BEVERLY HILLS, Cal., Dec. 21. – As Mayor of Beverly Hills I arrived today amid big demonstrations. They mistook me for Ormiston. If not a success as Mayor, they offer to change City Hall into a tabernacle—me to preach, and Doug and Tom Mix and Bill Hart to take up collection; Ben Turpin to run radio, so there will be no chance of a scandal.

Honest, they gave me a great welcome, and I want to thank everybody from the bottom of my heart and President Coolidge for a lovely nice wire. Also Al Smith and my opposition, Jimmy Walker of New York; also Hiram Johnson and Shortridge.

The only Mayor that hasn't made a mistake so far—his honor of Beverly Hills. The best town west of Nantucket Lightship,

*Will Rogers.*

## 119 Mayor Rogers Of Beverly Hills Takes Note Of Army Troubles

BEVERLY HILLS, Cal., Dec. 22. – I see where Brig. Gen. Reilly says that American soldiers are deserting at the rate of a thousand a month.

Well, we have one consolation. A thing like that can't last for over a couple of months. We are refunding to the taxpayers more soldiers than we are taxes.

It's a good thing for us that the last war was the last one.
HIS HONOR THE MAYOR OF BEVERLY HILLS, CAL.

*Will Rogers.*

P. S. – Thank Charley Dawes for a nice wire. May Morpheus never overtake him during an emergency.

## 120 Will Rogers' Christmas Advice And A Tribute To Ty And Tris

BEVERLY HILLS, Cal., Dec. 23. – I am too busy replacing presents to write today. I bought some mechanical and electric things for the kids and wore 'em out playing with 'em myself. Don't forget to lay by a few presents today for those who you didn't think would send you anything. You may not have to use 'em anyway. Yours,

*Will Rogers.*

P. S. – I want the world to know that I sincerely wish Tris and Ty the same as I have always wished them over an acquaintanceship of fifteen years. If you are crooked it shouldn't take you twenty years' hard work to get enough to retire on. If they been selling out all these years I would like to have seen them play when they wasn't selling.

## 121 Greetings From Will Rogers And Some Advice To Men

BEVERLY HILLS, Cal., Dec. 24. – Merry Christmas, my constant readers, both of you.

No scandal today. There is some, but it will be more scandalous by tomorrow.

Men, act surprised this morning as if you didn't know the tie was coming.

Yours,
*Will Rogers.*

## 122 Will Rogers Has Bad News About Celebration Of Christmas

HOLLYWOOD, Cal., Dec. 26. – It's going to take four days to bury all those who celebrated Christmas.

If Nicaragua would just come out like a man and fight us, we wouldn't have to be hunting away off over in China for a war.

See where Tunney, the champion prize-fighter, fell in the water and it was all a Boy Scout could do to rescue him.

The Mayor of Beverly—the Claremore, Oklahoma, of the West Coast,

*Will Rogers.*

## 123 Will Rogers Has His Own Plan For Disposing Of The Surplus

BEVERLY HILLS, Cal., Dec. 27. – Congress is arguing, this whole short session, over what to do with the $378,000,000 surplus. It seems odd that nobody has ever thought of returning it to the source they saved it from, the army, navy and aviation. Through not spending anything on them is how we got it.

The first political party that is far-sighted enough to buy airplanes instead of votes is going to be setting mighty pretty the next few years. That's what Beverly Hills is doing—preparing. I just today had to hire another cop for Saturdays and Sundays.

Yours, executively,

*Will Rogers.*

## 124 A Few Nicaragua Aphorisms From Mayor Rogers Of Beverly

BEVERLY HILLS, Cal., Dec. 28. – A few slogans for our latest war:

"Join the army and take the old Nick out of Nicaragua."

"Join the navy and try and help America find Nicaragua."

"Join the aviation. We are sending our plane to Nicaragua."

"The 1932 Legion Convention will be held in Nicaragua."

"Let's make Nicaragua free for 100 per cent. Americans to live in."

"We have lost our first combat there, but wait till our Spring drive starts against Nicaragua."

"Stop Nicaragua while there is time."

Recruitingly yours,

*Mayor Rogers.*

## 125 WILL ROGERS ANALYZES EUROPE'S BEING 'SORE AT US'

LOS ANGELES, Cal., Dec. 29. – They say all nations are sore at us, but unfortunately for us they didn't get sore at us quick enough. If they had, we would have saved money. We are the ones that should be sore at them for not getting sore at us quicker. Them's the Mayor's sentiments.

*Will Rogers.*

## 126 NOBLE CHANCE FOR A REPUBLICAN WITH MAYOR ROGERS AT BEVERLY

BEVERLY HILLS, Cal., Dec. 30. – Say, you talk about a prosperous town. We can't find a Republican poor enough to be Postmaster here. Even Democrats got money in this town and won't take the job.

Here is an opening for Butler of Massachusetts, Vare or Smith.

The Mayor of a town in distress,

*Will Rogers.*

## 127 MAYOR ROGERS COMMENTS ON OFFICIAL 'MURDER BY THE QUART'

BEVERLY HILLS, Cal., Dec. 31. – I see the Government has worked out a plan to fix the liquor that they sell the bootleggers from the warehouses so it won't totally exterminate the ultimate consumer. Even the prohibitionists are in favor of diluting it, as it depleted their ranks during the holidays.

Something has to be done. You want customers that will live at least for two or three sales. Governments used to murder by the bullet only. Now it's by the quart.

Yours,
*Will Rogers.*

P. S. –Read Judge Gary's message to the country on optimism.

## 128 Will Rogers Finds Mexico Fair In The Matter Of Earthquakes

HOLLYWOOD, Cal., Jan. 2. — See where America and Mexico had a joint earthquake. That's the only thing I ever heard that we split 50-50 with Mexico.

Lucky for Mexico that she didn't grab off more of the earthquake than we did or she would have got a note from Kellogg.

It's the influence from Moscow that is causing all this earth's upheaval.

Yours for reciprocity in earthquakes,

*Mayor Rogers.*

## 129 Will Rogers Names Chaplin As His Lieutenant Mayor

GALLUP, N. M., Jan. 3. — In the Mayor's much regretted absence from Beverly Hills, I hereby and hereon do this day appoint as Lieutenant Mayor Charles Spencer Chaplin, who is temporarily out of a wife, and can therefore devote all his humor to the office.

I want also to thank my beautiful town for the law-abiding spirit in which they acted during the holidays. We did not lose an inhabitant by death, which proves conclusively that the Eighteenth Amendment was strictly adhered to. We can behave ourselves better than lots of more moral towns can.

Going back to Claremore. His later Honor,

*Will Rogers.*

P. S. — Let me know how Aimee and Asa come out. Want also to thank everybody who so kindly came out and got pneumonia on the day of my arrival in the land of perpetual sunshine.

*Will.*

## 130 Mr. Rogers On Poison Rum As A Weapon In Our Next War

DODGE CITY, Kan., Jan. 4. — Talk about America being unarmed and unprepared for the next war. Why, say, we are setting pretty.

Give the enemy a party the night before the war starts and serve Government booze. Government statistics prove they are running about five funerals to the quart.

If you can't make 'em obey, kill 'em.

The rambling Mayor,

*Will Rogers.*

P. S. — And we are the country that wants to outlaw poison gases in war, for humanitarian reasons!

## 131 Rogers Losing Confidence In Even War Being On The Level

CHICAGO, Ill., Jan. 5. — Been listening all day here to baseball testimony. Just discovered ex-court-martialed soldier who swears Germans were bought off by Pershing in last series on Marne. I am losing confidence in even the Civil War having been on the level.

Yours,

*Will Rogers.*

## 132 Mr. Rogers Muses On Red Tape After War And Bullets In War

DETROIT, Mich., Jan. 6. — I see where a lot of banks are refusing the soldier boys loans on their adjusted compensations on account of too much red tape to handle. Not quite as much tape for them as it was to him to go to war, though there is at least no bullets in it.

Thank goodness there will be no more wars. Now you tell one.

*Mayor Rogers.*

P. S. — Am in Detroit to get a patrol wagon that will haul actors with dignity and comfort.

## 133 Mayor Rogers Classifies The University Of Michigan

ANN ARBOR, Mich., Jan. 7, 1927. — Am lecturing before University of Michigan tonight on "Better Government by Poorer

Officials." The great biologist, Professor Little, is President of the school. He took the position so he could combine the study of students with that of guinea pigs. Yours mayorally,

*Mr. Rogers.*

P. S. – You will remember this school more readily when I tell you it's the one that Benny Friedman and Benny Oosterbaan are building the new stadium for. Michigan's scholastic standing is a field goal better than any university in the Middle West.

## 134 Will Rogers Sees Washington Competing With Humorists

RICHMOND, Ind., Jan. 9. – You want to know why we are so funny to the rest of the world? Here we are sending warships to tell Nicaragua who to seat after their election and we haven't got a Senator that was elected here last Fall that will be allowed to sit down. I wish I was as funny as that is. My opposition is getting unusually keen in Washington just in the last few days. The Mayor is being driven slowly into the drama.

*Mr. Rogers.*

P. S. – What did you do, father, in the great war of Nicaragua?

## 135 Will Rogers Remarks

ST. LOUIS, Mo., Jan. 10. – We say that Diaz is the properly elected president of Nicaragua, but Brazil, Argentina, Peru, Chile, Mexico, Ecuador, Costa Rica, Cuba, Guatemala, Colombia, Uruguay, Paraguay—all those say that the other fellow is the properly elected President. It's funny how we are the only ones that get everything right. I'd rather be right than Republican.

*Will Rogers.*

## 136 Mayor Rogers Explains His Presence In Chicago

CHICAGO, Ill., Jan. 11. – Seems odd two messages hit the papers the same day. Mister Coolidge indicts Nicaragua and Mrs.

Chaplin indicts Charlie. Looks like they both got good grounds for complaint. Nicaragua is the Hollywood of Central America.

I am here studying the modern modes of crime. A progressive Mayor,

*Will.*

## 137 NOT ALL OF US LIKE CHARLIE, SAYS MAYOR ROGERS OF BEVERLY

GRAND RAPIDS, Mich., Jan. 12. – I knew something would happen the minute I got away from Beverly Hills and not attending to things personally.

Charlie has gone and ruined us just when I thought I had everybody all signed up to the pledge. But I want you to know that we are not all like Charlie. He is the only one that has sixteen million dollars, even if he had it.

Lita, take the children out to the old Mayor's house. I will feed 'em till you jar him loose from a few millions.

*The Mayor.*

## 138 WILL ROGERS SHOWS HENRY FORD HE HAS CONFIDENCE IN HIM

DETROIT, Mich., Jan. 13. – Been listening all day to the Ford stockholders' trial, where, after Mr. Ford had made each $100 share worth a half million, the shareholders thought he wasn't running his business right and sold out.

To show him that I have confidence in his business ability still I just told him personally out at his home today that I was willing to put a hundred in with him and string along even now. He certainly did seem to appreciate such confidence, so he and I are going to build some airplanes.

The aerial Mayor,

*Will Rogers.*

## 139 MR. ROGERS STUDIES A STADIUM; PRESENTS A FEW STATISTICS

COLUMBUS, Ohio, Jan. 14. – Dr. Wilce, the Ohio State coach,

just showed me their new stadium, seating 100,000, built by hard study and excellent scholarship.

They can seat 200 students to every book in the university. They lost to Michigan by a kick after touchdown. He has 400 students practicing day and night in relays to kick goals.

A product of the old book mode of education,

*The Mayor.*

P. S. — I suggested they practice making another touchdown, then they wouldn't have to worry about the goal kicking.

## 140 Will Rogers Falls In Love With The Blue Grass Country

LEXINGTON, Ky., Jan. 15. — I have seen today some of the most beautiful stock farms in America. I don't think there is another place in this country quite like the blue grass region around Lexington.

It's more like English country life than any place, and English country life is just about the best there is. Can't give London much, but those old birds out in the country sure do know how to live, and I tell you these old guys here, with their fine horses that we read about every Summer in all the big races, they got some great horses here and they know how to scramble a bran mash for a horse and a corn mash for a human that just about excels any hospitality in America.

Beverly Hills and Claremore have a close rival.

*The Mayor.*

## 141 Will Rogers' Dispatch

LEXINGTON, Ky., Jan. 16. — Been reading up on the early lives of our prominent men of today and find that Secretary of State Kellogg was scared very badly when a mere baby by a big ruff Russian.

*Will Rogers,*
The Meandering Mayor.

## 142 Will Rogers Says A Word About The Evolution Theory

CHATTANOOGA, Tenn., Jan. 17. — The Supreme Court of Tennessee down here has just ruled that you other States can come from whoever or whatever you want to, but they want it on record that they come from mud only.

Darwin's living illustration, the Mayor of what we think is a town, but may be a zoo.

*Will Rogers.*

## 143 Mr. Rogers Offers Florida A Little More Advertising

KNOXVILLE, Tenn., Jan. 18. – Wake up, Florida, and get some advertising! You've got a channel. I hereby offer $30,000, also made from chewing Wrigley's gum, to the first swimmer who lands from Cuba, bringing with him something besides his bathing suit.

*The Mayor.*

P. S. – Good luck to my friend Dan Moody, the new Governor of Texas, who has to start in from the bottom and capture his own prisoners.

## 144 Note From Mayor Rogers On Cruisers And Elections

SPARTANBURG, S. C., Jan. 19. – See where the Senate voted three new cruisers. We had to have 'em to deliver our marines around on our various battle fronts.

Those three cruisers will settle three more foreign elections. How many will they have to build to seat Smith and Vare?

Awaiting anxiously,

*The Seated Mayor.*

## 145 A Few Thoughts On Elections From Mayor Rogers Of Beverly

NORFOLK, Va., Jan. 20. – The Republican Senators whose side spent most of the money want Smith seated, but the Democrats, on account of their shortage of money, think it would be a bad precedent. Our elections will keep on till they are as uncertain as Nicaragua's.

Elected without protest or reason,

*Mayor Rogers.*

## 146 MAYOR ROGERS OF BEVERLY MUSES NEUTRALLY ON PROHIBITION

LESTER, W. Va., Jan. 21. – Prohibition has been in effect seven years this week, and what's living on both sides are celebrating.

*The Neutral Mayor.*

P. S. – One thing to be said for it, prohibition will work if you drink it.

## 147 WILL ROGERS IS INSPECTING PRESIDENTIAL CANDIDATES

LYNCHBURG, Va., Jan. 22. – All I been doing the last week is playing to and instructing coming Presidential candidates.

Hit Governor Donahey of Ohio, who even the Republicans think is better than anything they got out there; they have elected him three times in a row. Then I went into Tennessee, and Governor Peay, another Democrat, has fooled 'em three times in a row down there.

Then last night into West Virginia, to Charleston, where I run into my first Republican official. It was Governor Gore, who introduced me to the gang as the sole surviving "Progressive." He is a farmer and if Cal and Lowden go into a deadlock, like Smith and McAdoo will, why you want to keep this boy's name on your 'phone list.

Next Wednesday night I am in Troy, N. Y. On account of not being a member of Tammany I couldn't get into Albany, but I hope to see or hear about by old friend Al Smith, and see what his horoscope reads for about June, 1928.

It just looks like if it wasn't for the Presidential candidates I wouldn't have any audience at all. They have been a godsend to me, so bring on more of them.

I don't care whether they are better or not, but let's have more candidates.

*Mayor Rogers.*

## 148 WILL ROGERS SAYS A WORD ON THE MEXICAN SITUATION

NEW YORK, N. Y., Jan. 23. – Mr. Coolidge says he is not going to submit the Mexican trouble to arbitration. He says he feels so sure we are right that there is no one he would trust to decide it in our favor.

*The Mayor.*

P. S. — Be sure you are right and then go ahead, but don't arbitrate.

## 149 Will Rogers Interprets Princeton-Harvard Attitude

UTICA, N. Y., Jan. 24. — This has been a brain-fagging day for the tabloid readers. With the Norris trial not ending and the "Peaches" one starting, it's just asking too much, and some day their minds will crack.

*The Mayor.*

P. S. — Princeton denies that they were rough with Harvard in football. They say they were firm but never rough, that it wasn't necessary.

## 150 Will Rogers' Dispatch

NEW YORK, N. Y., Jan. 25. — You are going to get nothing three times a day but "Peaches, mud and applesauce."

When a judge holds a case like that in public, when he knows all they want anyway is publicity, where's your recall and referendum?

And we are the country that's sending missionaries to China.

*Will Rogers.*

## 151 Will Rogers On Mothers-In-Law Reputations, Law And Alimony

NEW YORK, N. Y., Jan. 26. — Every sensational case nowadays has its mother-in-law. If these mothers protected their daughters as much before they get into court as they do after they get in there, they wouldn't get into court. Too bad they don't fight for their daughters' reputation as quick as they will for their daughters' alimony.

*Will Rogers.*

P. S. — The permanent wife is the one without advice.

## 152 Brief Notes By Will Rogers On A Few Current Topics

ATLANTIC CITY, N. J., Jan. 27. – The missionaries went over to announce to China that there was a heaven, and now the Chinamen want to kill them to give them a chance to prove it. But some of the missionaries are showing a little doubt themselves.

*The Rolling Chair Mayor.*

P. S. – I see where Judge Landis exonerated Tris and Ty today. He wasn't much late. All us paying customers exonerated 'em the day we heard it.

P. S. S. – I ordered apple sauce this morning and the waiter brought me peaches.

## 153 A Few Problems In The News Settled By Will Rogers

ALBANY, N. Y., Jan. 28. – They just had to postpone the "spoiled peaches" case these few days to give the constant followers of that case a chance to catch up. They couldn't read that fast. Even the pictures were coming so fast they couldn't mentally digest them.

*The Mayor,*
In Al Smith's Territory.

P. S. – This will set at rest all rumors as to where Speaker and Cobb are to go. Just conferred with both. Ty goes to the Claremore (Oklahoma) Giants and Tris goes to the Beverly Hills, California, nearly White Sox.

## 154 Mayor Rogers Looks Over Sesquicentennial That Was

PHILADELPHIA, Pa., Jan. 29. – Arrived in Philadelphia today to attend the "sesqui-next-year-after" centennial. I visited Chicago the next year after, St. Louis the year after, and I wanted to keep my record clean. I wanted to visit this afterward, as I would much rather see the grounds than the exposition.

Well, I couldn't find a single Philadelphian that could tell me where it was. Some had heard of it, but none of them had ever attended. Some was in favor of leaving the thing open, so it would get advertised around Philadelphia that it was there, but they didn't want to leave it up that long.

*A Visiting Mayor.*

## 155 Will Rogers Says President Is Right On Protection

NEW YORK, N.Y., Jan. 30. – My advice to Mr. Coolidge on preparedness is slowly bearing fruit. Here are his exact words in a speech Saturday: "What we need and all that we do need for national protection is adequate protection."

Couldn't ask for a clearer statement than that. What a hungry man needs and all that he needs for personal sustenance is adequate food and shelter. All even a Democrat needs for self-preservation is adequate votes. All the old Mayor needs is plenty of jokes and good audiences.

*The Mayor.*

P. S. – I am taking care of New York while Jimmy Walker is gone to Cuba to recuperate from Tammany politicians.

## 156 The World's Seven Wonders As Listed By Will Rogers

ROANOKE, Va., Jan. 31. – Am down in Old Virginia, the mother of Presidents when we thought Presidents had to be aristocrats. Since we got wise to the limitations of aristocrats, Virginia has featured their ham over their Presidential timber.

Visited their Natural Bridge today, the first of the seven wonders of the world. Niagara and the Grand Canyon are a couple more. Italy's poor marksmanship is one. Faith in prohibition enforcement is another, Claremore (Okla.) radium water and last and greatest the Democratic eternal hope.

*The Mayor.*

## 157 Rogers's Idea Of Conferences, Particularly On Disarmament

RALEIGH, N. C., Feb. 1. – Had a visit today at the home of ex-Secretary of the Navy Josephus Daniels. He had all the photographs of our navy, when we had a navy.

Wars don't diminish our navy. It's peace that's so devastating. When we were attacked by the disarmament conference we had even our lifeboats shot from under us.

Other nations were anxious to confer when we were building ahead of them, but now they are ahead, so why should they confer?

*The Mayor.*

P. S. – Congress ought to pass a law to prohibit us conferring with anybody on anything, till we learn how.

## 158 Will Rogers Finds Florida, Like Dempsey, Still Popular

DAYTONA BEACH, Fla., Feb. 2. – You know Dempsey never was as popular as he was after he had lost the championship. Well, that's just the way with Florida.

And, like Dempsey, they still got the same things that made 'em great, one time. The panic weeded the punks out; all the regulars are down here as usual.

You know it's a pleasure to meet these people when they haven't got a map in their hands. Now they are trying to please you instead of sell you.

*A Mayor.*

From a Couple of States that
Can Afford to be Generous.

## 159 Rogers Meets Mr. Rockefeller And Comes Out 20 Cents Ahead

ORLANDO, Fla., Feb. 3. – Had breakfast this morning with John D. Rockefeller, for which I received a fine breakfast and a brand new dime. Went out with him and watched him play eight holes of golf, for which I received another dime.

Made 20 cents clear. Received more jokes from him than I gave, as he is certainly keen and has a great sense of humor.

Had a very pleasant morning and would have stayed longer, but he run out of dimes. I am trying to get him to come to California for his second hundred years.

Who else will give me a dime to eat with them?

*The Mayor.*

## 160 WILL ROGERS SUGGESTS A COURSE OF ACTION IN CHINA

MIAMI, Fla., Feb. 4. – We will stop those Chinese from fighting among themselves if we have to kill them to do it.

*The Reading and Rambling Mayor.*

## 161 MAYOR ROGERS OF BEVERLY FINDS FLORIDA GOING STRONG

MIAMI, Fla., Feb. 5. – Say, where do some of these birds get the idea that Florida has blown up? Why, say, they are going strong down here. The lot-buying period is over, but now they are settled down to work and common sense and they are getting in fine shape.

It's the most beautiful weather you ever saw in your life here now—everybody walking around in Summer clothes and bathing and fishing and golfing. Of course, the Mayors here don't stack up with the California-type of Mayors, but outside of that they give us quite a run. The main place where we got 'em licked is in the Summer. California is better as a Summer resort than it is as a Winter one; but it's warmer here in the Winter than in California.

But don't start in feeling too sorry for these Floridians. They are getting along mighty fine. I see by this morning's paper that California had an earthquake yesterday. These papers here just keep earthquakes set up in type all the time, and it goes in daily that Cal has had one.

Well—just so we don't have one out there.

Yours,

*The Mayor.*

## 162 WILL ROGERS KEEPS CALM, DESPITE EARTHQUAKE REPORTS

MIAMI BEACH, Fla., Feb. 6. – See by the Florida papers today that California had another earthquake yesterday. I rushed right down to The Miami News to see what details they had, for my family was all out there. In looking it up in the pressroom we couldn't find any details, but we found the story on the press of the earthquake that we are having today, and that will be in tomorrow's paper, so I am not going to get excited till next Friday's earthquake. That's when they report a big one.

*Will Rogers,*

The Mayor of an Unshaken Town.

## 163 Passing Note By Will Rogers On Two International Events

ST. PETERSBURG, Fla., Feb. 7. – I am here in the only town in America where two world's series sporting events are held. The outdoor, under-a-shade checker championship and the horseshoe pitching finals are here.

It's the greatest climate in the world for open-air checkers. You can get into the king row here before you can make a move in other climates. And the mule-slipper heaver can do more with a horseshoe than a manicurist can with a drunk.

I'll have to get some grounds for these games out in old Beverly. We can play 'em while they are sleeping.

*The Mayor.*

## 164 Will Rogers Remarks:

PENSACOLA, Fla., Feb. 8. – Portugal is having revolution. Good joke on us. We haven't any more marines to cover that one.

*Will Rogers.*

P. S. – I flew 300 miles to get here. Hurrah for commercial aviation.

*Will*

## 165 Will Rogers Discusses British Parliament Opening

SARASOTA, Fla., Feb. 9. – The King opened Parliament yesterday. The Prince of Wales got his sword and his robe and his legs mixed up, and furnished what the papers called the comedy element. But get this one. I think the King furnished his quota of humor with the following:

"My relations with China are friendly and I have dispatched warships there to express my good feeling."

The King evidently gave more thought to his wardrobe than he did to his speech. This shows why Kings don't have jesters any more. They don't need 'em.

Yours,
*Tourist Rogers.*

## 166 WILL ROGERS IN PALM BEACH SO MORAL HE WAS UNINTERESTING

PALM BEACH, Fla., Feb. 10. – Terrible wave of immorality sweeping the stage. My performance in Palm Beach tonight was witnessed by jury of moralists composed of E. F. Albee, Lee Shubert, Marcus Loew, Adolph Zukor, Edgar Selwyn, Arthur Hammerstein, Joe Leblang, Mrs. Stotesbury and Ben Bernie. They pronounced the performance so clean that it was uninteresting.

*The Evangelist Mayor.*

P. S. – Length of season here depends on amount of your money. Mine lasted from 8:30 Thursday to 11 P.M. same day. I didn't think it worth while to take a cottage.

## 167 WILL ROGERS MEDITATES ABOUT FARMERS' RELIEF

TAMPA, Fla., Feb. 11. – One thing about farmers' relief: It can't last long, for the farmers ain't got much more to be relieved of.

A farmer that knows.

*Cocklebur Rogers.*

## 168 MAYOR ROGERS SENDS AN ITEM ON THE STATE OF FLORIDA

MACON, Ga., Feb. 12. – Just come out from a ten-day tour of Florida. Didn't see a real estate man on entire trip. Everybody in bathing suits, nobody bathing.

They are taking their misfortune like real sports and have reconciled themselves to being the second best resort State in America. They have drained the golf courses and you don't have to play with a ball that will float any more.

If they could ever starve those natives into working, Florida would be a second Germany. Even old Georgia has picked up since Ty was restored.

Touring the Rotary belt,
*The Mayor.*

## 169 WILL ROGERS PRESENTS HIS IDEA OF FARM RELIEF

AUGUSTA, Ga., Feb. 13. – Here is my Farm Relief bill: Every time a Southerner plants nothing on his farm but cotton year after year, and the Northerner nothing but wheat or corn, why, take a hammer and hit him twice right between the eyes.

You may dent your hammer, but it will do more real good than all the McNary-Haugen bills you can pass in a year.

*Old Doc Rogers.*

## 170 WILL ROGERS ON FARM RELIEF AND THE VALUE OF DAUGHTERS

COLUMBIA, S. C., Feb. 14. – The Senate relieved the farmers on Friday; the House of Representatives is supposed to relieve them tomorrow. Rotation of crops and less automobiles will relieve them whenever they decide to try it.

*The Mayor.*

P. S. – Just had lunch with the Governor of South Carolina. He has nine grown daughters. What would the wide-open spaces of the West give for some Governors like that? In a few years he will have enough grandchildren to vote him Governor for life.

## 171 AS TO PRESIDENTS, WILL ROGERS DISAGREES WITH DR. BUTLER

ASHEVILLE, N. C., Feb. 15. – I never thought we would live to see the day when Congressman Upshaw of Georgia knew more than President Nicholas Murray Butler of Columbia; but it has happened. The Doctor says our next President must be a wet. He may know schoolmarming, but he don't know American sentiment outside New York.

Mind you, I am very fond of the Professor. He said he was going to give me a degree just as soon as he can think of one to give me. Well, after the next election he can give me one for ignorance with a smattering of political insight.

From the Mayor who gathers other people's ideas all over the country instead of just expounding his own,

*Will.*

## 172 Will Rogers Meditates On Fisticuffs In Congress

PINEHURST, N. C., Feb. 16. – Two of my Congressional friends had a fight in Congress yesterday–Sol Bloom of New York and Blanton of Texas. That's three fights in there in three days, and nobody has been hit yet.

If their political sight is as bad as their aim, we better call for a new election. What this country needs is legislators that can both knock each other out for good. That's our only salvation.

The Mayor who won't give up his seat in Beverly Hills without being bought off.

*Will.*

## 173 Will Rogers Not Worried Over Recall Talk In Beverly

FLORENCE, S. C., Feb. 17. – Haven't paid much attention to that talk out in Beverly Hills about going to recall the Mayor. I am not afraid of that. Thay can't let me out. I know too much. Why, I will rock the very foundation of the social strata of screen, oil and realtor business.

*The Mayor From Now On.*

P. S. – If they monkey with me I will undo all the good that Will Hays has done for years.

## 174 Will Rogers Makes A Plea To Heflin's Constituency

MONTGOMERY, Ala., Feb. 18. – Senator Heflin of Alabama held up all Senate business yesterday for five hours. That's a record for narrow views.

Tonight in his home capital I am pleading with Alabama to please not exterminate all Catholics, Republicans, Jews, negroes, Jim Reed, Al Smith, Wadsworth, Mellon and Coolidge and the Pope.

Of course, my plea will do no good, for Tom knows the intelligence of his constituency better than we do.

*A Missionary Will.*

## 175 Mr. Rogers In Mississippi Muses On Farm Politics

JACKSON, Miss., Feb. 19. – I am here in the native igloo of Senator Pat Harrison. The only way I get booked in Mississippi is to tell them I am a friend of Pat Harrison's.

They sure are strong for Pat down here, and say, you would be surprised to see what they are doing. This old State is up and going– diversified farming, and talking politics. Lowden has been down here, and he sure made a hit with these old Democrats. I believe they will vote for him.

What's Cal going to do about the Nary-McHaugen bill? I am betting he vetoes it. Lowden against Harrison in 1928.

*Will.*

## 176 Will Rogers Sees Big Job Ahead For Aimee McPherson

HOT SPRINGS, Ark., Feb. 20. – Headlines this morning said: "Aimee to Reform Texas." Naturally I thought it meant "Pa" Jim Ferguson and Amon G. Carter. I read on and found it referred to "Texas" Guinan and Mayor Jim Walker. If Aimee can save them, her days in the desert for publicity are at an end. An Arkansaw traveler for the next few days.

*Will.*

P. S. – Ban Johnson and Harry Wills are both here training for return matches with Judge Landis and Jack Sharkey.

## 177 Thoughts On Evolution From The Mayor Of Beverly

HOT SPRINGS, Ark., Feb. 21. – Arkansaw took the literacy test just this week, with an evolution bill. They just did make it. Tennessee and Texas couldn't pass.

I don't know why some of these States want to have their ancestry established by law. There must be a suspicion of doubt somewhere.

Outside of the Legislature's action, why, old Arkansas is certainly booming. Hot Springs is crowded with guests. They are exhibiting me here at the Arlington Hotel.

*Will Rogers.*

## 178 WILL ROGERS ENTHUSIASTIC ABOUT THE ARKANSAS OZARKS

FAYETTEVILLE, Ark., Feb. 22. – I didn't get to buy any of Valentino's personal objects and works of art, but when they bring them to Claremore, Okla., for an auction there, I think I will buy some rare old pieces. Yours,

*Will Rogers.*

P. S. – Say, if you want to visit the most beautiful country in the United States, don't overlook these Ozark Mountains. In these are where I grabbed off my only wife. So you will pardon me for bragging on Arkansas.

## 179 DIRT FARMER ROGERS'S VIEW OF THE PRESIDENT'S SPEECH

FORT SMITH, Ark., Feb. 23. – Say, that Mr. Coolidge is a smart man. He delivered an oration on the life of Washington, and all he talked about was how good a farmer George was. He insinuated Washington made all his money farming and never asked for reiief.

I don't know myself, but I believe George's fighting got him further than his farming. But it just shows you how far ahead Calvin figures.

Yours with fifteen hundred acres of Oklahoma waiting for relief, an automobile dirt farmer,

*The Mayor.*

## 180 ROGERS, DOWN IN TEXAS, REPORTS CAPITAL EVENTS

BRECKENRIDGE, Tex., Feb. 24. – Mr. Coolidge isn't keeping the great American people in suspense on that farming bill purposely. It takes time to feel out the whole country and see which side has the most votes.

A farmer without a surplus,

*Will Rogers.*

## 181 Will Rogers Gives Credit To Coolidge As 'A Big Man'

BROWNWOOD, Tex., Feb. 25. – Well, Calvin vetoed the "Mary McHaugen" bill. One thing, nobody can ever accuse the President of being a "yes" man. I am with him on this. I never could see why the bill raised the price on a hog and not on a cow, raised it on an ear of corn, but not on a potato.

You see, that shows you where class will tell. The old Congressmen and Senators got scared by the vetoes back home, but Cal went through. That's the difference between a big man and a little one.

A dirt farmer who has to fertilize.

*Will.*

## 182 Will Rogers Sees Help For The Farmer In Radio

AMARILLO, Tex., Feb. 27. – Mr. Coolidge killed the Farm Relief bill, but the farmers broke about even. The "Better Radio" bill passed. Farmers are buying more batteries than they are seeds.

A radio farmer,

*Old Bill.*

P. S. – Hurrah! Only four more days of Congressional burglary on the Treasury.

Another P. S. – I am on my way home to take up any loose divorces that may have accumulated in my municipality during my absence. I am stopping in Arizona, I want to see the State that produces the Senators that can talk for three days and nights.

## 183 Will Rogers Says We Handle A Few Mandates, Ourselves

ALBUQUERQUE, N. M., Feb. 28. – Just drove 125 miles over to Santa Fe to speak before New Mexico's Legislature. It's the only one in America where everything is carried on in both Spanish and English.

You know New Mexico is handled under an American mandate–the same as we handle Nicaragua, Mexico, Tacna-Arica and China.

Only three more days and the country is free again. Congress is adjourning. Soothing syrup for sick Senators.

*Will.*

## 184 BRIEF NOTE FROM MAYOR ROGERS REGARDING AFFAIRS IN MEXICO

EL PASO, Tex., March 1. – Just returned from Jaurez, Old Mexico. Liquor smuggling is going on the other way now. They are crazy about our new drinks and claim they receive twice the insensibility for one-third the amount of drinking.

I have to disappoint Mr. Kellogg, but I didn't see a single Russian Bolshevik plotting against us. Mexico had received their morning note from our State Department telling them how to run their country.

Headed for Beverly Hills to protect my honor.

*Will.*

## 185 ROGERS TAKES HIS OATH ON THE SUBJECT OF DAMS

TUCSON, Ariz., March 2. – Arizona says dam California; if they want a dam let 'em dam their own river as much as they dam please, but Arizona bedams if she is even going to split a dam so dammed bad; let 'em dam their climate or dam Frisco or dam something. Why pick on us to dam? We don't want to be vulgar, but in plain words, dam California. But they are not going to dam us or Arizona's Colorado River at any dam place, any dam time. And our dam senators will tell the dam world as long as they have a dam bit of breath left, so that's the whole dam business in a dam nutshell.

This is from the dammed best mayor in Beverly Hills.

*Will Rogers.*

## 186 MR. ROGERS SURVEYS THE NEWS AND FINDS IT WARLIKE

TUCSON, Ariz., March 3. – Captured boat from China, landed more marines in Nicaragua, sent new demand to Mexico.

Looks like Mr. Coolidge will run on his war record.

*Will Rogers.*

*Mayor Will Rogers inspects Beverly Hills police force.*

## 187 WILL ROGERS CELEBRATES ADJOURNMENT OF CONGRESS

BEVERLY HILLS, Cal., March 4. – Don't ever tell us Friday is unlucky. Didn't Congress adjourn today?

The Republicans died fighting to keep from being investigated. The voters would like to investigate both parties as to their sanity the last few weeks. And there would be no hung jury as to their decision.

*The Homing Mayor.*

## 188 MAYOR WILL ROGERS OF BEVERLY FINDS DIVORCES JAM HIS OFFICE

LOS ANGELES, Cal., March 5. – Arrived home. Mayor's office clogged with divorces. Have to get rid of some of them before we can have any new marriages.

Regards to the two Reed boys of Sixty-ninth Congress fame.

*Will.*

## 189 ROGERS SAYS WE PAID SENATE FOR WISDOM AND GOT WIND

HOLLYWOOD, Cal., March 6. – I notice all newspapers call it the adjournment of the Senate. It wasn't adjournment. They just give out. The big blow in Florida was a great local misfortune, but the big blow in the Senate was a national calamity. Even the Red Cross can't repair their damage. We got wind where we had paid to get wisdom.

Reviewed my Police and Fire Department this morning. Boy, we got a town! We are putting an immigration quota on millionaires now, they getting too thick.

On the job.

*His Honor.*

## 190 ROGERS FEAR LACK OF HUMOR NOW CONGRESS HAS ADJOURNED

BEVERLY HILLS, Cal., March 7. – Well, I just seem lost for comedy since Congress adjourned. I would keep them in session the year round for my business, but I have some consideration for people, so I sacrifice my needs for the good of the country.

I don't know where we will get our laughs from until next December, so if I am not funny it's because I have no example.

Yours downheartedly,
*William Penn Rogers.*

## 191 Will Rogers Comments On Southern Primary Decision

BEVERLY HILLS, Cal., March 8. – See this morning where the Supreme Court says negroes in Texas have the right to vote at Democratic primaries.

Certainly will seem funny to see the negroes and the whites voting the same ticket. First thing you know they will be allowing a white Republican to associate with a white Democrat in the South. It's before the Supreme Court now.

Yours for quality in politics regardless of quantity and color.
*Will.*

## 192 Mr. Rogers Has A Suggestion For Mr. Coolidge's Vacation

BEVERLY HILLS, Cal., March 9. – Everybody out here is all excited about where Mr. Coolidge will spend his vacation.

Put him on a farm with the understanding he has to make his own living off it, and I bet he will give the farmers relief next year. I offer mine for the experiment, and if he makes a go of it he is not a President, he is a magician.

*Farmer Bill.*

## 193 Will Rogers Interprets A California Whiskey Law

FRESNO, Cal., March 10. – California State Legislature passed bill yesterday to make whiskey stills unlawful unless operating under State permit. This makes police permits null and void. The plan is to try and get people to do their drinking under the auspices of the State Government instead of under just anybody.

*Will.*

P. S. – Certainly want to thank the neighboring village of Los Angeles for turning out in such paying quantities to see a Mayor who is funny purposely, and not unconsciously. Sorry my friends Tom Mix and Doug Fairbanks couldn't be with us, but they were both running pictures of themselves at their homes and couldn't leave. I took my own fire and police protection with me. I wouldn't trust that Los Angeles bunch.

Thanks.

*Will.*

## 194 Will Rogers Is Stirred By Our Stand On Airplanes

SAN FRANCISCO, Cal., March 11. – See by the newspapers this morning Secretary Wilbur says there is no danger from Europe from airplanes. When we nearly lose the next war, as we probably will, we can lay it onto one thing and that will be the jealousy of the army and navy toward aviation.

They have belittled it ever since it started and will keep on doing it till they have something dropped on them from one, and even they will say it wasn't a success.

*Will.*

## 195 Will Rogers Says Dawes Has Been Vindicated

OAKLAND, Cal., March 12. – Everybody is just sitting tight out here in California, waiting till the next term of Congress to get Boulder Dam. They figure that Senators Ashurst and Cameron of Arizona can't talk during the whole of next session.

It looks like Dawes has been vindicated. He has always said there was a taint of hookworm in the Senate and that it should be administered to.

Say, Dawes is kinder looking up for President. Did you know it? I hear a lot about him in case Coolidge abdicates.

Tell Florida California never looked more beautiful. I am headed for Borah's range in a few days.

*Will.*

## 196 Will Rogers Gives His View Of The Chinese Situation

OAKLAND, Cal., March 13. – All we ask of the Chinese is that they settle down and let us and England keep on collecting and running their customs for them. I don't see why they should refuse a little thing like that.

China owes us four million and we take over their custom revenue. France owes us four billion and we are afraid to send them a bill for it. What a great difference in diplomatic relations an army and navy make!

Refereeing from the side lines.

*Will.*

## 197 Will Rogers Finds Haiti Ideal Because Senatorless

SAN JOSE, Cal., March 14. – See where they don't allow an American Senator to land in Haiti. Who would ever have thought that Haiti would be the first ideal country? Watch its population double right now.

This is the champion prune town of the world. I was reported to the police this morning for ordering grapefruit.

*Will Rogers.*

P. S. – I never saw California looking more beautiful. The tremendous rains out here have washed away all the real estate signs.

## 198 Opinion Of Will Rogers On The Legal Conscience

SACRAMENTO, Cal., March 15. – Just addressed the California State Legislature and helped them pass a bill to form a lawyers' association to regulate their conduct.

Personally I don't think you can make a lawyer honest by an act of the Legislature. You've got to work on his conscience. And his lack of conscience is what makes him a lawyer.

Met the Governor. He tried to sell me a lot. So California has a typical Californian as Governor.

The evangelist among State Legislatures,

*Will.*

P. S. – Tomorrow I invade Nevada and may get to Weepah.

## 199 Will Rogers Reports On Legislation In Nevada

CARSON CITY, Nev., March 16. — Just delivered free public advice to the Governor, Senate and State Legislature of Nevada.

They killed the License Gambling bill here today. The gambling element killed it. They voted against paying a license. With all other States gambling free, there was no reason they should pay a license here.

*Will Rogers.*

P. S. — This is the solar plexus town; ask my friend Corbett. Also the old stamping ground of Mark Twain. Going now to Virginia City.

## 200 Mr. Rogers's View Of Reply Mellon Sent To Princeton

SALT LAKE CITY, Utah, March 17. — Hurrah for Mellon for answering, today, the Faculties of Columbia and Princeton on debt cancellation. It almost takes a sense of humor for college professors to advise Mellon on money matters.

When our country does accidentally stumble on a competent man why don't they let him alone? That's why Notre Dame has the best football team in America every year—because they concentrate on the business of a college and not on the business of a Government.

What Columbia and Princeton need is open field runners and not canceled debts.

*Pedagogue Rogers,*
Of the Claremore Third Grade.

P. S. — Just flew in here 300 miles from Elko, Nev., by airplane. Got lost over the mountains in a snowstorm. Oh, boy, we got real aviators in this country, even if the Government don't think they are useful.

## 201 Will Rogers, Out In Idaho, Sends Impressions Of Borah

POCATELLO, Idaho, March 18. — It took me forty-eight States to do it, but I finally arrived in one where every one knows who one of their Senators is.

I go to Borah's home town tomorrow. I want to see this place before it is made a shrine for honoring the only man in public life in his time with independent thought, when everybody else's ideas are as standardized as Ford parts.

What's best for the political machine is best for the politician. What's best for America is best for Borah. Ask Mr. Coolidge how far wrong I am.

*Will.*

## 202 Will Rogers Fails To Find Any Democrats In Boise

BOISE, Idaho, March 19. — I blow into this town of Borah's wanting to hold my usual conference or caucus with the Democrats about next year's nomination and I find there are no Democrats here. Borah is the only one they have.

Haven't been out to look the town over, but I bet it's rotten. Anything that is all Republican is no good. Anything that is part Republican isn't much good. You have to have some decent element.

They built a new depot for Borah to go out from and come in to. He's gone out of it, but has never come back yet. I got a wire from him welcoming me to his town; also one from Alice Longworth. So I see that the Republican Party is still intact.

I'm going to Oregon tomorrow looking for a Democrat. Love to all the faithful.

*Will Rogers.*

## 203 Will Rogers Pays Tribute To A Governor Of Mississippi

PENDLETON, Ore., March 20. — Last year I was entertained in the home of a fine old Southern gentleman. He came to my little performance. This year he phoned me: "Will you have time to come and tell the jokes? I can't get over." And I did.

He was a plain, lovable character and he handed me out much homely philosophy. I will miss him next year when I go back, and his State will miss him. He was just a plain Governor of the great State of Mississippi.

You missed a lot by not knowing Governor Whitfield. We don't raise any more like him, for conditions have changed.

*Will Rogers.*

TACOMA, Wash., March 21. – Just flew in here from Portland. Beautiful country and it's the only way to see it. When Brisbane and I get our aviation we can make all trips like this. Was met by newsboys with extras telling of Peaches losing alimony. I think to save readers' time and courts', too, all alimony should be stipulated in marriage contract. Course she has still got her faithful mother and the movie rights. If old Daddy don't pay alimony he is just liable to not land any more Peaches. It's a bad year for fruit.

Yours,
*Will.*

## 205 ON SELF-DETERMINATION AS ROGERS SEES IT IN CHINA

PORTLAND, Ore., March 22. – Headline says "British Kill Fourteen Chinamen in Shanghai." If our missionaries had already saved these fourteen, why that ought to make it all right, but it certainly will be terrible if they died heathens.

Hurrah for self-determination of nations. Yours,
*Will.*

P. S. – This is written from Portland, the red hot rival of Longview. I can remember when Seattle was their rival.

## 206 WILL ROGERS FINDS PROOF OF THE GENIUS OF HENRY FORD

ABERDEEN, Wash., March 23. – We have often heard it said that Henry Ford was just lucky. Well, picking up all those odds and ends and pasting 'em together and getting 'em to run right have been lucky. And when they kept on running all these years, that might come under the head of perpetual luck. But when a man goes out and hires Jim Reed for his lawyer–that's inspired genius. The other side needs Moses to compete with him.

*Will.*

P. S. – I have seen so many saw logs the last few days that I will go out of this country barking.

## 207 Will Rogers Discusses Wars And Our War Ports

SEATTLE, Wash., March 24. – Just had a pleasant chat with Seattle's woman mayor. She seems to be one woman who has lived up to expectations in public office.

Seattle is the nearest port of debarkation for our latest war in China. The port is what New Orleans is to our Nicaraguan festivities. I am anxious to see what port our gunboats and marines depart from to cover the Italian Yugoslavian war.

Palm Beach ought to get that trade. Every port will soon have its own war trade. Yours,

*The Male Mayor.*

P. S. – Klondike sourdoughs are all going South to Weepah.

## 208 Mr. Rogers Has A Poor Opinion Of Disarmament Conferences

YAKIMA, Wash., March 25. – I see we are off to another disarmament conference. I never saw a country that wanted to get rid of their army as bad as we do. We should have been born a cockroach, then the present Administration wouldn't have such a time getting rid of our arms. Yours,

*Will.*

## 209 Will Rogers, Still Wandering, Reports From Spokane, Wash.

SPOKANE, Wash., March 26. – Just blew into Spokane. This is a beautiful city.

Was met at train by Senator Dill. He is the one that just got married. His wife is awfully smart; that is, she was supposed to be.

I tell you it seemed good to run onto a Democrat again. This is the town that has the Davenport Hotel and Restaurant. That's the Mussolini of hotels. It's the Bobby Jones of American hotels.

Third term not so strong up here. Next week I penetrate Wheeler and Walsh territory. Just think of finding two Democrats in one State.

So long. Tomorrow war news.

*Will Rogers.*

## 210 Will Rogers's Comment On Course Of Events In China

SPOKANE, Wash., March 27. — Smedley Butler has arrived in China. The war may continue but the parties will stop.

Yours,

*Will.*

## 211 Will Rogers's Opinion Of Americans In China

MISSOULA, Mont., March 28. — Any person that will stay in the middle of a civil war for six months and don't know enough to even send his family out, it won't do much good to rescue him. You bring him back home and he will run right in front of a Ford. We had to shell that Chinese town to let our people know it was time to come out and be rescued.

Yours for home missions.

*Will.*

## 212 Mr. Rogers Moralizes A Bit On International Relations

BUTTE, Mont., March 29. — A nation is just like an individual. If a man's neighbors all hate him and he is continually in trouble, and all his fights and troubles are always over in the other fellow's yard, he must be wrong.

If he won't stay at home what he needs is a good licking or a muzzle. Yours,

*Will.*

P. S. — Flew in here two miles high over the snow-covered mountains from Missoula and just been down a mile under the ground. There's nothing to see on the level any more.

## 213 Mr. Rogers Sees Us Disarming If We Have To Do It Alone

HELENA, Mont., March 30. — France and Italy won't join us in disarmament, but that don't worry us. We will do it alone.

If nobody wants to disarm with us, we will show 'em we are right. We will shame 'em into it—if we have to sink our last life preserver to do it.

Yours,
*Will.*

## 214 Our West Like Switzerland If Our Farmers Would Yodle

GREAT FALLS, Mont., March 31. — Just flew into this great little Western city, late home of Charles M. Russell, the painter. He will live in history as America's most famous cowboy. And his country talks about scenery.

I flew over mountains today that make Switzerland look like a prairie dog town. If we could get our mountain farmers to wear feathers in their hats and yodle, we would be as picturesque as Switzerland.

Maybe the farmers will yodle when they get relieved. They will have time to learn, anyway.

Yours,
*Will Rogers.*

## 215 Mr. Rogers Suggests Means Of Identifying Advertisers

BILLINGS, Mont., April 1. — Say, Henry Ford getting hurt in a Ford car was kind of a knock against the Lincoln, wasn't it?

Since we found out Ford uses his own product I suppose every man we see eating corn flakes we will think is Kellogg, every guy chewing gum is Wrigley. If he shaves himself we will think it's Gillette. If he is well powdered it's Mennen.

If it's three fellows with store clothes on it will perhaps be Hart, Schaffner and Marx, and if it's a bird nearly naked it's Mr. B. V. D.

Yours,
*Will Rogers.*

## 216 Will Rogers Gets Information About The Great Northwest

BROKEN BOW, Neb., April 3. — Just returning from very successful educational lecture tour of the entire Northwest. No English lecturers had been in there and spoiled the field. They can't make railroad fare to get that far away.

Not even a politician has insulted their intelligence publicly lately. Politics is dead there. Only thing they are interested in of a foreign nature is Ford's and Charlie Chaplin's trials.

They are near enough to Canada that prohibition is not an issue, and far enough away from Washington that they don't care if Upshaw was President.

Yours for outside information,

*Will.*

## 217 CHICAGO'S ELECTION SLOGAN AS MR. ROGERS INTERPRETS IT

HASTINGS, Neb., April 4. – Everybody is excited over who will win the election in Chicago. The side with the most machine guns will win it.

We send marines to Nicaragua to tell them how to run an election and send missionaries to China. No wonder we are funny to the rest of the world.

The slogan in Chicago is "Shoot 'em before they can vote."

Yours for law and order–in China,

*Will Rogers.*

## 218 MR. ROGERS FEARS WE'LL START DEHORSING OUR CAVALRY NEXT

MANHATTAN, Kan., April 5. – Just today visited Fort Riley, our advanced cavalry school. I saw all the cavalry in Europe, but these boys have got it on all of them.

I suppose, though, as soon as we get all our ships sunk at the disarmament conference we will start dehorsing our cavalry.

Yours,

*Will.*

P. S. – Everybody sit around the radio this evening to hear casualty reports of killed and wounded at Chicago.

## 219 MAYOR ROGERS IS DOUBTFUL OF CHICAGO'S BETTER ELEMENT

DES MOINES, Iowa, April 6. – Congratulations to the other cowboy mayor, Bill Thompson of Chicago!

They was trying to beat Bill with the better element vote. The trouble with Chicago is there ain't much better element. Reminds me of the time John W. Davis run on honesty.

There was no shooting in Chicago election day, but it will drop back to normal right away.

Flew here this morning from Fort Riley, Kansas. Brought and escorted by real aviators (wish we had a thousand of them).

This is Iowa, the incubator of Southern California.

*Mayor Rogers.*

## 220 Thoughts By Will Rogers On The Philippines Veto

MILWAUKEE, Wis., April 7. — See by the papers today that the Philippines wanted just to vote to see if they wanted independence. But we told 'em "No, you can't even vote to see if you want it or not, and furthermore we urgently request that you don't even be seen thinking about it."

What was that slogan the whole country was shouting just exactly ten years ago today? Does this sound like it, "Self determination of small nations."

Yours for memory,

*Will.*

## 221 Thoughts By Will Rogers On New Visual Telephone

WORTHINGTON, Minn., April 8. — With this new telephone photography life has no privacy any more. Suppose your 'phone bell don't work, somebody may be calling you up and looking you over, and you not knowing it.

And remember, don't run direct from the bath tub to the telephone. It also pictures everybody and everything that's in the room, so why hire a detective, when you can get evidence for a nickel?

We don't know yet whether it's a scientific discovery or a Wayne Wheeler invention. One lucky thing is gin photographs like water.

Yours for the good old days when they couldn't even tell where you were when 'phoning. There will be none installed at Beverly Hills.

*The Mayor.*

## 222 Will Rogers In Minnesota Sends Advice To Coolidge

MINNEAPOLIS, Minn., April 9. – Just been over today and addressed the Legislature of the great State of Minnesota. A fellow named Johnson interpreted for me. I didn't go to Norway, Sweden, and Denmark last year. I didn't think there was any use as I knew I was going to play here this year.

They are still hollering for farmer's relief and are trying to throw out Senator Shaw, who is in the United States Senate, and bring back Magnus Johnson, the best milker that ever hit Capitol Hill.

Mr. Coolidge has been invited here to this State, but if I were him I would be afraid to come.

Yours,
*Will.*

## 223 Will Rogers In Chicago Discusses Politics And Crime

CHICAGO, Ill., April 10. – Bill Thompson is a fast worker. Elected two days ago, he decided he would like to start Mayoring about tomorrow. No lame duck Mayors in this burg. When the votes are counted your hat is waiting. Congress and the Senate ought to do that. Why give 'em six months to repent on salary? This is the Rogers and Dawes plan.

Yours,
*Will.*

P. S. – Buried a bandit here yesterday. Had thirty-five thousand dollars' worth of flowers. It's the florist that's backing this crime wave. Undertakers advertise their high-priced coffins: "Fit for a bandit." Glorified crime.

## 224 Will Rogers Is Anxious To Help Out Somehow In China

DANVILLE, Ill., April 11. – I hereby offer myself and services to our Government as the first $1 a year man in our great war to make China cosmopolitan.

Unselfishly yours,

*Will.*

P. S. – I will run a railroad or supervise shipbuilding—in fact, any little errand just to help out.

## 225 Novel Prohibition Debate Proposed By Will Rogers

VINCENNES, Ind., April 12. – It's all the rage now to hold a debate on prohibition, if you can find a crowd drunk enough to pay to hear it.

I hereby challenge Billy Sunday on the subject: "Resolved, That the talk and arguments used for and against prohibition are worse on the public's morals than the drinking." Billy can take either side, affirmative, negative, progressive or farmers' relief.

At the finish we will split 50-50. He can take the decision and I will take the gate receipts.

Yours for getting this settled by the right people,

*Mr. Rogers.*

P. S. – Let me hear from this, Billy, over in Aurora, right away. If you don't take me, why, Aimee will.

## 226 Will Rogers, Dirt Farmer, Sees No Hope In McNary Plan

BEDFORD, Ind., April 13. – Senator McNary of McNary-Haugen farm relief fame dined at the White House yesterday. McNary says he would like to be given another chance to draw up another bill. He says he can draw up one without the objectionable features of the last one. If it eliminates the objectionable features it won't be any good, for it will eliminate the relief.

A dirt farmer.

*Will Rogers.*

## 227 Will Rogers Sees A Lesson In Aviators' 51-Hour Record

LAFAYETTE, Ind., April 14. – Hurrah for our aviators that broke the continuous flight record. Fifty-one hours! That breaks the Arizona Senators' continuous air record in the last Senate filibuster. That was not a contribution to science like this was. Theirs was just a tribute to poor Senate rules.

No automobile ever went fifty hours without stopping or refueling or meeting a train at a grade crossing or something, yet we spend a billion dollars on good roads for them. Why not a subsidy to commercial aviation? Congress is waiting two more wars to see if they are practical.

This better make us think. Fifty hours—they can send 'em here from any nation in Europe.

Regards from George Ade and Purdue.

*Will.*

## 228 Mr. Rogers Marvels At Certain Aspirations Of Cleveland, Ohio

CLEVELAND, Ohio, April 15. – Can you imagine? This town of Cleveland wants the Republican and Democratic conventions both in 1928.

A town that don't know any more than that is liable to ask for a sesquicentennial. The Republican convention will be held further West, for that's the way they are going to relieve the farmers—to let 'em see a convention. And as for the Democratic one, a sanity test will follow any town purposely asking for it.

From the Burgomaster of Beverly Hills,

*Will Rogers.*

P. S. – Cleveland's new depot has the front finished, but has made no arrangements about any trains or tracks coming in. If you know of a railroad that needs a depot, communicate with Cleveland.

## 229 Will Rogers Sends A Comment On China And Disarmament

CLEVELAND, Ohio, April 17. – We are holding another disarmament conference in Geneva. America and England have to wait every morning till we get the war news to see if we will have to sink the ship or has China sunk it for us.

The war correspondent,

*Will Rogers.*

## 230 Rogers Tells What He Finds In Governor Smith's Statement

CLEVELAND, Ohio, April 18. – If you want to read one of the only real straightforward statements ever issued by a politician, read Al Smith's, out today.

He explains that if elected President all Protestants would not be exterminated; that even a few of the present Senators would be retained, including Tom Heflin; that the Knights of Columbus would not replace the Boy Scouts and Kiwanis; that mass would not replace golf on Sunday morning, and that those that were fortunate enough to have meat could eat it on Friday.

It's no compliment to a nation's intelligence when these things have to be explained.

*The Old Burgomaster of Beverly.*

## 231 Views On Tolerance From The Burgomaster Of Beverly

WARREN, Ohio, April 19. – It was amusing this morning to read the various comments on Al Smith's statement.

Carmi Thompson, Republican, who was supposed to be so broadminded he decided the destiny of the Philippine nation, said of the Smith article: "I haven't read and don't intend to read it."

Congressman Burton, Republican, Ohio, said: "I wouldn't make any statement."

Now which is the narrowest, religious intolerance or political intolerance? Politicians think an umpire's decision is based on "What will my decision do for the party."

The old Burgomaster of Beverly,

*Will Rogers.*

## 232 Rogers On The Snyder Trial, Mr. Hoover And Other Topics

PITTSBURGH, Pa., April 10. – All I can see in the papers here today, by artificial light in the daytime, is that the Snyder murder trial is turning out to be a typical tabloid affair. They only have one juror and he is a press agent. They are trying to get eleven more press agents.

Again my judgment has been vindicated by no less a person than Mr. Coolidge. He says "Mr. Hoover could fill any Cabinet position." I go even further in my estimation of him. I say he could preside over the Cabinet in a pinch.

Yours,

*Will Rogers.*

P. S. – Who said Will Hays's job was a cinch? Think with what apprehension he picks up the paper every morning.

## 233 SHAKESPEARE AND POLITICS; A FEW REMARKS BY MR. ROGERS

MORGANTOWN, W. Va., April 21. – This is the home State of John W. Davis, the last Democratic sacrifice on the altar of "no policy to run on." Notice to Democrats–Get a policy and stick to it, even if it's wrong.

See by the papers that Mr. Davis is toastmaster tomorrow night at the Ambassador Hotel, New York, at a dinner to Shakespeare. He is not only the only West Virginian that would have known anything about Shakespeare, but the only Presidential candidate we ever had that could call his name without referring to his notes.

From the old Burgomaster of Beverly,

*Will Rogers.*

P. S. – Shakespeare is the only author that can play to losing business for a hundred years and still be known as an author.

## 234 WILL ROGERS VENTS OPINIONS AND A PROPHECY ON COOLIDGE

HARRISBURG, Pa., April 22. – I see where the wise guys are going to try and smoke Mr. Coolidge out with an open letter about how he stands on the third term.

They can write him till his mail looks like Santa Claus's, and all they will have to show for it will be ink on their fingers.

Why should he tell 'em? What would you tell anyone that asked you what you would be doing Nov. 4 a year and a half from now?

Yours,

*Will Rogers.*

P. S. – The following is not an editorial opinion, because they are always certain of what they write. This is only a fool's opinion, but it will be backed with money, made from being a fool. Coolidge will not only run; but he will win by so much he won't even stay up to listen to the count over the radio.

## 235 WILL ROGERS FIGURES RESULT OF THE PROHIBITION DEBATE

NEW YORK, N. Y., April 24. – Clarence Darrow and Wayne B. Wheeler debated here last night on prohibition. Darrow won, so the country stays wet. Wheeler said "The country ought to be dry." The farmers says "we ought to have relief."

Say, I just now saw the movie "The King of Kings." This is not an ad. It's a duty to let you know of it. The only way you could make a greater picture would be to have a better subject, and I doubt if there will ever be a better subject during our lifetime than the story of Christ.

A small town Mayor in a big city.

The Burgomaster.
*Will Rogers.*

## 236 ROGERS PLEADS THE CAUSE OF THE FLOOD SUFFERERS

PHILADELPHIA, Pa., April 25. – I don't believe our people that have never been around a flood area realize the tremendous need of these sufferers down on the Mississippi. It's by far the worst thing that has happened in this country in years.

A fire don't start to do the damage that a flood does. We have helped every nationality in the world. Now we have a chance to help the poorest people we have in America, and that is the renter farmer.

Most of the people need help, even when there is no flood, but they have always been too proud to ask for it. Mr. Ziegfeld has generously given me his wonderful new theatre in New York City, and I am going to put on my little one-man dogfight for this great cause next Sunday night. So even if you don't like cowboy gum chewers on the stage, come anyway and help out a real cause.

They will get every cent that comes in, if there is nobody there but my wife—who will have to pay to get in.

The old Burgomaster,

*Will Rogers.*

## 237 McCORMACK JOINS WILL ROGERS TO HELP THE FLOOD SUFFERERS

HIGH POINT, N. C., April 26. – It certainly does pay to have friends. John McCormack heard that I was giving a benefit performance for the flood sufferers at Mr. Ziegfeld's new theatre next Sunday night, and he called me on the phone just now, from out in Illinois, and said he would come clear in to New York to sing; that "he thought it was the greatest need by the largest number of people of anything that had ever come up."

Now, outside of being a good fellow, he is not a bad singer. So it will be "McCormack and Rogers, those two nifty boys in funny songs and sentimental jokes." But what the whole country has got to do is wake up and give. These people are going to need assistance for months.

Actors will help you in every town to give shows and raise money. They don't fail. And neither do the people, when they know the need.

Yours,
*Will.*

## 238 President Coolidge Has Partly Convinced Mr. Rogers

WINSTON-SALEM, N. C., April 27. – Mr. Coolidge said that newspaper men should stand by the Administration's foreign policy.

Now I will admit there has been times when he and I differed on Nicaragua, Mexico and China, but when I read his angle of it all, why, it sounded plausible.

They say a smart man changes his mind, but an editorial writer never does; so I have been convinced that I would rather be wrong with the Administration than right against it.

The Old Burgomaster of Beverly,
*Will Rogers.*

## 239 Will Rogers Makes A Plea For River Flood's Homeless

RICHMOND, Va., April 28. – There's hundreds of thousands of people being driven from their homes—homes that won't be there when they come back.

These poor people have never harmed a soul or broke a law. Yet Mrs. Snyder's picture has occupied more space in some of the papers than the whole State of Mississippi fighting for its life. There are ten reporters and photographers at the trial to one at the flood.

Just think of the extra amount of money that could be raised if that array of special writers, with their various talents for describing dramatic scenes, could be sent to the flood instead of the trial. There is more heart interest in one house-top with its little family flowing down the river on it than in all the corset salesmen in the world.

Yours,
*Will.*

## 240 Mr. Rogers, In The Shenandoah, Muses On Democratic Chances

STAUNTON, Va., April 29. – Been traveling today down through the beautiful Shenandoah Valley of Virginia—and boobs are leaving to see Europe! Just saw the birthplace of Woodrow Wilson.

They got a great young Governor here they are priming for the Democratic nomination for President in eight years from now. I am in favor of not nominating any in the meantime, and by that time the party will have time to think of an issue.

I tell you, you can't do nothing until this fellow Coolidge is overtaken by age.

Yours for travel, weather and political news,
*Will Rogers.*

## 241 Will Rogers, Here By Airplane, Urges More Red Cross Giving

NEW YORK, N. Y., May 1. – I just flew in here from Beckley, W. Va., where Casey Jones, the famous Curtiss aviator, landed me on the field after just two hours and twenty minutes from Washington, D. C. They had the big Bellanca plane out on the field and Chamberlin, the pilot, who is to take it to Paris, took me up in it. It's a great sample. All we need is thousands of them.

It looks like a big night at our show tonight. McCormack and I are arguing over who will open the show. Mr. Coolidge is going to make another Red Cross appeal for more funds. Don't stop at your quota. This is the biggest need we ever had in this country. Thank you.

*Will.*

## 242 Will Rogers Gives Thanks For Aid To His Flood Benefit

NEW YORK, N. Y., May 2. – Well, our benefit turned out fine. We got $17,950, and more checks still coming in. Want to try to thank everybody from all over the country that helped out.

Now don't slack on this stuff because New Orleans is out of danger. That doesn't alter the need of those hundreds of thousands of others who will have to be supported till a crop is raised. My old friend Ring Lardner, along with a contribution, sent the following suggestion as to how to stop the flood.

"Send out all the levees in New York."

Yours,
*Will.*

## 243 MR. ROGERS, IN ALBANY, THINKS AL MIGHT BE INDUCED TO MOVE

ALBANY, N. Y., May 3. – Just speeding along the old Hudson River the last three hours. I was thinking how many millions and millions of dollars would be raised overnight if it was out of its banks and doing the same amount of damage that the old Mississippi is.

Makes a lot of difference where a thing happens.

The old bounding Burgomaster,

*Will Rogers.*

P. S. – This is Albany, the official home of Al Smith, New York's hereditary Governor. Al likes the old place here, but I believe he could be persuaded to move.

## 244 WILL ROGERS MUSES A BIT ON THE HABITS OF A NEW YORKER

NEW HAVEN, Conn., May 4. – I was in Albany, the New York State Capital, last night. They didn't know any more news about Al Smith up there than we do in Claremore, Okla. He hadn't been there in weeks. You can't keep a native New Yorker away from home.

Can you imagine Senator Borah, Nick Longworth, Pat Harrison, Jim Reed and Tom Heflin having to go to Tammany Hall on Fourteenth street to confer at a White House breakfast?

Yours,
*Will Rogers.*

P. S. – I am addressing Yale tonight on the subject "Which is More Beneficial to Colleges, Suicide or Football?"

## 245 Mother's Day, Next Sunday, Gives Will Rogers An Idea

NEW HAVEN, Conn., May 5. – Every edition tells of more levees breaking and more people in danger.

This Sunday is Mother's Day—a beautiful thought, whoever started it. Now what could please your Mother more, either living or dead, than to mail one dollar to your nearest Red Cross for the flood sufferers?

Even if you have given, give again, just because it's in memory of your mother. Spend one more dollar on our own unfortunates. And if your mother is living write her and tell her what you have done and that you have enclosed a dollar for her. Come on, editorial writers, you ask them to do it.

Yours,

*Will Rogers.*

P. S. – And when you write your mother, if you don't think the shock will be too great, you might enclose her some money just for a change.

## 246 Rogers's First, Last And Only Opinion On The Snyder Case

PAWTUCKET, R. I., May 6. – This is my first, last and only opinion on the brassiere case:

The moral of Gray's testimony, as I gather it, is that no matter what town you are in you can get liquor, and the whole mystery of the case, as I see it, is how did he buy all this liquor on $5,000 a year?

Both parties claim they were tempted by the other. Well, after looking at pictures of both of them, I have decided that neither one had much resisting power in the first place.

The tabloid readers are still reading Mrs. Snyder's testimony. The case is moving faster than they can read. So long!

*Will Rogers.*

P. S. – Guess all the sob writers will move over to the Peaches Hempel case now.

## 247 Thoughts From Will Rogers Up In Coolidge's Country

MONTPELIER, Vt., May 7. – Well, here I am for the first time up in "Calvin's country." I have passed through here coming down from Canada lots of times but I never stopped off here. Have had the most beautiful trip today from Boston on the Central Vermont Railroad up the White River.

I won't know until tonight how I am going to make out up here with these Vermonters when I open up with my riddles on "Cal." Of course they aren't so terribly strong for him because he left here and went over to Massachusetts; so about all he ever did for them was to be born here.

If you are doing some motoring this Summer, why, don't overlook this part of the country, it is beautiful. Then, you see, you are near enough to Canada to make it mighty interesting to over 98 per cent. of Americans.

There is nothing thickens one like travel.

Yours,
*The Mayor.*

## 248 Rogers Draws A Parallel With Robinson Crusoe

NEW YORK, N. Y., May 8. — Mr. Butler, Mr. Coolidge's Friday, just returned from a reconnoitering tramp over on to the west end of Crusoe Island and reported to Robinson that from the looks of what had been washed up on the beach from mishandled Democratic crafts that Crusoe should have plenty to subsist on for another four years.

Yours,
*Will Rogers.*

P. S. — We all would like to see our boys the first to make the Paris flight, but as the Frenchmen have started they are carrying the good wishes of everybody over here.

## 249 Will Rogers Says Today:

SPRINGFIELD, Mass., May 9. — It would be better for American aviation that the French cross first. If we crossed first we would think we done all that could be done and just stop. Didn't we invent aeroplanes and then think after we had invented them that that was all you was supposed to do with them?

Look at that Italian, flew half way around the world, lost his plane and cabled Mussolini collect. Mussolini shipped him another plane that night, now he is off again. Picture one of our boys with a burned up plane over in Europe cabling Coolidge collect. The message would never reach destination. And then he wouldn't not only not have a plane to ship him that night or any other night, but Congress would have to meet and filibuster for two weeks before we could possibly be able to provide the money to send the boy a ticket home.

European nations might not have our foresight for amassing the dollar, but they know what altitude of the elements the next war will be held in.

Yours,
*Will Rogers.*

P. S. — All power to those two great Frenchmen, but we got boys.

## 250 Rogers In Coolidge's Town And Takes A Peep Ahead

NORTHAMPTON, Mass., May 10. — Made a speech here in Coolidge's home town last night. He was Mayor here one time .

They all said that my speech was as good or better than what he used to make at the Mayor stage of his career, and the town is no better than Beverly Hills, or Claremore, so they are kinder predicting here that I might get to live off the Government in some capacity some day.

Smith College is here. It's the college that replaced Princeton on Harvard's schedule when Princeton wouldn't quit swearing at Harvard on the field.

Yours with a political ear to the ground,
*Will Rogers.*

P. S. — I guess Hoover will have to go out and find the lost aviators. He is doing everything else that is being done out of Washington.

## 251 Rogers Predicts A Soft Answer To French Anger

BENNINGTON, Vt., May 11. — France is raving at us because the flight was not a success. What did they expect us to do, move New York over near them until it was over? I am in favor of us retaliating on France for this ill feeling by blaming them for our farmers' relief not getting to where it started.

You can bet Nungesser and Coli won't blame us when they are found. And they will be found, for they are too game to be lost. They have gone through hundreds of things worse than this.

It would be a good thing if our boys would fool Paris and go on to Constantinople and land. This only shows you the feeling in those countries the minute any little thing comes up. Then we have folks that say "Cancel the debts."

Yours,
*Will.*

## 252 WILL ROGERS WIRES AN OPINION ON THE SACCO-VANZETTI CASE

BOSTON, Mass., May 12. – I am the only person in Boston who has not expressed an opinion on the Sacco-Vanzetti case. All I know is that it should not take a nation or a State seven years to decide whether anyone committed a crime or not. It's a good thing they were young men when the crime was committed, otherwise they wouldn't live long enough for justice to make up its mind.

The Mayor in the cradle of liberty.

*Will.*

## 253 MELLON HAS DONE PRETTY WELL ON NOTES, MR. ROGERS RECALLS

RUTLAND, Vt., May 13. – Have just been reading some English papers commenting on Secretary Mellon's attitude toward the note they sent him about the debts. Fine chance England has of getting the better of Mellon on notes. That's how he got what he has now —out of notes. Notes are one of the best things he handles.

Yours,
*Will.*

P. S. – I am tired of reading about "our town has reached its quota of flood relief funds." There isn't any quota! A new break is reported every day and thousands more are in need. If you were hungry and some one gave you a sandwich would you have your quota? Can that quota gag and keep on working!

## 254 Mr. Rogers Has Discovered Why Chinese Dislike Us

PROVIDENCE, R. I., May 15. – When American diplomacy gets through messing us around over in China, I can tell them what has caused this hate of us over there. It's our missionaries who have been trying to introduce "chop suey" into China. China didn't mind them eating it there, but when they tried to call it a Chinese dish that's what made them start shooting at us.

Yours for corn bread, chitlins and turnip greens.

*Mr. Rogers.*

P. S. – This is Rhode Island, the place where half their Legislature went out of the State and hid one time, and the State never run better in its life than it did then.

## 255 Will Rogers Reveals A Sure Drawing Card For Lectures

ONEONTA, N. Y., May 16. – When I am playing in a town and it looks like there is not going to be much of a house, I announce through the papers that that night I will read passages from "Elmer Gantry," the Baptist sheik, and the house will be packed with Methodist and Presbyterian women. Old Elmer sure had It.

Yours,

*Will.*

## 256 Will Rogers Hails The News That Bootleggers Must Pay

BRATTLEBORO, Vt., May 17. – The biggest news that has hit the financial section of this country was yesterday, when the Supreme Court of the United States ruled that a bootlegger had to pay income tax.

We ought to have our national debt paid in a couple of years now. If he is a married bootlegger he can charge off $3,500 for his wife and $200 for every baby bootlegger in the family.

He is also allowed to charge off his payment to revenue officers and for all loss from breakage and explosions.

Yours for the latest news,

*Will Rogers.*

## 257 ROGERS ADMIRES COOLIDGE FOR HIS "PRETTY LANGUAGE"

PITTSFIELD, Mass., May 18. – Calvin Coolidge doesn't say much, but look how pretty he writes. This was his message yesterday to the medical society.

"As human beings gain in individual perfection so the world will gain in social perfection, and we may hope to come into an era of right thinking and right living, of good will and of peace, in accordance with the teachings of the Great Physician."

Gee! That sounds like one of those birthday greeting cards. With those beautiful thoughts there must have been a third term breaking through the cloud.

Yours in appreciation of beautiful language, even if it doesn't mean anything—but those old doctors sure ate it up.

*Will Rogers.*

## 258 WILL ROGERS NOTES A POINT OF DIFFERENCE WITH CHINA

HARTFORD, Conn., May 19. – We are still trying to make China see things our way, even if their eyes are not shaped like ours.

Yours,

*Will Rogers.*

## 259 NO JOKES FROM ROGERS TILL LINDBERGH ARRIVES

CONCORD, N. H., May 20. – No attempt at jokes today. A slim, tall, bashful, smiling American boy is somewhere out over the middle of the Atlantic Ocean, where no lone human being has ever ventured before. He is being prayed for to every kind of Supreme Being that has a following. If he is lost it will be the most universally regretted single loss we ever had. But that kid ain't going to fail, and what could be better to celebrate his arrival than another donation to over 600,000 of our very own, that are not even fortunate enough to be flying over water, but have to stand huddled upon the banks and look into it as it washes away their lifetime's work.

They didn't even have enough to buy a paper to know that he had gone. Nothing would please him better than for you to help them in his honor, for he comes from the banks of the Mississippi, and he knows what it can do.

Yours,
*Will Rogers.*

## 260 The Moral Will Rogers Draws From Lindbergh's Great Feat

NEW YORK, N. Y., May 22. – Of all things that Lindbergh's great feat demonstrated, the greatest was to show us that a person could still get the entire front pages without murdering anybody.

Nobody knows what he will do now, but he has had an invitation to return to America and address the regular weekly luncheon of the Kiwanis Club of Claremore, Okla.

Boy, that Prince of Wales better not appear in the same crowd as this bird and expect anybody to look at him.

One of his ardent admirers,
*Will Rogers.*

## 261 Will Rogers Mourns The Lack Of Democrats In Maine

PORTLAND, Me., May 23. – I am in Maine for the first time. Now I have showed in every State, this year, including New Hampshire.

Maine is beautiful now and Portland is a great old town. Fine harbor that used, in the good old days, to harbor not only some great lumber fleets, but some Democrats. Short-sightedness has killed off both industries.

Maine is and will be more so a very historic State, being the first State that ever broke a prohibition law. This town will be pointed out in years to come as the home of the original American bootlegger.

Yours for historical and human interest stuff,
*Will.*

P. S. – Daily Lindbergh item: Lindbergh is the greatest American since Theodore Roosevelt, and that statement don't belong in a joke column either.

## 262 How To Reward Lindbergh; Ideas From Will Rogers

BOSTON, Mass., May 24. – There is a hundred and twenty million people in America all ready to tell Lindbergh what to do. The first thing we want to get into our heads is that this boy is not our usual type of hero that we are used to dealing with. He is all the others rolled into one and then multiplied by ten, and his case must be treated in a more dignified way.

In the first place, the Government should reward him handsomely with a life pension and a high position in our Government aviation program. Second, instead of us paying money to see him on the stage or screen (where he don't belong), take that admission money and make it into a national testimonial that will provide a fund for he and his mother for life. Let him have his entire time open to assist aviation, then he will be a blessing to us and not a side show.

We don't ask our retiring Presidents to go into vaudeville and we would resent it if they did. England don't allow their Prince of Wales to go on paid exhibitions. Well, this lad is our biggest national asset. He is our Prince and our President combined, and I will personally play benefits for him the rest of my life to keep him from having to make exhibitions out of himself. We only get one of these in a lifetime.

Yours, one of the hundred million advisers,

*Will Rogers.*

P. S. — And listen: While waiting to do something to honor Lindbergh, make another contribution to the flood. That will please him more than anything you could do. Six hundred thousand are being fed and cared for by the public. It's our worst calamity in our lifetime.

## 263 Rogers On The Black Hills As Coolidge Vacation Ground

GLENS FALLS, N. Y., May 25. — The President is going to the Black Hills of Dakota.

Everybody in the West that does anything and wants to hide out until the thing blows over, goes into the Black Hills. He won't be as bad as some that will be in there, but he will be waiting for more to blow over than any one in "them thar Hills."

Yours,

*Will.*

P. S. — Another levee broke today; another hundred thousand standing on the banks. Don't forget that when you eat your big dinner and sleep in a nice dry bed tonight.

## 264 France Taught Us, Rogers Says, To Appreciate Lindbergh

CHARLOTTESVILLE, Va., May 26. – I see where Mr. Coolidge says "Lindbergh's feat grows on him." I wonder, if we should really be honest with ourselves, wouldn't we admit over here that the way France has appreciated the feat and honored him had something to do with waking us up to its real importance. You know they appreciate good aviation and know it when they see it.

We didn't offer him any U. S. crusier the day after he landed there. We didn't talk of all these things we were going to do until after France showed us how. Give them a little credit. Yours,

*Will Rogers.*

## 265 Will Rogers Sends Out Another Flood Appeal

BLUEFIELD, W. Va., May 27. – So many prominent Frenchmen have been kissing "Lindy" on both cheeks that it will be worth seeing when he meets Cal. If Coolidge and Jimmy Walker kiss him, they will have to stand on a stool.

I hate to keep digging on it, but we still have 600,000 of our own whose homes are now floating toward Nicaragua. We can't seem to get the Government interested in them financially. I wish you would send some checks to the Red Cross of New Orleans. I am going there next Wednesday night, June 1, to give a benefit, and it already has more money assured than any one given in any part of the country. Why? Because they are right there and they know the needs of the people.

If 600,000 people had lost their all and were being fed by charity in the East they would raise fifty millions in a day. Come on, let's help them, even if they are not Armenians. They can't help it because of their nationality.

I will tell you about it when I get down there.

Yours,

*Will.*

## 266 Will Rogers Passes Comment On Flood, Lindbergh And Kings

NEW YORK, N. Y., May 29. – Didn't I tell you Saturday that there were 600,000 people needing help? And that it would take more money than they had asked for? Now today Mr. Hoover says there are 700,000, and he is asking for only 2,000,000 more dollars. This whole thing has been underestimated from the start. Why not ask for some real sum? It couldn't be too high. Remember Wednesday night to send a check to the New Orleans Red Cross. We want to break all records at that benefit.

*Will.*

P. S. – That Lindbergh is certainly showing up the diplomats in knowing what to say. No diplomat wrote any of his speeches. They haven't been able to think up any that good for themselves. He hit it right yesterday with the King of the Belgians. I suppose when he meets King George tomorrow he will say "Glad to meet you; I have heard quite a bit of your eldest son."

## 267 Will Rogers Notes A Clean Town And Comments On The News

HERSHEY, Pa., May 30. – If I knew your address I would send you some fine chocolates. This is the cleanest and best run town I ever saw. It is run and operated entirely by Mr. Hershey, the most modest and the greatest philanthropist of any man in America.

The Jess Livermores held a social robbery at their beautiful home on Long Island last night. Evidently every one attending were members of the same set.

On my way to New Orleans tonight for the benefit. Send some money. The flood proper has not reached Southern Louisiana. Kick in with this other two million, and if Hoover didn't ask for enough I will let you know.

Yours,
*Will.*

## 268 Mr. Rogers Muses On Speeches By Lincoln And By Others

ATLANTA, Ga., May 31. – Another Decoration Day passed and Mr. Abraham Lincoln's 300-word Gettysburg Address was not dethroned. I would try and imitate its brevity if nothing else. Of course, Lincoln had the advantage; he had no foreign policy message to put over. He didn't even have a foreign policy. That's why he is still Lincoln.

Yours for shorter and better speeches,
*Will.*

P. S. – The Government has advised Lindbergh to come home.

We are afraid that every nation that treats him good will want something off their debt.

## 269 Rogers Finds New Orleans Our Most Appreciative City

NEW ORLEANS, La., June 1. – I thought they had mistaken me for Lindbergh here today. This is without doubt the most appreciative city I have ever seen.

This whole valley's appreciation to all the rest of the United States is wonderful. I am not going to tell you about the show and how much we got until tomorrow, but it will beat any benefit given for the cause anywhere. Thanks to friends from all over America for checks.

Hoover has done a wonderful work down here. Tomorrow I am flying all over the new part where the water has broken through and is still rising. Just saw today the cut they made to save the city and saw the refugees. If you could see this you would double your donations.

Remember, we are a million and a half shy yet.

Yours,

*Will Rogers.*

## 270 Rogers In Flood Zone, Saw More Water Than Lindbergh

BATON ROUGE, La., June 2. – I have flew over more water today than Lindbergh did, only this had housetops sticking out of it.

New Orleans broke the record with their benefit last night. Forty-eight thousand dollars! That's more than double any other one given, anywhere. They know the needs of it here.

Want to tell you more about it and who all sent checks in an early Sunday article. Thanks everybody.

*Will Rogers.*

P. S. – See where Cal Coolidge won the first political skirmish from Al Smith. Lindbergh is landing in Washington before New York.

## 271 Will Rogers Visualizes Flood Victims' Home-Coming

SPRINGFIELD, Mo., June 3. – On my way home to Oklahoma. What's happier, especially if people have forgot what you used to be?

Flew over hundreds of miles yesterday and saw the advance guard of 700,000 people returning home. Home to what? To a great, big, flat mud-hole. No houses, no barns, no fences, no plows, no seed, no work, no stock, no stoves. What a home-coming!

Also yesterday received personal telegram from John Barton Payne, the head of the Red Cross, America's great possession, in which he made this amazing statement:

"We are still a million and a half short of our quota."

Remember that there has been a new quota set for you in the last week, so get busy. What did we rescue them for? So they would have the pleasure of starving later?

*Will Rogers.*

## 272 Calling Lindbergh "Lucky" Arouses Will Rogers's Ire

CLAREMORE, Okla., June 5. — I hate societies. That's what's the matter with this country now. It is societied to death. But I would like to organize one, and will even go so far as to be sponsor for it.

It is called the Society to Boycott Any Newspaper in America That Has as a Headline or Allows to Be Used in the Article the Word "Lucky" in Regard to Mr. Lindbergh's Name. It's the politest way of lessening the glory of his feat that they could possibly think up.

The only requirement necessary to belong to my society is that you write to your editor and tell him why you didn't buy the paper that day.

Yours,
*Will.*

P. S. — This is Claremore, Okla., a town in physique but a city at heart.

Another P. S. — Through mistake in printing figures the paper reported eighty thousand raised at New Orleans benefit. It was forty-eight thousand.

## 273 Will Rogers Set To Be First To Cross Atlantic By Bridge

DODGE CITY, Kan., June 6. — Three weeks ago Sunday I was up with Chamberlin in this same plane. If I had known he was thinking about taking an outsider over I would have joined out myself. Then I would have been the first scared comedian to go over.

He is a fine, modest young man—another Lindbergh—and a great aviator, too. That he didn't jump weeks ago was no fault of his. He was the victim of rows and fusses in which he had no part.

Don't take any of the credit away from him because he was just the second one over. Say, the second plane can drop in that ocean just as easy as the first.

Well, never mind, I will be the first one to go over on a bridge.

*Will Rogers.*

P. S. — I am on the crack California train going West. There are several moving picture promoters on here that are just like Chamberlin—"they are just going on till their gas runs out."

## 274 Coupla Quips By Will Rogers On Topics In Current News

WINSLOW, Ariz., June 7. — I guess if Mr. Coolidge ever vetoes a movie relief bill he will have to spend the following Summers in Hollywood.

Water is going down in the Mississippi Valley and the politicians are coming up now.

Yours,

*Will Rogers.*

P. S. — Home to Beverly to collect the taxes and see Pola's new husband.

## 275 Rogers Tells The Proper Time For Preaching Prohibition

BEVERLY HILLS, Cal., June 8. — See where Mr. McAdoo made a prohibition address to a graduating class down in Tennessee. It's too late to preach prohibition to them when they are graduating. It's when they go into long pants and short dresses that's the time to get at 'em.

Yours, the homing Mayor.

*Will.*

P. S. — The old town here looks fine. I never saw the jail as empty.

## 276 Mr. Rogers Pours His Scorn On Men Who Think They Know

BEVERLY HILLS, Cal., June 9. – There are two types of men in the world that I feel sincerely sorry for. One is the fellow that thinks he "knows women," and the other is the one that is always saying "I know the Mississippi River."

The Bolsheviks used to sponsor bomb throwing. That's when they were doing the throwing. Now that they are on the receiving end, it's inhuman.

Yours, the Mayor on the job,

*Will.*

P. S. – Will H. Hays is here supervising production and divorces.

## 277 Mayor Rogers Suggests A New Career For Lindbergh

BEVERLY HILLS, Cal., June 10. – I know Lindbergh has had all kinds of offers, but has he ever had an offer to be a Democrat?

He may be one. People who do strange and unusual things generally are. If he will run for the Democratic Presidency it will release for more or less practical work Al Smith, McAdoo and eighty-eight others. Then when Cal is summering with the farmers, let Lindy summer at Newport among people whose votes really count.

My only interest is in having elections competitive again.

*Mayor Will.*

## 278 Transocean Flights Bring Out A New Lesson For Will Rogers

HOLLYWOOD, Cal., June 12. – I don't think people have realized yet the most important thing these ocean flights have brought out, and that is the quicker transporting of our marines to other people's wars.

In the last year transportation has held us back, sometimes a week or so late. But with airplanes there's no excuse. So our slogan will be now: "Have your civil wars wherever and as far away as you want, but on the opening day we will be there."

If Lindy will come here I will be glad to show him Mary Pickford's home.

The Burgomaster,
*Will Rogers.*

## 279 Will Rogers Sends A Word Of Consolation To Democrats

BEVERLY HILLS, Cal., June 13. – Democrats should never complain again. I thought they were worse off than anybody, but they are not. Look what happens in Russia to the party that criticizes their Government. Over here they are condemned–but not to death.

Yours,

*The Busy Mayor.*

P. S. – We are just sitting here in California right now doing nothing. Just waiting for two things–Lindy and Henry Ford's new model.

## 280 Thoughts From Will Rogers On National Disarmament

BEVERLY HILLS, Cal., June 14. – They sure are disarming fast at the disarmament conference in Geneva. Japan insists on being allowed to have a navy equal to ours. I sometimes wonder if Mr. Coolidge does take these conferences seriously.

For two weeks last Summer I sat at Geneva and listened to one argument on disarmament, and if I could reproduce it on the stage I would have a better show than Ziegfeld ever had. Of all the fool things that we go into (and we don't miss any) why, these disarmament conferences will go down as the prize.

No nation can tell another nation how little it shall protect itself.

*The Burgomaster.*

## 281 Will Rogers Finds We Haven't Quite A Corner On Democracy

BEVERLY HILLS, Cal., June 15. – Our President left for a quiet vacation with twelve carloads of cameramen, reporters, cooks, valets, maids, butlers, doctors, military and naval attaches. I saw King George when he left Buckingham Palace in London last Summer for his vacation, and you could have put all he and Mary both had in a Ford truck.

We ain't got exactly what you would call a corner on democracy.

*Will.*

P. S. – A stomach ache which the Mayor inherited from the last Administration was erroneously reported in the press today as nervous indigestion. It has been found to be nothing but the effects of home cooking. I've started eating in a different restaurant every meal now, and my stomach thinks I am in a different town every day, so I am back to normal again. Thanks for wires. One doctor thought I had had a prosperous enough season to call a bellyache appendicitis.

## 282 FORTHCOMING OPERATION A JOKE TO WILL ROGERS

BEVERLY HILLS, Cal., June 16. – Here is where the joke writers and everybody get even with me.

When the doctors found it was not appendicitis, knowing me personally, they said it must be gall or cholelithiasis. So I am in the California Hospital, where they are going to relieve me of surplus gall, much to the politicians' delight.

I am thrilled to death. Never had an operation, so let the stones fall where they may.

*Will Rogers.*

## 283 ROGERS, IN HOSPITAL, ENVIES ONLY REBECCA, PET RACCOON

CALIFORNIA HOSPITAL, 11 o'clock Friday morning, June 17. – When you lay in a bed you naturally feel sorry for yourself. Then you get to thinking of other people and how bad off they are.

So right now I can't think of a soul that I would change places with, except Rebecca, Coolidge's pet raccoon. Who would have ever thought that coon would get to summer in the Black Hills?

*Will Rogers.*

P. S. – Well, here comes the wagon. I do hope my scar will not suffer in size with other, older and more experienced scars.

## 284 JUST A LINE FROM WILL ROGERS ON HIS BED IN THE HOSPITAL

CALIFORNIA HOSPITAL, HOLLYWOOD, Cal., June 19. – "Relax–lay perfectly still, just relax."

*Will Rogers.*

NOTE – Mr. Rogers was operated on in the California Hospital on Friday and last night was reported to be making steady progress toward recovery.

## 285 Rogers Hears From President And He 'Does Appreciate It'

CALIFORNIA HOSPITAL, LOS ANGELES, Cal., June 21. – I got this today:

Executive Office
Rapid City, S. D.
June 20, 1927

Mr. Will Rogers, Beverly Hills, Calif.:

I am sincerely sorry to hear of your illness and trust that your recovery may be speedy and complete.

Calvin Coolidge.

Well, I certainly do appreciate that. It was mighty thoughtful, and I hope he and that wonderful wife have a wonderful Summer.

And I got lovely wires from Senators Borah, Jim Reed, Pat Harrison and Capper; also Alice and Nick and all my friends. Everybody that I make a living kidding about seemed to be watching for some turn in my illness.

People couldn't have been any nicer to me if I had died.

Yours,
*Will Rogers.*

P. S. – If an automobilist has lost two inner tubes, if he will communicate with me he will learn something to his advantage.

## 286 Mr. Rogers Extends His Own Invitation To Col. Lindbergh

CALIFORNIA HOSPITAL, LOS ANGELES, Cal., June 22. – Every town in the world is urging Lindbergh to come there and be entertained, to make speeches and drive for hours through cheering crowds. In other words, they absolutely guarantee that he will be all in when he leaves their town.

As down-and-out Mayor of the "best little town" between Los Angeles and Sawtelle, I hereby officially write Colonel Charles A. Lindbergh to visit Beverly Hills, and guarantee we will give him no parades, he is to make no speeches, thank us for no medals and attend no privately arranged parties.

We just want him to come and buy a lot.

*His Honor Will Rogers.*

P. S. — Just saw the scar. If they charge by the inch, that operation will be the serious one.

P. S. — Harry Carr—I want to thank you—you know us joke fellows don't get many thanks for nice things we sometimes say about people and I sho' want to thank you.

## 287 Will Rogers Comments On Tenderness For The Worm

CALIFORNIA HOSPITAL, LOS ANGELES, Cal., June 23. — The West sho' has tamed. The Society for the Protection of Single and Unmatured Worms won't let Calvin load his hook with one.

Next they'll be requiring an anesthetic be given the fish. Why, anybody that knows Cal knows he wouldn't harm a fish or a worm.

Besides, who knows when they will grow up and have a vote? Stranger things are voting now.

Yours,
*Will.*

## 288 Will Rogers Muses A Bit On A World Of Operations

LOS ANGELES, Cal., June 24. — One half the world may not know how the other half lives, but if all the letters and telegrams I get are not liars, I can tell you what the other half have been operated on for.

They have sewed me up with so much cat I am having a back fence built at home and will use that instead of a bed.

Yours, the howling Mayor,

*Will Rogers.*

P. S. — I guess I am not missing anything by being laid up because all of my prominent friends have left town any how waiting for the grand jury indictments.

## 289 WILL ROGERS SEES ONLY ONE WAY TO HAVE A NAVY IN THESE DAYS

LOS ANGELES, Cal., June 26. – Didn't I tell you what would happen at that disarmament conference? The reason the Washington one did anything at all was because we did all the sinking. England is not going to sit quietly around a table and agree to let somebody have as big a navy as hers. You don't get navies that way.

There is about only one practical way of getting a navy nowadays. That is to go out and build one.

*Will Rogers.*

## 290 WILL ROGERS TELLS ABOUT A RECENT MOVIE WEDDING

LOS ANGELES, Cal., June 27. – Rod La Rocque and Vilma Banky, the popular movie stars, were married in one of my churches in Beverly yesterday.

Sam Goldwyn, producer of the wedding, called me up and said he thought it would be a good publicity idea to hold it in a church. I said: "What denomination, Sam?" He replied, "Oh, any kind, just so it has a steeple high enough to pick up in the picture."

The novelty everybody experienced in the church was the big kick of the wedding.

*Will Rogers.*

P. S. – I knew I would get in somehow on these transatlantic flights. I just today booked a great-grandson to go over with Commander Byrd.

## 291 MR. ROGERS PENS A FEW NOTES ON HIS OPERATION AND OTHERS

LOS ANGELES, Cal., June 28. – I didn't know it at the time, but every old friend that I would lose track of for a while I know now where they were; they were having the same operation as mine. If you would place all our scars end to end it would make a cute strawberry pink line that would take six hours to pass a given point.

*Will Rogers.*

P. S. – They did not remove my gall bladder as they did not want to eliminate all chances of my entering politics.

## 292 WILL ROGERS DISCUSSES THE BYRDS AND THEIR RECORD

LOS ANGELES, Cal., June 29. – Say, this Byrd family is going to put old Virginia on the map where she used to be during Washington and Jefferson time. You want to look up their history. It reads like a romance.

Just a bunch of old Virginia country boys. Yet they, every one, have done something great. One is Governor of Virginia now, who will be Democratic nominee for President in 1932. As sure as my scar itches.

*Will Rogers.*

P. S. – Oh, Lord! Here she comes with the castor oil again.

## 293 MR. ROGERS FINDS SAFE FLIERS ANYTHING BUT SCARCE HERE

LOS ANGELES, Cal., June 30. – All an American aviator has to do these days is to have a helmet, put in some extra gas and two chicken sandwiches and be met next day by the Mayor of Honolulu or Paris or Berlin or Shanghai. The tough part nowadays with aviation is to think up some place to go.

I always told you we have the aviators. Just give them the planes. I have flown in the past year with at least a dozen boys whom I wouldn't be afraid to start to Siberia with.

*Will Rogers.*

## 294 ROGERS KNOWS HOW IT FEELS TO HAVE YOUR RADIO GO BAD

LOS ANGELES, Cal., July 1. – Wasn't it great about Commander Byrd and his gang landing safe?

Don't tell Mrs. Byrd, but my nurse says he is better looking than Lindbergh. I can imagine how humiliated he was when his radio went on the bum. Mine went fluey during the ninth inning of a tied world series game, and I wished I had had an ocean to drop it into. Yours,

*Will.*

P. S. – Lost my last tube today and have no interior mechanical connection with the outside world. In fact I've lost my outside aerial.

## 295 Will Rogers, Out Of Hospital, Suggests New 'Non-Stop Flight'

HOLLYWOOD, Cal., July 3. – I will give $500 for the first Ford car "non-stop flight" from Claremore, Okla., to Beverly Hills, Cal., or vice versa, whichever way yours runs better, east or west.

Remember, no stops for gas, oil, red lights, trains or loose-armed traffic cops. You can come alone like Lindy or you can have a Levine, just so you keep coming.

This is for scientific purposes. I would have offered more, but after the operation! Yours,

The Returned Mayor,
*Will.*

## 296 Fourth Of July Reflections By The Sage Of Beverly Hills

BEVERLY HILLS, Cal., July 4. – Well, this is the Fourth of July and my kids popping these giant crackers haven't been any great patriotic solace to my old battle scarred tummy.

This is Coolidge's and Georgie Cohan's birthday. Georgie writes his country's songs and Calvin writes its speeches. Georgie started out waving a flag and Cal the ballot. Shows you which one will get you the farthest.

I was born on Nov. 4, which is election day, and if it hadn't been for election day there would have been no Coolidge in the Black Hills. My birthday has made more men and sent more back to honest work than any other days in the year.

At that, I wish both of them well. They are both good kids, even if they do both talk with a whine.

Yours,
*Will Rogers.*

## 297 Mr. Rogers Has His Own Flight, With Terminus In Beverly

BEVERLY HILLS, Cal., July 5. – Dozens of inquiries by wire want to know if this non-stop Ford flight from Claremore to Beverly Hills, or vice versa, is on the level. It certainly is.

I will deposit the five hundred with any reputable man. The only trouble, since the Julian oil scandal, we have no reputable man here. You can come straight across or follow the great circle by the way of Newfoundland. You can steer by dead reckoning or telephone book. You can receive weather reports on fog, mud or sheriff's attachments.

It must be between these two cities, no other trip will get a nickel.

Yours,
*Will Rogers.*

### 298 Mr. Rogers's Views On China And The Geneva Conference

BEVERLY HILLS, Cal., July 6. – The war in China seems to be about over. Neither side could read the names in the casualty list. When you can't read the names in the papers, there ain't much use killing anybody, when nobody knows who you killed.

Yours,
*Will.*

P. S. – Two more disarmament conferences and there won't be enough ocean to hold all the cruisers they all want to build.

### 299 Mr. Rogers Likes Mr. Coolidge In 'Those Cowboy Clothes'

BEVERLY HILLS, Cal., July 7. – Calvin sho' does look good in those cowboy clothes. I never liked him in that yachting cap. And that old Mother Hubbard apron that they had him pitching hay in, for the pictures, up in Vermont that time, was terrible.

But those chaps will sure bring out the dude rancher vote. If he keeps on taking on all these mannish ways, why it looks like the old mechanical horse is liable to be for sale.

Yours,
*Will Rogers.*

P. S. – The Fords are lining up in Claremore to run for the $500.

### 300 Mr. Rogers Also Apologizes, But With Reservations

BEVERLY HILLS, Cal., July 8. – I certainly was glad to read Mr. Henry Ford's statement this morning in the papers in regard to the Jewish people. It was a fine thing for a big man to do. It takes big men to admit a fault publicly, and it has been a lesson to me.

From now on I am going to lay off the Republicans. I have never had anything against them as a race. I realize that, out of office, they are just as honest as any other class and they have a place in the community that would have to be taken by somebody. So I want to apologize for all that I have said about them and henceforth will have only a good word to say of them.

Mind you, I am not going to say anything about them, but that is not going to keep me from watching them.

Yours, the repentant Mayor,

*Will.*

## 301 Mr. Rogers On Motor Plans And Movie Developments

HOLLYWOOD, Cal., July 10. – It don't make much difference now whether Mr. Ford ever announces the specifications of his new car. They can be built like an ox cart and they will sell. He has all his small old customers back again.

Yours,

*Will Rogers.*

P. S. – Lasky announced a 10 per cent cut in movie stars' salaries. That reminded the Government of cutting, so they announced that there would be a small 100 per cent cut in Lasky's theatre building program.

## 302 Will Rogers Thinks Ireland Still All Right For Tourists

BEVERLY HILLS, Cal., July 11. – I knew that Vice President of Ireland that was murdered very well. He was a fine, able, conscientious man. I picked him then as one of the coolest, nerviest customers I ever met.

Hope this don't stir up trouble for Ireland, for they were just coming along fine. Tourists, don't miss it this Summer. If you do, you will miss more real hospitality and scenery than in any country in Europe. Yours,

*The Conversing and Convalescing Mayor.*

P. S. – Say, the Anti-Saloon League was about to let Calvin and Andy Mellon out, there one time. Guess they would have put Wayne B. Wheeler in as President and Billy Sunday as Secretary of the Treasury.

## 303 Observations By Mr. Rogers On Angling In South Dakota

BEVERLY HILLS, Cal., July 12. – They don't no more than stop Cal fishing with worms than he goes out with flies and catches even more. If they stop his using flies, why, he is getting so Western that he is just liable to pull out his .44 and shoot a flock of fish, or take down his old lariat and four-foot enough for dinner. There's no stopping the man. He is a modern Roosevelt.

Yours, a fisherman with a seine,

*The Mayor.*

P. S. – Judge Ben Lindsey is in Hollywood. His companionable marriage idea created no stir there at all. The idea is as old and commonplace out here as traffic lights.

## 304 Rogers Notes An Invasion Of Fords From Oklahoma

BEVERLY HILLS, Cal., July 13. – Say, stop that Ford-Claremore-Beverly Hills flight. They are coming in here from Oklahoma so thick we can't see the movie stars for Oklahoma Fords.

Every time I hear a noise outside I know it is another Ford car. They have made some great time. They have come over 1,800 miles in around three days and nights.

I will be careful with my jokes after this. It's costing me more to joke than I get for them. So if there are any more Fords coming please turn back. Imploringly,

*The Mayor.*

## 305 Will Rogers Acknowledges His Red Cross Life Membership

BEVERLY HILLS, Cal., July 14. – Today I got my official document from the Red Cross headquarters of being made a life member. Well, sir, I am just crazy about it for two reasons.

One, of course, is that it is the greatest organization in the United States (including the world). I think it's greater than the Republican Party (including Government salaries). But the other reason is it looks like a diploma.

You know I never had any kind of diploma. I never finished from anything. I always did want something that looked important. I never even had an oil share.

I waited all these years to get something to frame. And if Congress don't help the Mississippi Valley this next term I will devote my few remaining years to telling the truth about them.

Yours,
*Will.*

P. S. — The pay season on Oklahoma Fords entering Beverly Hills is closed, sine die, positively.

## 306 FIGHT, BUT DON'T CONFER, SAYS ROGERS, FEELING ENCOURAGED

BEVERLY HILLS, Cal., July 15. — This morning lots of people will feel discouraged over the disastrous ending of this disarmament conference without doing anything. But I don't.

I think it was the most successful conference we ever attended. It's the only one where we lost nothing, promised to give up nothing. It's the first one in our history where we come out as strong as we went in. If we would just do nothing at all of them, I wouldn't mind us attending them.

And the minute these other nations find we have nothing to give up, why they will gradually quit holding them, and with no international conferences the world would be peaceful and perfect.

That's where they learn to hate each other, is at the conferences. So, hurrah, we are back home without the loss of a boat.

Fight, if necessary, but don't confer.

Yours,
*Bill.*

## 307 ROGERS CREDITS BEST LAUGH OF THE DAY TO WILL H. HAYS

HOLLYWOOD, Cal., July 17. — Today's best laugh was by my old friend, Will H. Hays, who said films are made in Hollywood by the best thoughts of the real thinking people of all nations.

Bless your heart, Bill. If you get away with that you could be campaign manager for a Democrat President, and have him elected. That's the height of ability.

Mind you, I am not kicking on the statement, for it gives Ben Turpin, myself and Bull Montana about our highest rating.

Yours,
*Will.*

P. S. – If people are dying in the East by suffocation as bad as the Los Angeles papers state, then there is no use me sending this dispatch to my Eastern papers, as there is none of you living to read it.

## 308 Mr. Rogers Finds Our Strategy Commendable In Nicaragua

BEVERLY HILLS, Cal., July 18. – I see where our bombing planes down in Nicaragua bagged fifty natives yesterday.

The natives put up a pretty good fight. They threw rocks and knives at the planes, but our forces were too cunning for them. They wouldn't fly low enough to be hit.

Strategy has won many a war and it may pull us through this one.

Yours,
*Will.*

## 309 Will Rogers Remarks:

BEVERLY HILLS, Cal., July 19. – See where they've been making raids on all the new bootleggers at the new summer capital at Rapid City. Of course, we all know Cal is dry every way, but it's the men that are associated with him that have to drink.

*Will Rogers.*

## 310 Will Rogers Gives His Idea Of The Coming Prize Fight

BEVERLY HILLS, Cal., July 20. – Sporting writers have been so universally wrong about every big prize fight that all they are saying this time is "if this happens" and "if that happens." They are afraid to trust their judgment by announcing where the fight will be held for fear they might be wrong. The winner will be the one that will draw the most money with Tunney.

Tex Rickard can sell you tickets for that fight now with the names of the fighters on it.

Yours,
*Will.*

## 311 Thoughts On Monarchies By Mayor Rogers Of Beverly

BEVERLY HILLS, Cal., July 21. – When they crowned the little King Michael yesterday over in Rumania the only words he uttered were: "Come on mamma, let's go home. I am hungry."

That's the truest words ever uttered by a King, for the best thing they do is eat. However, I saw the movies of the last inauguration and Mr. Coolidge looked so bored it looked like he said: "I wish they would hurry up and get done here, Grace. I am getting hungry."

Lots of people over here think the Rumanian King is too young. You can't get 'em too young. The younger they are the better Kings they make.

Yours,
*Will.*

## 312 Quickest To Lick Dempsey With A Lawsuit, Rogers Says

BEVERLY HILLS, Cal., July 22. – This fight proves one thing: You can lick Dempsey quicker with a lawsuit than you can with a boxing glove.

Tunney better start hiring Kearns to drag out the old injunctions. Give me a lawsuit against him with enough figures on it and I believe I can lick Dempsey.

Sharkey lost, like thousands lose out in life every day, because he stopped to argue. He put his hands down to gab with the referee when he ought to have had them up. And naturally Dempsey pasted him.

I tell you a prize ring is no place for superfluous conversation.

A born referee.

*William.*

P. S. — I know the papers don't mention it and maybe I shouldn't, but let's be truthful out here among ourselves, ain't it hot?

## 313 Will Rogers Puts In A Word For The Preachers' Wives

HOLLYWOOD, Cal., July 24. — Since Judge Lindsey's ceremonial upheaval preachers are all trying to prove that the old-time marriages are the best and point to their own as example.

That's fine; but how about the preachers' wives' opinion? I want to hear from them. I believe there is some of those deserving sisters, if they had had a trial marriage, wouldn't be where they are today.

There's a race of people that I would like to see something done for, even before we exterminate Nicaragua!

A friend of the preacher but a true sympathizer with the wives.

*Deacon Rogers.*

## 314 Mayor Rogers Tells That He Is Ready To Marry Bud Stillman

BEVERLY HILLS, Cal., July 25. — Mrs. Stillman and the girl sweetheart's family are trying to tip each other's canoe. Mrs. Stillman says they are very primitive people. The Canuck family say, "It ain't Bud we are leary of; it's too much mother-in-law that scares us."

Now I wouldn't call a suspicion like that exactly primitive. Ma Stillman says she wants the girl to keep on learning. The girl figures if she knew enough to cop Bud she knows enough to hold him.

Bring 'em to Beverly. I will marry 'em.

*The Mayor.*

P. S. — On account of the visibility, it took Lindbergh two days to find Portland, Me. He will be so old his whiskers will catch in the propeller before he can see Pittsburgh.

## 315 Political And Pugilistic Comment From Mayor Rogers

BEVERLY HILLS, Cal., July 26. — My old friend Nick Longworth is out here setting some traps. Nick has been seeing what it is you can promise a farmer that will relieve him. Whatever it is, Nick will promise it to him.

With Longworth and Dempsey both here, the local Rotary and Chamber of Commerce are all set for talent. Dempsey hit Sharkey so hard in the jaw that he had to stop talking. Sharkey claimed he was fouled.

Any time you stop Sharkey talking he has been fouled.

*The Mayor.*

## 316 Will Rogers's Own Idea Of Two National Melodies

BEVERLY HILLS, Cal., July 27. – Lots of people don't know the difference between the two songs of America and England–"Columbia, Gem of the Ocean," and "Rule Britannia, Britannia Rules the Waves." Here is the difference: "Britannia Rules the Waves," is a fact; "Columbia, Gem of the Ocean," is just a song. Yours,

*A Diagnoser of Songs.*

## 317 Will Rogers Provides His Own News Summary, With Comment

BEVERLY HILLS, Cal., July 28. – Here is the world events as they happened in the press yesterday:

President Coolidge attended his daily rodeo, where a team of horses put on a runaway for him, the only new things done at a rodeo in years.

King of Rumania had oatmeal and castoria for breakfast.

Aimee declares the temple is as strong as ever; that the only thing can ruin it is poor collections.

Nick Longworth, in his Los Angeles speech, said he was glad this was a democratic country, but he seemed to be pretty well pleased that Republicans are running it.

Yours,

*Will.*

## 318 Will Rogers Gives Advice On Real Need In Aviation

BEVERLY HILLS, Cal., July 29. – Lindbergh is doing great work. He is visiting each town one day trying to interest people in aviation. When he gets through it wouldn't be bad to have him visit

Washington for at least a week and try and interest them. Don't get the idea because three of our planes flew to Europe and made it that we are ahead in aviation. It's not how far can three men fly, but what have you got for the other hundred and ten million to fly in; and where are they to land when they come down?

Yours,
*Will.*

P. S. — August the second, which is Tuesday, don't forget the national anniversary celebration of Walter Johnson at Washington, D. C. He is the other Swede that Lindbergh copied in showing the world how to be great and still be modest. Do something to help round out a great sportsman's career. Remember next Tuesday the only man in America that stayed a hero for twenty years.

## 319 WILL ROGERS SENDS COMMENT ON THREE NEWS EVENTS

HOLLYWOOD, Cal., July 31. — John Roach Straton should match the winner of the Tunney-Dempsey go against the winner of the Ma McPherson-Aimee McPherson fight, the bout to be staged in Babe Ruth's tabernacle.

The Prince of Wales landed in Canada. But not until Lindbergh had gotten out of there.

China lost 100,000 people in one quake and could only make one edition of our papers. One robbery could beat that. Yours,

*Will Rogers.*

## 320 WILL ROGERS GETS LIGHT ON MODERN FARM VALUES

BEVERLY HILLS, Cal., Aug. 1. — A farm in the country is judged now by how many blocks it is away from a filling station.

Yours,
*Will.*

## 321 CHAMBERLIN'S NEW FEAT IS A GREAT ONE, WILL ROGERS SAYS

BEVERLY HILLS, Cal., Aug. 2. — That was a great feat of Chamberlin's yesterday off the Leviathan. In some respects he showed a better record crossing the ocean than Lindbergh. Lindbergh only had to contend with the elements.

Yours,
*Will Rogers.*

P. S. — The deer season just opened. Any one driving an automobile on Beverly Boulevard or Mulholland Drive should wear red coats and carry an American flag.

## 322 Will Rogers Sees Coolidge Accepting The Nomination

BEVERLY HILLS, Cal., Aug. 3. — I think Mr. Coolidge's statement is the best-worded acceptance of a nomination ever uttered by a candidate. He spent a long time in the dictionary looking for that word "choose," instead of "I will not."

It don't take much political knowledge to know that a man can get more votes running on the people's request than he can running on his own request.

Mr. Coolidge is the shrewdest politician that ever drew Government salary.

Yours,
*Will Rogers.*

## 323 No Wonder Coolidge Was Pale, Will Rogers Says

BEVERLY HILLS, Cal., Aug. 4. — All the newspaper men that were in the room when Mr. Coolidge handed them out his statement have written about his being very serious and very pale. When a New England Yankee gives up $75,000 a year the surprise is not he was pale but that he didn't faint.

Yours,
*Will Rogers.*

P. S. — A deer hunter in Ventura county brought in his first man yesterday.

## 324 Will Rogers Sees Coolidge Drafted, But By The Sioux

BEVERLY HILLS, Cal., Aug. 5. — The Disarmament Conference ended by us blaming England for knowing enough to keep their country protected. That's like blaming Jack Dempsey for knowing how to box. When we have had as many wars as they have our statesmen may know as much as theirs, but I doubt it.

Yours,
*Will Rogers.*

P. S. – Mr. Coolidge attended his daily rodeo and the Sioux Indians made him big chief of their tribe. He said he didn't choose to be chief again, but he was drafted.

## 325 Will Rogers Comments On Fools And The Sacco Case

HOLLYWOOD, Cal., Aug. 7. – I haven't expressed an opinion on the Sacco-Vanzetti case, because I don't know any more about it than the people that have expressed an opinion on it. A fool that knows he is a fool is one that knows he don't know all about anything, but the fool that don't know he is a fool is the one that thinks he knows all about anything. Then he is a dam fool. People are trying to tell you all that happened in a case that happened seven years ago, when they couldn't tell you all that happened yesterday.

Just ten weeks ago I spent an hour in Governor Fuller's home discussing the case with him, and I do believe whatever he did he conscientously believed to be justice.

Yours,
*Mayor Emeritus.*

## 326 Will Rogers Says Dawes Speaks Plainest English

BEVERLY HILLS, Cal., Aug. 8. – Say, did you get Dawes blaming England right to the Prince's face? That's one thing about Charley, there is no wondering what he meant when he said so and so. He may not speak the best English, but he speaks the plainest English in American politics today. There is no word "choose" with Dawes, it's either will or will not, and here's hoping that his political hat didn't go over Niagara Falls.

Yours,
*Will.*

## 327 Will Rogers Sees Trucks As Best Peace Bridge Symbol

BEVERLY HILLS, Cal., Aug. 9. — The papers can't get over Dawes getting the press notices over such speakers as Baldwin, England's Premier, which is really their President, the Prince of Wales and Secretary Kellogg. Up to the time of Dawes the Vice President's speech was always the following: "Gentlemen, the President wishes me to convey to you his sincere regret at not being able to be with you here and to tell you that his heart and soul is in this noble cause of yours."

The loaded trucks couldn't wait till the speech was over before they were crossing the new bridge with their best wishes. That will cement more good relations than all the apple sauce spilled on the speakers' stand.

Yours,
*Will.*

## 328 Will Rogers Sees Great Navy From Conference Failure

BEVERLY HILLS, Cal., Aug. 10. — Who said the disarmament conference was a failure? Didn't Mr. Coolidge yesterday issue orders to start in on a secret building program? There is some sense to a return from a conference and start building and not sinking. If that's a failure we can have a great navy some day just out of such failures. Good boy, Cal.

Yours,
*Will.*

## 329 Will Rogers Is Enjoying Pre-Movie California

SANTA BARBARA, Cal., Aug. 11. — Up here attending the beautiful Santa Barbara fiesta, showing the life in California before Fords, movie salaries and realtors in knee-breeches made a Coney Island out of the State.

Yours,
*Will Rogers.*

P. S. — The weather was not unusual.

330 No Coolidge News Without A Rodeo, Will Rogers Says

SANTA BARBARA, Cal., Aug. 12. – Didn't read anything about Mr. Coolidge today. Guess there was no rodeo yesterday. Twelve planes were to have left for Honolulu today, but they are waiting till Tuesday, which is always a better day for flying.

Yours,
*Will Rogers.*

331 Rogers Sees Republicans Controlling The Elements

HOLLYWOOD, Cal., Aug. 14. – Biggest crop in years is reported to Mr. Coolidge. That man is in league with the Lord to give the farmers relief without letting it go through Congress. I tell you the Republicans are controlling the elements. Watch election year for even bigger crops than this year.

Yours,
*Will Rogers.*

332 Will Rogers Declares A Tie For Brains On Stage, Screen

BEVERLY HILLS, Cal., Aug. 15. – Doug Fairbanks stated yesterday in an interview that there are more brains on the screen than on the stage. After viewing some of the productions put on lately by both screen and stage, I think most people will agree that in the matter of brains displayed it's an absolute tie between the two.

Yours, a disciple of both,
*Will.*

333 Will Rogers, Ex-Mayor, Gives Out A Warning

BEVERLY HILLS, Cal., Aug. 16. – The State Legislature of California passed a law saying that no one not a politician could hold office. And I hereby notify the world that Beverly Hills has left my bed and board and I will not be responsible for any debts contracted by said municipality. I don't want to knock but the town never was as dead. There hasn't been a Beverly date line about a divorce since I got out, not a shooting, not even a swimming pool built. I didn't choose to be Mayor in the first place but they drafted me.

Just a good man looking for something better,

*Will.*

## 334 Will Rogers Keeps Up His Interest In Aviation

BEVERLY HILLS, Cal., Aug. 17. – California is awful lonesome this afternoon with everybody that is anybody flying to Honolulu.

You can't beat those Germans for efficiency. They flew over to the edge of America, and it looked kinder foggy, and they couldn't see the landing field very good, so they turned around and flew back.

I saw a late picture of Lindbergh. That banquet chicken is slowly getting him.

Yours,
*Will Rogers.*

## 335 Will Rogers Sees Hoover As Doctor For Sick States

BEVERLY HILLS, Cal., Aug. 18. – Herb Hoover is out here among us. He is just waiting around between calamities. When we, as individuals, get sick or hurt we send for a doctor. But when whole States get sick we send for Hoover. He is America's family physician. He is a great guy, is Doc Hoover, and I hope they don't spoil him by putting him into politics.

If my good friend, Mr. Ford, don't hurry up with his new model the next national catastrophe Hoover will be called on to rescue will be the Ford dealers.

Just Plain Citizen,
*Will Rogers.*

## 336 Ocean Air Races Bring A Protest From Rogers

BEVERLY HILLS, Cal., Aug. 19. – After my Ford nonstop promotion I may never be able to promote or back anything else, but if I was backing an entry for an ocean airplane flight I would certainly think enough of the people's lives taking the chance for me to put a radio sending apparatus on there for them the first thing. Then if I had any more money left I would get some gas and a propeller for it. Then I would have a law passed to choke the guy that promotes a race out of these hazardous trips. You know everybody that we got flying is not a Lindbergh.

Yours,
*Will.*

337

## Will Rogers Finds The West Looking 'Greener And Finer'

COLUMBUS, N. M., Aug. 21. – Just crossed Arizona and New Mexico. I never saw 'em looking greener and finer. Coolidge's coming to the West certainly has been a Godsend to this country. 'Course he may be wasting a lot of rain on such few voters but right now these States are standing in grass up to their waists and "choosing" him for "'28." The Democrats, with their usual foresight, had already sold their cattle.

Regards to Dan Moody and Amon Carter.

Yours,
*Will.*

P. S. – The only advantage that I can see in one land airplane looking on the ocean for one that's down is that if he finds it what's he going to do? If he leaves 'em and comes back they will float away from where he left 'em and if he comes down with 'em there will be just two lost instead of one.

338

## Will Rogers Is To Be Head Of Ex-Mayors' Association

TOPEKA, Kan., Aug. 22. – This is Topeka, the home of both Kansas Senators. Capper's life has been dedicated to the farmers, and Curtis on the helping of the Indians. Both denominations, the farmers and the Indians, are now destitute.

Tonight in Kansas City I am to be made President of a large body of men, the Ex-Mayors' Association, an earnest bunch of men trying to come back, all placed where they are by the honesty of the ballot. What this country needs is more ex-Mayors.

Yours, President of the Ex-Mayors' Association,
*Will Rogers.*

## 339 Will Rogers Says He Shies At Taking Billy Sunday's Job

CRESTLINE, Ohio, Aug. 23. – Passed through Chicago today. It was raining bad and practically all the shootings were confined to indoors. A few who had raincoats were outside plugging away at each other, but, take it all in all, it was what would be known as a dull day for du Pont.

Had a pleasant hour on the train chatting with Billy Sunday, the male McPherson. Billy is a nice fellow and Ma is wonderful. Billy wants to retire and wants me to take over his practice.

I am afraid I would get to defying the devil to come up through the platform some time, and it would just be my luck that he would come up before the collection.

Yours,
*Will Rogers.*

## 340 Rogers Examines White House Doubts Coolidge Will Leave It

WASHINGTON, D. C., Aug. 24. – Arrived in Washington today to examine the new White House roof. If it don't fall on me, why Mr. Coolidge can quit teasing those little perch and come on home and get to vetoing. Fixing up and spending $400,000 on that house is just another one of the dozen things that makes me know he is going to run again. Can you see him spending that much dough out of his Administration to fix up a house for somebody else to live in? Don't be silly. It's fixed great. He will be crazy about the old homestead when he sees it. He won't want to move out in 1932.

Yours, official Presidential house examiner,
*Will Rogers.*

## 341 Will Rogers Explains One Joke Is On Him

WASHINGTON, D. C., Aug. 25. – Good joke on me. I left Hollywood to keep from being named in the Chaplin trial and now they go and don't name anybody. Not a name was mentioned but Charlie's bank. Charlie is not what I would call a devoted husband, but he certainly is worth marrying.

Yours,
*Will Rogers.*

P. S. – When the papers spoke about Mr. Coolidge visiting "Old Faithful" I thought they meant Mr. Stearns.

## 342 Will Rogers Finds Washington Better With Congress Away

WASHINGTON, D. C., Aug. 26. — Tourists, you are missing something if you don't visit Washington while the politicians are not here. You have no idea the difference it makes. The bootleggers have followed their constituents back home. The embassy bars are closed; even Washington's national pest, the lobbyists, have gone home to take up another collection. Why, if they could get this Capitol moved away from here this would be one of the best towns in America. I think there are people in this city smart enough to vote.

Yours, boosting for a town that's not to blame for its shortcomings,

*Will Rogers.*

P. S. — There hasn't been a cuspidor used since Congress adjourned.

## 343 Will Rogers Now Speaks As Congressman At Large

WASHINGTON, D. C., Aug. 28. — Bobby Jones is to Atlanta what the movies are to California and Lindbergh is to America. If golf players took a speck of pride in what they do, Jones's playing should really be a help to humanity. After seeing him play, thousands of able-bodied men should be shamed into doing some useful work.

Yours,

*Congressman at Large,*

*Hon. Rogers.*

P. S. — My first official duty as Congressman at Large, which was bestowed on me last night, is to change the library of the overhauled White House into a fishing pool. That's economy for the taxpayers.

## 344 Will Rogers Sees Humor In Customs Search Of Fliers

WASHINGTON, D. C., Aug. 29. — I see the customs authorities in England searched the round-the-world fliers when they landed. I guess they thought the boys had smuggled over a couple of baby grand pianos or some early Oklahoma period furniture. I was there last

Summer when Gertrude Ederle swam in and they searched her. Figured she had brought in some cigars or cigarettes or millinery in the pockets of her bathing suit, I reckon. People tell you England has no humor. Why, they are funny even when they don't try to be.

The Congressman at Large,

*Will Rogers.*

P. S. – Did you ever see two people as much alike as Levine and Lindbergh? Both their names begin with an L.

## 345 Will Rogers Would Make Every Golf Course An Airport

WASHINGTON, D. C., Aug. 30. – Bobby Jones, Atlanta, Ga.: Bobby, you can be the means of saving a lot of human lives. The big problem of aviation is having emergency places to land. Now you insist on every golf course having one fairway long enough and level enough to land a plane on, all marked with crosses to show it. Every golf club should be patriotic and humane enough to do this.

Think what it would mean to an aviator with a missing engine to know that every golf course was a life preserver. If they don't do this voluntarily the Government will make 'em do it some day.

Now all you got to do, Bobby, is to say you won't play on a course that won't go to that much expense for their country and their fellow-man. If you do this you will do as much for aviation as Lindbergh.

Yours,

*Will Rogers.*

## 346 Rogers Scoffs Somewhat At Integrity Of Congress

WASHINGTON, D. C., Aug. 31. – Just finished taking scenes here in Washington for a movie of the old stage play, Hoyt's "A Texas Steer." It was the story of a man elected to Washington on bought votes. We are bringing it up to date by not changing it at all. In the stage version he didn't know what to do when he got in Congress. That part is allowed to remain as it was. He used to play poker more than legislate. That's left in. There was a little drinking among the members at that time. For correct detail in our modern version that has been allowed to remain in.

Yours for government buy the people,

*Congressman at Large,*
*Rogers.*

## 347 Will Rogers Is Pulling For "Flying Princess"

HARRISBURG, Pa., Sept. 1. – We certainly are pulling for that lady aviator. Just because we can't pronounce either barrel of her name won't lessen our reception of her. She is the only titled person we ever heard of that did anything. If a lady 63 years of age can fly across the ocean it certainly ought to muster up nerve enough in the rest of her sex to look a mouse in the face.

*Will Rogers.*

## 348 Will Rogers Sees Dempsey, But Not In The Ring

CHICAGO, Ill., Sept. 2. – Just spent the day at Dempsey's camp. Watched him train. He is in great shape. He went out in 55 and came in in 69. Leo Flynn, his sparring partner, went out in 41, came in in 42.

It looks like from what I saw they will send in Flynn against Tunney instead of Dempsey.

Yours,
*Will Rogers.*

## 349 Will Rogers Pays Tribute To A Mexican Aviator

EL PASO, Tex., Sept. 4. – We haven't got any corner on air feats. A young Mexican Army flier flew into Juarez, the sober end of El Paso, yesterday, from Mexico City, 1,200 miles, in less than ten hours, an average of 125 miles an hour, with a German engine.

One wing caught fire. He saw a rainstorm, flew over into it and put it out. That's doing some Lindbergh thinking, ain't it? If we find out they got some airplanes down there we are liable to quit picking on 'em.

Yours, the Congressman,
*Will Rogers.*

P. S. – Whoever located this town of El Paso where it is was looking far ahead.

## 350 Will Rogers Compares Airplanes And Auto Deaths

BEVERLY HILLS, Cal., Sept. 5. – Every paper is raving about legislation to stop ocean flying because thirteen people have been lost, just a fair Sunday's average in auto deaths. From ten to fifteen is just about the number that are always in a bus when it meets a train at a grade crossing, yet you never see an editorial about relief from that. You may not die as spectacularly in a machine as you would if you dropped in the ocean, but you are just as dead.

Yours back in a town that don't look so good since a certain party ain't mayor. Mind you, I am not knocking.

Congressman-at-large from the whole United States,

*Will Rogers.*

## 351 Will Rogers's Tributes To Loew And Wheeler

BEVERLY HILLS, Cal., Sept. 6. – Wayne B. Wheeler and Marcus Loew died. I happened to know them; Loew intimately for twenty years. Now a man has died in the movies that all the hysteria and eulogies that they generally bestow can rightly be used on. Marcus Loew was a man. He would have stood out in a legitimate business.

Wheeler will be hard to replace. He made a strong political party with nothing to start out with but a caucus. He was to the League what Mussolini is to Italy and what Mr. Coolidge is to the Republican party. The best fight a man can put up is to have his enemies say if he passes out in the thick of the fight: "Well, I am glad he is out of the way."

Yours, the Old Congressman,

*Will Rogers.*

## 352 Will Rogers Throws Light On Farm Offer To Coolidge

BURBANK, Cal., Sept. 7. – The good people of Dakota offered to give Calvin a farm if he would live on it. I wouldn't advise you to give those people too much credit for generosity. There is not a farmer in any State in the West that wouldn't be glad to give him a farm if he will paint it, fix up the fences and keep up the series of mortgages that are on it. And if you think Coolidge ain't smart, you just watch him not take it.

Yours, Congressman-at-Large,
*Will Rogers.*

P. S. – That wasn't a philanthropist that made him that offer. That was some comedian.

## 353 How To See The Big Fight As Will Rogers Plans It

BEVERLY HILLS, Cal., Sept. 8. – Notice – How to save money if you are going to the big prize fight: If you live in the West get your seats in the west side of the ring and get off at Omaha. New Yorkers take the 10,000 east ringside seats and detrain at Toledo. Ushers will seat the South at Louisville. Canada will occupy the northern ringside section with nothing between them and the fight but the Great Lakes.

One fighter will be painted white and the other black. Don't crowd after the fight is over. Ushers will pass among you and announce the winner.

The standing joke of the next century will be the man that came home and said "I had a ringside seat to the Dempsey fight."

Yours,
*Will Rogers.*

## 354 Will Rogers Has A Query About These Ocean Air Trips

BURBANK, Cal., Sept. 9. – I just want to ask one question. When I get it answered it will relieve me and perhaps others. If a flier was going from New York to San Francisco, where it is all overland—you never see them do it with a hydroplane where they can land only on the water. Then why is it they take a land plane across the ocean. No one has disappeared yet over water in a hydroplane.

Yours,
*Will Rogers.*

## 355 Will Rogers Gives A Tip To Aspiring Democrats

HOLLYWOOD, Cal., Sept. 11. – The trouble with the Democrats is that they all want to run for President. If they had somebody on their side that would announce he didn't choose to run, why he would be such a big novelty that he would be nominated by acclamation.

Yours,
*Will Rogers.*

P. S. – A few $10 seats for the fight still left, with radio attachments.

## 356 Will Rogers Figures Profit Of A Jones-Hagen Match

BURBANK, Cal., Sept. 12. – Tunney and Dempsey training on golf will draw over $3,000,000. If they can ever get Bobby Jones to fight Walter Hagen it ought to draw $6,000,000.

There is a lot of suspicion of this fight. That is on account of Tunney speaking perfect English. Any time an American speaks perfect English he is under suspicion. We know he is covering up something.

Yours,
*Congressman Rogers.*

## 357 Will Rogers Picks A Spot For A Coolidge Summer Home

FIRST NATIONAL STUDIO, BURBANK, Cal., Sept. 13. – I want to be the first to offer the Coolidges a Summer home. It's located at Claremore, Okla. Oklahoma is a doubtful State. That is, it is doubtful if it is allowed to stay in the Union if it don't mend its political ways.

We have the ranch house screened to keep the fish out. We have had as many as 10,000 fish in one rodeo there. We will guarantee him a Wild West show and Indian war dance twice a day. If a farmer mentions relief in his presence he will be shot at sunrise.

Remember this offer is for either next Summer or the four following ones.

Yours,
Congressman at Large
*Will Rogers.*

## 358 WILL ROGERS SENDS ALONG A DEFINITION OF AN OPTIMIST

FIRST NATIONAL STUDIO, BURBANK, Cal., Sept. 14. – Been talk of calling an extra session of Congress to care for the Government's business. What's the use of doing that? Ain't Borah and Coolidge already there? Coolidge won't call any extra session. If he had his way, he would postpone the regular opening indefinitely and we'd all be better off.

Yours,
*Will Rogers.*

P. S. – My idea of an optimist is a near-sighted man in a five-dollar seat at the big prizefight.

## 359 WILL ROGERS SAYS FIGHTS ARE NO NOVELTY TO DAWES

FIRST NATIONAL STUDIOS, BURBANK, Cal., Sept. 15. – I see where Vice President Dawes refused a ringside seat free to the fight. It's no novelty for him to have a ringside seat to see a national argument, just between two. He has to watch ninety-six in one ring and gets paid for it, and should.

My old friend Mayor Bill Thompson of Chicago is out here with us. He is making speeches on the Mississippi flood. Knowing Bill was generally on the opposite side from the crowd, we kinder figured he would speak in favor of floods. But he didn't. He was agin 'em right from the first word.

Yours,
*Will Rogers.*

P. S. – A few five-dollar seats left around States bordering Illinois.

## 360 WILL ROGERS STUDIES EFFECT OF A MAN LOSING A MILLION

BEVERLY HILLS, Cal., Sept. 16. – Just been over visiting Charlie Chaplin at his studio, and watching him work. I wanted to see how a man acted that had just been separated from a million. That would be the supreme test of a comedian. He is funnier than ever. He showed me the new picture. If the next wife settles for a cent less than two and a half million, she is a chump.

Yours,
*Will Rogers.*

## 361 Will Rogers Sees McAdoo As Another "Draft" Horse

HOLLYWOOD, Cal., Sept. 18. – At the prize fight in Chicago the usual Chicago rules will prevail, guns instead of boxing gloves. Chicago has offered free ammunition to all out of town visitors.

Lindbergh is coming here tomorrow. He is the one man in this world that I would stand on a soap box on the corner and try to get a peek at. I got my box and my corner picked out.

I see where my good friend W. G. McAdoo has followed Coolidge's example and announced he is eligible for the draft. Two draft horses may pull against each other at the next election.

Yours,

*Will Rogers.*

## 362 Will Rogers Will Wait To See Next Year's Fight

BEVERLY HILLS, Cal., Sept. 19. – Tunney and Dempsey are letting up on their training, just going nine holes on the links instead of their previous strenuous eighteen. On Wednesday and Thursday they will just do a little light putting and a couple of simple questionnaires.

Amon Carter invited me to the fight, but I would rather wait and see them fight next year. That will be the third and maybe for the championship. I hope we can hear the shooting over the radio from Chicago that day.

*Will Rogers.*

## 363 Thoughts By Will Rogers On Aviation And Pugilism

FIRST NATIONAL STUDIO, BURBANK, Cal., Sept. 20. – Leaving tonight to go to San Diego to make a speech at Lindbergh's banquet. It wouldn't be so hard to speak if you knew anything of importance he had ever done.

Yours,

*Will.*

P. S. – See where the aviator and the lion landed O. K. and remained friends. That's the pilot that might get along with Levine.

P. S. – Can't tell you how to bet on the fight yet, as I haven't heard from Abe Attell.

## 364 Will Rogers Is Thrilled By Lindbergh's Airplane

SAN DIEGO, Cal., Sept. 21. – Lindbergh has been welcomed to all his various old homes, but today I saw a sight worth remembering. It was the other half of "We" landing on the field where she was made.

San Diego can rightfully claim a great credit in the flight. But you can't beat Los Angeles. They had to get in on it somehow. They claim they raised the pigs that the ham sandwiches were made from that Lindy took to Paris.

The pig was raised on Hellman's ranch and the ham cured by Joe Toplitsky.

Yours,
*Will Rogers.*

P. S. – In five years this town will have grown till it reaches Tijuana, Mexico. Then it can rightfully be known as the best city in America.

## 365 Will Rogers Takes A Flight With Lindbergh As His Pilot

BURBANK, Cal., Sept. 22. – I couldn't go to the fight today, but there is not one of that mob there that wouldn't have traded places with me.

I flew in a plane piloted by "Slim" Lindbergh, from San Diego to Los Angeles. You have never seen him at his best till you sit out in the pilot's seat by his side. When he has a plane in his hands there is no careworn or worried look. That's when he is in his glory.

He brought eleven of us, including my wife, on a wonderful trip in a giant three motored Ford plane.

When Ford takes to the air, aviation is assured.

Yours,
*Will.*

## 366 The Richer The Ambassador The Better It Suits Rogers

BURBANK, Cal., Sept. 23. – I want to announce to President Coolidge that the appointment of Dwight Morrow as Ambassador to Mexico is perfectly satisfactory to me. Andy Mellon has disproved the

*Will Rogers and Charles Lindbergh, September 22, 1927.*

popular Democratic theory that a rich man can't possibly be any good. I am going to Mexico next month, and the richer the Ambassador the better it will suit me.

Yours for more wealth in office. They might turn honest just for the novelty.

*Will.*

P. S. – Slow counting was all that beat Hollywood out of a championship. The Chicago referee would have begun counting quicker, but he couldn't think what number to begin with. Then he counted halves, too.

## 367 ROGERS DOUBTS GERMANY DISARMED WITHOUT URGING

HOLLYWOOD, Cal., Sept. 25. – Arthur Brisbane says that 11 people died listening over the radio to the fight. They just committed suicide waiting for the announcer to quit announcing the list of papers and tell them who won the fight.

Germany, this morning in the papers, wants everybody to disarm, saying they disarmed. Yes, but look what it cost to disarm 'em. Is it worth that, making a nation disarm? Besides, disarming only prolongs wars. Both sides fight till they get 'em. We didn't have any when we went in the last time. Less diplomats is what you want, not less arms.

Yours,
*Will.*

## 368 WILL ROGERS SEES NO ISSUE IN THE PROHIBITION ROW

BEVERLY HILLS, Cal., Sept. 26. – Jim Reed says prohibition will not be the issue with the Democrats, and, as usual, Jim is right.

How are you going to make an issue of it? The drys want it in the Constitution and it's in there.

The wets want a drink and they get it.

So what's all the argument about?

Yours,
*Will.*

## 369 WILL ROGERS FOR BOULDER DAM, BUT FLOOD VICTIMS COME FIRST

BEVERLY HILLS, Cal., Sept. 27. – One of our Western Senators says: "The Mississippi flood people say theirs is a national problem. Well, so is the Boulder Dam, and I will fight any effort to set it aside in favor of the flood."

Well, there is no difference in the two problems to a politician; but to a human being there is this difference: One is to do nothing but save lives and property, while the other is to develop a dam for cheap power and water, the same as dozens of other projects on other rivers are developed every day, without dragging in the Mississippi.

If the Colorado ever overflowed you can turn it out across the land anywhere on its lower course, and there is enough sand to soak up the Atlantic Ocean. The dam should be built, but not as a club over the Mississippi sufferers.

Yours,
*Will.*

## 370 WILL ROGERS COMPLIMENTS MAN WHO KISSED HIS OWN WIFE

BEVERLY HILLS, Cal., Sept. 28. – Some old boy got $3,500 damages for kissing his own wife publicly. His defense at the trial was that it was mistaken identity and that the moon drove him to it. Give him credit for one thing, he didn't lay it on to drink.

The American Legion is coming home from France. Somebody will have to meet them with doughnuts and tickets.

*Will Rogers.*

P. S. – Seven Governors of States are in Denver arguing and fussing over who owns the Colorado River. Mexico, where the river goes to, of its own free will, ain't saying a word.

## 371 WILL ROGERS SAYS DEMPSEY MAY WHIP TUNNEY SOME YEAR

BEVERLY HILLS, Cal., Sept. 29. – I saw the fight pictures last night. I don't see why Dempsey shouldn't whip Tunney some time. He keeps getting nearer to it every year. Tunney seems to be getting older faster than Dempsey. When the knockdown comes you can go out of the theatre and get a drink and come back before the counting starts.

The entire audience gave Dempsey the decision, so it looks like the old act will go on again next year, bigger and better than ever, same cast, same management, same boobs for an audience.

Yours,
*Will Rogers.*

## 372 MEXICAN RELATIONS PLEASANT OVER 'PHONE, SAYS WILL ROGERS

HOLLYWOOD, Cal., Sept. 30. – Mr. Coolidge just talked to the President of Mexico over the phone. Everything was pleasant and fine, but wait till Mexico opens its mail tomorrow morning and gets its daily note from Kellogg.

You read about the disaster in St. Louis and what the Red Cross did. No matter what happens or where it goes to happen they are the first there. That's why everybody in America should belong to it.

Yours,
*Will Rogers.*

## 373 WILL ROGERS SEES HOW RICKARD WOULD STAGE WORLD'S SERIES

HOLLYWOOD, Cal., Oct. 2. – If Tex Rickard sold 40,000 ringside seats to an event that took place all within twenty feet, how many would he sell around a baseball field to a world's series? He would have them play in the center of the Mississippi Valley and seat 'em all around the Rockies and Alleghanies.

It sure does good to have an athletic event approaching and not have to read about how the contestants played golf to get in shape for it. If Pittsburgh walks Ruth and Gehrig every time they can beat 'em.

Yours,
*Will Rogers.*

## 374 WILL ROGERS DISCOUNTS AN OVERSEAS CRITICISM

BURBANK, Cal., Oct. 3. – I see our papers quote a sarcastic criticism from a British paper about our Legion boys' visit to London, saying "We've had enough of this Yankee flag waving." Now that was only one paper said that. That's like England saying "America's form of government was all cockeyed" just because they had read in the paper where I had said it was.

Yours,
*Will Rogers.*

P. S. — I will feel there's something missing when I visit Tennessee next time. Monkey business might have gained Governor Peay national prominence, but being a real human being made him three times Governor of Tennessee.

## 375 Will Rogers Indicates A Little Home Prosperity

BURBANK, Cal., Oct. 4. — I unconsciously broke an American record of five years' standing yesterday. I bought a new car and didn't trade an old one in.

Yours,
*Will Rogers.*

## 376 Will Rogers Listens In Vain For A Home Run By Ruth

BURBANK, Cal., Oct. 5. — I had heard so much about this fellow Ruth and his homers that I listened in on the rodeo today and I never was so disappointed in my life at any one. Why, he only hit three singles, I thought he was supposed to knock home runs. We are proud in Oklahoma of our favorite sons, the Walloping Waners. We have produced the only two brothers that ever helped each other in a pinch.

Yours,
*Will Rogers.*

P. S. — You know yesterday I told you about breaking a record by buying a new car and not trading one in; well, if I just had paid cash for it I would have broken a real record, but I didn't.

## 377 Will Rogers Finds Movies Not Classified In Labor

BURBANK, Cal., Oct. 6. — See where Secretary Kellogg sent word to Mr. Borah that we were not only going to personally conduct the next Nicaraguan election, but if necessary the marines would do a little voting on the side themselves.

Secretary of Labor Davis was out to the studio here yesterday. He told me he can't find any classification of labor to put the movies in. Put 'em with politics, and they still won't be in any classification.

Yours,
*Will Rogers.*

P. S. – Pittsburgh will win tomorrow.

## 378 Will Rogers Still Predicts Pittsburgh Victory 'Tomorrow'

BEVERLY HILLS, Cal., Oct. 7. – I told you yesterday that Pittsburgh would win tomorrow and it looks like that's the day they will win. With Lazzeris, Bengoughs, Pipgrasses and Cvengroses playing no wonder Babe Ruth is popular. His is the only name we can pronounce.

Well, it's just as well to get the baseball over with, for the boys that are working their way through football are all ready to break a leg for big gate receipts.

Yours,
*Will Rogers.*

## 379 Will Rogers Will Bet $5,000 That Coolidge Will Run Again

HOLLYWOOD, Cal., Oct. 9. – This is to my friend, Arthur Brisbane:

Now, Arthur, here is the proposition: You keep saying Coolidge won't run. I have always said he would, not because he wanted to, but because he has to. Now, I am not for a moment conceited enough to think my opinion is as good as yours on any subject, but you writers can write one way and believe another. But no man bets one way and believes another. In fact, the only way to back an opinion is by some deed or some money, not by an editorial.

So, I will bet you $5,000 that he runs; no ifs about it. I bet he runs. You bet he doesn't. The winner to give the $5,000 to charity, preferably to form a society for the advancement of political knowledge.

Yours,
*Will Rogers.*

P. S. — Have Hearst indorse check. There is such a thing as a man becoming land and property poor.

P. S. — This whole thing is not any joke either. When a comedian bets $5,000 it's a serious business.

## 380 Plenty Of Advice On How To Use Surplus, Will Says

BEVERLY HILLS, Cal., Oct. 10. — See the United States Chamber of Commerce has advised Mr. Mellon how to divide up the government's $400,000,000 surplus. They don't tell him how to enforce prohibition or any of those hard things, but the minute there is some money to be split up they are there with the suggestion.

*Will Rogers.*

P. S. — If you didn't happen to read their first proposal to Mellon, it was that their members should get three hundred and ninety of the four hundred million.

Another P. S. — Will hear from Arthur soon. He is always a couple of days late with the news.

## 381 Mr. Rogers On French Tariff; He's Also Still For Coolidge

BEVERLY HILLS, Cal., Oct. 11. — See where we are sore at France now for imitating us and putting on a tariff against our goods. Kinder puts us at a disadvantage on account of the size of France.

If it was some South or Central American country, we could claim it was unlawful and make 'em take it off.

Haven't heard from Arthur yet. I doubt if he has seen it. I don't guess he slums much in his reading.

If the Republicans don't run Coolidge, history will repeat itself. You saw what happened to Pittsburgh when they thought they could win without Cuyler.

Yours,
*Will Rogers.*

## 382 W. R. Hearst Takes Up Will Rogers's Bet That Coolidge Will Run Again Next Year

BEVERLY HILLS, Cal., Oct. 12. — I have received this:

Will Rogers, Beverly Hills, Cal.:

Dear Will: Since you have brought me into the Rogers-Brisbane controversy as to whether President Coolidge will run again in spite of his definite declaration that he will not, let me say I will accept your bet of $5,000 and moreover, will give you odds of 2 to 1; in other words, I will wager $10,000 to $5,000 that President Coolidge will not run in 1928.

I have no inside information, but I know the President to be a truthful, honorable gentleman and a high-minded patriot who wishes to stand, and deserves to stand, with Washington, Jefferson, Madison, Monroe, Jackson, Cleveland, and all the great Americans who have been unwilling to endanger the republican character of our American institutions by substituting a dictatorship for a democracy by breaking the eight-year limitation, the more than two-term restriction, established by the Father of our country.

Moreover, the people have shown their devotion to the principles of Washington by voting out of office the party and the public men who violated his injunction against foreign entangling alliances, and I firmly believe that the public would be equally drastic in their action concerning any public man who thought more of his petty personal ambition than he did of Washington's patriotic injunction against the dangers of a protracted Presidential term.

William Randolph Hearst.

All right, Mr. Hearst, it's a bet. I can understand your position. You, as a Democrat, don't want him to run. Neither does any other Democrat want him to run. But it's the Republicans that he has to listen to, and not the Democrats. It's not "his petty personal ambition." It's that he has to run to protect the party that has kept him in office all his life. You say he will be defeated. Now, I will outdo you in generosity. I will bet you 5 to 1 that if he runs he will be elected.

I base this belief on the ground of the Democrats splitting, which is the surest ground in the world, especially if a wet is nominated. And if a wet is not nominated the wet Democrats will go Republican. So they split either way they jump.

Now, Mr. Hearst, it wasn't you I was after at all. It was Arthur I was fishing for. I base both bets on two things—Republicans needs and Democratic precedent. Now, when I start collecting, W. R., I hope this don't make you short. The charity which I will devote the winnings of the last bet to, is the upbringing of the Rogers offspring, so they won't have to rely on public office for sustenance.

Arthur got out of this pretty lucky.

Yours,

*Will Rogers.*

## 383 Rogers On What Might Be With Reed In White House

BEVERLY HILLS, Cal., Oct. 13. – Say, did you read this morning what Jim Reed called the Republicans? Why, you would think if they had any pride at all they could come out and deny it. I guess they would if they could.

It took Missouri seven years to find out that Jim was right. I hope the nation can catch on quicker than that. I would love to see Jim in that White House. He would sure have some of those old rich boys going in and bringing sticks out of the water for him.

*Will Rogers.*

P. S. – I only got one more bet to make and then I'm through. I'll bet one million dollars everything Jim said about the Republicans was true.

## 384 Will Rogers Says Girl Fliers Should Find More Useful Jobs

BEVERLY HILLS, Cal., Oct. 14. – We wish some girl would make it across some ocean. It might encourage all these others that are trying to be first across to take up some more useful employment. Look at the English Channel swimmers. The last two women to swim it lately didn't even get a chance to advertise the grease .

See Queen Marie's daughter is reported to have eloped with a Rumanian naval Lieutenant. There's a mistake there somewhere. He can't be a Rumanian Naval officer, unless they just kept one for decorative purposes.

Yours,
*Will Rogers.*

P. S. – Coolidge lectured yesterday on art and Mellon on Pittsburgh.

## 385 Rogers Says Ruth Elder's Motto Is "Save The Lipstick"

HOLLYWOOD, Cal., Oct. 16. – Outside of Notre Dame there is not much to brag about in the papers today.

Kamal Pasha or somebody is making a speech in Turkey that is lasting for five days and nights. He must be arguing whether to put prohibition in their platform or not.

Ruth Elder, that dutiful and home-loving wife, says "save the lipstick first." So the plane was lost.

Yours,
*Will Rogers.*

## 386 Firemen's Home On Desert Makes Rogers Wonder Why

BEVERLY HILLS, Cal., Oct. 17. – Had lunch today with Mr. Brisbane. He seems sure Coolidge won't run. He thinks it will be Mellon or Hughes against Smith. He thinks next year will be very prosperous in spite of election. Brisbane has built a home on the edge of the Mojave Desert. He is going to build some homes there for retired firemen. Can you imagine a fireman retiring to go to the Mojave Desert? He will think he is fighting a fire yet. He is strong for California, but he says the real money in real estate is to be made between Thirty-fourth and Fifty-ninth streets, New York.

Yours,
*Will Rogers.*

## 387 Will Rogers Sends A Note On Western Aviation Progress

SALT LAKE CITY, Utah, Oct. 18. – While you are talking about progressing aviation, don't overlook this company, the Western Air Express.

One year and a half ago they started with only twenty pounds of mail. Today, in here packed around me, is 550 pounds. We are coming into Salt Lake. Only been six hours from Los Angeles.

They have flown 650,000 miles, with only four forced landings and no one hurt.

Brigham Young might have seen more women than I have, but I have seen more of Utah today than he ever saw. Who said this country was all settled up? Tonight we will see how it feels to fly at night.

Yours,
*Will.*

## 388 Rogers Contributes A Note On An Airplane Journey

LEWISTOWN, Pa., Oct. 19. – Breakfast at home in Beverly yesterday (Tuesday) and dinner in New York tonight (Wednesday).

Only one bad feature on whole trip. Got lost in the pistol smoke over Chicago.

Yours,
*Will Rogers.*

P. S. – Going to New York to match up some dress material for my wife.

## 389 Will Rogers Illustrates Air Travel As A Time Saver

CLEVELAND, Ohio, Oct. 20. – Left New York at 1 P. M. today; am at Cleveland at 5 P. M., and will be in Beverly tomorrow night for corn bread and beans.

No special planes, just regular mail planes; fare $400 each way, and you save two days each way.

So, if your time is worth anything, travel by air. If not, you might just as well walk.

Yours,
*Will Rogers.*

## 390 Will Rogers Chases Wolves On His Flight Back Home

LAS VEGAS, Nev., Oct. 21. – Had the greatest kick flying this morning I ever had. All the way across Wyoming we chased wolves and antelopes. Will be home for dinner. Left Tuesday morning, spent one night and half a day in New York City and back in Beverly Friday afternoon. Have only been away three nights. If you had left Los Angeles on the train at the same time I did you wouldn't even arrive there till Saturday morning, and, boy, what pilots those air mail babies are. Lindbergh came from a great school.

Yours,
*Will Rogers.*

P. S. – This Las Vegas you will hear a lot of it when Boulder Dam is built. We just flew all over and around it. It certainly should be built. The man that never saw it by air never saw it.

## 391 Will Rogers Backs Morrow Against Mexican Bandits

HOLLYWOOD, Cal., Oct. 23. – Dwight Morrow is on his way to Mexico to become a diplomat. His diplomacy started early; in fact, at the border, when he got into an armored train. We needn't worry about him. Those Morgan boys can generally take care of themselves. If the train is held up by bandits, I bet you the outlaws come out second best in any financial transaction. If the worst comes to the worst he will float a loan and take their guns and horses as collateral.

These are anxious hours for Old Amherst. Cal will stick by his classmates. It's too bad he hasn't got a war to send some of them to.

If Dwight gets away with Mexico in good shape, I hereby propose him as first ambassador to Russia.

Yours,
*Will Rogers.*

## 392 Will Rogers Suggests New Plan To Mrs. Grayson

BEVERLY HILLS, Cal., Oct. 24. – Morrow got to Mexico O.K. He was only an Ambassador and not a candidate.

Poor Mrs. Grayson, to save wear and tear on bidding her friends good-bye so much, won't be on the ship on its next two starts.

If they ever get Prince Carol on the throne in Rumania they could use Madam Lupescu as lady-in-waiting. It's funny to me they don't get that guy on the Mann act.

Yours,
*Will Rogers.*

## 393 Bankers Are Happier Than Borrowers, Rogers Implies

BEVERLY HILLS, Cal., Oct. 25. – The American Bankers' Association are holding their annual benefit at Houston. It's their biggest benefit year. The government has contributed permission for them to consolidate to freeze out the little fellow. The public, of course, will contribute everything else, so really the only problem before the convention is "how much bonuses on loans will we make 'em pay above the legal rate of interest?"

Branch banks are all the go now. They realize they have got to bring the bank nearer the robber. He won't be annoyed by driving through traffic just to rob one bank. The branch bank is the robbers' only salvation.

Yours,
*Will Rogers.*

P. S. – Every banker that could afford a failure in the last year is there.

## 394 WILL ROGERS GIVES HIS VIEW OF THE MAGRUDER INCIDENT

HOLLYWOOD, Cal., Oct. 26. – The navy called in Admiral Magruder. He said the navy was spending too much money.

There is only one unpardonable thing you can say either in navy, army or politics, and that is to propose to cut down its expenditure. You can accuse them of negligence and even laziness, but to suggest spending less money! Well, he just lost his compass in mid-ocean.

On the Riviera in France they found a bunch of people wearing no clothes and not particularly caring who they were married to and they called it a cult. Over here we call it society, and lack of dress is standard equipment.

Yours,
*Will Rogers.*

## 395 WILL ROGERS COMMENDS SENATOR CURTIS'S POSITION

BEVERLY HILLS, Cal., Oct. 27. – I liked Senator Curtis's announcement in the papers this morning better than any Presidential ones we have had.

He said he would accept it if he was elected, but that he wouldn't accept the nomination unless he was elected. I think that's a most straightforward and clear-sighted decision. If more men wouldn't run for offices unless they can get 'em we would have fewer races and politics would improve a thousand per cent.

I am strong for Charley because he's an Injun, and he is close enough to Oklahoma to understand the farmers' problems.

Yours,
*Will.*

## 396 WILL ROGERS HOPES TO JOIN THE FESS-MAGRUDER CLUB

BEVERLY HILLS, Cal., Oct. 28. – Col. T. Coleman Du Pont, United States Senator from Delaware, has lost use of his vocal cords. Now I feel sincerely sorry for his personal discomfiture, but if his ailment could be made contagious and he distribute it among his brother members of the Senate his illness would prove to be a tremendous national blessing.

Since Senator Fess has been reprimanded for complimenting Coolidge, and Magruder has Philadelphia sunk from under him, I have been accused of being lax in my national criticism for fear of exile. I want to say that I am only trying to think up something terrible enough to say.

Yours,
*Will Rogers.*

### 397 WILL ROGERS ON RANCHES, CONGRESSMEN AND CATTLE

SAN SIMEON, Cal., Oct. 30, 3:50 P. M. – The fellows that keep saying big ranches are all done away with ought to see this one, 300,000 acres.

If this was back East they could call it Delaware, Maryland, Connecticut and Rhode Island, and eight Senators and twenty-five Congressmen would have to live off it. Out here that much beautiful land don't have to support a thing but wonderful cattle and horses. You can just tell the difference when you look at land that has to support a Senator or a white-faced bull.

Yours,
*Will Rogers.*

P. S. – Yours for more cattle and less Congressmen.

### 398 WILL ROGERS MAKES CONTRAST BETWEEN AUTO AND PLANE DEATHS

SANTA BARBARA, Cal., Oct. 31. – Five people killed in plane yesterday and it is headlined today in every paper. Saturday in Los Angeles at one grade crossing seven were killed and six wounded and the papers didn't even publish the names.

It looks like the only way you can get any publicity on your death is to be killed in a plane. It's no novelty to be killed in an auto any more.

Yours,
*Will Rogers.*

### 399 WILL ROGERS ASKS $20 FEE TO JOIN 'AMERICA ONLY' CLUB

BEVERLY HILLS, Cal., Nov. 1. – Mayor Bill Thompson of Chicago has started a society called "America First." You send $10 to defray the expenses of trying to keep it "first." Bill has the nucleus of a good idea, but, like any good idea, it's the improvements that make it.

So I hereby offer stock in a society called "America Only" at $20 a share. Why be only first? Let's be the whole thing. Why spend $10 to be in front when $10 more will put you in front, behind and in the middle all at the same time? If everybody in America will give me $20 I will be more than glad to show them where we are the "only nation in the world." Besides, this money will not all revert to me. A small percentage will be spent in exterminating all other nations.

Who'll be the first to display super-patriotism and join "America Only"?

Yours,
*Will Rogers.*
Founder and Treasurer.

## 400 Will Rogers Gets Moral Aid, But No Dues For His Society

FIRST NATIONAL STUDIOS, BURBANK, Cal., Nov. 2. – I am hearing already from my "America Only" Society. Have received several wires, collect. Everybody is interested, but nobody has sent dues.

I have yet to find a legitimate excuse for any other nation existing at all.

Yours,
*Will Rogers.*

P. S. – Just received applications from two Washington jurors.

## 401 Reflections By Will Rogers On Our High Standard Of Living

BEVERLY HILLS, Cal., Nov. 3. – Bureau of something or other in Washington announces that "America has reached the highest standard of living ever reached by any nation."

Yes, and if they will just cut down on the original payments we have to make from a dollar to 50 cents we will show you some living. It's an injustice to ask a hard-working people to pay a dollar down. It should be 50 cents down and 50 cents when they come to try and find it to take it back.

Course, we don't get meat as often as our forefathers. But we have our peanut butter and radio.

Yours,
*Will Rogers.*

P. S. — You wait till Henry Ford's new car comes out. You ain't seen any high living yet.

## 402 WILL ROGERS EXPECTS TO SEE HENRY FORD GIVING 'EM AWAY

BEVERLY HILLS, Cal., Nov. 4. — Everybody is just tickled to death over the new Ford plan, but I was just a little disappointed in it. I thought sure, after his waiting all this time, that he was going to give 'em away.

Of course, renting 'em ain't bad. I bet you the next time some other concern gets to crowding him he will give 'em to us.

I hereby put in my order for the first one that lights in California. I think I will get two or three. I always did want to go out in the morning and choose my car.

Yours,
*Will Rogers.*

P. S. — Thanks for the birthday greetings. I was trying to keep it quiet.

## 403 WILL ROGERS IN IDLE TIME TURNS TO THE NAVAJO COUNTRY

ADAMANA, Ariz., Nov. 6. — For the first time in my life had nothing to do and nowhere to go, so I says to the balance wheel: "Did you ever see the petrified forest, the Navajo Indians, the Cliff Dwellers and all those interesting things?" She said no.

So here we are just prowling around making no speeches, doing no act, just trying to buy a Navajo blanket from a Navajo; in other words from the producer to the ultimate consumer without a middle man.

It's a beautiful country and the same climate California charges you for.

Yours,
*Will Rogers.*

## 404 WILL ROGERS SAYS NAVAJOS DON'T PROFIT BY OIL ROYALTIES

LAGUNA, N. M., Nov. 7. — They struck oil on the Navajos' land three years ago. I foolishly asked how often they get their payments for their oil royalty. Well, they hadn't any yet. They took a million of it to build a bridge across the Little Colorado River so tourists wouldn't have to drive so far around to see the Grand Canyon. The Navajos paid for the bridge and there has never been a Navajo crossed it yet.

If the Indians' oil royalties hold out they will have enough to build the Boulder Dam for the whites.

I suppose I will be recalled for telling this, like Magruder and Summerall.

Yours,
*Will Rogers.*

## 405 Will Rogers Has An Idea About Terms For Governors

SANTA FE, N. M., Nov. 8. – Just messing around seeing some of our wonderful country. Here in Santa Fe, the oldest town in America, the tourists say, "Oh, aren't the people quaint and unique! I wonder what they do and think about."

Well, today they are voting on the same thing New York State is—whether to keep a Governor two years or four. So, wherever there is politics, people have the same worries. I think a good, honest Governor should get four years and the others life.

As we become more enlightened we will extinguish our office seekers every two years.

Yours,
*Will Rogers.*

## 406 As Will Rogers Views Results Of The Election

SANTA FE, N. M., Nov. 9. – News of the day about Tuesday's elections: Smith carried New York through force of habit. Vare carried Philadelphia through something. It may not have been just habit alone. Cleveland, Ohio, admitted they needed a Mayor and New Mexico here voted that if any man couldn't get it in two years in this State that there was no use giving him four.

Kentucky decided it was all right for the State to have some of the money bet on horse races, that the profit should not all go to the bookmakers.

Yours,
*Will Rogers.*

## 407 A Few Notes By Will Rogers On Agricultural Conditions

TOPEKA, Kan., Nov. 11. — Been a-coming through a Kansas cornfield all day. This country is so busy gathering corn they can't get 'em to town to holler for relief.

Down South the bo weavil eat 'nough cotton to keep it high priced. Cattle couldn't wait for election year to go up in price.

If Cal can give 'em one more year of rain and bo weavil, I'll cop William Hearst's ten thousand.

What other man has the Republicans got that can control the weather and the insects like that? John Roach Straton and his divine healing is the only one I can think of offhand.

Yours,

*Will Rogers.*

## 408 Will Rogers Sizes Up Mayor Thompson And Chicago

CULVER, Ind., Nov. 13. — Had a long chat with Mayor Thompson in Chicago yesterday. A smart guy that, and don't you believe otherwise.

The thing of playing George Washington against King George; he knows it's a lot of applesauce better than you do. Bill don't dislike the King personally, but they have been kinder giving George Washington the worst of it in the Chicago second and third readers. If it had been in the fifth or sixth readers, Chicago never would a noticed it.

P. S. — Notre Dame's defeat yesterday in New York was the first setback Al Smith has had. I am going up to South Bend tonight to help cheer Knute up.

*Will Rogers.*

## 409 Will Rogers Sends A Beat About The New Ford Car

DETROIT, Mich., Nov. 14. — Here is the biggest news I have ever gathered. It's a real beat on the rest of the press.

I have spent the whole day with Henry Ford, saw and drove in the new car. And here is what you have been waiting for for years; get ready, everybody.

HE HAS CHANGED THE RADIATOR!

I didn't even notice whether it has four wheels or five, two doors or twenty, whether it uses horses or is pulled by a motor. When I saw that radiator changed, I was just so tickled and overcome I couldn't tell you if the thing has got fenders or wings.

I am to meet him early in the morning again, and may be more composed. Then I can tell you tomorrow more about it. But what more would anybody want to know?

Yours, Old Sleuth,
*Will Rogers.*

## 410 WILL ROGERS IS ENTHUSIASTIC ABOUT THE NEW FORD HE RODE IN

CHICAGO, Ill., Nov. 15. — Start building more roads, for you can announce to the world that Uncle Henry Ford has a conveyance. Cops, mount your steeds, for this new baby will do seventy miles. Wire wheels, four-wheel brakes.

I tell you, breeding and association will tell; she looked like a Lincoln. The only Fordy thing about it is the fellow that wrote the name on it—it is the same handwriting as old Lizzies.

Yours,
*Will Rogers.*

P. S. — Just flew in here from Detroit with twelve others in big three-motored Ford plane. Great trip! If you like aviation don't miss seeing it take the air. I went clear to Detroit to see it.

## 411 MR. ROGERS FOR SEX EQUALITY IN POST-NUPTIAL SHOOTING

DODGE CITY, Kan., Nov. 16. — Headline in papers here today said "Ruth Elder bids good-bye to husband and sends him back to Panama."

More women envy Ruth over that than anything she has done. Thousands of women wouldn't care to brave the Atlantic but would love to send their husbands to Panama.

I think this fellow Remus, who is on trial, should be a hero to us men. He is the only man in our time that has had the foresight to shoot his wife first.

Yours for equality in sex in firearms practice after marriage,
*Will Rogers.*

## 412 Thoughts By Will Rogers On Floods, Hoover And Hold-Ups

WINSLOW, Ariz., Nov. 17. – I happened to be playing up through New England last Spring when the Mississippi flood drive was on, and they were very, very generous, never dreaming that they would ever need help. But they did, and there is the old Red Cross, and old Doc Hoover is at their bedside.

I get what the wheat farmers are sore at Hoover about. He wouldn't let them hold up the people for bread during the war. Their excuse is that everybody else held us up, so why pick on them?

They were the only ones he could catch.

Yours,
*Will Rogers.*

P. S. – Coming home. After seeing the Navajos and the Ford cars, what else is there?

## 413 Mr. Rogers Sees New Signs That Mr. Coolidge Will Run

BEVERLY HILLS, Cal., Nov. 18. – Did you read Mr. Coolidge's acceptance speech of next year's nomination in the paper this morning?

Why, say, if we are doing only just a third as well as he says we are doing, why, we wouldn't no more let him leave us, no matter what his own chooseclinations are. Why, I hadn't read the speech half way through till I paid a dollar down on half a dozen things I didn't need.

We'll show the world we are prosperous if we have to go broke to do it.

Yours,
*Will.*

## 414 Will Rogers Discusses Football Season's Results

HOLLYWOOD, Cal., Nov. 20. – The football season is about over. Education never had a more financial year. School will commence now.

Successful colleges will start laying plans for new stadiums; unsuccessful ones will start hunting a new coach; cheer leaders will join the Rotary luncheons for hog-calling contests. Heroes have been cheered that will never do anything to be cheered again.

We are trying to arrange a post-season game between Harvard and the motion-picture leading men.

Yours,
*Will Rogers.*

## 415 Mr. Rogers Draws A Moral From Washington's Diary

BEVERLY HILLS, Cal., Nov. 21. – Say, did you read what Rupert Hughes dug up in George Washington's diary? I was so ashamed I sat up all night reading it.

This should be a lesson to Presidents to either behave themselves or not keep a dairy. Can you imagine, 100 years hence, some future Rupert Hughes pouncing on Calvin's diary? What would that generation think of us?

Calvin, burn them papers!

Yours for the suppression of scandal,
*Will Rogers.*

## 416 Will Rogers Tells The World What To Do About A Surplus

BEVERLY HILLS, Cal., Nov. 22. – Mellon, foolishly and unpolitically, saved up a little money out of our national "jack pot." Well, a forthcoming war or a colossal national pestilence couldn't have stirred up half the excitement among entire America as what to do with this little dab of money.

Half of Congress met three weeks early, not to solve the Mississippi floods nor to build Boulder Dam, but to split up the "jack pot." We owe thirty billion dollars, but we couldn't think of applying it on that; it's too near an election.

I am beginning to believe that Mellon is the poorest Treasurer we ever had. I would like to be Treasurer. Here would be my policy, and you see if it wouldn't be the best thing for America:

Save nothing, have nothing in there. Then Congress and the entire nation could have nothing in view only what they made themselves.

*A Candidate.*

## 417 WILL ROGERS REVIEWS A THANKSGIVING LIST

HOLLYWOOD, Cal., Nov. 23. – This is Thanksgiving. It was started by the Pilgrims, who would give thanks every time they killed an Indian and took more of his land. As years went by and they had all his land, they changed it into a day to give thanks for the bountiful harvest, when the boll-weevil and the protective tariff didn't remove all cause for thanks.

So here is what the Republicans have given us the past year: A war in Nicaragua and China, and a rehearsal in Mexico, two floods and a coal strike, and pictures of the Black Hills.

And all we got in return is the promise of a new Ford car and lower taxes.

Yours,
*Will Rogers.*

## 418 WILL ROGERS ON OUR WEALTH AND OUR GAMBLING RULES

BEVERLY HILLS, Cal., Nov. 24. – If you think we are not prosperous and cuckoo both, read these: "Three hundred thousand dollars for seat on Stock Exchange." You pay that for a seat where nobody sits down. They stand and yell and sell something they haven't got, and buy something they will never get. You can get on the Curb for forty thousand. All you have to do is make signs to a guy in a window, and try to keep from being run over by a truck.

In the next column we read "Kentucky prohibits betting on races." You can gamble on how high people pay for their bread but you can't bet on how fast a horse will run. We must appear odd to the foreigners.

*Will Rogers.*

## 419 WILL ROGERS FINDS A COMMENT IN THE DAY'S NEWS FROM EUROPE

BEVERLY HILLS, Cal., Nov. 25. – All the day's news comes from Europe.

Rumania's dictator died. So that helps Prince Carol's case. He is only two wives removed from the throne now.

Another headline says, "One Hundred Million More Men Under Arms in Europe than 1914." "England sends word to Italy to lay off Jugoslavia."

It's taken a long time for Europe to get back to normal, but it's slowly doing it.

Yours,
*Will.*

## 420 WILL ROGERS DESCRIBES THE EUROPEAN FOOTBALL GAME

LOS ANGELES, Cal., Nov. 27. – The Balkan nations have gone into a huddle. It looks like Bulgaria's ball on Rumania's ten-yard line. Poland was penalized ten yards for being offside against Lithuania. Mussolini is the triple-threat man of the game. It will all wind up like the last one, just another incompleted war. They will have to bring it back and line up again.

Yours,
*Will Rogers.*

## 421 WILL ROGERS HAS AN IDEA ABOUT THE ACTIVITY OF THE DRYS

DOUGLAS, Ariz., Nov. 28. – See by the Arizona morning papers that the biggest bunch of drys ever collected are staggering into Washington to try and keep Congress from nominating Al Smith. If he is elected it will take away millions and millions of dollars now appropriated among them for law enforcement. It's not more teeth that's wanted in enforcement acts, it's more money.

Arizona is fat and prosperous and all set for another Winter's argument on the dam.

Yours,
*Will Rogers.*

## 422 WILL ROGERS' DISPATCH

SAN ANTONIO, Tex., Nov. 29. – The head of the Democratic ticket is just about set outside the machine, so I want to start early with my Vice Presidential nomination. It's Dan Moody, the Governor of this little province.

Now Dan this is not just what I would like to offer you, but it may lead to something worth while. To any guy that can run Texas, America ought to be a pipe.

The newspapers have dug up another sensational murder trial. Man and Woman and Dead Husband. Watch the sales double.

Yours,
*Will Rogers.*

## 423 WILL SHOULD SEND OBREGON A WIRE JUST LIKE THIS ONE

LAREDO, Tex., Nov. 30. – Going into Mexico just as a tourist, not as a critic, and want it publicly known not as a candidate.

Yours,
*Will Rogers.*

## 424 WILL ROGERS FINDS MORE FORD THAN FIGHTING DOWN IN MEXICO

MEXICO CITY, Dec. 1. – Been traveling two days and one night in Mexico. Just as well been crossing Kansas as far as excitement was concerned.

The world is a small place after all. This whole nation is just waiting tonight to see what Ford will charge for his car. If it is cheap, tomorrow will be declared a feast day—"Los Fiesta de Fords."

Yours,
*Will Rogers,*
*Aragon Hidalgo.*

## 425 WILL ROGERS, DOWN IN MEXICO, PRAISES AMBASSADOR MORROW

MEXICO CITY, Dec. 3. – Am on Presidential train and with Ambassador Morrow have just inspected Government agricultural schools and big water project. I am interpreter between Mr. Morrow and President Calles.

Say, this fellow Morrow has made a big hit down here. He's going to do some real good. He is a great fellow.

I don't generally send dispatches for Sunday papers, but this is an exception.

Yours,
*Will Rogers.*

## 426 Will Rogers Sees A Bull Fight, But Declines To Take Part

ON THE PRESIDENTIAL TRAIN SOMEWHERE IN MEXICO, via Laredo, Tex., Dec. 5. – Having a great trip but can't find any revolutionists.

Yesterday the President, out on one of the big ranches where we were entertained, went into the bull ring himself and fought the bull. He had no weapons and didn't hurt the bull. He tried to get me to go in, but the bull was still armed, so I stayed in the grand stand.

It was bull fighting that would have pleased Americans. No horses and no bulls hurt; only a couple of men.

Yours,
*Will Rogers.*

## 427 Will Rogers, From Mexico, Says He Hears No Shooting

ON BOARD PRESIDENTIAL TRAIN, Somewhere in Mexico, via Laredo, Tex., Dec. 5. – Ambassador Morrow and I, just today, saw a dam and irrigation plant that will irrigate two hundred thousand acres. That's as big for Mexico as the Boulder Dam scheme is for the United States, and they have three others like this one under construction, so they are doing something down here besides shooting at each other.

Morrow has learned five words of Spanish and is eating chili. Over a hundred and fifty American civil engineers down here on all this work.

Haven't heard a gun fired since I left San Antonio.

Adios Amigos,
*Will Rogers.*

## 428 Will Rogers Anxious For News Of Government Matters Here

ON BOARD THE PRESIDENTIAL TRAIN, coming into Mexico City, Dec. 6. – Just getting in off a great trip. Ambassador

Morrow and President Calles had a great time and it gave them a great chance to get better acquainted without the usual formality.

Did Congress open yesterday and why? Did Calvin tell 'em anything, and what and for why?

Yours,
*Will Rogers.*

## 429 WILL ROGERS HOLDS TO HIS BET THAT COOLIDGE WILL RUN

MEXICO CITY, Dec. 8. – Arrived in Mexico City and found President Coolidge has issued another "choose." My bet with Mr. Hearst still holds. He means well, but necessity is where I will win my bet. He told the Republicans to search vigorously, and they will have to. Mexico was pleased with his message.

If Vare and Smith fall down on the American Senate have them get in touch with me and I can get them in the Senate here.

The farmers in the Middle West wanted relief so the Republicans gave them the Republican Convention.

Who in the world are the Republicans going to run? I can come home if necessary.

Yours,
*Will Rogers.*

## 430 TRUTH NOT SO BAD AS RUMORS IN MEXICO, SAYS WILL ROGERS

MEXICO CITY, Dec. 9. – They just last night removed the censorship on news from Mexico, and now I don't know anything to say. From now on you will get the truth, and I'll bet you the truth is not as bad as the rumors.

I am having dinner tonight with General Obregon, the sole surviving candidate of all parties. Just think, if you had to eat with every Presidential candidate of both parties at home you would be eating out the rest of your life.

Yours,
*Will Rogers.*

## 431 Guadalupe Day Pleases Rogers, But He Can't Stand A Bull Fight

MEXICO CITY, Dec. 12. – Witnessed a sight today, the greatest and oldest thing of its kind on this continent–Guadalupe Day.

There must have been 200,000 come from all over Mexico to worship at the birthday of Mexico's patron saint. It takes more than laws to change beliefs.

Let me know when Lindy is coming; I got to get out and give up my bed at the Embassy.

Went to a bull fight yesterday, but when the horses commenced dropping I couldn't stand the gaff. However, it's the only thing starts on time.

Yours,
*Will Rogers.*

## 432 Will Rogers Finds The World Praying Again For Lindebergh

MEXICO CITY, Dec. 13. – Just flew over and looked right down in crater of Popocatepillar. It's easier to fly over than it is to pronounce. They have some good fliers here. The whole country is crazy about Lindbergh's flight. He is the first thing that America has sent here that was not in the form of a note. He will get a great reception and I will lose a good bed.

That kid has the whole world praying for him again tonight.

Here's hoping,
*Will Rogers.*

## 433 Will Rogers Yields 'Post' To Lindbergh

MEXICO CITY, Dec. 14. – Lindbergh is right here–just left him in the next room. Didn't have to give up my room at the embassy; the Ambassador gave up his. Said mine wasn't good enough for Lindy.

He has just this minute talked with his mother in Detroit. He couldn't hear very well and Mr. Morrow did the talking. He invited her down here for Christmas, and she said, ask her son, and he told her to come on. So it looks like she may be here to spend Christmas with him.

He don't seem very tired. He was twenty-seven hours in the air. I saw over 200,000 people, including the President and all his Cabinet, wait for eight hours to welcome him, and even our own country couldn't equal the welcome. They went cuckoo.

Any other aviator in the world would have come down to see where he was, but that determination made him stay up there till he found the name of a hotel, one building, and found it on the map, and then laid a compass route from there.

You people up there can't realize what this trip of his means to the two countries. An American audience couldn't have been any more sincerely worried during the time we heard he was lost. When we heard he had found his way and was coming on, I was standing by President Calles and he said:

"What a brave and great man he is!"

To give you an idea of the ardorous nature of these people in comparison to America and Europe: In France and America they like to tore up the plane to tear off souvenirs. Here hundreds took it up on their own shoulders and carried it to the hangar.

Here instead of being bombarded with ticker tape the streets were two inches thick with flowers.

The Ambassador has been working on this flight since he was first appointed. He was just in my room and said he was the most pleased man in Mexico tonight.

Tell the doubtful ones that Lindbergh will not be taken to a bull fight, that there are other amusements here. He is resting now and says he don't want to go to sleep till night comes.

Morrow and I have resigned as Ambassadors in Mexico. Now there is only one when he is in the country.

The Ambassador gave me a dinner here in the embassy last night at which the President and all the Cabinet attended, the first time a President of Mexico ever was in the American Embassy. We had many a laugh. These are real people down here if we only knew them.

Yours,

*Will Rogers.*

## 434 Will Rogers Tells The World What A Hero Eats For Breakfast

MEXICO CITY, Dec. 15. — Somebody could have been President yesterday without a revolution if they had just thought about it while he was at the aviation field with all the soldiers in Mexico. They could have taken the palace, sent out their laundry and announced that they was President.

While we were having breakfast this morning at the embassy somebody told Lindbergh that he ought to stay and see some of Mexico while here. He said:

"I saw all Mexico yesterday but the Gulf of Lower California."

To show you the modesty of this fellow, the Ambassador was reading how the whole world printed extras of his trip. He said: "The papers ought to give me a prize for getting more sensational headlines for less reason than any one ever did before."

If you have wondered what a hero eats for breakfast, he had fruit, ham and eggs and toast and coffee, just about what a common feller will eat when he can get it.

Yours,
*Will.*

P. S. – Has the Senate found out who gave the Senators the money down here? I want to see if there is any left .

## 435 WILL ROGERS, UP WITH 'LINDY,' SAYS HE'S A GREAT FLIER

MEXICO CITY, Dec. 16. – Just been flying over the city with Lindy in a Mexican plane. It don't make any difference to that baby what the nationality or the breed as long as it's got a propeller. He is going to take up President Calles and also Obregon.

He says he is going to stay here till after Christmas so he won't have to buy all his friends back home presents. I think he will go to some of the other South American republics from here and then make Cuba.

Lindy says they take him to a show to watch the Spanish girls dance and then everybody gets around him and talks to him so much he can't see her.

So Tom Heflin is finally getting Republican ideas.

Yours,
*Will Rogers.*

## 436 WILL ROGERS TELLS ABOUT LINDBERGH AND BULL FIGHTS

TAMPICO, Mexico, Dec. 18. – Just flew in here by plane from Mexico City. Flying to Brownsville, Texas, in the morning. Left Lindy at the rodeo. He was going to the bull fight from there. Don't believe he would have gone at all if there had not been so many fanatical requests not to, even before he thought about it. Being a guest of the country there was hardly no way he could keep away from it. Besides he really wanted to see one.

That's the way with all Americans, but we seldom want to see another. I stayed away two Sundays and they killed twice as many horses as they did the Sunday I went, so staying away don't do any good. There is only a certain class of people that go, but they go every Sunday. The only way they ever lose a fan is by death, but baseball is replacing it.

Yours,
*Will Rogers.*

## 437 Will Rogers Says Flying Is The Only Way To Travel

SAN ANTONIO, Tex., Dec. 19. – Flying is the only way to travel. Left Mexico City at 3 o'clock yesterday afternoon, spent the night at Tampico, lunch in Brownsville and Kelly Field, San Antonio for dinner.

Mexico is as excited about Mrs. Lindbergh's arrival as they were Charlie's. Had no more need for me in Mexico after Ambassador Morrow's appointment had been ratified.

Flew over the Rio Grande Valley, which is wonderful. The only thing the matter with it, they say the Republicans are about to take it.

Yours,
*Will Rogers.*

## 438 Will Rogers Doesn't Want All Oklahoma To Be Foolish

YUMA, Ariz., Dec. 21. – Well, ain't Oklahoma making a fine mess of itself? Now, I don't want this to be taken as sour grapes, or a jealous dig, but I thought I was supposed to represent about all the foolishness from that State, as that's what I get paid for.

But I do feel sincerely grieved that a great State like we have thinks they have to contribute nothing but laughter to the rest of the Union. If they are going to do the comedy, you will pardon me for turning sad. But I do want the rest of the world to know that we have

*Will Rogers in first Model A, given to him by Henry Ford in 1927.*

something down there besides political clowns, even if we haven't shown anything else.

Yours for a Warden instead of a Governor for our State,

*Will Rogers.*

## 439 Will Rogers, Home Again, Has The First New Ford Car

BEVERLY HILLS, Cal., Dec. 22. – Mr. Henry Ford told me he would make me a present of the first new Ford car, and sure enough, when I got here today, here she is. It's the first one delivered for actual use, and believe me I sure am using it. Nobody is looking at these Rolls-Royces here in Beverly.

Here is hoping that Mrs. Lindbergh has a good trip and lands in Mexico today. She will get a great welcome. Her coming after Charley will be like a wonderful dessert after a great meal for them. They never saw a three-motored ship down there.

Got to get back in my Ford.

*Will Rogers.*

## 440 Will Rogers Has For Sale Some Mexican 'Documents'

BEVERLY HILLS, Cal., Dec. 23. – I got some Mexican documents I want to sell if I can. They are mostly pictures, so you won't have to be able to read to understand 'em. On that account I want to sell to some tabloid newspaper.

One shows a bullfight, and one bull's name is "Sam" and another bull was named "Uncle." Now that looked like they were trying to kill "Uncle Sam," and I think it calls for intervention.

Another picture is of two men talking to each other. One has money in his hand and the other has a wrinkled brow and his shoulders are stooped from much responsibility. Which leads me to believe he is at least a United States Congressman.

In addition to price of documents I want railroad fare and expenses to any and all investigations.

Yours,

*Will Rogers.*

## 441 Will Rogers Plays At Pessimism For A Day

BEVERLY HILLS, Cal., Dec. 25. – Well, the neckties were all red and the sox were all too small. So there is practically nothing I can do but just sit and wait for another holiday. If Santa has failed us this time we will see what he brings us on next Nov. 4. I am just afraid it will be another red necktie.

Yours pessimistically,
*Will Rogers.*

P. S. – It is just an ideal Xmas day here in California—a cold, drizzling rain all day. I was in hopes the weather would be "unusual" and the sun would shine, but it didn't.

## 442 Mr. Rogers Has A Suggestion For Lindbergh's Flight

BEVERLY HILLS, Cal., Dec. 26. – Lindy is leaving Wednesday to go to Guatemala and from there on down to Nicaragua.

He was talking before I left down there about how he could tell which side of the battle line to land on when he got there; the American Marines are on one side and the rebels on the other. He said he guessed he would have to come down in "no man's land" to remain absolutely neutral.

We are still settling that election for them down there. Mexican stocks have gone up since Lindy flew into Mexico. Why don't the farmers get him to fly over their place?

Yours,
*Will Rogers.*

## 443 Rogers Sure That Mussolini Will Fix Those Earthquakes

BEVERLY HILLS, Cal., Dec. 27. – See where Rome had an earthquake yesterday. You watch Mussolini get out and issue a decree against those things. He will make 'em sorry they ever hit that country.

France will be scared to death for fear he will pass it on to them.

Yours,
*Will Rogers.*

## 444 Will Rogers Gets A Bank Loan, And Seems Surprised At It

BEVERLY HILLS, Cal., Dec. 28. – You have all heard of the tremendous success of a bank called the Bank of Italy. Well in yesterday's papers was a very unique statement by its founder, Mr. Gianini. He said he was making no personal fortune from it, didn't want to, that he only wanted to help other people, and wanted to die poor. Well, when I read that I went right down to his main bank to see how he would help other people. I put in a bid for a loan, to try and do all I could to make him die poor, and the funny part about it is that this fellow is on the level with it, he really is practicing it. I got the loan; so hurry up and get in, everybody, before he turns banker.

*Will Rogers.*

## 445 Will Rogers Sees New Value In The Lindbergh Flights

BEVERLY HILLS, Cal., Dec. 29. – Lindbergh's Central American tour will do more than establish good relations, it will make people study maps that haven't studied anything but golf scores and menu cards in twenty years.

Speaking of advanced aviation, yesterday on the battleship Pennsylvania I took my first catapult in a plane from a ship. From a standing start, on a runway only sixty feet long, you are doing sixty miles an hour at the end of it, shot by compressed air. Just watch your head and see that you don't leave it behind you. Maybe you don't know it, but every one of our battleships carries three or more planes.

We are going great now if another disarmament conference don't hit us, via airplanes.

*Will Rogers.*

## 446 Will Rogers Couples Cameras And Murderers

BEVERLY HILLS, Cal., Dec. 30. – I was in Milwaukee last Winter when the following happened:

Early in the morning a man killed his wife. He was captured right away, tried before noon and was taken ninety miles away and lodged in jail, awaiting execution before sundown of the same day.

Course you couldn't do that on a well-advertised murder trial for you wouldn't have time to take enough pictures, and what's the use of a young man murdering anybody if he couldn't see his pictures in the papers. The camera has made more criminals than bad environment.

Yours,
*Will Rogers.*

## 447 WILL ROGERS SEES CONGRESS ANXIOUS TO 'SPLIT IT UP'

BEVERLY HILLS, Cal., Jan. 1. – Secretary Mellon has asked Congress to please wait till after March 15, when the new income taxes come in, before passing any legislation, as he don't know how much there will be, if any.

But Congress says, No, we are going to divide it up now, whether there is any to divide or not. What do you suppose we are in Congress for, if it ain't to split up the swag? Please pass the gravy.

Yours,
*Will Rogers.*

## 448 WILL ROGERS WANTS TO HEAR FROM A NON-MILLIONAIRE

BEVERLY HILLS, Cal., Jan. 2. – Did you read all the New Year's optimism and apple sauce in the papers today by all our leading men and bankers? Same gang every year. Every one either a millionaire or an officeholder.

Now, there is 30,000 millionaires in the country and 110,000,000 that are not yet. You never see a New Year's prediction by one of the 110,000,000. Looks like just for the novelty one paper would print just what some poor man saw in store for the coming year.

Yours,
*Will Rogers.*

## 449 WILL ROGERS ASKS WHY ROAD NEAR MEXICO MUST BE 'MILITARY'

BEVERLY HILLS, Cal., Jan. 3. – See where they got a bill in Congress to make a road from Brownsville, Texas, up along the Rio Grande to El Paso, then on out to San Diego along the Mexican boundary.

It's a good idea and should be built, but it's called in the bill a military highway. Now, if we was building a road along the Canadian border we wouldn't insult our neighbors by calling it a military road. Can't you get Government aid without calling it military?

No wonder it takes all Lindbergh's time to try and make friends, as fast as our statesmen's lack of courtesy loses them for us.

This case is like calling a hospital "the home for incurables." There is a tactful title for you.

Yours,
*Will Rogers.*

## 450 Will Rogers Says 'Lindy' Has New Task In Nicaragua

BEVERLY HILLS, Cal., Jan. 4. – "Lindy" lands in Nicaragua tomorrow. He has kept us out of wars. Now we will see if he can get us out of one after we are already in it. That's asking a good deal of the boy.

If we would get out of there and let the Nicaraguans alone they might like us by the time we got ready to build the canal.

Yours,
*Will Rogers.*

## 451 Will Rogers Defends Navy And Would Bar Investigations

BEVERLY HILLS, Cal., Jan. 5. – Everybody is hopping onto the navy as though they purposely had the submarine sunk. They blame the navy for the bad weather. They blame the navy for having a submarine in the water at all.

The Mississippi flood happened last year, and nothing has been done about it yet by Congress. Yet if a boat sinks they think the navy ought to have it lifted to the surface by daylight. Don't you suppose the navy feels worse about it than we do? Why pick on a mourner?

We would rather see it not investigated. Then the causes will be remedied. But anything that is ever investigated, nothing is ever done about it.

Yours,
*Will Rogers.*

## 452 Will Rogers Looks Forward To The Jackson Day Dinner

BEVERLY HILLS, Cal., Jan. 6. – Leaving here tonight for the Jackson Day dinner in Washington, D. C., where we will open bids for the Democratic nomination. Al Smith can't come, as a New Yorker has never been that far away from home. He sent a message of 90,000 words, which the toastmaster will read.

I am not interested in who they nominate that night or in anybody's message of regrets, but I do hope they will have plenty to eat.

Yours,
*Will Rogers.*

## 453 Will Rogers Is Skeptical About National Conventions

NEWTON, Kan., Jan. 8. – Been passing all day through Kansas, and reading Kansas City papers. They are pretty sore about having the Republicans coming there next June and manging the town all up.

I guess at the Jackson Day dinner in Washington we will draft some town to hold the Democratic one in. Nobody has applied for it. Naturally, I certainly hope Claremore don't draw it. We are just getting on our feet good there now.

I am going through Senator Curtis's range now. He will be hard to beat in this roasting ear belt.

Yours,
*Will Rogers.*

## 454 Will Rogers Praises Chicago's Handling Of Crooks

GARRETT, Ind., Jan. 9. – Just passed through Chicago today. Wanted to go up and see my old friend Mayor Thompson, but had had English breakfast tea for luncheon and afraid he would smell it on my breath.

You can kid about Chicago and its crooks, but they have the smartest way of handling their crooks of any city. They get the rival gangs to kill off each other and all the police have to do is just referee and count up the bodies. They won't have a crook in Chicago unless he will agree to shoot at another crook. So viva Chicago!

Yours unhit,
*Will Rogers.*

## 455 WILL ROGERS SPECULATES ON DEMOCRATIC CONVENTION CITY

WASHINGTON, D. C., Jan. 10. – I haven't spoke to a one of my Republican friends. The minute the dinner and the convention city is picked, I can take up any Republican offer.

Say, the Democrats are flocking in here from all over. Cleveland, Chicago and Frisco are the three cities they will pick from, and Frisco is the only one with a certified check. So it looks like we gather there from June to December.

Cleveland wants it because they never saw a Democrat, but everybody is pulling for Frisco.

Visited the Senate. Yes, nothing.

Yours,
*Will Rogers.*

## 456 WILL ROGERS SENDS REPORT OF HOTEL LOBBY NOMINATIONS

WASHINGTON, D. C., Jan. 11. – I know you are anxious to know who is to be nominated on both tickets. Well, here's who was nominated in the lobby of the Mayflower Hotel in less than an hour's listening:

"Hoover is the fellow they will put over." "Dawes is the man. The banks will take Dawes." "Watch Lowden. The farmers are naming the man this year." "They will tie up for a week, somebody will mention Coolidge, and that will be the pay-off."

"Well, they better name Smith. That's our only chance." "Smith can't win. The country's dry." "Jim Reed, he's the best yet." "Look out for Heflin if they don't nominate a Catholic." "George of Georgia is the dark horse." "Donahey can carry Ohio, even if he ain't running."

Now, don't tell me I didn't tell you the news.

Yours,
*Will Rogers.*

## 457 LOOKS LIKE GESTURE TO SMITH TO JOIN THE KLAN, ROGERS SAYS

WASHINGTON, D. C., Jan. 12. – As usual, the Democrats fooled everybody, including themselves, and Houston got the convention. I certainly did what I was sent here to do; I kept it out of Oklahoma.

They went to Texas on account of it being a doubtful State. It looks like a gesture to Al Smith to join the Klan. But don't let 'em bluff you, Al. You go on down there, you will be received great, and I will bet you get a square deal if you can call getting the nomination on the Democratic ticket a square deal.

Save me a corner room at the Rice Hotel with plenty of windows, an electric fan and mosquito netting.

Yours,
*Will Rogers.*

## 458 He Didn't Offend Mr. Coolidge, Rogers Says; Has A Letter From The President To Prove It

WASHINGTON, D. C., Jan. 13. – I found on my arrival in Washington that some people had censored me severely for leaving the impression the other night that Mr. Coolidge was on the radio. Well, the idea that any one could imagine it was him uttering the nonsense that I was uttering! It struck me that it would be an insult to any one's sense of humor to announce that it was not him.

So I wrote Mr. Coolidge a note explaining, and received a two-page letter within thirty minutes from him, written all in his own longhand, saying that he had been told of it, but knew that anything I did was done in good natured amusement, and to not give it a moment's worry. He also thanked me for my kind reference to him on various occasions of which he had heard.

I knew my man before I joked about him. It's as I have often said: You can always joke good naturedly a big man, but be sure he is a big man before you joke about him. What I did over the radio on Mr. Coolidge I did an entire year on my tour of every State last season, and I knew it didn't offend good taste.

I want to here publicly thank Mr. Coolidge for that lovely letter, for I am personally very fond of him. With an election coming on, I know of no man connected with either party who I have ever had the pleasure of meeting for whom I have a greater regard.

When there is no malice in your heart, there can be none shown in your homes. But between you and I there is a lot of people in this country who should never be so absent-minded as to refer to their sense of humor.

Yours,
*Will Rogers.*

## 459 Will Rogers Is Stirred To Comment On Nicaragua

HAVANA, Cuba, Jan. 15. – What a beautiful sight as the Texas steamed into this flag and crowd draped city on a beautiful Sunday afternoon! It made you proud and showed what a friend we could be to the whole world if we would only let them all alone and run their various countries the way they think best.

This was a great thing, the President coming here, and we have a great delegation representing us. With these men looking after our interests in Central and South America I think we could send our Nicaragua delegation home.

It takes quite a sense of humor for these people to understand us shaking hands with one hand and shooting with the other.

Yours,
*Will Rogers.*

## 460 Rogers Cites, For President, Lindbergh's Punctuality

HAVANA, Cuba, Jan. 16. – The President made a good speech. He didn't say that we would do anything for these countries, but, on the other hand, he didn't say that we would do anything against them. So it was what you might call a conservative speech.

He was an hour late arriving here and a half hour late to deliver his speech. Now, here is a tip for him if he is going to be an Ambassador:

Lindbergh, the best Ambassador in the world, is never late. If he says I will arrive in Siberia at 3:30, at 3:29 he will be there. So no man, even a President, can do better than to follow the example of Lindbergh.

Yours,
*Will Rogers.*

## 461 Effect Of The Cuban Climate Upon Reporter Will Rogers

HAVANA, Cuba, Jan. 17. – It seems kinder lonesome around the old town since Calvin went away. He lit out this morning before Cuba got up.

Secretary Hughes spent the afternoon at the races. The two Democrats on our delegation, Judge O'Brien and Senator Underwood, held a harmony dinner last night and got the party down to two factions.

Ambassador Fletcher of Rome calls up Mussolini every night. Morrow is here to see that Mexico gets a square deal.

The conferences are all being held in the Biltmore Hotel yard.

Yours,

*Will Rogers.*

## 462 WILL ROGERS FOR ONE ANTHEM THAT WILL DO FOR ALL NATIONS

HAVANA, Cuba, Jan. 18. – We stood while twenty-one nations played their national anthems. The conference is already a standing and musical success.

I have one suggestion to offer for international good-will, that is, have an international national anthem that goes for everybody when it is played. It's for all; the Chink, the Limy, the Wop, the Zulu, and even the Rotarians. Make it short and it will please every nation. Some of these anthems today were longer than their countries' records. I propose Irving Berlin as its composer.

When you have stood in the tropical sun for twenty-one national airs you are about ready to vote for your nation to annex the other twenty.

Yours, groggy from martial music,

*Will Rogers.*

## 463 MR. ROGERS NOTES POLITENESS OF NEIGHBOR NATIVES AT HAVANA

HAVANA, Cuba, Jan. 19. – President Coolidge made a speech here and our diplomats are all here, so that means that Lindbergh will have to follow soon and get the people in a good humor again.

I do know that these other nations are the politest people in the world. We have all been here five days and not a one has mentioned Nicaragua.

It's like Dempsey being in a crowd and having no one mention Tunney.

Yours,

*Will Rogers.*

P. S. — Suppose you read about what Michigan did with their child murderer. They sent him to jail for life before the newspapers could make him famous.

## 464 Will Rogers Bespeaks Hearty Welcome For Cosgrave

KEY WEST, Fla., Jan. 20. — Talking about visiting Presidents and welcomes, don't forget our guest, the President of Ireland. He is a great fellow, and if his welcome here is as cordial as his country gives to Americans, his tour will be a triumph. Show him a good time, Jimmy Walker. I'll keep Heflin off.

Yours,
*Will Rogers.*

## 465 Will Rogers Finds Florida Needs No Sympathy Now

JACKSONVILLE, Fla., Jan. 22. — I never like to pick on anybody when they are down. That's why I have laid off the Democrats, and for over two years I have not told a joke against Florida. I knew the people and I felt sincerely sorry for them.

But I have just seen the State and noticed the conditions down here now, and my sympathy is getting back to the old envy again. With this climate and this close to sixty million people, Florida needs the sympathy of no one, and the jokes of no one can hurt it. Game people, these Floridians! But you can afford to be game when you know you've got the goods.

This Mayor here sold Coolidge a lot while showing him the city Wednesday.

Yours,
*Will Rogers.*

## 466 Will Rogers Sees Little Hope Of Flood Relief From Congress

LAFAYETTE, La., Jan. 23. — Just passed through the lower Mississippi flood district again, first time since last May. Congress has taken up the tariff, farm relief, big navy, Al Smith, Ku Klux, Nicaragua, Cuban independence, Mexican oil, Boulder Dam and Tom Heflin, but nothing has been said about building the dikes higher. They will wait till the night they adjourn and then pass a resolution against another flood.

*Will Rogers.*

## 467 WILL ROGERS SETS FORTH WHAT HE'D DO TO RELIGION IN SENATE

YUMA, Ariz., Jan. 24. – If we are going to have an amusement hour in the Senate every day I want a chance at it. I would denounce the Catholics Monday; the Baptists Tuesday; the Methodists, both North and South, Wednesday; the Presbyterians Thursday. Friday would be society day—the Episcopals. Saturday would be a general summing up against any denomination I had forgot during the week. Not that I have it in for any of these, but if religion must be the butt of our legislative amusement, I would at least stick to our Constitution and be unbiased.

A Senator in waiting,

*Will Rogers.*

## 468 WILL ROGERS GIVES OUTLINE OF MODERN MURDER CASE

BEVERLY HILLS, Cal., Jan. 23. – This murderer out here, Hickman, confessed, so that means a long-drawn-out trial. It's going to be a fight to a finish between the alienists and the photographers.

American murder procedure is about as follows: Foul enough to commit a crime, dumb enough to get caught, smart enough to prove you was crazy when you committed it and fortunate enough to show you was too sane to hang.

Yours,

*Will Rogers.*

## 469 WILL ROGERS GETS A LAUGH FROM A LINDBERGH STORY

BEVERLY HILLS, Cal., Jan. 26. – Got a laugh the other day by some fellow writing from Panama, saying that Lindbergh was "showing signs of nervousness, that he would pick up a book and then lay it down and not read it."

I saw him do the same thing in the embassy in Mexico, but I just thought to myself, there is another example of this boy's splendid judgment. If he had read any of the books that he picked up, I would begin to have doubts about his condition.

If more people laid down books without reading them we would have more Lindberghs and fewer Loebs and Leopolds.

An honest author,
*Will Rogers.*

## 470 WILL ROGERS TELLS HOW HUGHES EXPLAINED NICARAGUA TO HIM

BEVERLY HILLS, Cal., Jan. 27. – You know we are doing lots of hollering on various sides of this Nicaragua now. One night at a little dinner in Havana last week, Secretary Hughes explained the whole thing to me in such plain language that even I could understand it. And, by the way, if we just knew that man like he really is, he would be President by acclamation. He is just as common as any of us if it wasn't for his learning.

He says the way the play come up we had to go in there, and that nobody wants us out of there half as bad as we want to be out. I am only quoting you a man that ought to know.

Yours, second handedly,
*Will Rogers.*

## 471 NOT DEALING IN REALITIES AT HAVANA, SAYS WILL ROGERS

HOLLYWOOD, Cal., Jan. 29. – Somebody at the Havana conference Saturday brought up the question of revolutions, what, when and how to treat 'em. The delegates want to vote to make revolutions unlawful. That is, while they are in, but, when they are out, have them declared legal again.

It's rather embarrassing, for all the delegates are there by grace of a revolution at some time. Even Mr. Hughes. But he settled the argument in his usual tactful way by announcing: "We are not here to deal in realities. What kind of a conference do you think this is?"

Yours,
*Will Rogers.*

## 472 Will Rogers Gives His Views Of Marriage And Divorce

BEVERLY HILLS, Cal., Jan. 30. – Dr. M. S. Taylor and Judge Ben Lindsey are debating tonight in Chicago on "Companionate Marriages," and knowing that I had been in the "Follies" and out here in Hollywood they wanted my opinion.

I think marriages should be companionate. I hate to see them meet and marry when they are not friends at all. And as for divorce, I think people put too much dependence in it. You don't see many cases where the parties did any better the second time than they did the first or the third and fourth or the fifth and so on marriages.

It just looks like the people are grabbing at a straw.

Yours,

*Will Rogers.*

## 473 Will Rogers Meditates On The News Of The Day

BEVERLY HILLS, Cal., Jan. 31. – News of the day:

Coolidge in a speech told what the budget system had saved, and Congress sat and licked their chops. They could see a new post-office in every line.

The papers says Dempsey's eyes are bad. You shake Tunney and a half million check in front of him and you will find he can still put on enough glasses and gloves to see both objects.

Been reading about the weather in the East. We have had it bad here—two heat prostrations yesterday, and one bather went out too far.

Yours in a Panama hat,

*Will Rogers.*

## 474 Will Rogers Wants Hoover To Keep Charge Of Flood Relief

BEVERLY HILLS, Cal., Feb. 1. – See in the paper this morning that there is some talk of Mr. Hoover resigning from the Cabinet. Certainly would be too bad, for we would have to draft him back again in April and May to take care of the flood situation on the Mississippi.

If he had charge of that relief work for a few years continuously he could have that whole country trained so they would leave the South and move North for two months every year. They would only have to do this till the year 1950, when Congress would vote relief.

Yours,
*Will Rogers.*

## 475 Will Rogers Not A Candidate This Year; His Phrase Is 'I Do Not Contemplate'

BEVERLY HILLS, Cal., Feb. 2. – There was a piece in the paper this morning where somebody back home was seriously proposing me for President. Now when that was done as a joke it was all right, but when it's done seriously it's just pathetic. We are used to having everything named as Presidential candidates, but the country hasn't quite got to the professional comedian stage.

There is no inducement that would make me foolish enough to ever run for political office. I want to be on the outside where I can be friends and joke about all of them, even the President. As long as it is all right with him, why my conscience is clear.

So I hereby issue my statement, which is as follows:

I don't contemplate becoming involved in a political conflict of any nature during the Autumn of 1928.

Yours,
*Will Rogers.*

P. S. – Should the Democrats, however, become successful I would accept the postoffice in Beverly Hills and Claremore, Okla. I can take care of both letters.

## 476 Will Rogers Steers Clear Of The Hickman Murder Trial

BEVERLY HILLS, Cal., Feb. 3. – I want to die claiming only one distinction, the only writer to refuse newspaper offers to cover the Hickman trial. Instead of being ashamed of it, it looks like every town tries to make their murder the biggest one of the year.

Alienists always furnish humor, if no facts, to a case. Here was one's testimony yesterday. "I find Hickman to have two gold teeth, and sore adenoids."

So the moral is, keep away from gold teeth and watch your adenoids.

Yours,
*Will Rogers.*

## 477 Will Rogers Fails To React To Big Toe Insanity Test

HOLLYWOOD, Cal., Feb. 5. – Well, the alienists in the murder trial again took the comedy honors yesterday. One testified that Hickman was insane because when he tickled the bottom of his feet, his big toe turned up instead of down. So take off your shoes and have somebody tickle you and see which way your toes go, north or south. I tried it and mine didn't pay any attention to it. So I guess I am a cross between crazy and sane.

Say, did you read what Calvin told the newspapers? He said while you are bragging on nations, give this one a boost.

Yours,
*Will Rogers.*

## 478 Will Finds A Slight Flaw In Aerial Dining Service

BEVERLY HILLS, Cal., Feb. 6. – I want to do all I can to further aviation. A good Jewish friend of mine wrote me from Newark, that he made the trip East by plane from here, had a wonderful trip, but all the box lunches that are handed you on the way by the company have nothing but ham sandwiches. Now this is a thing that I will see is remedied, so our slogan will be "food for all races."

Yours,
*Will Rogers.*

## 479 Will Rogers Suggests Some More Non-War Treaties

BEVERLY HILLS, Cal., Feb. 7. – America and France signed a treaty that they wouldn't fight each other. Now, if we could just sign one with some nation that there is a chance of having war with, why it would mean something. This is too much like New Hampshire signing one with Arizona. The four babies we want to get one with are England, Japan, Mexico and Nicaragua.

Yours for better understanding with our enemies than with our friends,

*Will Rogers.*

## 480 Mr. Rogers Sees Unanimity In Welcoming Lindbergh

BEVERLY HILLS, Cal., Feb. 8. – Lindbergh made Havana today. I can just imagine the welcome he got, for I was there a month ago and watched them rehearse for his reception.

The Pan-American Conference is still in session there. They will no doubt pass a resolution welcoming him, and that will be the only unanimous resolution they will pass during the entire conference.

For fairer treatment to our sister republics, then we won't have to hold conferences.

Yours,
*Will Rogers.*

## 481 John D. Right As Far As He Goes, Will Says

BEVERLY HILLS, Cal., Feb. 9. – Did you read young John D. Rockefeller's plea to the oil men. He implored them to tell the truth, or tell something, whether it was the truth or not, but to please not just sit there, as that made the whole industry not only look dumb, but guilty.

Poor young John D.! He is trying to do what is right, but his Bible class should include all his holding companies.

Yours,
*Will Rogers.*

## 482 Will Rogers Sympathizes With Candidates Beset By Borah

BEVERLY HILLS, Cal., Feb. 10. – My good friend Bill Borah makes life miserable for these Presidential candidates. Every time a new one shies his helmet into what he hopes will be the Presidential ring why Borah floors him with the question, "How do you stand on the prohibition question?" And the poor fellow, not knowing which side the most votes are on, is stuck before he starts.

There are men bareheaded in this race now that will be sunstruck before even the heat of Kansas City and Houston hits 'em.

Yours with a hat on,
*Will Rogers.*

## 483 Will Rogers Sees Senate Action As A Slap At Coolidge

HOLLYWOOD, Cal., Feb. 12. – Talk about me even joking about our President while the dignified United States Senate went clear out of its way to take an unnecessary slap at him with a resolution that he shouldn't run again. Now, off hand, you would think that a Senate resolution meant something, but they carry no more authority than a Chamber of Commerce one does.

The Senators voted that Coolidge shouldn't run again, but that each one of them were eligible. They wanted to show that the country was not entirely destitute of great men, that there were ninety-six men that could improve on Cal at any minute.

Yours,
*Will Rogers.*

## 484 Will Rogers Gives Praise To Rockefeller And Hoover

BEVERLY HILLS, Cal., Feb. 13. – Young John D. issued a straightforward statement Saturday that it didn't sound like a rich man at all. He is liable to shame some of these other big men into being for the country, and if he does that will do more good than his gifts have.

Hoover is formally in the race now. He is the only candidate in either party by acclamation. The others are candidates by personal desires. It will be interesting to see what kind of race a known qualified man can make. This election will decide whether qualifications are an asset or a liability.

Yours,
*Will Rogers.*

## 485 Will Rogers Sees Need For Lindbergh Again In Cuba

BEVERLY HILLS, Cal., Feb. 14. – Guess Lindbergh will have to go back to Cuba. He hadn't reached Key West before the Argentine and United States delegation at the Pan-American Conference were hissing each other.

So that Nicaragua can have a fair election next Fall and no candidate spending too much, why, we have the marines on horseback down there now watching the voters. It's a great idea for Nicaragua, but we haven't got enough marines and enough horses to even patrol the Pennsylvania and Illinois precincts.

Yours,
*Will Rogers.*

## 486 WILL ROGERS THINKS WE WON IN NOT LOSING AT HAVANA

BEVERLY HILLS, Cal., Feb. 15. – See where the Pan-American Conference is to break up next Monday. A lot of people feel discouraged that there was no more accomplished, but I tell you the United States did mighty well. They didn't give up anything, and any time we can attend a conference and come out as good as we went in, why we are ahead.

They will quit holding conferences the minute they find we are not going to give any more than any other nation. A conference is a place where countries meet and find out each other's short comings and form new dislikes for the new conference.

Yours,
*Will Rogers.*

## 487 WILL LEARNS A RAISE IS NOT TO BE HAD FOR THE ASKING

NEWTON, Kan., Feb. 17. – Had visits from two of my "bosses" just before leaving California. Mr. Lorimer, who was out drumming up subscriptions for his Saturday Evening Post, and his charming wife and two fine grown sons come out to our shack slumming. We settled the Republican nominations. The next day Mr. Adolph Ochs, owner of the New York Times, and his gracious wife and entertaining sister-in-law spent the day with us. We took up the hardships of the Democrats. He thinks, of course, Al will be nominated, and my friend Jesse Jones of Texas for Vice-President. Aided by Mrs. Rogers I coyly hinted for a raise from both gentlemen, but even socially they are always the business man. So it looks like I just fed two hungry editors for nothing. Once a sap, always a sap.

Yours, underpaid,
*Will Rogers.*

## 488 Will Rogers Sees Evidence Of Democrats Getting Wiser

CHICAGO, Ill., Feb. 19. – The bill of Senator Walsh of Montana the other day to investigate the power trust kinder put the boys in the Senate on record as to who was on the payroll. I was glad to see some Democrats among those favored, for it shows the old party is learning enough to not just sit as usual and let the Republicans grab everything. Fine chance that bill had passing before the campaign funds were made up.

The older Democrats are getting smarter every day. They wanted in on the campaign contributions, too. It's a great country if you got the influence.

Just a tax payer,
*Will Rogers.*

## 489 Will Rogers Again In The Air Praises Planes And Pilots

OMAHA, Neb., Feb. 20. – Left Chicago last night at 10 o'clock in a snowstorm and flew to Omaha. These mail babies go through. They can get through weather that most people couldn't find their way from the house to the garage with a well-lighted course. Good planes and good pilots!

It's safer and more gratifying than running for a Presidential nomination, which seems to be the other popular fad nowadays.

The farmers out here threaten to keep Norris as Senator in Washington till they get relief. If I was you, Mr. Coolidge, I would take care of the farmers at once.

Yours,
*Will Rogers.*

## 490 Rogers Seeking Gov. Bulow To Run Him For Something

SIOUX FALLS, S. D., Feb. 21. – Am here in South Dakota. Coolidge found it in the Summer time, but I guess I am about the only one who ever came here in the Winter.

I am looking for that Democratic Governor of theirs who made such a big hit at the Jackson Day dinner in Washington. He is the fellow that said they had a big game preserve up here and they just built a high fence around it and turned Calvin in there and gathered him in and shipped him back to Washington in the Fall.

I am going to bring that old boy out of these hills and run him for somethin'.

Yours,
*Will Rogers.*

## 491 WILL ROGERS SENDS A NOTE ON THE ROADS OF IOWA

DES MOINES, Iowa, Feb. 22. – I am here in Iowa looking over the future Californians. We are just picking the best. We are not letting 'em all come like they used to, it's restricted immigration now.

This State has been trying for seven straight years to get an election held to vote bonds for roads. The election requires half the voters to vote. Well, the roads have been so bad they have never been able to get the voters to town. So now they have called an election for the month of May.

That gives them an entire month to come in on horseback and vote.

Yours,
*Will Rogers.*

## 492 WILL ROGERS TAKES A FLING AT MISSOURI LEGISLATORS

ST. LOUIS, Mo., Feb. 23. – Just passed through Jefferson City, Mo., the home of the State Prison and the State Capitol. The worst in the State is sent there. The Sheriff was on our train and he had two men who had escaped, and he was taking them back to the Legislature.

You remember Missouri got so sore at Jim Reed one time because he wouldn't let 'em join the League of Nations that they was going to hang him. Well, they are naming the Missouri River after him now. And maybe the Mississippi.

Yours for the news,
*Will Rogers.*

## 493 WILL ROGERS SEES HOOVER AS A CLEVER POLITICIAN

WATERLOO, Iowa, Feb. 24. – Say, that Hoover is turning out to be a better politician than everybody gave him credit for. He is the only man since prohibition has been in that is for the drys, but not against the wets.

Both sides been studying it and the more they read it the more it looks like it is for both of them.

Passed through Chicago this morning. Since this bomb throwing at officials started Mayor Thompson went to Washington to see about flood relief.

*Will Rogers.*

494

## Will Rogers Finds Farmers Hopeless Of Relief Measures

OMAHA, Neb., Feb. 26. — Just been prowling around up in this country with the farmers. They have about given up hope of getting farm relief and have decided to fertilize instead.

*Will Rogers.*

P. S. — Hope Harry Brooks was not lost. A fine boy and great pilot.

495

## Will Roger Calls Attention To Robinson As A Candidate

PINE BLUFF, Ark., Feb. 27. — At the conventions pretty near every State will waste a complimentary vote on some useless native son. Of course, most of them will have to do so with a smile, but when the great old State of Arkansas shouts, "18 votes for Senator Joe Robinson," why they won't have to apologize to nobody.

Joe is for you or agin' you, whichever you want. He'll play you poker or golf, kiss you or fight you. Whenever he makes a speech he makes you think he is going to bite you. He is tougher than a top sergeant, but a Senator and a statesman combined, a rare combination.

The Democrats could nominate a lot worse and the chances are they will.

Yours,
*Will Rogers.*

496

## Rogers Makes A Suggestion To The Coal Mine Owners

CAMDEN, Ark., Feb. 28. — If I was a coal mine owner and couldn't understand my help any better than they do, I would resign and announce to the world that as an industrial leader I was a "bust." And I would devote my life to seeing that the world burned cow chips.

*Will Rogers.*

P. S. – Say, do you know this little city has a $6,000,000 plant where they make wrapping paper out of post oak and black jack trees? Arkansas has made wonderful improvements in lots of lines, but I doubt if I could get a better wife out of the State today than I did twenty years ago.

## 497 Will Rogers Has A Good Word To Say For The Policemen

MEMPHIS, Tenn., Feb. 29. – Right here in Memphis today over twenty-five policemen went to a hospital and volunteered to give blood transfusions to a kid that was near death. I know that I am out of order in speaking of the good things that cops do, but I am one of the old-fashioned people who believe if somebody pounced on me, I could holler for one and he would come and help me out without me having to pay him anything.

The poor fellows can't catch many criminals as our towns have them too busy marking cars that have been parked too long.

Yours,

*Will Rogers.*

## 498 Mr. Rogers Discusses Politics And Muscle Shoals Project

FLORENCE, Ala., March 1. – Spent the day looking at the marvelous Muscle Shoals dam and projects. Everybody should see it. It's a monument to the neglect of our politicians. It was built to manufacture nitrates for fertilizer. It's the only idle nitrate plant in the world. Every country is building new ones.

When you see a $150,000,000 plant lying here idle it gives you an idea of the pull in legislation that the power trust exerts. They say "If we don't get it nobody else will."

The Madden bill settles it right, and the farmers will get fertilizer, but you watch the same gang kill it that killed Walsh's resolution, including Heflin and George.

*Will Rogers.*

## 499 WILL ROGERS SAYS WILL HAYS AMUSED HIM BY TESTIMONY

BIRMINGHAM, Ala., March 2. – My old friend, Will Hays, took Patrick Henry's old phrase and cleaned up on it. "Give me Liberty bonds or give me checks." Bill says he got $260,000 but gave some of it back. As bad as I felt, I had to laugh at that one.

Then he says he got it back again, that sounds more plausible. Then he says he gave back some more. That brings on another doubt. Then he says he held the other but didn't want to use it. He is resorting to fiction again.

Finally, Sinclair was so flabbergasted at Will returning any of it that he took it and gave it to the Democrats where he knew none of it would ever come back.

Just a sore-headed voter that didn't get any of it,

*Will Rogers.*

## 500 WILL ROGERS PRAISES ALABAMA FOR ITS SCHOOLS

MONTGOMERY, Ala., March 4. – Say, Alabama is sure humming on good schools. That one in Auburn will compare with anybody's university, and coming over here I spent the morning at Tuskegee, that living monument to Booker T. Washington.

They have a great idea there that some of our schools are copying. They teach the pupils that they are going to have to work, and how to work. Our old mode of college education was teach 'em so they think they won't have to work.

And singing! Oh, boy! After hearing 1,500 of those colored pupils sing negro spirituals, I feel sure I will shoot the next white person that I hear try to sing one.

Say, Tom Heflin and I are all O. K. again. We realized there wasn't enough Democrats to afford to fall out.

Yours,

*Will Rogers.*

## 501 WILL ROGERS CRITICIZES SMITHSONIAN AIRSHIP STAND

ALBANY, Ga., March 5. – Caught a tail wind and flew in here from Montgomery, 160 miles, in seventy minutes, brought by Major Weaver and Lieuts. Cote and Ott. I would have been a whole day making the trip on the train.

Just read the Smithsonian Institution's explanation about the Wright flying machine. They say the trustees decided Langley's machine could have flown first but didn't. I could have flown to France ahead of Lindbergh but I just neglected doing it. I had a lot of other things on my mind at the time.

Those trustees remind me of the Senator that votes on something and then hears from back home afterwards. These heard from the whole of America when that plane went to England.

Yours,
*Will Rogers.*

## 502 The Cynical Will Rogers Sees Judgeships As Silencers

CHARLOTTE, N. C., March 6. – Congressman Green, Chairman of the Ways and Means Committee and in favor of strong inheritance taxes for the rich, has been made some kind of judge at an increased salary. It's funny the Administration never thought of giving Borah or Jim Reed or Walsh some judgeship where it would keep them from ferreting out so much Republican devilment. I'll bet all three of them could get appointments to the Supreme bench tomorrow if they would take it.

Yours,
*Will Rogers.*

## 503 Will Rogers Sees Big Future For Smoky Mountain Park

ASHEVILLE, N. C., March 7. – Spent the day in the mountains with my eastern Cherokee brothers, the ones that old Andrew Jackson wasn't able to run out of this country. They are pretty poor and their land is poor, and they don't get anything from the Government, but they are not hollering for relief.

Was also in the Big Smoky Mountain Park that Rockefeller just gave $5,000,000 to today. It's going to be the Yellowstone of the South. It's beautiful and can't help from being a big success as a public park for tourists. They got the stills in there already. All they got to do now is to get the roads into 'em.

Yours,
*Will Rogers.*

## 504 Rogers For Less Supervision Of Other Peoples' Elections

GREENSBORO, N. C., March 8. – The Senate says that the marines were sent to Nicaragua to supervise an election and have to stay until it's held, which is next October.

In the meantime the marines are doing all they can to see that there are fewer votes to supervise and Sandino is doing all he can to see that there are fewer marines to supervise.

The next time we go wet nursing some ambitious republic's election, why go in so early? Go in on the day of election. We are the only nation that ever supervised anything a year before it was supposed to come off.

Yours for shorter and fewer supervisions,

*Will Rogers.*

## 505 Rogers Sees A Big Turnover Coming In Automobiles

SAVANNAH, Ga., March 9. – Has somebody with a knack for statistics kept track of how many times they have been told the joke of a "certain small make car" catching up with a big car going seventy miles an hour and asking "Do you know how to get this 'certain small make car' out of second gear?"

We can save half the wasted time in this country if we can get people to quit telling that joke. I hereby offer a substitute:

All automobile prosperity is based on what they call the "quick turnover." Well, with all these cheap make cars developing sixty and seventy miles an hour and our improved roads and many sharp turns, you are going to see the greatest turnover in the automobile business this country ever witnessed. Undertaker shares will go higher than General Motors.

Yours for the airplane, where it's safe,

*Will Rogers.*

## 506 Will Rogers Is Critical Of Political 'Lame Ducks'

MIAMI BEACH, Fla., March 11. – Congress killed the "Lame Duck bill." A lame duck is a Senator or Congressman who has had his official position shot from under him by the excellent judgment of the voters back home.

Now, wouldn't you naturally think if a man was told by a majority of his voters that he wasn't wanted any more that he would naturally step out and say, "Why certainly; put in the man who has defeated me"? Now, that would be the case in any other business in the world, but not with these political babies. They say, "You may beat me in November, but I will be on your neck till the following December."

Viva politics!

Yours,
*Will Rogers.*

## 507 WILL ROGERS SENDS $5 TO MAKE FIVE REPUBLICANS RESPECTABLE

ORLANDO, Fla., March 12. – See by today's paper where Senator Borah made an appeal to the country to donate a dollar or more each to save the respect of the Republican Party. I just mailed $5 to make five Republicans respectable. Wish I could afford more, but this continued prosperity has just about got me broke.

Yours,
*Will Rogers.*

## 508 MR. ROGERS IS TAKING NOTES UNDER SUNNY SKY OF FLORIDA

ST. PETERSBURG, Fla., March 13. – Everybody used to argue over who was the greatest ball player, Sisler or Hornsby. Well, I saw them play against each other here today, nine innings, nothing to nothing. The Braves have a great team and so has Washington.

Everybody in shirtsleeves and straw hats. And I think it's snowing up North.

Yours,
*Will Rogers.*

## 509 WILL ROGERS SEES RED CROSS NOBLY AT WORK AGAIN

JACKSONVILLE, Fla., March 14. – There's your wonderful Red Cross on the job again. Be it Mississippi Valley, Vermont, Florida or California, no one knows when their section may be next. Just think, four Sundays ago I drove all over that beautiful and peaceful valley in California and visited the Harry Carey ranch.

Florida has been mighty nice about it. Yesterday they headlined it as an earthquake just through force of habit, but today they have stuck to the truth.

We have great sectional rivalries, but it don't take much to wipe it out when something happens.

Yours,
*Will Rogers.*

## 510 WILL ROGERS COMPARES PARTY 'CORRUPTION' RESULTS

DAYTONA BEACH, Fla., March 15. — The Democrats are having a lot of fun exposing the Republican campaign corruptions, but they would have a lot more fun if they knew where they could lay their hands on some of it themselves for next November. The difference in corruption in the two parties was 7,000,000 votes last election, so the Democrats have got to investigate and find out how to improve their corruption.

Yours,
*Will Rogers.*

## 511 WILL ROGERS MEETS JOHN D. AND A DIME CHANGES HANDS

TAMPA, Fla., March 16. — You can never tell in this world when positions will be reversed. Last night, in Daytona Beach, John D. and young John D. and family came to my little show.

I was invited to the house for breakfast this morning. On arriving the elder John D. made no effort to give me the customary dime, whereupon I took out one and gave it to him. He took it. I'll say he took it. I guess this prosperity in big business is overrated.

I went around the course with him. He is the only man I will watch play golf—there is some excuse for him playing it.

Yours,
*Will Rogers.*

## 512 WILL ROGERS REPORTS WALKER REACHED PALM BEACH ON TIME

PALM BEACH, Fla., March 18. – Mayor Jimmy Walker just blew into Palm Beach, the Winter residence of New York's Mayors, on time. I am here giving a benefit for the Salvation Army tonight and Jimmy has graciously agreed to introduce me. That shows you that these Mayors stick together even if one has been thrown out.

I think that town out West (you never hear its name any more) made a mistake by canning me, and New York would make a bigger mistake if they ever let Jimmy go. He is a great ad for Tammany Hall. He is to them what the Prince of Wales is to England without the falls.

Yours,
*Will Rogers.*

## 513 WILL ROGERS SEES REASON IN CAPPER'S REQUEST TO PARTY

OCALA, Fla., March 19. – Did you read Senator Capper's appeal this morning to the Republican Party "to please clean up before election?" He intimated that they could get back to normal after election but to kinder lay off till some of this has blown over. Now that's not an unreasonable demand to make of a party—to remain decent one year out of four.

The farmers not only didn't get any relief during this Administration, but they don't seem to have got any of the relief handed out before the election.

Yours,
*Will Rogers.*

## 514 ROGERS GLAD THAT LINDBERGH TOOK PRIZE FROM THE MARINES

THOMASVILLE, Ga., March 20. – Certainly glad to see Colonel Lindbergh got the Wilson Prize "for the greatest contribution to international peace and good-will." I thought for a while there that the marines would get that; they are the only Americans that have been in as many countries as Lindbergh.

I am glad he is taking the Senators and Congressmen flying. If he can get them "air broke," why, they will all be boosters for it. That was a smart trick doing that.

Well, that's about all he does.

Yours,
*Will Rogers.*

## 515 WILL ROGERS SAYS SMITH MADE THOSE FELLOWS 'LAY OFF'

RALEIGH, N. C., March 21. – With Pilot Yost of Pinehurst caught a tail wind and flew in here from Atlanta, over 400 miles, in less than four hours. This is the line they are going to put an air mail route on to New York. Certainly need one through line to the South like they have to the Coast.

Having dinner tonight with Josephus Daniels, who used to handle the navy before we contributed to the social success of a conference and sunk ours, thinking we would shame somebody into following suit.

Say, Al Smith kinder made those fellows lay off somebody's name when they couldn't prove what they said, didn't he?

Yours,
*Will Rogers.*

## 516 WILL ROGERS SEES OPPOSITION IN THE FIELD OF BEING FUNNY

ATLANTA, Ga., March 22. – Why try to be funny when an association does it for you? This week's prize for humor goes to the Maryland Racing Association for barring Harry Sinclair's horses from races. Be a good joke if the Senate investigated them.

I suppose all the touts at the Maryland tracks will have to live at the Y. M. C. A. and the book-makers will have to show their church cards. They will have Governor Ritchie making prohibition speeches.

It's a great country when you are down and out. Well, Harry, I hope Oklahoma don't get so pure that they refuse your taxes. If they do we will all the rest of us go to work.

Yours, but not a sportsman,
*Will Rogers.*

## 517 WILL ROGERS THINKS OUTLOOK IS PRETTY GOOD FOR HOOVER

PINEHURST, N. C., March 23. – Things must look pretty good for Hoover. This fellow Bascom Slemp, after considering for months the best offer from Coolidge, Lowden, Al Smith, Jim Reed, and even Willis, has finally decided to go with Hoover. He don't generally decide till it's practically in the bag.

After the three women in Congress went up first, why, all the legislators want to go up now with Lindy.

Nicaragua voted the other day not to have us supervise their election, but that's not official, as we didn't supervise that vote.

Yours,
*Will Rogers.*

## 518 WILL ROGERS PUT HIMSELF ON THE OIL WITNESS LIST

WASHINGTON, D. C., March 25. — I was called to Washington before investigation committee to explain about the dime I gave to Rockefeller. Even porters are afraid to take tips here now. There is politicians acting honest now that never acted that way in their lives.

Senator Borah was at the depot taking up collection to get lysol to scrub Republicans.

I am hiking right out to see Alice. I will have all the dope by tomorrow on who the candidates will be.

Yours,
*Will Rogers.*

## 519 WILL ROGERS FINDS CONGRESS DOING OTHER PEOPLE'S BUSINESS

MANSFIELD, Ohio, March 26. — Blew through Washington yesterday. Everybody that I tried to talk to about the nomination was a candidate himself, so all their opinions were sorter biased.

Both houses spent all last week arguing politics. Congress spent the week on Ohio politics. Suppose they will take up Indiana next, and that will keep 'em all Summer.

The Senate spent the week discussing Al Smith. Suppose they will take up Ritchie next week.

Did you ever figure it out? They are the only people in the world that are paid to do one job and do every other one there is but that. If business men strayed that far from their actual business, we would have the prosperity of India.

Yours,
*Will Rogers.*

520 WILL ROGERS IN PENNSYLVANIA, NOTES TWO OUTSTANDING FACTS

PITTSBURGH, Pa., March 27. – Am here in Pittsburgh, but am the only person that didn't come to investigate the coal situation.

Henry Ford is paying $8 a day and having no trouble in his mines. Ain't it funny when it looks like a business can't be run right, he bobs up and shows that it can. I believe that fellow could make a farm pay.

Talk about Andy Mellon's great Treasury record, you ought to see his State political one. He is the only man, since Mussolini in Italy, that controls both the Republican and Democratic delegations to both conventions. I think he will instruct both delegations for Coolidge.

Yours,
*Will Rogers.*

521 WILL ROGERS FINDS A JAIL T'WOULD BE DISGRACE TO GO TO

CLEVELAND, Ohio, March 28. – Seven times Cleveland has voted down bonds to rebuild a jail that was built in 1866.

In company today with every prominent minister in the city, Catholic, Jewish, Protestant and Baptist, we went through the jail. Honest, it would be a disgrace to serve a term in it. It will have to be rebuilt by outside subscription from humanitarian cities like Akron, Hamilton, Columbus, Cincinnati, Oberlin and Detroit.

I think it and Borah's fresh air fund to cauterize the Republicans are the two outstanding charities of the hour.

Yours,
*Will Rogers.*

522 WILL ROGERS UP IN A BLIMP IN DEBATE WITH JUDGE LINDSEY

AKRON, Ohio, March 29. – This town of Akron is responsible for the most aggravating invention that ever was let loose on modern civilization. It's spoiled more perfect days than rain and bad weather. There is 110,000 people in some part of the world every minute of every day just fixing punctures in Akron tires, part of 'em rubber.

*Will Rogers with prominent Cleveland, Ohio, ministers and foreman of the grand jury inspects Cuyahoga County jail built in 1866. Seven times Cleveland had voted down bonds to rebuild it.*

I just took my first trip in one of these blimps that Mr. Goodyear makes. It is shaped like a gall bladder. It makes me think of my operation. Judge Lindsey and I went up together and discussed companionate marriage, which was over the heads of most people.

Yours,
*Will Rogers.*

## 523 WILL ROGERS SUGGESTS MORROW AS A CANDIDATE

CINCINNATI, Ohio, March 30. – When you get through discussing all the Republican candidates and it comes out what's the matter with each one, why not pick out one that nothing is the matter with–Dwight Morrow? Being President is child's play compared to pacifying Mexico. He gave up something to be of service to his country. He is the biggest ad Wall Street ever sent out. He almost makes 'em look respectable. If there ever was a regular guy, he is it.

I have no ulterior motives in his election outside of the Ambassadorship to Mexico myself, which few would envy me.

Yours,
*Will Rogers.*

P. S. – The above nominations don't belong in a joke column either.

## 524 IT'S NOW COL. WILL ROGERS, SUH, BY ACT OF KENTUCKY GOVERNOR

LEXINGTON, Ky., April 1. – Today the Governor of Kentucky made me aide on his staff with the rank of colonel. I thought I would get out of Kentucky without being made a colonel. But luck was against me. This Governor is a Republican, and I do hope people will not think anything changed hands but the commission.

His name is Sampson, a very strong man. He certainly slayed the Democrats "with the jawbone of an ass." His Democratic opponents ran on "no horse racing in Kentucky," thereby not only supplying Mr. Sampson with the jawbone, but making themselves the whole animal by thinking that Kentucky would vote against horse racing.

So it's Colonel Rogers, suh. Boy, put a sprig more mint in that julep.

Yours,
*Will Rogers.*

## 525 Col. Rogers Gives Advice On Campaign Contributions

ANN ARBOR, Mich., April 2. – You hear a lot of talk about the campaign this year being awful cheap, and maybe on the level, but I want to tell you that I would hate to offer $160,000 to either side. I'll bet it wouldn't have to be in bonds. They would grab at a promissory note or even an anonymous check.

So don't be afraid to contribute. Both sides are doing business at the old stand.

Yours,
*Colonel Rogers of Kentucky, Suh.*

## 526 Mr. Rogers Moved To Eloquence Over Battle Creek, Mich.

BATTLE CREEK, Mich., April 3. – What a place this is. The home of the sensitive stomach. It's the rendezvous of everybody with an ailment between the chin and hip.

Everybody is getting along fine. Cheerful and just saturated with sanitarium scandal. Cure you by giving you everything to eat but food. These patients' idea of a wild party is to get their hands on two slices of bacon or just an old lamb chop bone.

Showed me through the breakfast food factories, and I thought here is where I find out something about what it is. They showed me how the boxes were made and how they shipped them out—in fact, everything but. So I leave here just as ignorant as the other one hundred and ten million.

But they can sure overhaul a stomach that's been missing.

Yours,
*Will Rogers.*

## 527 Will Rogers Suggests Indiana Humorists As Candidates

LAFAYETTE, Ind., April 4. – Indiana is noted for its great crop of humorists—George Ade, Kin Hubbard and a flock of others. Indianians, jealous of these men's reputations, used to say, "We have people in Indiana besides humorists." And sure enough they did have, but they were all in jail but the humorists. So why don't they elect some of them?

George Ade would redeem your State in national esteem. He is a graduate of Purdue, a university that can't beat Amherst doing anything. You would have to draft him the same as the Republicans will do with Coolidge. Abe Martin for Lieutenant Governor in case Ade laughed himself to death when he saw the inside workings of the State.

Yours for candidates that can win,

*Will Rogers.*

## 528 WILL ROGERS OFFERS ADVICE TO WOMEN CANDIDATES

INDIANAPOLIS, Ind., April 5. — Illinois is faced with another one of its clown elections. There is a woman running over there for Congress that Alice Longworth told me one time had the keenest political mind of any one in Washington and was the most able woman that could possibly enter politics.

It's Mrs. McCormick. Now, if you elect her she will be seated, and when she is she will be heard from. She is not like other women that go into politics who get up and tell you about the "woman's angle." She tells you about the people's angle. When you women enter a man's game there is only one angle.

Yours for information on real candidates,

*Will Rogers.*

## 529 WILL IS LONG ON AVIATION AND THE FUTURE OF U. S. A.

INDIANAPOLIS, Ind., April 6. — I am going to beat my friend Brisbane to this one. I read: "Aviator flies in seven hours over Timbuctoo and Sahara Desert. It takes five months to make the trip overland."

So, if you are going to Timbuctoo, that's all the more reason why you should have an aeroplane. And don't sell America short; get some good stock and hold it till it's worth more and then sell. But don't gamble.

Yours,

*Will Rogers.*

## 530 Will Rogers Says Red Cross Will Be Ready At Chicago

LOUISVILLE, Ky., April 8. — As a life member of the Red Cross we are rushing doctors and nurses to Chicago with all speed to have them there when the bombing starts Tuesday morning. We are establishing first-aid stations just about where we figure the voting booths will be blown to.

I am covering the Chicago election for the Nicaraguan press. As we are putting on their election for them in October they are anxious to learn what it will be like. The roads away down here are packed with refugees leaving Chicago.

*Colonel Rogers.*

Aide to Governor Sampson of Kentucky, suh, should he ever need aid.

## 531 Will Rogers For Town Signs As An Aid To Aviation

COLUMBUS, Ohio, April 9. — Flew 220 miles from Louisville over here with the Cardinal Aircraft Pilot Gast. We got a head wind and made it in 1 hour and 45 minutes. Takes all day on train.

Say, you luncheon clubs, stop eating and singing songs long enough to get you some paint and a brush and go out and put the name of your town on the biggest roofed building you got. It would be a tremendous aid to aviators. Lots of towns can't afford an airport, but any of you can do this. You Kiwanis's or Rotary's could do it some day and not miss over half of some speech.

Pray for any friends in Chicago tonight.

Yours,
*Will Rogers.*

## 532 Will Rogers Sees Longworth As A Good Ohio Candidate

CINCINNATI, Ohio, April 10. — You have heard about Ohio's favorite sons. Well, I have been all through the State, and if you take it from me, the most popular native son they have had there is Nick Longworth.

So what's the matter with Nick for candidate? He is the most able and popular speaker the House has had. In fact the greatest since Alexander Hamilton.

Everybody talks about what a great campaign Al will make. Well, Nick can stay with him, I don't care how late he campaigns.

*Colonel Rogers,*
Late of Kentucky.

P. S. — Did you read about those great Kentucky basketball players?

## 533 WILL ROGERS IN A NEW ROLE AND SIGNS HIMSELF SHAMUS

CLEVELAND, Ohio, April 11. — See where Henry Ford wouldn't visit Ireland till they took their tariff off something or other. That ought to keep about everybody from visiting this country. I think Uncle Henry has a tough time competing with those jaunting cars in Ireland. He can make a billion cars, but he will never make as good ones as those little donkeys—no overhauling, no tire trouble, no carburetor adjustment, no insurance, no depreciation, no upkeep, and they can carry more and pull more than any Ford ever built. In fact, those donkeys is where Ford got his idea of his car. Viva Ireland!

Yours,
*Shamus Rogers.*

## 534 WILL ROGERS BELIEVES AVIATORS 'ARE GOING TO MAKE IT'

ROCHESTER, N. Y., April 12. — As I wire this from Rochester we haven't heard anything from the German and Irish flyers, but I am leaving here after my sermon tonight and will be in New York standing with Casey Jones on Mitchel Field all day tomorrow.

I don't know, but I just believe they are going to make it. I met this Irishman over in Ireland and I just can't picture him anything but alive.

Politics can wait. This is important business we got to think of today. I am going to be a-looking, a-hoping and doing a little amateur praying.

Yours,
*Will Rogers.*

535 **WILL SPENDS THE DAY WATCHING FOR FLIERS**

PHILADELPHIA, Pa., April 13. – I stood on that field all day, and if you could have seen those anxious faces, good old homely German people and Irish with buoyant hope! It's a shame if brave fellows like that are lost.

But no wonder they had trouble coming west. Lieutenant Balfour had a hard time getting our ship from Mitchel field here against that strong west wind.

But it's not too late to hope.

Yours, hopefully,
*Will Rogers.*

536 **WILL ROGERS FINDS INTEREST IN FLIERS, SMITH, ANDY COHEN**

NEW YORK, N. Y., April 15. – That certainly was nice of that Irishman to let those two Germans stay in there with him when he saw that the load was so big they couldn't make any time against that wind.

You folks thought I was kidding you when I have been telling you all this time about these head winds. The reason they make it going the other way is because they got Congress behind 'em. The only sure way to have a successful trip made this way is to have our Congress meet in Ireland.

There is no politics in it, but Smith is the only fellow that ever went South for a vacation in the Summer time.

I am going out to see Andy Cohen. He is bigger than Aimee McPherson out home.

Yours,
*Will.*

537 **WILL ROGERS SAYS NOBLE IDEAS DON'T GET ANYWHERE IN POLITICS**

NEW YORK, N. Y., April 16. – I received my $5 back from Senator Borah that I sent him to clean up five Republicans. I even named the five that he was to clean up. He wasn't able to raise the fund because people realized that it was a lost cause. You can't make the Republican Party pure by more contributions, because contributions are what got it where it is today.

This was a noble idea of Borah's, but noble ideas don't get anywhere. Look at Dawes's original idea of cleaning up the Senate! I doubt if he can remember even trying it now. Noble ideas don't belong in politics.

Yours,
*Will Rogers.*

## 538 WILL GETS RING LARDNER TO WRITE SOMETHING FREE

NEW YORK, N. Y., April 17. – Ring Lardner and I are seeing New York tonight and he has promised to say a few words of cheer to you. All I do is pay for the theatre tickets and when the show drags I will laugh at him. Mr. Lardner now speaking:

"Good evening newspaper fans. I used to have to write in the newspaper for a living, too. It must be awful hard. Georgie Cohan is producing a new baseball play of mine which I hope you get more laughs out of than I do going around with Will Rogers. I have a song hit in it sung by a Scotchman entitled, 'I Would Give a Thousand Dollars to Be a Millionaire.' That's all I will write for this guy for nothing. Yours, Ring Lardner."

*Will Rogers.*

## 539 WILL ROGERS AGAIN FLIES, THIS TIME IN FRED STONE'S PLANE

HAGERSTOWN, Md., April 18. – To give you an idea of what private aviation is advancing to, I left New York this morning at 8 o'clock against a head wind, in Fred Stone the actor's new plane with his private pilot, Campion. Fred is over 50, yet he has learned to fly his own plane.

Say, have you been reading about that Claremore (Okla.) boy, Payne, in that walk, trot and single-foot derby from Hollywood to Hoboken? He led them into Claremore yesterday, which, by the way, was half way. When they all saw the town they didn't want to leave.

Yours for home talent,

*Will Rogers.*

*Actor Fred Stone and his private pilot with the Rogers family following landing on polo grounds at the California ranch.*
(L to R: Pilot Johnny Campion, Mary Rogers, Fred Stone, Jimmie Rogers, Will Rogers, Betty Rogers and Will Rogers, Jr.)

## 540 Will Rogers Finds Variety Of News In West Virginia

PARKERSBURG, W. Va., April 19. – Was in Maryland last night. Everybody can get a drink there but Sinclair's race horses. They have closed the saloons to them.

Say, this Senator Goff of West Virginia is pulling Jim Watson down here. He kinder acts like he is serious about this Republican Presidential nomination. This State is worried more about how to make a coal mine pay than it is about Presidential candidates.

The D. A. R.'s canned William Randolph Emporia White as speaker and used President Coolidge as substitute. Mr. Coolidge that night stole Governor Ritchie's act, State rights, and didn't do it as good as Ritchie, so now the D. A. R.'s want to reinstate White.

It is about time for this Ohio River to get up, as there has been no flood relief passed I am going to get out of here.

Yours,
*Will Rogers.*

## 541 Will Rogers Not For Peace, But For Good Show At Houston

FAIRMOUNT, W. Va., April 20. – I am here in Clem Shaver's, the head of the Democrats, home town. He tells me that the Democrats are going to be so peaceful and hungry for harmony at their convention that you won't hardly know they are Democrats.

Well, if I go there and they are as he says, I certainly will ask for my money back. They have worked for years to bring their conventions up to a show and now they want to crab it.

I have been investigating the condition of the coal mines all day. They are not nearly as bad as the condition of the second-hand automobile dealers.

Yours,
*Will Rogers.*

## 542 Will Rogers Finds Another Woman Who Belongs In Politics

INDIANAPOLIS, Ind., April 22. – Say, you know I wrote you the other day about a wonderful woman politician who has since been nominated, Mrs. Ruth McCormick of Illinois, daughter of Mark Hanna.

Well, there is a live Democratic woman, too, and that's Ruth Bryan Owen, daughter of William Jennings Bryan. She is running for Congress in Florida from the Miami district and she is another woman that really belongs in politics, for she was bred to politics. That will be two daughters of two great politicians.

Who are the Republicans going to nominate for President? They are liable to furnish the comedy this year.

Well, Sinclair come clear. Now, if his horses in Maryland can just prove they are innocent.

Yours,
*Will Rogers.*

## 543 WILL ROGERS FINDS CHICAGO QUIET AND KIND TO ENGLISHMEN

CHICAGO, Ill., April 23. – Say, Chicago is as quiet—only one big murder headline today, and Englishmen are allowed to use their own accent on the street again.

The League of Women Voters are here in convention demanding these planks in the next platform: Democratic women want birth control for Republicans, and Republican women want equal corruption for both sexes.

Yours,
*Will Rogers.*

## 544 WILL ROGERS DISCOVERS A TUNNEY LITERARY TEST

CHICAGO, Ill., April 24. – Gene Tunney just lectured before Yale's class on Shakespeare. He said he read Shakespeare ten times before he could get what he meant.

Now that brings up the question: Is there something wrong with Shakespeare or with Gene? If everybody has to read his stuff ten times, why Shakespeare is not the author he is cracked up to be. But if somebody else can read him and get him the first time, why, Tunney is not the high-brow that *he* is cracked up to be.

So read my stuff at least ten times, and if you can't get it, why, you are neither a Shakespeare or a Tunney.

Yours for simpler authors and harder hitting fighters,
*Will Rogers.*

## 545 Rogers Advises Investors To Look Into Egg Business

CHICAGO, Ill., April 25. – Speaking at a banquet here tonight at the opening of a beautiful seventeen-story building built by the butter and egg men. It's a monument to the American people who can't tell a good egg from a bad one. It's a tribute to what a rooster and a churn can do.

You can buy eggs on this market the same as you can buy General Motors stock. So, get you some eggs and hold 'em. Somebody will eat 'em no matter how old they are and if you can't pay your cold storage bill hardboil 'em and sell 'em for picnics.

Yours a cacklin',

*Will Rogers.*

## 546 Rogers Expects Another Flood To Reach South Before Relief

ST. PAUL, Minn., April 26. – I am just sitting here looking out over the Mississippi River, and it's up pretty high. So I am just giving all my friends down South warning. Now, it will take this raise a long time to reach away down there, but it will get there ahead of Government relief. So get ready. This water has got to go somewhere. Have your Fords made into amphibians.

Yours,

*Will Rogers.*

P. S. – It looks like the only thing can stop Hoover now is crooked politics, and it will just about do it.

## 547 Will Rogers Finds Old Friends In Flying Around Iowa

CEDAR RAPIDS, Iowa, April 27. – Just flew in here in a new Ryan monoplane against a terrific head wind with Pilot Livingstone. Talk about meeting great people. I had breakfast in Des Moines with "Ding," the great political cartoonist. He won't leave Des Moines. That's where he gets all those wonderful rube ideas. The streets are packed here today with farmers' automobiles waiting for relief.

This is the home of Quaker Oats and Cherry Sisters. I am going out to see the sisters. They were really the inspiration of me going on the stage.

Tomorrow Topeka, the home of Charley Curtis, and he would make a great President.

Yours,
*Will Rogers.*

## 548 Will Rogers Takes Early View Of A Convention City

KANSAS CITY, Mo., April 29. – Out of all the States I have been in, and out of all those that have ambitious Presidential sons, I take a straw vote every night. Curtis is the only one who really has the backing of his State. These others are just family support, but old Kansas is for Charley.

I am right now in the room of the Meulbach where the nomination will be held and I can see Convention Hall, where the delegates will be notified who has been nominated. It's their main suite of rooms here and they are in here now working on ice boxes, sawdust and cuspidors.

It's a great life if you take it serious.

Yours,
*Will Rogers.*

## 549 Will Rogers Hopes The Press Will Be Kind To Aviation

SALINA, Kan., April 30. – When will the newspapers commence giving aviation an even break? There were eight people killed all over America in planes Sunday and it's headlined in every newspaper today. If there was a single State that didn't get that many in automobiles yesterday it was simply because it fell below its average.

I see where Tunney has gone into training for that fellow Heeney. He trained on Shakespeare and Homer for Dempsey. But he just took a set of Zane Grey and Harold Bell Wright to get himself in condition for Heeney.

Yours,
*Will Rogers.*

## 550 Will Rogers Gets A New Kick Out Of Aviation In The West

CHELSEA, Okla., May 1. – I got the real kick of my life out of aviation today. Left western Kansas and flew down to Oklahoma and landed right on the old ranch I was born on. First machine was ever in there. When I was raised there, I never thought there would ever be anything faster than a horse get in there.

I ask you and plead with you again, you luncheon clubbers, will you please paint the name of your town on top of your building? I will pay for the paint if you will do it. We were lost today, and all the towns in Kansas had no names we could make out till we got to Bartlesville, Okla., who had their name out.

Are you ashamed of your town?

Yours,
*Will Rogers.*

## 551 Will Rogers Sees Congress In A Generous Mood

OMAHA, Neb., May 2. – Just flew in from Chelsea, Okla., bucking a head wind. See by the papers that every appropriation bill is being passed. Too bad you didn't ask for something. You would have gotten it.

Suppose four different groups from four different parts of the country all want something and all trade votes with each other so that everybody gets theirs. What chance has the Treasury got? There is times when it looks like the James boys got their robbery reputation on mighty scant evidence.

If all these appropriations go through, then Judd Gray and Ruth Snyder were innocent.

Yours,
*Will Rogers.*

## 552 Will Rogers Flying Back Home To Oppose Any Recount

ROCK SPRINGS, Wyo., May 3. – Left Omaha this morning for a little flight and as we happened to get a tail wind just kept on coming. Will soon be in Salt Lake. Make Beverly Hills tonight. That's rambling.

Going to California to see that they don't have a recount on Smith and Hoover like they did on Hughes that time.

Yours,
*Will Rogers.*

## 553 Will Rogers Says Will Hays Earns His Pay In The Movies

BEVERLY HILLS, Cal., May 4. – Say, those that thought Will Hays was over in Europe just to get away from the Republicans are mistaken. No wonder Bill draws such a big salary from the movies. He earns it.

Did you see what he did yesterday in France? France was about to bar our movies and Bill made 'em sign a contract where they not only retain our movies but for every seven of ours the French see they will have to look at one made in France. That satisfied the French producers; all they wanted was to make theirs compulsory.

Yours,

*Will Rogers.*

P. S. – Say, I run out of paint. Some towns were painting their own homes with it.

## 554 Will Rogers Praises Walsh For His Honesty And Frankness

BEVERLY HILLS, Cal., May 6. – Senator Walsh issued a statement that on account of its extreme novelty has not received the proper amount of publicity that it should. He resigned as follows: "There just don't seem to be any burning desire on the part of the people for my nomination. I feel sure they want Smith."

We may not owe Mr. Walsh the Presidency but we certainly do owe him something for his eyesight, honesty and frankness. Jim Watson is still wearing smoke-colored glasses.

Yours,

*Will Rogers.*

P. S. – Owing to shortage of funds I am limiting my offer to supply paint for names of towns with not more than four letters.

## 555 Will Rogers Discusses What Carol Offers Rumania

BEVERLY HILLS, Cal., May 7. – See today where Prince Carol says that "Rumania is the laughing stock of the world," but he insinuates that if he can get on the throne he will add just the amount of dignity and wives that it has been lacking. He says the girl friend,

Mme. Lupescu, is perfectly willing to share him with the needy Rumanians. She is broadminded that way.

Been reading Sunday's casualty lists from automobiles. It looks like everybody gets run over but Presidential candidates. Is there no justice in the world?

Yours,
*Will Rogers.*

P. S. — Paint has been put down to towns of three letters. Ada, Oklahoma, for instance. Mooselookmeguntic, Me., sent me a bill for $79. They had to put a letter on each house and borrowed three houses from Connecticut.

## 556 WILL ROGERS ANALYZES A FEW CAMPAIGN EXPENSES

BEVERLY HILLS, Cal., May 8. — They examined some of the Presidential candidates yesterday to see what they had spent on their campaigns. Norris made the best showing. He had only spent $6 for an ad in a country newspaper and has the Wisconsin and Nebraska delegation to show for it, which proves that cheap advertising pays.

Goff has spent $90, but received nothing definite so far. George of Georgia has spent $100 and has Georgia—that's about $4 a delegate. Walsh receipts were $1,075 and the expenditures $1,090.65, so he is in the red $15.65. Curtis spent $11,000. It cost money to get William White and his gang to vote for anybody.

Now, none of these men have spent much, but on the other hand they haven't got far. So it just shows you can't get something for nothing.

Yours,
*Will Rogers.*

## 557 WILL ROGERS SAYS IT'S CHEAPER TO BE PRESIDENT THAN SENATOR

BEVERLY HILLS, Cal., May 9. — The Senate is still examining the expenditures of Presidential candidates. The humor of the thing is that you can be elected President of this country on one-tenth what it costs to be elected Senator.

Old Prince Carol is still on the front page, so I can see a lecture tour in America next Fall for him.

Tax relief, farm relief, flood relief, dam relief—none of these have been settled, but they are getting them in shape for consideration at the next session of Congress with the hope that those needing relief will perhaps have conveniently died in the meantime.

Yours,

*Will Rogers.*

## 558 Will Rogers Shows Surprise At The Result In Indiana

BEVERLY HILLS, Cal., May 10. – When Indiana votes that Jim Watson would be a more competent man for President than Herb Hoover, there just ain't nothing you can say. Mind you, Jim is a good fellow as far as politicians go, but I leave comment in the hands of George Ade, Kin Hubbard and Booth Tarkington and Jesse Andrews. Old Perdue, it looks like you have failed.

Yours,

*Will Rogers.*

## 559 Will Rogers Offers Advice To John D. Rockefeller Jr.

BEVERLY HILLS, Cal., May 11. – I hate to be the first to make notice of it, but I believe that it is a record. Japan and China have been fighting now for one solid week and we haven't entered our marines. What's the matter, are they barred? Maybe they are eliminated on account of being professionals.

I don't want to tell young John D. Rockefeller his business for he is a friend of mine. But if he wants to get rid of anybody why don't he stop their pay. That's more successful than writing them letters.

Yours,

*Will Rogers.*

## 560 Will Rogers Comments On Mellon And The Nomination

BEVERLY HILLS, Cal., May 13. – Did you read where Mellon says "Hoover is the best man, and has the most qualifications for the job of being President?" But he did not want the Pennsylvania delegation instructed for him. He wants to go to Kansas City and wait for the best offer. In other words, he will take an inferior man if the inducements are better.

You can't blame men like Jim Watson for wanting to have their State delegation to trade off, when one of our biggest men, like Mellon, wants to do the same thing.

And the poor fellow voting in the primary still takes it serious and really thinks he has something to do with the nomination.

Yours,
*Will Rogers.*

## 561 Will Rogers Asks For Credit For Long-Distance Foot Racers

BEVERLY HILLS, Cal., May 14. – It's about time somebody give a real endurance test some credit–this foot race to New York, and a 20-year-old kid from Claremore, Okla., leading it. It's all right to kid it and call it bunions, but no athlete in any other branch of sport could get up every day for three straight months and run from forty to seventy miles.

Sporting writers write pages over some football player's seventy-yard run. Our champion prize fighters can only fight thirty minutes every two years. There is not a golf player in America that could have stood this same trip in an automobile. You will find it's the grit and heart that's doing this more than bunions or ingrowing toe nails, so be fair and give 'em a break.

Yours from Claremore,
*Will Rogers.*

## 562 Mr. Rogers Sees Prosperity In The Increase Of Divorces

BEVERLY HILLS, Cal., May 15. – Somebody is always quoting figures to prove that the country is prosperous, and it takes a lot of quoting; but the only real bona fide indication of it was in the paper today: "Divorces in Reno have increased over 105 per cent in the last year."

Now, that's prosperity, for you can't be broke and get a divorce. That's why the poor have to live with each other. There is nothing that denotes prosperity quicker than to hear that "so and so and his wife ain't getting along."

I maintain that it should cost as much to get married as it does to get divorced. Make it look like marriage is worth as much as divorce, even if it ain't. That would also make the preachers financially independent like it has the lawyers.

Yours for the downtrodden,

*Will Rogers.*

## 563 WILL ROGERS DISCOVERS THE PERFECT PUBLIC DINNER

BEVERLY HILLS, Cal., May 16. — A big step forward in modern civilization was made last night here in Los Angeles (the last place you would expect civilization to advance). It was a dinner given at $100 a plate, with the distinct understanding there would be no speeches. The place was sold out and everybody tickled to death. The funds from the dinner were divided among those who wanted to make speeches but were not allowed. Everyone in the hall received $100.

Yours,

*Will Rogers.*

P. S. — Jack Dempsey told me tonight he would fight Tunney in September if he got enough money for it. I told Jack I would fight Tunney myself if they gave me enough money, and time to brush up on my English and Shakespeare.

## 564 WILL ROGERS FORSEES LIVELY ELECTION IN THE SOUTH

BEVERLY HILLS, Cal., May 17. — An ex-Governor and State leader had a fist fight in South Carolina. One called the other a Republican. Had the accused killed him for calling him that it would have been hard to convict him in any court where justice is really dealt out. If they are fist fighting in the primaries what will it be in the election? You stock buyers better be buying Du Pont Powder and Winchester Arms.

Say, Oklahoma just pulled a good stunt to advance fields and aviation interest. They rounded up all the planes in their State and toured the whole State.

Hoover went fishing in Pennsylvania and caught twenty-eight delegates in New Jersey. Some fishing!

Yours,

*Will Rogers.*

## 565 WILL ROGERS BLAZED TRAIL FOR QUICK TRIP TO COAST

BEVERLY HILLS, Cal., May 18. – In an article over three months ago I told you of this proposed trip to the Coast by train and airplane combined. Now the papers are just full of it. Guess they thought on account of mine being a joke column that it was the bunk. I should have relayed the news to an editorial writer and let him tell about it. Then it would have been authentic.

The only thing I see about the scheme that is not practical is why would you get off the plane and onto a train just because night had come. We never got off a train and into a wagon just because it's dark.

Yours,
*Will Rogers.*

P. S. – Overestimated my resources when made offer to furnish paint. It was typographical error. I meant I would send brush to any town who would paint name.

## 566 WILL ROGERS STILL THINKS 'DON'T CHOOSE' MEANS 'WILL'

HOLLYWOOD, Cal., May 20. – When a word comes out and you don't know what it means, you rush to old man Webster. But when one comes out and even Webster don't know what it means, why our only chance to learn what it means is to ask the man that used it, but when he only replies "it means what it means," why we are not any better informed than we were at first. So we just have to wait till something happens that makes him divulge his secret.

Well, in Kansas City three weeks from Tuesday it happens, we will learn for the first time on any stage if "choose" means "yes," "no," "maybe," "I can't tell yet," "who knows," "search me," "probably" or "perhaps."

I claim that it means "will under proper pressure," so don't argue; just wait three weeks.

Yours,
*Will Rogers.*

## 567 WILL ROGERS THINKS CONGRESS ALL WRONG ON BOULDER DAM

BEVERLY HILLS, Cal., May 21. – Wasn't this your idea of what the original founders meant Congress and the Senate to be,

"When a bill is introduced, let it be voted on, and either approved or rejected by a majority"? It was never meant that by political manoeuvring any bill could be prevented from being voted on. Yet that's the standing of Boulder Dam in the Senate. In other words, you don't find out if the prisoner is innocent or guilty; you just keep him in jail till he dies.

Yours,
*Will Rogers.*

P. S. – Another notorious case out here of a young girl and a rich man, assisted, as usual, by the fond mother.

## 568 WILL ROGERS SEES REAL HUMOR IN OUR ATTITUDE TO GAMBLING

BEVERLY HILLS, Cal., May 22. – Big headline in the paper says, "Three newspaper men arrested in connection with horse-race betting." In the adjoining column, "Wall Street stock market reaches another four million; call money is the highest in its history."

You don't have to look much further in the paper for humor than that. And we call Latin American Governments primitive for allowing lotteries. We only have one rule: If you can build a business up big enough it's respectable.

Just a sorehead because I didn't have any General Motors.

Yours,
*Will Rogers.*

P. S. – Did you know those foot-racers run seventy-six miles yesterday? That's three full-length marathons in one day. Try to ride a horse seventy-six miles in one day and you'll truck him back home.

## 569 WILL ROGERS SEES LINDBERGH ABOUT TO SETTLE DOWN

BEVERLY HILLS, Cal., May 23. – Several weeks ago I told you that "a certain fairly well-known aviator would be connected with this railroad and air line." Well, this morning the papers are just full of "Lindy's" acceptance. The whole country seems tickled to death that that boy is going to settle down and go to work, quit gadding about and finally see if he can't amount to something.

In this new job all he has to do is to pick out the planes, the pilots, the route and the fields, about the same type of job that it took

Jay Gould and Jim Hill a lifetime to work out. Wonder who gave Lindy a letter of recommendation for this job?

Yours for opportunities for young men,

*Will Rogers.*

## 570 WILL ROGERS GIVES COOLIDGE FULL CREDIT FOR CONSISTENCY

BEVERLY HILLS, Cal., May 24. – By golly, you got to give Calvin credit for consistency. He told 'em a year ago that he thought this farm bill was wrong, they took it back and took out the word "hog" and replaced it with "pork" but he still wouldn't fall for it. Politicians couldn't understand any man vetoing a bill with an election coming on.

I have always claimed that the farmer will get no relief by legislation, for there is more people eating than there is raising, so he is a minority before he starts. His belief should come through taxes. When a farm don't pay anything it shouldn't be taxed.

I am not worrying about Andy Payne winning the race, but I am worried if he will win anything else.

Yours,

*Will Rogers.*

## 571 WILL ROGERS HAS LITTLE FAITH IN PROMISES BY CONGRESS

BEVERLY HILLS, Cal., May 25. – News of the day: Congress has promised the country that it will adjourn next Tuesday. Let's hope we can depend on it. If they do it will be the first promise they have kept this session. If they only hadn't promised it, there might be more grounds for hope.

They just distributed $225,000,000 of Andy's hard earned savings. If your part of the country didn't get your share it's because your Congressman didn't take a bag with him.

Andy Payne of Claremore, Okla., wins foot race, but is liable to have to run back to Los Angeles to get his money.

They got Henry Ford running foot races now. He must have left home in one of his own.

Yours,

*Will Rogers.*

## 572 Will Rogers Sees More Politics Than Relief In The Farm Bill

HOLLYWOOD, Cal., May 27. – You can always tell when the Senate is getting near a close–the Boulder Dam bill will come up. Some day somebody with the interest of that bill at heart will bring it up the first day of Congress, and then if some Arizona Senator can talk from then to the close, why it will be a record and not just a repetition.

They knew Coolidge would veto the farm bill. Well, if they had help this Summer, why didn't they have some kind of a compromise bill ready that he would sign. No sir. There was more politics than relief in that bill.

Yours,
*Will Rogers.*

## 573 Will Rogers Gives Advice To Bunion Derby Winner

BEVERLY HILLS, Cal., May 28. – Breeding and ancestry hasn't got a thing to do with this boy Andy Payne. His daddy and I grew up together about the same age, and he was raised on an outfit next to ours. He never run in his life. He always rode horseback. He has another kid that was named for me, and I am certainly going to try and keep him from running down to Buenos Aires or up to Alaska or somewhere. If Andy don't get this prize money, this certainly ought to be a lesson to him to never run far unless he is sure. If I was him, from now on I would just enter some short sprints of maybe just fifteen hundred or two thousand miles.

Yours,
*Will Rogers.*

## 574 Rogers Finds A Prediction About The Senate Fulfilled

BEVERLY HILLS, Cal., May 29. – I told you not to be too optimistic about the Senate resigning. They filibustered all last night. We pay for wisdom and we get wind.

Andy Payne didn't get his money but they took him to Washington and let him see Mr. Coolidge. That will go down in history as the $25,000 look. If he didn't see Mrs. Coolidge he was stuck.

Charley Paddock, the great runner, was in the East training for the Olympics, and they drag him clear back to Los Angeles to make him run a special race to raise money.

I guess the most professional thing we have in America is an amateur association. A dollar is valued more than a stride.

Yours,
*Will Rogers.*

## 575 Will Rogers Has A New Idea Of How To Build Boulder Dam

BEVERLY HILLS, Cal., May 30. – How would this do as a compromise way to build Boulder Dam?

Put California Senators and Congressmen on their side of the river and Arizona's on their side and let 'em start throwing boulders at each other, and in a year there would be enough rocks in the river to make Boulder Dam.

The boys are all on their way home now to take care of their campaign contributions.

It's a tough year for the voter. Every man is trying to be elected as cheap as possible. Even Pennsylvania and Illinois votes was never bringing as little as they are this year. It don't hardly pay a man to vote.

Yours,
*Will Rogers.*

## 576 Rogers Warns That 'Goff' Is Just A Senator, Not A Game

BEVERLY HILLS, Cal., May 31. – Headline says "Goff wins over Hoover in West Virginia," but as soon as the West Virginians find it's only a Senator and not a game they will call for a recount.

Another Decoration Day passed and Lincoln's speech is still untouched. But Mr. Coolidge made a mighty nice speech, and what he said about this international peace that Kellogg is working on was news. People had no idea that it has progressed that far.

The balloon race must work right with the weatherman. If they didn't they couldn't start just before a storm like they always do.

Yours,
*Will Rogers.*

## 577 Will Rogers Discovers Quick Change In News Values

BEVERLY HILLS, Cal., June 1. – Shows you how quick even a President's plans can drop from public interest. Last Summer Mr. Coolidge's vacation place was the one big news of the year. Now everybody's interest in "Where will Al spend next Summer?"

One thing, they can't accuse Coolidge of trying to cater to the voter by going to a doubtful State. Wisconsin is never doubtful. You can always depend on it doing just exactly what the other forty-seven don't. If the fish are as queer as the voters, he will eat steak all Summer.

Yours,
*Will Rogers.*

## 578 Will Rogers Says A Word About The International "But"

HOLLYWOOD, Cal., June 3. – Just when Secretary Kellogg had his "no-more-war-plan" all going good and about ready to sign up, why, England, Japan and France came through with the old usual diplomatic clause which says, "We agree in principle, but–." Well, there was the but. "We are heartily against all wars, unless, of course, we should see fit to do a little fighting ourselves. Then, of course, this agreement would be null and void. But we certainly join you in preventing others from having the pleasure of fighting."

If Kellogg can get all us four big nations to agree that Monday follows Sunday without them having "I agree in principle, but –" in it, he will be the world's greatest diplomat.

Yours, just an amateur diplomat,
*Will Rogers.*

## 579 Rogers Tip To Speculators: Don't Sell Democrats Short

BEVERLY HILLS, Cal., June 4. – I see by this morning's papers that Mr. Coolidge is sending somebody to Kansas City to protect his interest. If I had any interests to be protected in any political convention I believe I would send the marines. Be a good joke on the Republicans if they go and nominate somebody else if Coolidge would veto the nomination. He is liable to do it just through force of habit.

With everybody's mind on stock selling and buying I just want to give you a tip. The way things are looking don't sell the Democratic Party short.

Yours,
*Will Rogers.*

## 580 Flying To The Fiji Islands Rogers's Idea Of The Best Way

BEVERLY HILLS, Cal., June 5. — When four men in a three-motored plane and carrying all that gas can fly 3,200 miles over the ocean in one hop and keep in communication with the world every minute of the time, why aviation has really arrived. If I went to the Fiji Islands that's how I would want to land—in a plane and be ready to get away in case they looked hungry.

Yours,
*Will Rogers.*

## 581 Will Rogers's Own Version Of His Airplane Accident

SALT LAKE CITY, Utah, June 6. — Wheel broke when she come down and turned over and lit on her back. Am the first candidate to land on his head, and being a candidate, it didn't hurt the head.

Grabbed another plane and on into Salt Lake City on the way to where these Republicans meet. Anyhow, if we had landed twenty feet further, we would have hit in Boulder Dam. On to Kansas to draft Coolidge.

Yours,
*Will Rogers.*

## 582 Mr. Rogers Takes A Survey Of The Day's Happenings

CHICAGO, Ill., June 7. — Had a fine trip in from California on the air mail. Arrived in Chicago twenty-four hours after leaving old Beverly.

Iowa and Nebraska are just planting corn. What the farmer needs is for a convention to be held some time when he is not so busy.

All the politicians are trying to stop Hoover, and all the people are for him, so lay your bets.

They blew up a Russian cafe in Hollywood and like to got all the movie stars that had been educated up to caviar. I would like to have seen Charlie's exit when he found it wasn't a movie blast.

Yours, on to the convention,

*Will Rogers.*

## 583 Will Rogers Sees Mr. Mellon As Naming Party Candidates

JACKSON, Mich., June 8. – Flew up from Chicago today to round up some anti-bunk party delegates. Am taking off at daylight in the morning for Kansas City, where the Republicans are gathering to await word from Mr. Mellon as to who will be nominated.

If Mellon really had the economy of the country at heart, like he says he has, he would have mailed everybody a post card and told them, instead of having them go clear to Kansas City to await his announcement.

I went last night to an endurance dancing contest in Chicago where they have been going for six days and nights. I watched 'em all night. I was training to listen to the keynote speech in Kansas City.

Yours,

*Will Rogers.*

## 584 Mr. Rogers Seeks Religion In Politics And Finds It Not

KANSAS CITY, Mo., June 10. – Today being Sunday (even in a political convention), I just got an idea I would see just how religious all these politicians really are, as I had heard that religion might play some part in the Fall festivities. So I grab a cab and rush from one church to the other all over town, and not a single candidate, or delegate, or even delegates, was among the worshipers.

Still, this Fall, in the campaign, you will hear them get up and shout "Our religion is the bulwark of our great and glorious country; we must continue to be God-fearing people; our Church is our salvation." Well, our Churches are our salvation, but some of those babies won't be among those rescued.

Yours,
*Will Rogers.*

P. S. — Everybody is just sitting at the depot waiting for "Uncle" Andy Mellon to come and tell 'em who will be nominated. He is the "head man" in this show.

## 585 Will Rogers Summarizes The Convention Tips He Gets

KANSAS CITY, Mo., June 11. — Here is the tips that are going the rounds today; Hoover on the first ballot; Coolidge on the second ballot; Dawes on the third; Lowden on the fourth; Curtis on the fifth ballot. Then, in case there is a deadlock, why it will go into a hat and all the Senators draw for it.

Just talked with Borah and he says he don't care who gets it, as long as he can disagree with him.

Kansas City is a-doing herself proud. They did have some pickpockets here when it started, but they all starved out.

I am still for Mrs. Coolidge on a vindication platform.

Yours,
*Will Rogers.*

## 586 'Stop Smith,' Will Rogers Says Has Replaced 'Stop Hoover'

KANSAS CITY, Mo., June 12. — We met this morning for no reason, and adjourned for the same. When Andy Mellon come in, everybody stood up, as though a lady had entered the room. Rather an effeminate move I thought.

The best thing at the convention was Schumann-Heink singing. Oh, what a grand old lady she did look, and how she sang!

I wish she had sang Fess's keynote speech.

It looks like they met this morning just to take photographs. Every delegate had his photographer. The keynote now is, not to "Stop Hoover" but to "Stop Smith."

I think we will have the boys out of the hotels by Thursday, so let's go on to Houston, where they at least know how to fuss.

*Will Rogers.*

## 587 Mr. Rogers Calls For A Hand For A Great Flier, Carranza

KANSAS CITY, Mo., June 13. – Say, while a lot of your minds are sorter half-way taken up with this Republican applesauce, I hope there is enough sanity left to give this Mexican aviator, Carranza, a hand; the one that flew to Washington. I knew him down there; he is a great flier in any man's country.

We spent all day here today on resolutions. I wish some one would pass one that they adjourn and go home. Moses made a speech this morning and denounced Smith, and incidentally eliminated himself from the Vice Presidency.

If Smith ever gets after him in the campaign, he will make him wish that Pharaoh's daughter had never dug him out of those bullrushes.

Yours,
*Will Rogers.*

## 588 Rogers Links Convention With A Bank Robbery

KANSAS CITY, Mo., June 14. – Bank was robbed just before the convention opened this morning. Chicago and Indiana delegations are under surveillance. Towns will book these conventions.

Young Bob La Follette made the only real speech that has been made in the convention. He spoke in favor of the people. He was listened to, but his amendments were not adopted. They kept in the Wall Street ones. If there is enough banks to rob, there is no telling when the convention will adjourn.

It's Heflin for Vice President to "stop Smith."

Yours,
*Will Rogers.*

## 589 Mr. Rogers Pays His Respects To Mr. Curtis, The Candidate

KANSAS CITY, Mo., June 15. – Well, it's over here. That's one thing about these Republicans, they don't allow things to clog up. I been telling you for days that Curtis would be the one. He is a Kaw Indian and me a Cherokee and I am for him. It's the first time we have ever got a break—the only American that has ever run for that high office.

Watch your campaign. It will be America as typified by the West, or America as typified by Eastern immigration. So, hurrah for you, Charlie. A real two-fisted bird who used to be a jockey.

Come on, Injun! If you are elected let's run the white people out of this country.

On to Houston to the biggest show on earth.

Yours,

*Will Rogers.*

P. S. — Kansas City, you did yourself proud. It's Oklahoma that supports you and makes you a city, but I didn't hear a complaint about you. Of course, the show at times was terrible, but no show can be better than the cast.

## 590 CONVENTION AFTERTHOUGHTS WHICH COME TO WILL ROGERS

KANSAS CITY, Mo., June 17. — Did you ever see a town after they had just finished sweeping out a convention?

The Republicans have all gone back home to collect. You know, they don't pay off till after you have voted. The farmers that were supposed to be so mad are all in a good humor now. They got a good rain today. That's their only relief.

The Republicans picked absolutely the strongest ticket they could have. Hoover has a tremendous popularity with the people; it was the politicians that were against him. He licked them. Now watch 'em start telling how great he is.

On to Houston to nominate a Vice Presidential candidate.

Yours,

*Will Rogers.*

## 591 WHY WILL ROGERS IS GLAD MISS EARHART SUCCEEDED

PAWNEE, Okla., June 18. — Having a little visit with my old friend Pawnee Bill here, on his buffalo ranch.

Oklahoma sure looks fine. Greatest wheat crop in years. If there just wasn't any new cars for sale farmers would be out of debt this Fall.

Certainly glad that girl made the ocean trip. Now the rest of these other women can devote their time to steady thinking of some other way to make the front page.

Yours,
*Will Rogers.*

## 592 Mr. Rogers Sees Gov. Ritchie As An Ideal Vice President

CLAREMORE, Okla., June 19. – Andy Payne, the foot racer, has just come home, and Claremore has given him a big welcome. I had to rush home to protect my own interest. I am about to lose my favorite-son standing.

I just had a talk with Andy. He is a fine, modest young kid. He promised to run out to California and see me sometime.

I see where Governor Ritchie of Maryland withdrew. There is your real, legitimate Vice President. If they nominate a dry Vice President the Democrats will maintain their comedy reputation.

Yours,
*Will Rogers.*

## 593 Rogers Advises The Farmer To Turn His Mind To Golf

CLAREMORE, Okla., June 20. – Say, what do you know about Claremore having a golf course? I tell you turning your land into a golf course is the salvation of the farmer. That's the only thing to do with land now, is just to play golf on it. Sell your land and caddy.

Say, there is a lot of people down here that haven't paid their bet against Smith yet. I have been led to believe that it was all over.

I am flying tomorrow to Fort Worth, the ranchman's post office. Hurrah for Amon Carter, West Texas, and Dan Moody! Jesse Jones get me some chili ready, and a ticket to the hall where they are exhibiting the New York delegation.

Yours,
*Will Rogers.*

P. S. – Claremore's got a manicurist. Here's the town for the Democrats in '32, if they meet again.

## 594 Mr. Rogers Arrives In Texas And Notes Its Hospitality

FORT WORTH, Tex., June 21. – Just flew in from Vinita, Okla., against a head wind. On to Houston in the morning.

Was met at the field by the champion host of the world, Amon G. Carter; also by H. L. Mencken. Mencken says, after seeing the South, he is going to start picking on the North.

We are holding a preliminary convention tonight at Shady Oaks Farm (all of us party advisers). It looks like a dry Vice President. Then those that are wet can go to the President's dinner and those that are dry can go to the Vice President's.

Texas starts entertaining you when you hit the State line. I thought the convention was held here, the way they act. It ain't just Houston, it's Texas that will show you something.

Yours,
*Will Rogers.*

## 595 Rogers For Vice President, With Slogan 'Scalp The Kaws'

HOUSTON, Tex., June 22. – Say, I got a great new political scheme. Captain Hickman, Captain of the Texas Rangers, wants me to run as Vice President on the Democratic ticket, me being Cherokee Indian, and Charley Curtis a Kaw Indian.

Hickman's theory is that the Cherokees have always licked the Kaws, and that there is many more Cherokees than Kaws. Pretty sound reasoning, and besides, nobody knows how I stand on prohibition. Coolidge was President six years and nobody knew how he stood. Religion–I am a holy roller. Farm relief, I never voted for, against, or even read the Mary McHaughen bill.

Vote for Rogers and scalp the Kaws.

Yours,
*Will.*

P. S. – Great trip in here by air from Fort Worth on the Texas Transport Mail Line. See Houston from the air. Jessie Jones has a sky line.

## 596 Rogers Lists Some Matters That Interest Conventions

HOUSTON, Tex., June 24. – The following three events have caused more talk at the conventions than Keynoter Fess forgetting his speech:

First, Mary Pickford nicking the Government for three thousand bucks. Mary is not only our sweetheart, but our best bargain hunter.

Then Mae Murray, with no preliminary advance notices, has a baby sixteen months old, which was thought an unheard-of feat even in the movies.

Then Tom Heflin's platform collapses. That was the first platform crash of the political season. Two others will follow in order.

Yours,

*Will Rogers.*

P. S. – Houston is as cool and sober as Beverly Hills.

## 597 Will Rogers Gives A Tip To Radio Listeners Today

HOUSTON, Tex., June 25. – Say, listen. I want to give you all a little tip. The minute you read this in the morning, run right to the radio and get the Houston Convention.

Now I know they are all terrible to listen to, ordinarily, but get the keynote speech of this bird, Claude Bowers, Tuesday evening. I was the first one that suggested him for this job when I followed him at the Jackson Day Dinner in Washington last Spring. He is a bear.

You haven't heard the Republicans called anything till you hear this fellow—comedy, oratory, facts and sense. Shut off on all the others, but you will thank me for tipping you off to this guy. He makes the Republicans pretty near as bad as they are. That's how good he is.

Yours for straight tips,

*Will Rogers.*

## 598 Will Rogers Is Sweating For Democracy At Houston

HOUSTON, Tex., June 26. – The principles of the Democratic Party were never listened to with more heated brows and perspiring necks than is paying its bodily tribute here. I have perspired for Jefferson, sweated for Jackson, fainted for Tilden and am dying slowly for Smith. I don't know that we are helping democracy, but we are certainly perspiring for it.

Yours,

*Will Rogers.*

## 599 WAITING FOR THE BENEDICTION IS WILL ROGERS'S VIEW OF IT

HOUSTON, Tex., June 27. – The Democrats always do the unusual. They come here with the reputation that they never can get a convention finished, and here we are at one and its main problem is how to keep the thing going till Houston gets its flag money back.

Smith has been practically approved on the floor of the convention three different times, and Joe Robinson for Vice President once. Still they won't go ahead and have it done officially. We are all just sitting here waiting for the benediction.

The platform it looks like they will adopt is wet on week days and dry on Sundays.

Yours,
*Will Rogers.*

## 600 SMITH IS ELECTED, SAYS ROGERS, IF ALL HIS SECONDERS VOTE

HOUSTON, Tex., June 28. – The only thing I got against Al was his seconders. If so many hadn't seconded him we would have been home a week ago. If his seconders all vote for him he will walk in.

And don't let anybody kid about the heat here, especially from Eastern cities. There is always a dandy breeze and it's cool at night. It's the hotel lobbies that are the black holes of Calcutta.

Let's see, this is Thursday. The elevators in the hotels are going up today.

Democracy has found a candidate. Now they are looking for a drink.

Yours,
*Will Rogers.*

## 601 'ALL OVER, HARMONIOUS,' WILL ROGERS'S CONCLUSION

HOUSTON, Tex., June 29. – She is all over, and don't let anybody kid you that the Democrats didn't nominate their best possible ticket and the same applies to the Republicans, so it will be a pleasure to just sit back and watch four fine men run.

Joe Robinson will make a great presiding officer over the Senate. I got a wife out of that State, and they do know how to tell somebody else when to hush and sit down.

The whole thing ended so harmonious that they acted more like friends than Democrats. If they could just hold the election now, before they have time to go home and think up something to call each other!

Houston and Kansas City both did fine jobs.

Yours drowsily,
*Will Rogers.*

## 602 WILL ROGERS FINDS TEXAS HAS WORLD'S BIGGEST RANCH

KINGSVILLE, Tex., July 1. — Just leaving to fly to Kelly Field, the training field of the world's best aviators. Had a great two days visiting at King's ranch, the biggest ranch in America—and the hospitality is bigger than the ranch.

Texas is getting ready to vote for Al. They kinder wanted a dry candidate, but they would rather have a wet than lose the post-offices.

Since these nominations have been made Coolidge could catch a whale and not land on the front page.

Yours,
*Will Rogers.*

## 603 WILL ROGERS FOR ONE SPEECH AND FOR STAYING WITH IT

MARFA, Tex., July 2. — See by this morning's paper where Al Smith is going to make sixteen speeches, all different.

Now off-hand, that looks like a pretty hard thing to do, but it's not. You could put sixteen different interpretations on the Democratic platform and still not exhaust half the alibis. And Hoover could speak incessantly on that Republican promissory note.

If I was a politician I would pick out one good reason and one good speech and stay with it. Lindbergh only made one speech all over America, and is a hero yet. But if a politician was that smart he wouldn't be a politician.

Yours,
*Will Rogers.*

## 604 Airplane Meditations By Convention-Weary Rogers

BEVERLY HILLS, Cal., July 3. – Just flew in home. If you want a pretty trip, fly over the Imperial Valley and the Salt Sea, then over the desert, mountains, fig orchards, then 10,000 acres of grapes in one orchard.

No wonder both parties did a nose dive when prohibition was mentioned. Oranges, lemons, alfalfa, filling stations, real estate offices, all this after looking for one solid month at delegates with nothing on their mind, only to get their side in office.

No wonder they only hold these things every four years. It takes that long to get a straight face for the next one.

Yours,
*Will Rogers.*

## 605 Will Rogers, Losing $5,000, Offers Another Coolidge Bet

BEVERLY HILLS, Cal., July 4. – I got to figure some way of laughing Mr. Hearst out of that $5,000 that I lost on Calvin. I don't know just how five thousand bucks worth of jokes is going to strike him. He don't need the money, and on the other hand, he may say he don't need the jokes. I will repeat to him the nominating speeches made at both conventions. The Republicans and the Democrats paid a couple of hundred thousand for them, so they ought to be worth five.

By rights Coolidge should be made to pay half this bet. He layed down on me. If he will pay half, I will pay half in money, or here is another way out. I will bet the five I owe that Mr. Coolidge will "choose" to run in 1932 in case Al or Herb (whichever one gets in) don't turn out to be what they are cracked up to be, so I hereby go on record as being the original "Coolidge for 1932" man.

Yours,
*Will Rogers.*

## 606 Will Rogers Discusses The Fourth And Tammany

BEVERLY HILLS, Cal., July 5. – Fireworks was sure popping last night. The Fourth has turned out to be a national benefit for the du Ponts.

Some guy went over Niagara purposely yesterday and run Coolidge, Hoover and Smith all off the front page. Shows what hard work, preservance and taking advantage of your opportunities will do for you.

Did you read Al's eulogy on Tammany Hall yesterday? It was mighty touching. He said any one was welcome, rich or poor, just so they was a Democrat. So it looks like the campaign issue this Fall will be "Who has done more for humanity, Tammany or the Red Cross?"

Yours,
*Will Rogers.*

## 607 Will Rogers Sees Great Demand For Front Page Places

BEVERLY HILLS, Cal., July 6. – I tell you these are sure hard times for fellows fighting to stay on the front page. Coolidge had to catch two fish on one line on his birthday to make the grade. A Belgian millionaire had to jump out of his plane and light running in the English Channel. If it had been two Summers ago he would have drowned a Channel swimmer.

Mayor Walker is out here in Hollywood trying to get in the movies. Hoover says the farmers have got him wrong, that he has always been especially fond of them, and I myself hope that Hearst will be reasonable. I know if I had won I certainly would have been lenient with him. The only thing is Brisbane is liable to want his commission out of it.

Yours,
*Will Rogers.*

## 608 Mr. Rogers Sets Out To Inform Dr. Work On Prohibition

BEVERLY HILLS, Cal., July 8. – I see where Mr. Work, Mr. Hoover's head man, says that prohibition will not be brought out during the campaign; that "the campaign we propose to follow will be informative and constructive."

Now, Mr. Work, I don't want to tell you your business, for you just left a good job to take up this one. But when you start in "informing" or "educating" the country on anything, you got you some job. There is millions more people in this country interested in a drink than are interested in political knowledge.

You start out with a drink and a lecture on statistics, and see which one you can dispose of first.

Yours,
*Will Rogers.*

P. S. — Say, didn't Clem's wife throw a cat into the electric fan, though?

## 609 WILL ROGERS PRESENTS A FEW VIEWS ON SPORTS AND POLITICS

BEVERLY HILLS, Cal., July 9. — This foot runner Paddock certainly is a professional, as far as the amateur association is concerned, they have been running him all over America to raise funds to send over runners that nobody would pay to see run.

It's unfortunate for Paddock that America don't share in the gate receipts in Holland. If they did, our association would let him go over. He was an amateur when he was running for the same money, but to go to Europe and run for nothing he is a professional.

See where Vice Presidential nominee Joe Robinson is visiting Al Smith, to wish him health and good fortune till March 5 next.

Yours,
*Will Rogers.*

## 610 ARCTIC EVENTS SLIGHTLY BEWILDER WILL ROGERS

BEVERLY HILLS, Cal., July 10. — It's been a terrible thing those airship men up north getting lost. But I want to tell you it's been pretty near as bad a hardship on us here trying to keep track of the whole thing. Who was lost? Who was found? Who is lost hunting who was lost? Who was lost hunting for those that were searching for those who were lost hunting the original rescuers? That North Pole from what little I can gather is kinder over-rated anyhow. If those brave men would devote their time and energy to electing a good Democrat, that wouldn't advance science but it would help a race of people get some postoffices.

Yours for science that pays,
*Will Rogers.*

## 611 Look For Candidates Near A Radio Outfit Says Rogers

SANTA MONICA, Cal., July 11. – Every man that was nominated to something or other during the late party uprisings are having trouble trying to pick out a place to be notified in that he was nominated. In case they have trouble locating any of these candidates I would suggest they look in front of some radio broadcasting outfit. They will be there from now to November.

Say, Mayor Jimmy Walker give a lot of the film people an awful roasting out here for being Republicans, and I am like Jimmy. I think any of us that are in the amusement line should naturally be Democrats.

Yours for reciprocity among comedians,

*Will Rogers.*

## 612 Will Rogers Sees Sense In New Democratic Move

SANTA BARBARA, Cal., July 12. – Say, did you notice who the Democrats grabbed off for stage manager? They are finally getting some sense and quit trying to appeal to the poor people with poor people. They figured let us grab off some rich men and make our party look like somebody had something.

There is nothing impresses the "common folk" like somebody that ain't common. This fellow took General Motors when it was nothing but a few bent axles and some old carburetors and put it on Wall Street and got away with it. Now, if he can combine all the loose nuts of the Democrats he is liable to repeat.

Yours for money in politics,

*Will Rogers.*

## 613 Will Rogers Takes Note Of Two Items In The News

SANTA BARBARA, Cal., July 13. – See where Tammany Hall has told her boys to work at home, where their line is understood. They are taking no chances on it being a liability.

See where Peggy Hopkins is going to marry an Englishman. If nationalities hold out Peggy ought to have quite a future–the bride of all nations.

Yours,

*Will Rogers.*

## 614 Will Rogers Deplores The Loss Of Carranza

HOLLYWOOD, Cal., July 15. – Just flew in from Santa Barbara and found a real, legitimate use for my polo field. We landed on it.

And speaking of aviation, I sure feel bad about this boy Carranza. I had flown with him in Mexico City. He spoke English, and he and I got very chummy down there. He was a fine aviator and a great young fellow. Mexico will feel mighty bad, for they were sure proud of him, and they had a right to be.

That's one of the sad things about it. There has been and will be lots of fine pilots lost in developing aviation to such a point that it will be safe for a lot of folks less useful to the world than these fine young fellows are.

All America grieves with Mexico, for the boys like him belong to the world and not to one country.

Yours,
*Will Rogers.*

## 615 More Notes By Will Rogers On Aviation And Politics

BEVERLY HILLS, Cal., July 16. – We all know what the aeroplane has done in war, commerce, science and business, but today we get a touch of it from the social angle.

Fred Stone, our most respected and versatile actor, arrives from New York City in his own plane to pay myself and family a visit. He carries a pilot, but he can steer the thing himself. There is nothing that guy can't learn.

Hoover called on Dawes yesterday. Charley told him, "Hell and Maria, I am glad I won't have to listen to that gang another four years."

Today Herbert runs into Calvin. Now wouldn't you just like to really know what those two say? Fish with goiters get a rest today.

Yours,
*Will Rogers.*

## 616 Will Rogers Has Decided It's A Hard Thing To Be A Hero

BEVERLY HILLS, Cal., July 17. – This poor explorer Nobile, the way they are talking about him it's hard to tell whether he was saved or lost. This thing of being a hero, about the main thing to it is to know when to die.

Prolonged life has ruined more men than it ever made.

Well, we can't tell much about election till the boys are both notified. I don't believe there will be much doubt, however, but what they will take it. We will soon be seeing whether preachers have influence or just endurance.

Yours,
*Will Rogers.*

## 617 REMINISCENCE OF OBREGON COMES FROM WILL ROGERS

GALLUP, N. M., July 18. – I had just finished writing about Carranza, my little Mexican friend, when now comes the death of another.

Nobody that enjoys humor could help but be crazy about Obregon. I never met a public man in any country with as many laughs tucked away as he had. After escaping one assassination while I was there he spent over $1000 answering congratulatory telegrams on his escape. He said to me:

"I can't afford to be missed again. It's cheaper to be hit."

He gave me a beautiful memento of my Mexican trip and came to the flying field to see me off. I think Mexico has lost a real patriot.

That country certainly don't deserve all this hard luck.

Yours,
*Will Rogers.*

## 618 WILL ROGERS THINKS SMITH HAS MADE A MASTER STROKE

NEWTON, Kan., July 19. – Al Smith did a thing the other day that I don't think has received enough publicity. It was a Godsend to America, and the smartest thing a candidate ever said.

Some photographers wanted him to pose in the act of laying bricks and he said:

"I can't lay bricks, and any bricklayer that saw it would know I couldn't. That's a baloney picture, and I am not going to stand for any baloney pictures during this campaign."

Now he may lose the photographers' vote, but he will gain the entire picture reading public instead. I will always claim that those Coolidge cowboy baloney pictures last Summer drove him out of the White House four years early.

Yours,
*Will Rogers.*

## 619 Will Rogers Finds Humor In Amateur Associations

TOLEDO, Ohio, July 20. — That lawn tennis association didn't monkey with Tilden long when they saw he couldn't win, did they? The rules say "You can write articles, but not on the same day you play." They figure it's too hard on an amateur to write and play the same day. It takes a professional to have that much endurance.

Outside the Maryland Racing Association, who barred Harry Sinclair's horses for running on an oiled track, I don't suppose there is any body of men in America that are as consistently humorous as these amateur associations.

Saw Amelia in Chicago.

Yours,
*Will Rogers.*

## 620 Will Rogers Is On A Tour Of The Training Camps

HEMPSTEAD, N. Y., July 22. — Flew down today to see Heeney training. That's the first one of the four camps I have visited—going to Al Smith's next. The way the whole thing looks to me, I don't see how this fellow Raskob can lose. He can sell every Democrat a car.

See by the papers today that Al don't know when he will accept the nomination, as they are having trouble getting the radio for him to accept over. That's a bigger thing nowadays than the election is—"When can I get the radio?"

Be funny if the night some candidate accepted there was static, and the audience couldn't tell if he accepted or not.

I sometimes wonder how Lincoln ever let the people know he was in a mood to do some running.

Yours,
*Will Rogers.*

## 621 Will Rogers, In Newport, Tells How It Impresses Him

NEWPORT, R. I., July 23. – Well, here we are in Newport. They won't let an actor bathe at Bailey's Beach. I just come to show 'em that actors didn't need to bathe at Bailey's Beach. Keep the place for them that need it.

In flying from New York we flew low here over the beach and beautiful homes. That's one way they can't keep the riffraff from looking in. If this exclusiveness looks to me like a good thing I am going to take it back and introduce it in Beverly Hills. We screen folks won't let a mere millionaire land in our town, but Newport is a great old place. If you are not a sailor or a millionaire you feel out of place here.

Flew over beautiful Montauk Point today. Say, don't miss that. It's a wonderful place.

Yours, in Newport, but out of place.

*Will Rogers.*

## 622 Political And Fistic Notes From Will Rogers In Boston

BOSTON, Mass., July 24. – It looks like this State of Massachusetts is going for Smith. If it does, it will be a blow against Harvard's English department. They are becoming discouraged anyway. Our English is getting worse than our habits.

Tunney is going to fly to the fight. Just before every fight Gene flies there. He would be a great booster for aviation if he fought often enough. He does that to disconcert the other fellow. That left hand of Gene's will disconcert Heeney more than even Lindbergh's flight did.

I told Heeney he should go to the fight in a captive balloon. Good luck to you, Graham McNamee, and here's hoping you don't have static.

Yours,

*Will Rogers.*

## 623 Remarks From Will Rogers On Politics, Finance, Sport

NEW YORK, N. Y., July 25. – Don't sell General Motors short just because they have gone Democratic. Raskob resigned and the stock went up five points.

Dempsey is to second Heeney. The people will pay more to see Dempsey as second than Tunney as fighter.

Tilden is an amateur again till the French tournament get their money back.

Yours,
*Will Rogers.*

## 624 WILL ROGERS TAKING PART IN A RELIGIOUS GATHERING

WINONA LAKE, Ind., July 26. – Am here at Winona Lake. It's to the Presbyterians what the River Jordan was to those foreigners over there in the old days. These meet here to wash their sins away every Summer. Will Hays will be here as soon as he comes from Hollywood.

Billy Sunday lives here, and I am really pinch-hitting for him. I am preaching not only on the evils of liquor but the evils of the stuff they sell for liquor. Billy takes up a collection. Being a Methodist, I won't trust these Presbyterians that far. I want mine before they get in.

Yours,
*Will Rogers.*

P. S. – This is the only place I have visited that Mayor Walker has not arrived as yet. Late again.

## 625 NEW VIEW OF MAYOR THOMPSON FROM WILL ROGERS IN CHICAGO

CHICAGO, Ill., July 27. – Mayor Bill Thompson today said he was going to try and do better and make Chicago the happiest city in America to live in. I have a notion to stay here and live. He made it seem so beautiful, everybody is trading their machine guns for hymn books.

Yours,
*Will Rogers.*

## 626 OBSERVATIONS BY WILL ROGERS AS HE FLIES ACROSS COUNTRY

SALT LAKE CITY, Utah, July 29. – In flying out from the East I stopped over Saturday in Cheyenne to see the frontier days celebration—the one they all got their idea from. It's a great show and the people as much as the contestants make it.

No private plane; still flying air mail with two hundred and six dollars worth of stamps pasted on me from Chicago to Beverly.

People down on the ground tell me that it is very warm crossing these deserts. I just borrowed a pair of mittens from the pilot.

Yours,
*Will Rogers.*

## 627 MR. ROGERS GETS A SURPRISE IN A CALIFORNIA AIR FOG

BEVERLY HILLS, Cal., July 30. — Flew into a Los Angeles airport this morning to wait till the fog raised to get over to another one at Santa Monica, when all at once a plane dropped down through fog that was thicker than smoke in a Presidential nominating room. And who crawled out of the thing but the kid himself, Lindbergh!

Fog don't stop that lad. I asked him where he was going and he told me, "Confidentially, East."

Say, what do you know about my old friend William Randolph White? He asked Al a question and Al didn't answer. When they get Al to hesitating on an answer, why he looks bad. Many a public man wishes there was a law to burn old records.

Yours,
*Will Rogers.*

## 628 ONLY PROHIBITION IS LEFT US, ROGERS FEARS, AS OURS ALONE

SANTA MONICA, Cal., July 31. — All America used to have to do to win the Olympics was to buy some steamer tickets over there.

The thought never entered our head that any nation could beat us in field sports, because we were the first ones that specialized in one event and had trainers. Now they have all learned and are doing that, so we are no greater than any other nation, after they get on to our tricks.

Same way with our mass production and buying on credit. They are getting on to that now.

So it looks like prohibition is about all we have on 'em.

Yours,
*Will Rogers.*

## 629 Will Rogers Sees Disaster Ahead For The Night Clubs

SANTA MONICA, Cal., Aug. 1. – See where they are really stopping 'em selling booze in the night clubs in New York. That means that they just have to go out of business, for you can't look at those shows sober.

It's this woman Willebrandt that is doing all this and she is a Republican. The Democrats will say that it is just a political move, but when you take away an out-of-town yap's booze it's more than politics. It comes under the head of disaster, for how is he going to tell the folks back home what a devil he was in New York if he can't buy some courage?

Yours,
*Will Rogers.*

## 630 Will Rogers Sees Olympic Loss Due To The Automobile

SANTA BARBARA, Cal., Aug. 2. – Santa Barbara has the greatest old California fiesta and celebration you ever saw. Even W. G. McAdoo was in costume on a horse with all the old Catholic padres, which shows that he must be for Smith.

About the only way the United States can ever win a race at the Olympic Games is to annex Canada. The fact of every fourth person in the United States owning an automobile is having its effect.

Yours,
*Will Rogers.*

## 631 Will Rogers Says Hoover Is Shortening His Speech

BOHEMIAN GROVE, Cal., Aug. 3. – Just blew up from Los Angeles with a head wind all the way. This is that famous Bohemian Grove Club you have heard so much of. It's wonderful in these great redwood trees. I thought the place was very exclusive, but I run onto Harrison Fisher, Jimmy Swinnerton and even George McManus, and Hoover belongs.

He is busy shortening his acceptance speech. He is not going to promise as much as he first thought he would.

Yours,
*Will Rogers.*

## 632 Will Rogers Pays A Tribute To The Injured Fred Stone

BEVERLY HILLS, Cal., Aug. 5. – Just flew down from the Bohemian Grove. Hoover didn't show up at their great show last night. Some advisers came and he had to stay and listen to them. That must be the hardest part of being a candidate, to have to listen to their hooey.

Somebody must have taken the dessert away from our athletes in Holland, they are doing better.

If you ever said a prayer say one for the return of Fred Stone to the stage. He has given more people real, clean, wholesome laughs than any man that ever stepped on our stage. What a character of a man he is! To see him is to admire him, to know him is to love him.

Yours,

*Will Rogers.*

## 633 Will Rogers Chides Americans Who Fly Abroad, But Not Here

BEVERLY HILLS, Cal., Aug. 6. – I meet people every day who say, "I have never been up over here, but in Europe I had some wonderful trips." Well, I have just traveled to Frisco, where we have two different lines running daily three-motored, twelve-passenger planes 400 miles in less than three hours, yet they are not full. Why? Because there is not enough foreign tourists who trust our aviators with their lives in preference to trusting their own countrymen.

A foreigner feels that if he is taking a chance he would rather be killed by his own countryman, but with us it's different. "Let us fall in Paris, or fall in the Channel, and we will get a bigger death notice."

No safer, finer lines ever ran than these two. It must be the liquor that accounts for our bravery on the other side.

Yours,

*Will Rogers.*

## 634 Will Rogers Tells A Secret That Is Kept From Hoover

BEVERLY HILLS, Cal., Aug. 7. – A reassuring wire from Mrs. Stone says Fred is getting along fine. That's great news.

Here is a secret, but don't let it out. They are going to tell Hoover Saturday that he is to go into the finals against Al. His speech is to be shortened to forty-five minutes. That's a long time for a man just to say, "I am proud that my country has chosen me for their standard bearer and I hope that I will be able to live up to that high standard."

I see where Coolidge this morning says that Hoover will win. Cal has to issue almost a sensational statement nowadays to get in the papers. He can catch a whale now and never even land on the editorial page.

Yours,
*Will Rogers.*

## 635 Will Rogers Hopes To Catch Florida Home Blown His Way

BEVERLY HILLS, Cal., Aug. 8. – Florida had a stiff breeze yesterday, which has developed with each succeeding edition in our California papers till by this afternoon's extras the tornado is sweeping the whole State. I am going to set a net and perhaps catch one of the best homes that are reported to be blowing this way.

Well, Al has finally dignified the clergy by offering to debate with one. In the old days he would have kidded that off with one wise crack. That's the trouble with our candidates. After nominations they take things serious and lose the touch that put 'em where they are.

Yours,
*Will Rogers.*

## 636 Great Things Ahead With Motion Pictures By Radio

SANTA MONICA, Cal., Aug. 9. – Did you read in the paper this morning about 'em being able to broadcast the actual moving pictures over the radio? When a lot of us old timers are just a sitting staring into space, and look like we are day dreaming, or going cuckoo, our wives will holler: "What are you setting there gawking at. Come on to bed." Maybe we will be looking out into the universe watching Clara Bow disrobe in her latest photo radio drama entitled "You ain't Seen Nothing Yet."

Yours,
*Will Rogers.*

## 637 WILL ROGERS QUOTES MOSES AS HE MIGHT TALK TO HOOVER

SANTA MONICA, Cal., Aug. 10. — Moses come west today, not the Moses of bullrushes fame, but one from the granite swamps of old New England. He, tomorrow, is to strike the mountains of California and out will come a commandment which will read, "Go forth, Herbert, and preach even unto the destitute corners of this land the benefits of Republican prosperity; promise aid to the farmer who needs succor, and is one; preach to 'em the parables of the protected tariff, lay ye heavy on the evils of the wine when it is red. And, for God's sake, save the postoffices for the Republicans."

So sayeth the words of Senator Moses. Amen.

*Will Rogers.*

## 638 WILL ROGERS DECLARES HOOVER SPEECH SURPRISED HIM

BEVERLY HILLS, Cal., Aug. 12. — Well, the whole thing Saturday over the radio certainly was a surprise to me. I didn't think Hoover would accept, but he did. He says every man has the right to ask the following question: "Is the United States a better place for the average man to live in because the Republican Party has conducted the Government eight years?" If we are privileged to ask the question, I will be the first to bite. Is it?

In the first place, Herbert don't know all about human nature, or he wouldn't try to appeal to the average man. No man wants to admit that he is average.

Did you see the picture and specifications of that average man they located last year? That took all the joy out of wanting to be average.

Yours,
*Will Rogers.*

## 639 WHAT WILL ROGERS DISCOVERS IN HOOVER'S ACCEPTANCE SPEECH

BEVERLY HILLS, Cal., Aug. 13. — According to the Republican press of the country, Hoover's speech ranks right along with Washington's after-dinner effusions and some of Lincoln's monologues, but according to the Democratic press it was just another Republican press clipping and is in a "class with all Presidential seconding speeches."

But as an independent I could see much truth and novelty in it. He was against poverty and favored education, even if you couldn't get into a fraternity. He said prohibition was a noble experiment, and he believed in noble things, even if they were only experiments.

Yours,
*Will Rogers.*

## 640 WILL ROGERS TELLS HIS IDEA OF POLITICAL BOLTERS

HOLLYWOOD, Cal., Aug. 14. – In the old days some politician had to attack the trusts to get in the papers, then in these late years he either had to rob the Government or be killed by his wife. But the new way is to bolt your party and jump to the opposing candidate.

They always announce that they will take their supporters with them. Their support generally consists of a wife who didn't register and two children too young to vote.

Then if he makes speeches for his new party candidate that will more than offset his own vote, so I know either party hates to see a bolter coming his way.

Yours,
*Will Rogers.*

## 641 WILL ROGERS SAYS THE PARTIES ARE WORSE THAN THE CANDIDATES

BEVERLY HILLS, Cal., Aug. 15. – See where Mr. Lowden now is complimenting Hoover, and on the other side Charley Bryan, brother of W. J., and also Josephus Daniels, the man that took the cocktail shakers off the navy, are out for Al. They say he is accused of being a wet, but he has never been accused of being a Republican.

All of which shows that when the votes are counted this Fall that every party man will be about where he generally is. No matter how bad any candidate is, he can't possibly be as bad as the opposing party.

Yours,
*Will Rogers.*

P. S. – Hoover will be here tomorrow. I hope he promises us Boulder Dam.

## 642 Rogers Hopes Byrd Finds Land Seeing Need Of Golf Courses

BEVERLY HILLS, Cal., Aug. 16. – You been reading about Commander Byrd's expedition? Well, he is starting next week. That fellow looks like he makes the best and most thorough preparations to do anything of any person I ever heard of. If he fails there is no use for any one else trying.

It will break the politicians' hearts to see this bunch of men leaving before election; they wouldn't care what happened to 'em if they only voted for their side before leaving.

Let's hope they find some land, for we are going to be mighty short of golf courses before long; especially since we started allowing the poor to play.

Yours,
*Will Rogers.*

## 643 Will Rogers Sees Candidates As Acting Every Minute

BEVERLY HILLS, Cal., Aug. 17. – Hoover opened his tour of one nighters here tonight. He is breaking in the act that will either get him in the White House or into the most obsolete circle af all—men who have run for the Presidency.

From now till November neither of the boys can be themselves. They are on parade. They are eating and sleeping in a show window. They are acting every minute.

Coolidge is the only one nobody ever knew when he was acting and when he wasn't. He was like a ukulele. You can't tell when somebody is playing one, or just monkeying with it.

Yours,
*Will Rogers.*

## 644 Why Will Rogers Approves Curtis's Stand On Farm Aid

BEVERLY HILLS, Cal., Aug. 19. – Shows you what ends we will go to for amusement in this country nowadays. They are even having notification meetings to tell the Vice Presidential candidates they have been nominated. In the old days that come in the nature of a warning.

I like my Injun compatriot Curtis's stand on farm relief. He said: "Appoint a Congressional committee to study the problem and when they have found out about it pass legislation in accordance." Now who could have thought of a better way to sidetrack anything than to wait till some Congressmen and Senators found out anything about it. That they don't know anything about it in the first place is why they are Senators and Congressmen.

Yours,
*Will Rogers.*

## 645 Will Rogers Says Speeches Have Spoiled This Summer

SANTA MONICA, Cal., Aug. 20. – A day hardly passes without somebody being notified of something. Notification speeches have just about spoiled what otherwise would have been a very pleasant Summer.

If we got one-tenth what was promised to us in these acceptance speeches there wouldn't be any inducement to want to go to Heaven. Did you ever see such love and devotion to the farmer??

And Smith, when he accepts on Wednesday night (as he probably will), I bet he will tell how he and Tammany used to lay awake at nights just to think up ways to help the farmer skin the city slicker.

Yours in sympathy for those that fall for all this,
*Will Rogers.*

## 646 Rogers Would Notify Heflin That Smith Has Been Nominated

SANTA MONICA, Cal., Aug. 21. – Say, wasn't that some trip Goebel made. Good thing he didn't fly across Texas, or he couldn't have made that time. I tell you when you read about those fellows doing things like that, it kinder offsets what politicians are promising to do.

I see where Smith has answered White, the newspaper editor, and told the preacher to get back to his collections.

Now he is acting more like his old self.

During all these notifications, I wonder if you are not going to notify Heflin that Smith has been nominated.

Yours,
*Will Rogers.*

## 647 Rogers At A Snake Dance, Couldn't Hear Smith's Speech

FLAGSTAFF, Ariz., Aug. 22. – I would like to hear Al's speech tonight but my boys and I will be up to the Hopi snake dance. Al used bad judgment in picking a night for the Tiger to howl when the snakes were dancing.

This dance is an old Indian custom, almost as old as some of the gags that Al will use tonight about lower taxes and better conditions for the poor man and relief for the farmer.

Hoover ought to get all the votes at the dance, for that is no place for a wet.

Here's hoping, Al, the static don't crab you.

Yours,
*Will Rogers.*

## 648 Will Rogers Disappointed That All Candidates Accept

FLAGSTAFF, Ariz., Aug. 23. – This has really been a Summer of acceptances. There hasn't been a refusal all year. Why do we nominate men that are in such receptive moods? I believe we have men in this country that would promise to enter a lion's den, if they were notified to do so, by a committee of what is humorously called our best citizens, and before he entered the den, he could be allowed to make a speech of acceptance, length unlimited.

One snake was not notified that this dance was supposed to be religious and he bit an Indian. Intolerance is even an issue among the snakes.

Yours for the varsity drag from now on,
*Will Rogers.*

## 649 Will Rogers Advises Flight Over The Grand Canyon

GRAND CANYON, Ariz., Aug. 24. – Hadn't seen a newspaper in three days, and after seeing one I had not missed a thing.

To prove that the snake dance is a sacred thing before the last Indian had finished a two-step with a six-foot rattler in his mouth why drops of rain begin to fall. The only way an Indian spectator could see the dance would have been to climb up on some funny looking white woman's shoulder, for there sure was queer types there.

If you never take but one airplane trip in your life, make it the one where you fly over the Grand Canyon.

Yours,
*Will Rogers.*

## 650 WILL ROGERS FINDS POLITICS DEAD OUT IN CALIFORNIA

BEVERLY HILLS, Cal., Aug. 26. – I don't know whether you noticed it or not but Calvin is fishing later this Summer than he has in years. Politics is so dead out here that there wasn't but one sermon on it in the whole town today.

Yours,
*Will Rogers.*

## 651 WILL ROGERS OFFERS A PLAN TO WIN DURANT'S $25,000

BEVERLY HILLS, Cal., Aug. 27. – My good friend, Mr. Durant, offered $25,000 for the best suggestion as to the enforcement of prohibition. I would like to grab off that $25,000. Then I could pay Hearst that $5,000 that Coolidge laid down on me for.

Here is my plan. Have the Government pass a law making it compulsory for everybody to drink. People would rebel against it so that they would stop drinking.

That's a funny thing about American people, tell 'em they have to do anything, and they will die twice or do it. If I win I will drive nothing but a Durant car.

Yours,
*Will Rogers.*

## 652 THE POLITICAL ATMOSPHERE AFFECTS MR. ROGERS'S CAR

BEVERLY HILLS, Cal., Aug. 28. – I just found out by the papers today why Coolidge wouldn't run again. His humilation over his son John turning out to be a saxophone player was too much for him, but wait till he finds out John maybe belongs to a fraternity. That would be the last straw.

I don't know anything about politics and nothing about machinery, but I do know that since General Motors have gone Democratic that my Buick won't pull up a hill, and it is the same hill that it used to go up on high before Raskob went into politics.

Yours,
*Will Rogers.*

653

## Will Rogers Has A Scheme For Stopping All Wars

SANTA MONICA, Cal., Aug. 29. — This Kellogg peace treaty—a lot of folks don't seem to be enthusiastic about it, but it's based on a great idea, and if he does get away with it he deserves a lot of credit.

I have a scheme for stopping war. It's this—no nation is allowed to enter a war till they have paid for the last one.

This, as you remember, was to be a very economical campaign, but on account of the Democrats having something to offer besides speeches, a voter is going to be able to accept some competitive bidding for the first time in years.

Yours,
*Will Rogers.*

654

## Will Rogers Sees Tunney Offsetting Any Literary Loss

BEVERLY HILLS, Cal., Aug. 30. — I see by today's paper that Gene Tunney says "the only joy to be obtained by losing is by facing a man of physical and intellectual equality." So it looks like his two fights with Dempsey were a total loss as far as intellectual ecstasy were concerned. But I imagine the financial returns offset the literary loss.

Two explosions rocked Hollywood this afternoon and nobody knows who set them off. Evidently somebody had heard one of the talking pictures taken part in by screen actors.

Yours,
*Will Rogers.*

655

## Will Rogers Approves Of Curtis And Robinson

SANTA MONICA, Cal., Aug. 31. — Did you read about the wonderful reception that Ireland gave Mr. Kellogg? That's a mighty fine omen when Ireland comes out for peace.

Vice Presidential candidates Joe Robinson made an awful good acceptance speech in Little Rock yesterday. I don't mean to detract in any way from either of our fine Presidential men, but I tell you both parties have got just about as good Vice Presidents as could be had, and that's not taking anything away from Charley Dawes.

Charley wasted as fine a talent as has been wasted in years on a job that is really nothing but watchful waiting.

Yours,
*Will Rogers.*

## 656 Will Rogers Hails Calles As A Rare Politician

BEVERLY HILLS, Cal., Sept. 2. – President Calles of Mexico issued a very unusual statement. He said: "When my time is up I will get out. I won't accept the job of Provisional President till one is elected, and I also won't at any future time accept the Presidency of Mexico."

In all our 150 years of politicians we have never had one say that. On their dying bed they believe they will some day get back into office. But Ambassador Morrow always told me that this was a very unusual man, this Calles, and that he had none of the earmarks of a politician.

Wouldn't it be great if Mexico started electing by the ballot instead of by the bullet, and us electing by the ballot instead of by the bullion.

Yours,
*Will Rogers.*

## 657 Will Rogers Urges Towns To Get Airports Ready

SANTA MONICA, Cal., Sept. 3. – They are having the air races out here next week, with planes coming from all over America, so get your town marked with its name so an aviator can tell where you are, even if nobody else knows. And get you a flying field even if you have to trade your Chamber of Commerce for it, and paint your name even if you have to trade your Rotarys, Kiwanises, Lions, Tigers, Tadpoles, Civitans, Junior apes or any other organized form of eating for the paint to do it with.

So Babe wouldn't meet Hoover. Maybe he thought it was some new pitcher they was bringing into the league.

See where Straton got more votes for Al Smith again yesterday.

Yours,
*Will Rogers.*

## 658 Rogers Sees All Religions Handicaps In This Campaign

SANTA MONICA, Cal., Sept. 4. – I have been libeled by my friend Brisbane. In his editorial he says that at one time I was a Sunday school teacher. Now, he is wrong. I went, but I didn't teach. I didn't even take up the collection. Some banker always did that.

On account of me being a candidate he is trying to drag me into all this religious controversy. You see, if he can prove that I was connected with a Sunday school it will lose me the Catholic and Jewish votes, and if he can prove that it was a Methodist Sunday school it will lose me the Baptists.

All religion in this campaign seem such handicaps that I think it's better to claim you are an atheist.

Yours,
*Will Rogers.*

## 659 Will Rogers Says Campaign Has Passed Acceptance Stage

BEVERLY HILLS, Cal., Sept. 5. – Well, it looks like everybody has accepted that is going to accept. So now they can settle down to see what chance they have of receiving what they have already accepted.

Being associated with national calamities more or less for years, you would think that Hoover belonged on the Democratic ticket, wouldn't you?

Yours,
*Will Rogers.*

## 660 Will Rogers Says America Is Now 'Sitting Pretty'

BEVERLY HILLS, Cal., Sept. 6. – Politics are receiving a lot of attention because we have nothing else to interest us. We don't have to worry about anything. No nation in the history of the world was ever sitting as pretty. If we want anything, all we have to do is go and buy it on credit.

So that leaves us without any economic problem whatever, except perhaps some day to have to pay for them. But we are certainly not thinking about that this early.

Yours for more credit and longer payments,

*Will Rogers.*

## 661 WILL ROGERS HAS CHAMPION IN TRAINING ON SHAKESPEARE

SANTA MONICA, Cal., Sept. 7. – I got a wire today from Tex Rickard. He has booked the fellow that won the Olympic Marathon to come over here and race, and Tex wants to book him with Andy Payne of Claremore, Okla., best medium-priced town in America.

Andy is the boy from home that won the foot-and-mouth race from Beverly to Claremore. Why, Tex's man only run twenty-six miles. Andy used to run that far every morning limbering up, just to get ready to run sixty or eighty miles each day for a whole Summer.

Besides, I am going to make a Tunney champion out of him. I got him reading Shakespeare, and told him not to meet anybody that was not his equal. So we can't be monkeying with some foreigner.

Yours,

*Will Rogers.*

## 662 AS WILL SEES IT, FARMERS ARE NOT NEEDING RELIEF

NEWTON, Kan., Sept. 9. – The farmers starve three years out of four but the good year is always election year. It really looks like the Lord was in cahoots with the Republicans, but if He is that would make you almost lose faith in Him. Even up to nominating time this year the farmers wanted relief, now they are so prosperous they would be insulted if you suggested it to 'em.

Same way four years ago, La Follette was figuring on their support, and he run into a bumper crop. So the only way the Democrats will ever get the farmers' vote is to hold the election in the spring, when they are broke.

Yours,

*Will Rogers.*

## 663 Rogers Rebukes Tunney For Criticizing Home Brew

CLEVELAND, Ohio, Sept. 10. – Did you see this morning's paper where Gene Tunney was drinking beer in Paris and said he didn't drink beer at home because our home brew was terrible?

Now listen, Gene, you can criticize our boxing skill, you can make light of our intellect, you can denounce us as morons, but don't make light of our home brew. You are condemning the very spirit of our American homes. It's made by hand, not by factory. We have had nine years' practice and we don't want to be told we can't learn anything in that time.

So you stick to your books. You may know Shakespeare, but you don't know our beer.

Yours for home industry,

*Will Rogers.*

## 664 Will Rogers Sees Babe Ruth And Hears About Night Clubs

NEW YORK, N. Y., Sept. 11. – Got here just in time to see the Babe win his own game. Why these people back here are all excited over election, while out West everybody is tending to business.

The court here today just passed a ruling that the night clubs that they had padlocked here would have to be unlocked, that "where do you suppose people were going to go between midnight and noon?" The judge says, "What do you think this is, Arkansas or somewhere?" They claim it was a political move in the first place to deprive the Republicans coming to New York from getting a drink.

Yours,

*Will Rogers.*

## 665 Will Rogers Sees Lesson In Fred Stone's Recovery

NEW YORK, N. Y., Sept. 12. – Been up today to the hospital in New London, Conn., to see Fred Stone. He was hurt as bad as reported at the time, but is coming along great. If the world could see what that man is recovering from it would be worth the accident, just to prove to people what clean living and physical fitness will do for you when you really need 'em.

Anxious to see the Argentine-United States polo championship. Saw this week's United States team play, but haven't seen next week's team in action.

As Maine goes so goes New Hampshire.

Yours,
*Will Rogers.*

## 666 Will Rogers Adds A Whisper To The Campaign Debate

NEW YORK, N. Y., Sept. 13. – Our clever little movie star, Bebe Daniels, don't overlook many sporting events. On the eve of the international polo games here she has just denied that she is to marry Tommy Hitchcock. Just before the tennis match she denied an engagement to Tilden, and during the Olympics she publicly denied a betrothal to Charley Paddock. On November 4, I hope she has the good judgment to refuse both Smith and Hoover, and when Christmas rolls around, if she is going to marry Santa Claus, why keep it a whispering secret.

As Maine goes, so goes the opposite way Mississippi. Whisper that to your friends.

Yours,
*Will Rogers.*

## 667 Rogers On Gang Killings And Other News Matters

NEW YORK, N. Y., Sept. 14. – I think some of these crooks are just getting killed to show they can have a bigger and finer funeral than their rival had.

It's hard to tell whether there is more guns or flowers at the funeral. I would rather have the undertaker's privilege, with some good high-class gang, than to have a seat on the Stock Exchange. In order to outdo each other some gangs will start raising their own flowers.

Two railroad events took place this week for the first time: John Coolidge went to work on one and Al Smith starts to ride on one. John had to go to work in an old New England town. It's the only place where he could find a room in America for twelve dollars.

Al, don't try to sleep in that hammock!

Yours,
*Will Rogers.*

## 668 Will Rogers Sees Significance In Smith And Hoover Trips

NEW YORK, N. Y., Sept. 16. – Smith says that this prosperity thing is a myth, and left for the West last night in an eleven-car de luxe private train to prove it. Hoover comes tomorrow to the wettest part of New Jersey, which trip is not only a noble but brave experiment. His audience will run about a corkscrew to the listener.

They again postponed the international polo matches to give the United States Selection Committee a chance to recuperate from their hard Summer of selecting.

Paul Block's 15-year-old boy gave $1,500, his lifetime savings, to the campaign fund. Education should be made compulsory in this country.

Yours,
*Will Rogers.*

## 669 Will Rogers Praises Wives Of Edison, Firestone And Ford

NEW YORK, N. Y., Sept. 17. – Just had dinner tonight with Thomas Edison, Henry Ford and Harvey Firestone and their wives. Say, there is the ones you want to meet, these three famous men, we know all about them, but you ought to meet these wives that made them famous. No frills, no put on, just three lovely wholesome family folks. Talked children and grandchildren all evening.

And say, Thomas A. pulled a good one. As you all know he is very deaf; well, he walked over to the window overlooking Broadway, and says to us, "Broadway seems so quiet." I think he was looking at it to see if his lights was working O. K.

Yours,
*Will Rogers.*

## 670 Will Rogers Bespeaks Oklahoma Welcome For Smith

NEW YORK, N. Y., Sept. 18. – Oklahoma, Al Smith is coming down there tomorrow, and I want the old home to treat him right. He has been good to lots of us back here. Don't pull off any snipe shooting or badger fights, don't even break his derby. Show him the State produces something besides outlaws, bo-weevil and comedians.

Tell him what a great territory we had before we struck oil and Republicans, followed by mortgages, foreclosures and impeachments.

Yours,
*Will Rogers.*

### 671 WILL ROGERS HAS AN IDEA ON FARM DEBTS AND FARM VOTES

NEW YORK, N. Y., Sept. 19. – As I write it's pretty near farm relief time. About 8 o'clock every night they get relief over the radio. Last night Smith marketed their surpluses at a profit for 'em. Tonight, Hoover, through co-operative marketing, will assist them in payments on new cars. Then tomorrow night Smith will take 'em in hand again. But you notice nights when there is legitimate entertainment on the air and the candidates can't get on why they don't seem to care what happens to the farmer. So it looks to me like the candidates are trying to relieve the farmer of his vote, instead of his debts.

Yours,
*Will Rogers.*

### 672 WILL ROGERS MAKES A PLEA FOR AID TO FLORIDA VICTIMS

NEW YORK, N. Y., Sept. 20. – Let's lay off politics today and get down to something necessary and worth while. I don't think we are taking enough interest in this Florida and West Indies relief as we should. Florida is in real need. The Red Cross needs much greater funds than have been sent.

I know giving to campaign funds this year when the competition is so keen has about got everybody broke, but I think Florida is worth more to us than trying to get the postoffices for the next four years.

Yours,
*Will Rogers.*

### 673 ROGERS DOUBTS THE VALUE OF CAMPAIGN SPEECHES

NEW YORK, N. Y., Sept. 21. – It's too bad there is not some machine or way of registration just how many votes a political speech gets or loses. I claim if we had some way of finding out it would do away with political speeches.

Coolidge made less speeches and got more votes than any man that ever run. Bryan was listened to and cheered by more people than any single human in politics, and he lost. So there is a doubt just whether talking does you good or harm.

Take your campaign contribution and send it to the Red Cross, and let the election be decided on its merits.

Yours,
*Will Rogers.*

## 674 WILL ROGERS ENJOYS SMITH ATTACK ON "POWER TRUSTS"

NEW YORK, N. Y., Sept. 23. – In Omaha Al relieved the farmers, in Oklahoma (near Claremore) he bawled out the Baptists, but in Denver he reached his peak when he told the truth about the power trusts. It's no novelty to hear the farmers verbally relieved, and to reprimand a Protestant is nothing new, for they do that to each other, but when you hop on the power trusts you are standing on the very arches of the Republican Party.

I had a joke about the power lobby in the papers and I got so many letters from power magnets saying, "there was no power lobby," that it almost made me lose faith in rich men. So sic 'em, Al.

Yours for everybody owning their own river,
*Will Rogers.*

## 675 WILL ROGERS FINDS BASEBALL BIGGER THAN THE CAMPAIGN

NEW YORK, N. Y., Sept. 24. – The Republicans of New York have a very strong candidate for Governor, Mr. Ottinger from up-State. Now the Democrats have figured it out that on account of him being Jewish, and Mr. Smith Catholic, that what they needed to balance the ticket would be some Protestant from New York City, and they got to looking around and couldn't find one. John Roach Straton, the last survivor, had left.

You hear ten people back here ask, "Who is going to pitch for the Yankees tomorrow?" where you don't hear one ask, "Who is going to be elected?"

Yours,
*Will Rogers.*

## 676 Will Rogers Links Corruption And Golf As Always With Us

NEW YORK, N. Y., Sept. 25. – Al spoke in Montana on oil corruption. That subject can get more applesauce and less votes from an audience than any subject ever invented during our time. Jim Reed has made the subject so entertaining that the audience instead of going out voting against it, they start practicing it. Senator Walsh adopted it as a motto and eliminated himself from the race. It was an issue in 1924 and Calvin won by nine million.

Corruption and golf is two things we just as well make up our minds to take up, for they are both going to be with us.

Yours,

*Will Rogers.*

## 677 Will Rogers In A Mixture Of Baseball And Politics

NEW YORK, N. Y., Sept. 26. – Everybody you see is nutty figuring out mathematical possibilities. If Smith can carry New York and Massachusetts and hold the Cubs' heavy hitters, and McGraw wins a double-header today and can carry New Jersey, and the St. Louis Cards lose the Solid South, and Curtis swings the Cleveland Indians' vote, and the Athletics get all the farmers, why that will mean that Hoover and Robinson will have to win every game, even if the Selection Committee don't know who will play the Argentines while the Yanks are taking New England and holding the border States runless, and stop all the whispering, why then it looks like Mrs. Willebrandt won't be in the same league next season.

Yours for statistics,

*Will Rogers.*

## 678 Will Rogers Says Women Make Poor Political Speeches

NEW YORK, N. Y., Sept. 27. – The whole campaign has switched from Hoover and Smith to Mrs. Willebrandt. Now, I used to think that no one in the world could possibly make a poorer speech than some man politician, but after attending both conventions and various dinners and public affairs, I have found that any woman politician can make a poorer political speech than man any time they try.

I don't know why it is but it just looks like the wrong women are in politics, for I have heard other women on other subjects make brilliant speeches. I believe their cause would get further if they would just vote and not try to explain publicly why.

Yours,
*Will Rogers.*

P. S. — Charles Curtis's daughter at Kansas City was the only exception, and I don't think she is in politics.

## 679 Will Rogers Urges The Need Of Relief For Florida

NEW YORK, N. Y., Sept. 28. — None of the other candidates won't draw your attention to it in their speeches, where it would do tremendous good, but Florida is really in great need of much more money than has been raised. I got a wire from Judge Payne, the head of the Red Cross, and he says that the need is tremendous, and have just got letters and wires from personal friends in Florida who I know wouldn't misrepresent, and they say the same.

Sunday they are holding a funeral for 2,500. That ought to make us forget "whisperings" and "issues" and "promises"; so, Al, I wish you and Herb, along with your appeals every night, would include Florida.

Yours,
*Will Rogers.*

## 680 Will Rogers Boosts Polo, Adds A Word On Prohibition

SPRINGFIELD, Mass., Sept. 30. — Saw that polo game Saturday in New York. That was the greatest game ever played. The best men and the best horses in the whole two Americas. Don't miss the next one, Wednesday, no matter where you have to come from.

Al made one great mistake in his prohibition speech Saturday night. He said, "We can't expect anything from the Republicans." Well, I don't know how we could possibly expect more than we have unless a man has unlimited expectations.

But Herb won't answer. He is pulling a Coolidge and is getting the Democrats' goat.

Yours,
*Will Rogers.*

## 681 Will Rogers Still Silent On His Choice For President

SPRINGFIELD, Mass., Oct. 1. – I haven't made my announcement for either man yet. Myself and Coolidge, I guess, are about the last to come out for any body. Some think Calvin will go for Smith in the end, if he is paying Hoover back for what Hoover did for him in 1924. Why, Hoover must have either been sick or out of the country during the campaign.

The Democrats in New York State are gathered in Rochester tonight to try and find some body to nominate for Governor. A good many of them are for nominating Al Smith.

Yours,
*Will Rogers.*

## 682 Roosevelt Nomination Leads Will Rogers To Rumination

SPRINGFIELD, Mass., Oct. 2. – Al Smith unanimously nominated Franklin D. Roosevelt today for Governor of New York.

Roosevelt will always be remembered as the man that any time as many as three persons met, either in conference or convention, he would arise and nominate Al Smith for President. You could just wake him in the middle of night and he would start to nominating Al.

His nominating days over, he is now going to take up politics seriously. He is a Roosevelt by blood, but a namesake politically. If he had retained his splendid qualities and stayed with the Republican end of the family, he would have been President, but I doubt if he could have retained those qualities and been Republican.

Yours,
*Will Rogers.*

## 683 Will Rogers Discovers The Height Of Conceit

SPRINGFIELD, Mass., Oct. 3. – Well, Gene Tunney got married today and everybody wishes them good luck. I thought on account of his going to Europe to marry that maybe he was going to get Shakespeare to marry them.

What will become of that author that has been walking around with him? He will stroll alone now.

My idea of the height of conceit would be a political speaker that would go on the air when that world's series is on.

Yours,
*Will Rogers.*

684 WILL ROGERS SEES LINDBERGH AGAIN SHOWING HIS NERVE

SPRINGFIELD, Mass., Oct. 4. – Charles Lindbergh holds the world's record for length of time he remained a hero from the time he landed in Paris until yesterday, when he declared his preference for President. That took more real nerve for a man with his standing to do than his flight did, for with these people that take politics serious they don't believe there is any way in the world if you belong to the opposite party, that you could possibly be any good.

You watch Coolidge. You don't see him coming out for anybody, do you?

Yours,
*Will Rogers.*

685 WILL ROGERS HAS A FLING AT PARTY TREASURERS

SPRINGFIELD, Mass., Oct. 5. – I been hearing appeals over the radio for funds and I thought sure it must be for Florida or Porto Rico or some equally deserving cause and come to find out it was the Democratic campaign Treasurer seeking first aid.

Nights when the candidates don't talk over the radio, why their treasurers do, asking for money enough to pay for the radio for the next night for the candidate. Both parties have got to a point now where they will take old clothes or second-hand cars, or anything.

There is peculiar charities in this country.

Yours,
*Will Rogers.*

686 WILL ROGERS SEES HOOVER REFUSING TO BE THE COMEDIAN

NEW HAVEN, Conn., Oct. 7. – Hoover spoke Saturday, but he didn't answer any of Al's questions. He acted like he hadn't read 'em. On the stage we call the man that asks the questions the "straight" man and the one that answers them the "comedian." I guess Herb figures "well you are going to make no comedian out of me."

If St. Louis is as big a surprise in politics as they were in baseball, I look for the State to go for me on the anti-bunk party.

Yours,
*Will Rogers.*

## 687 WILL ROGERS FIGURES IT'S SAFER TO FLY THAN DRINK

NEW HAVEN, Conn., Oct. 8. – Seven people were killed in the whole of America over the weekend in airplanes, and the way the newspapers headlined it you would have thought Nicaragua had invaded us. Yet in New York City alone, fifteen was killed and seventy wounded with bad liquor, to say nothing about Chicago, so it's safer to take a flight than a drink.

So much money is being spent on the campaigns that I doubt if either man, as good as they are, are worth what it will cost to elect them.

Yours,
*Will Rogers.*

## 688 WILL ROGERS NOW CONVINCED THAT BASEBALL IS CROOKED

NEW HAVEN, Conn., Oct. 9. – These candidates on their rounds better not hit the same town as Babe Ruth or they will feel like they are running for Congress instead of President.

Yes, baseball is awful crooked. It was all fixed to stretch the series out to four games.

New York City is all excited over the poison liquor, and they are thinking of passing a city ordinance to make it unlawful to sell it.

Yours,
*Will Rogers.*

## 689 WILL ROGERS SEES NEED OF HOME-RUN CONTROL

NEW HAVEN, Conn., Oct. 10. – Hoover has always attended all our disasters, cheered the unfortunate and cared for the maimed. Where was he when Babe Ruth unleashed death and destruction on the upper Mississippi Valley? Who is going to take up the cause of home-run control? It certainly has taught St. Louis a lesson. I bet you they will be careful the next time to watch and not try to win a pennant on the same year that it looks like the Yanks will win.

Smith and Hoover are gradually creeping back on the front page again.

Yours,
*Will Rogers.*

690

## Will Rogers Discusses This 'Speakeasy' Business

NEW HAVEN, Conn., Oct. 11. – This "speakeasy" business must be the most independent and prosperous business in the world, especially in New York, for no other industry in the world could afford to kill its customers off like that. They must run an undertaking business on the side.

I will say this for the police. There are lots of these places they don't know where they are. The customer never lives long enough to tell the police where he got it.

New York has notified 'em that if they don't quit putting so much poison in their liquor they will revoke their license.

Yours,
*Will Rogers.*

691

## Will Rogers Sees Candidates And Zeppelin Off The Course

NEW HAVEN, Conn., Oct. 12. – With this Zeppelin 1,200 miles to the south of its true course, and Al Smith, a Democratic candidate, 800 miles south of his true course, and Hoover going to New England, 100 miles north of what should be his true course, it's a cinch with such poor navigation all around some of these are not going to reach their destination.

But did you ever see as much ground covered and as many speeches made as these two Vice Presidential candidates are making? It's out of all proportion to the position. One of them is going to get badly fooled, the one that is elected.

Yours,
*Will Rogers.*

## 692 Will Rogers Sees The Zeppelin And Thinks About Lindy

NEW YORK, N. Y., Oct. 15. – Everybody is always advising the Government not to go into business, yet the Navy football team played to 125,000 people in Chicago Saturday. That's not bad business even for a Government. I propose they keep them playing every Saturday the year round and buy their own battleships.

Just this minute watching that Zeppelin flying over New York. You know that's quite a kick to see something that has been in the air for days, and flew all the way from Germany by way of Cape Horn. Lindy would have been in hard luck if he had gone on it with only two ham sandwiches.

Yours,
*Will Rogers.*

## 693 Will Rogers Deplores Competition With Politics

NEW YORK, N. Y., Oct. 16. – We opened up our show last night. Putting on a Fred Stone show without Fred is about like Ringling bringing in his circus and announcing that he is sorry but that the elephants, clowns and horses were not with it. Lindy attended our opening to pay his respects to the clever daughter of his fallen aviator friend.

That's been Fred's greatest worry, that his fall, given such wide publicity, might injure the game, but an accident like that might happen to any one.

Hoover opens here next Monday night. It's pretty tough for us, getting six sixty, when the other candidates are showing all over the country for nothing. Their leaders even conscript people to make 'em go in and listen to them.

Yours,
*Will Rogers.*

## 694 Will Rogers Sees The Cost Of Saving Money Going Up

NEW YORK, N. Y., Oct. 17. – Smith in Sedalia, Mo., read some figures and records of Republican economy. The Department of Agriculture had spent $45,000,000 more in '27 than in '24. That means

*Will Rogers and Fred Stone's daughter, Dorothy, in scene from* "Three Cheers."

that cost of "promise of relief" has advanced that much. Mellon's department had saved some money, but it showed that it cost fifty million more to save it than it did the same department in '24, showing that even the cost of saving money has gone up.

They have also been printing Government documents on both sides of the paper. I don't know how any one ever found it out that they were using both sides.

Yours,
*Will Rogers.*

## 695 WILL ROGERS DISCOVERS WHAT AN ELECTION POLL SHOWS

NEW YORK, N. Y., Oct. 18. – The Literary Digest is taking a poll to see how many people there are in the United States who are interested in politics that can write their name. Up to now there has been about a third more Republicans that can write than Democrats. Course, when election day comes and all you have to do is make your mark, why I think the Democratic total will pick up. Republicans have to learn to write on account of signing checks, but Democrats never have to be bothered with that.

Yours,
*Will Rogers.*

P. S. – Only two more weeks for Coolidge to decide who to come out for.

## 696 WILL ROGERS PAYS TRIBUTE TO A LOST AIR MAIL FLIER

NEW YORK, N. Y., Oct. 19. – It was a dark, rainy, cloudy day on the New York end of the air mail. No planes through in two days. I wanted to get home to my family in California. I insisted on going. It wasn't bravery–it was dumb ignorance and an unlimited confidence in all air mail pilots.

"We will try to get through if you insist." And we got through, clear to Cleveland. Yesterday he didn't get through.

I kinder feel like his skill saved my life; so "Hoppie," old boy, here's hoping you are piloting the best cloud the Boss has got in His hangar up there, and you don't have to worry about low ceiling, engine missing, head winds, or even whether the old rip-cord will pull in case——

Yours,
*Will Rogers.*

## 697 WILL ROGERS ANALYZES PRESIDENT COOLIDGE'S SPEECH

NEW YORK, N. Y., Oct. 21. – Mr. Coolidge broke his long silence and spoke Saturday at the unveiling of a Civil War monument. There was very little politics in his speech. It was mostly about war and monuments. While he didn't exactly advocate another war, he did speak most highly of that one between the Republicans and Democrats. But he did come out strongly in favor of monuments (on account of the granite coming from Vermont). He favors bigger and better monuments.

A little politics sneaked in when he insinuated that it was the prosperity of the last six years that made the money for the monument possible, so it was after all another Republican achievement.

Smith spoke in Chicago on oil and corruption. If I spoke in Chicago I would speak on "Prepare to Meet Thy Keeper."

Yours,
*Will Rogers.*

## 698 WILL ROGERS SEES A JOKE IN CAMPAIGN MANAGERS' CLAIMS

NEW YORK, N. Y., Oct. 22. – Of all the comical things, the so-called local party leaders take the cake. Smith's leaders have assured him he will carry every State he has gone into. Meaning he could carry all of them, but he don't like to travel so much. Moses, the Republican apostle, told Hoover today that Smith wouldn't get ten votes even on Oliver Street, and that Hoover was a cinch for everything east of the Golden Gate, and a chance for a split in Honolulu.

How do they know what people are going to do? You would think they had a sworn affidavit of every voter. Of all the "yes" men they are the prize. If either candidate believes one half of 1 per cent what any of his henchmen say, then Hoover or Smith neither one are smart enough to be President.

Yours,
*Will Rogers.*

## 699 HOOVER'S SPEECH HERE WINS COMMENDATION FROM ROGERS

NEW YORK, N. Y., Oct. 23. – Hoover dug up a whole new subject last night, and made the best speech of his campaign.

It was about keeping Congress and the Senate from having anything to do with the nation's business. If he had gone a step further and come out for their entire abolishment, I believe he would have been elected unanimously on the spot.

Smith is always saying, "If I get in I will appoint a commission to look into so and so." That's what fills poorhouses—people that have waited for some Government committee to act.

Outside of traffic, there is nothing that has held this country back as much as committees.

Yours,
*Will Rogers.*

## 700 Will Rogers Is Curious About 'Jeffersonian Principles'

NEW YORK, N. Y., Oct. 24. – I hope the Democrats win this election just for one thing. I have heard 5,000 hours of "speeches" on a "return to Jeffersonian principles," and I want to see what "Jeffersonian principles" are.

Is it just an oratorical topic, or is it an economic condition? I know that Jefferson was for the poor, but in his days that was good politics, for practically everybody was poor.

I just want to tell you all when you get through raving about both of these candidates, that Coolidge could start tomorrow and beat both of them.

Yours,
*Will Rogers.*

## 701 Will Rogers Sees One Way To Make It An Election Tie

NEW YORK, N. Y., Oct. 25. – Al was good last night in Boston. Shows what he can do if he can get anybody arguing with him. But Hoover won't make the same mistake and leave another opening. His next big speech is the very last night before election, and before Al can answer it the voters will be staggering to the polls, voting dry to protect the other fellow against liquor.

If Hoover wins The Literary Digest vote and Smith wins the one on November 6, that would make it a tie and throw the election into Congress.

Yours,
*Will Rogers.*

## 702 Will Rogers Admires The Big Family In Politics

NEW YORK, N. Y., Oct. 26. – The best thing I've seen in a political speech was where Chairman Raskob said he had eleven children. That's wonderful. If more men in politics would raise children instead of issues, we would have a bigger and better country. No wonder Al wanted to swing him over to his side.

New York is getting their disguises ready, and memorizing the various names they are to vote under all day November 6.

Coolidge gave Mary and Doug lunch, but took nothing off their income tax.

Yours,
*Will Rogers.*

## 703 Will Rogers Discovers Just What's In The Air

NEW YORK, N. Y., Oct. 28. – Saturday all the papers headlined Al Smith saying, "There is something in the air. I don't know what it is, but there is something in the air."

I believe I can tell him what it is. It's at least 200,000 words of "applesauce" delivered every night by speakers from both parties over the radio. So that's all there is in the air.

If every radio set went static from now until November 6 it would be a godsend to a suffering public and no loss to political knowledge.

Yours,
*Will Rogers.*

## 704 Will Rogers Calls Prosperity One Of The 'Dumb' Issues

NEW YORK, N. Y., Oct. 29. – Smith is broadcasting tonight from Baltimore through WJZ, Hoover is broadcasting tonight from Washington through Senator Moses.

Of all the "dumb" issues that candidates bring up to try and influence people how to vote, I think "prosperity" takes the cake. How a speaker can convince a man that he is prosperous when he is broke or that he is not prosperous when he is doing well is beyond me. If a voter can't feel in his pocket and see if he is doing well without having some total stranger tell him, then this Government shouldn't be in the hands of the people. We might as well have candidates argue with us that we have a pain in our stomach.

Yours,
*Will Rogers.*

## 705 Will Rogers Comes Out For Coolidge In 1932

NEW YORK, N. Y., Oct. 30. – I will say one thing about this campaign: after running for months without an "issue" they have finally found one—that is, the Republicans have. It is Smith. That's their issue.

Al sure is drawing the crowds. If I was him I wouldn't care whether I was elected or not. He can go in vaudeville and make more than a President 'cause there is always plenty of things to denounce as long as there is a Republican Administration.

Coolidge won't come out for either side. He is afraid it will be held against him in 1932. Paste that in your hat and remember it. I am the original Coolidge-in-'32 man.

Yours,
*Will Rogers.*

## 706 Will Rogers Sees Little In Campaign Promises

NEW YORK, N. Y., Oct. 31. – Well, the promising season ends next Tuesday, and at about 8 o'clock that same night the "alibi" season opens and lasts for the next four years.

To show you what campaign promises amount to, can you remember back a few weeks ago when the promise was made on both sides that "the campaign was to be run on a high plane"?

This campaign ends Tuesday, but it will take two generations to sweep up the dirt.

Yours,
*Will Rogers.*

## 707 Will Rogers Tells About The Nicaraguan Election

NEW YORK, N. Y., Nov. 1. – We sent our marines not so much to supervise Nicaragua's election Sunday as we did to keep them from being at our election Tuesday and getting into real serious trouble. We won't vote on Sunday, as we are holding our last political sermons then.

I bet you those Nicaraguans are just about ignorant enough to have nothing in their election about bigotry, religion, prohibition, pro-British, brown hats, bad English, 100 per cent or any of those great issues that we know mean the life or death of our country.

Nicaragua is perhaps so backward and primitive that they don't know enough to believe in campaign promises.

Yours,
*Will Rogers.*

## 708 Will Rogers Has A New Idea About The Vice Presidency

NEW YORK, N. Y., Nov. 2. – Al paraded in his home town here today. His reception couldn't have been any bigger if he had swum the Channel or stowed away on an airstrip. He started the parade at 11:00 o'clock, so early that Jimmy Walker had to accompany him in boudoir cap and pajamas. Smith presented Walker with the keys of the city.

Mrs. Al Smith paid us a lovely compliment last night by attending our show. Al was speaking somewhere too, but I guess she wanted to come and listen to reason one night out of the campaign.

Only two more days, and Coolidge and I are still holding out, I am for Curtis and Robinson splitting the Vice-Presidency between 'em. It's really too much for one man to handle. They could take it time about, keeping their names before the public while the other one was acting as Vice-President.

Yours,
*Will Rogers.*

## 709 Rogers Comes Out For Himself To Offset Coolidge For Hoover And McAdoo For Smith

NEW YORK, N. Y., Nov. 4. – McAdoo finally come out for Smith, and to offset that Democratic gain, why Coolidge came out for Hoover.

So that leaves only myself in the open.

I have been studying the two parties and here is their difference: Hoover wants all the drys, and as many wets as possible. Smith wants all the wets and as many drys as he can get.

Hoover says he will relieve the farmer, even if he has to call Congress. Smith says he will relieve the farmer even if he has to appoint a commission.

Hoover says the tariff will be kept up. Smith says the tariff will not be lowered.

Hoover is strongly in favor of prosperity. Smith highly indorses prosperity.

Hoover wants no votes merely on account of religion. Smith wants no votes solely on religious grounds. But both would accept the Mohammedan vote if offered.

Hoover would like to live in the White House. Smith is not adverse to living in the White House. And in order to get in there either one will promise the voters anything from perpetual motion, to eternal salvation.

So I am out openly for myself.

If I have any religion I have at least not advertised the fact. If I want the Constitution changed, or if I want it left as it is, I know that is the people's business and not mine.

I have never spent twenty years abroad, nor have I spent twenty years in the shade of Brooklyn Bridge.

I have neither lived off tax payers, or corporations.

If I was born of poor parents, either in city or farm I have kept it a personal affair.

I am not the greatest "Administrator of all time" neither am I "The greatest executive a state ever had."

I have never fed the Belgians nor have I kept Tammany Hall from starving for 8 years.

In fact so little is known about me that I must be just about a normal American.

If defeated I will have less squawks, or alibies.

I have promised nothing, and am the only one of the three that can make good, so to offset Coolidge and McAdoo I come out for myself.

Yours,
*Will Rogers.*

## 710 WILL ROGERS OFF THE TICKET BUT IS NOT DOWNCAST

NEW YORK, N. Y., Nov. 5. – Owing to jealousy, and me not paying my entrance fees, I find my name has been left off the ballot.

Now here is how we will fool 'em. There is a fellow running somewhere on the ticket called Thomas. He is a Socialist, so vote for him in place of me, and in case he gets in we will split it, I will run the Government and he can do the fishing. So vote for Thomas and elect Rogers.

The election ain't over till 6 o'clock tonight, but it's been over since last June. Just think. We got people in this country that have to wait till votes are counted before they know.

This is going to be the greatest lesson in geography that New York City ever had. They never knew how many people live west of the Hudson River.

Yours,
*Will Rogers.*

## 711 Will Rogers Found It Quiet For A National Election

NEW YORK, N. Y., Nov. 6. – It's so quiet here today it's like Yom Kipper instead of election. Taxicabs are rushing back and forth taking voters from one precinct to another.

We have to put on a new version of our show after election. Got a Hoover and Smith version just waiting.

The South will give the Republicans no more votes than they ever did. Only this is the only time they have ever counted 'em.

Both men's fate tonight is in the hands of the counters. That's like trusting yourself to a woman jury. I would rather have counters on my side than "issues." I want to hereby be the first defeated candidate to claim "a moral victory."

Yours,
*Will Rogers.*

## 712 Will Rogers Would Sell Democratic Party Franchise

NEW YORK, N. Y., Nov. 7. – FOR SALE–Would like to sell, trade, dispose of or give away to right parties franchise of what is humorously known as Democratic Party. Said franchise calls for license to enter in national elections; said right of franchise is supposed to be used every four years, but if intelligent parties had it they would let various elections go by default when understood they had no chance.

If in right hands and only used in times when it had an "issue" or when Republican Party had split, think it could be made to pay, but present owners have absolutely no business with it. Under present management they have killed off more good men than grade crossings have. Address Raskob, back at Chevrolet workshop.

Yours,
*Will Rogers.*

## 713 Afterthoughts Of Mr. Rogers On Notable Election Results

NEW YORK, N. Y., Nov. 8. – Offers pouring in all day for the purchase of the Democrats. All want the title, but no one wants any of the cast.

I bet preachers are looking for a new act more than I am after election. It will take them months to get their minds back on religion. Nobody knows yet who is Governor in this State. There is a Jewish fellow running, and if he gets it and makes a good Governor for four terms, why, the religious issue won't come up again for President till 1936.

Smith carried all the Democratic States he didn't go into, and Hoover had a cinch in all the Republican ones he didn't speak in. I believe a dumb candidate could have beat 'em both.

Yours,
*Will Rogers.*

## 714 Will Rogers Finds The Reason For The Defeat Of Gov. Smith

NEW YORK, N. Y., Nov. 9. – When the editorial writers get all through analyzing all the various reasons for Smith's defeat – religion, prohibition, Tammany, brown hats, prosperity, wisecracks, Raskobs and all the rest of them–maybe one of them will accidentally hit on the real reason, a Democrat.

Hoover would have beat Coolidge, if Coolidge had been running on the Democratic ticket.

While in Northampton, Mass., the other day to vote Mr. Coolidge found a house that rented for $32 a month, and took it. He is not only a President, but a detective.

Yours,
*Will Rogers.*

## 715 WILL ROGERS EXPLAINS HOW HOUGHTON DIDN'T RETIRE

NEW YORK, N. Y., Nov. 11. – Arkansas voted last Tuesday against evolution and Republicans. They don't want anything taught about either subject in their schools.

Houghton goes back to London as Ambassador, it seems his resignation was lost in the mails and didn't reach Mr. Coolidge till just as they had finished counting the votes in New York, so Mr. Houghton owes the salvaging of his job to the inefficiency of the Republican postal system and not as some "catty" ones thought to Mr. Coolidge's favoritism.

Many a guy wishes he hadn't resigned by being misled by the promises of a lot of "dumb" party leaders. You never saw a smart fellow like Joe Robinson resigning, did you?

Yours,
*Will Rogers.*

## 716 ROGERS FINDS HE CAN COMMEND COOLIDGE, HOOVER AND SMITH

NEW YORK, N. Y., Nov. 12. – Big boost for three of our most prominent men today. Mr. Coolidge says "we can do our own cruiser building without any European supervision" and that "we have no alibis to offer to anybody." Atta boy, Calvin!

This trip of Mr. Hoover's to South America is the smartest thing ever done by a President-elect. That and the Orient is where our trade of the future will come from. Send Presidents down there instead of marines.

And tomorrow night when you hear Al Smith speak you will get the real human side of a great fellow. He won't have to be denouncing anybody, and will be at his best, and will make lots of friends.

So, no kick with any one of the three boys today.

Yours,
*Will Rogers.*

## 717 WILL ROGERS GIVES HIS VIEW OF EUROPE'S ATTITUDE

NEW YORK, N. Y., Nov. 13. – We got one of the most stubborn murder cases here in New York. It seems the fellow that shot Arnold Rothstein is just bullheaded and won't come in and give up.

There was some little talk of even going so far as to arrest him, but that's been squashed.

Been reading editorials on President Coolidge's debt and armament speech. Several papers have asked, "What would Europe do if we were in difficulties and needed help?" So this is in reply to those inquiries. Europe would hold a celebration.

Yours,
*Will Rogers.*

## 718 WILL ROGERS SAYS HOOVER WILL PICK OUT ABLE MAN

NEW YORK, N. Y., Nov. 14. – Ambassador Fletcher from Rome on his way to join Hoover's party was by to see me today. You know I told you politicians that if Hoover was elected that he would just about fool you all by surrounding himself with a lot of able men. Well, he did it. This fellow knows all about South America.

I would liked to have gone on that trip and I believe I could have been pretty useful and taken a lot of unnecessary work off Mr. Hoover's shoulders. I could have spoken at all the unimportant events, that is, I would have been the luncheon club speaker. It don't take very good speaking for that. That's the training table for after-dinner speakers. Then he could have gone on at nights.

Yours,
*Will Rogers.*

## 719 WILL ROGERS DISCUSSES PRESIDENT COOLIDGE'S FUTURE

NEW YORK, N. Y., Nov. 15. – Everybody has been wondering what Mr. Coolidge will do after March. Well, one thing certain, after issuing that Armistice Day speech, he had no idea of being made Ambassador to England or France.

I see they have promised this Rothstein murderer now if he will come in and give up they will give him a medal and his gun back. I think if he holds out they will do by him the same as the other prominent guests, they will give him the keys of the city.

Why does every peace envoy always go on a battleship? No wonder Lindbergh's trip was so well received.

Yours,
*Will Rogers.*

## 720 WILL ROGERS HAS AN IDEA FOR SAFETY IN SEA TRAVEL

NEW YORK, N. Y., Nov. 16. – Pardon a mere comedian for entering this sea controversy, but if I was going to South America and saw my boat wasn't going any too good, I would swing over and keep in next to the coast line.

Course that's just a rough idea of mine and perhaps is not practical. I got the idea from some excellent air pilots that I have flown with. When things don't look just right they go the long way round and keep over territory where they have the best chance of landing in case it's necessary. But that's why an aeroplane is safer than a ship, or a bus at a grade crossing.

Yours,
*Will Rogers.*

## 721 THE RELIEF OF THE FARMER AS WILL ROGERS SEES IT

NEW YORK, N. Y., Nov. 18. – It's been a great Fall for the farmer. No matter how much his mortgages were, he could always turn on the radio every evening and receive consolation. On Mondays, Wednesdays and Fridays Mr. Hoover would care for his every desire; on Tuesdays, Thursdays and Saturdays Mr. Smith would succor him.

This was up to November 6. Then Smith lost interest in him, Hoover discovered that it was the Argentine planter that needed aid, so it looked like the poor farmer was left with no relief from his radio but a jazz band. Then Mr. Coolidge rushed into the breach, and last Saturday night the old tiller of the soil got his usual relief.

Yours,
*Will Rogers.*

## 722 WILL ROGERS POINTS OUT HOW THINGS HAPPEN FOR THE BEST

NEW YORK, N. Y., Nov. 19. – I am a great believer in all things happening for the best. Now, take Raskob. I guess it's just as well he wasn't a success in politics, for don't he go right to work and put out the cheapest six-cylinder car on the market? A cheap car means more to the people than all the "burning issues of this great campaign."

Now, maybe after January 1 Al will settle down and get his mind on something practical.

Hoover has to hurry up and get to South America before Calvin makes a speech and declares war on 'em.

Yours,
*Will Rogers.*

## 723 WILL ROGERS SEES A TEST OF PUBLIC MEN IN GOLF PICTURES

NEW YORK, N. Y., Nov. 20. – Al Smith has gone South to play golf. That shows that there must be prosperity when even the Democrats can afford golf courses.

I attribute Hoover's success to the fact that we have never seen his picture on a golf course. Nothing outside of a Senatorial investigation can ruin a man so completely with the general public as golf pictures can.

That's why Calvin has remained so strong. You have seen him in every other costume imaginable, but you have never seen him in knee breeches.

Yours,
*Will Rogers.*

## 724 WILL ROGERS HAS A GOOD WORD FOR THE COOLIDGE FUND

NEW YORK, N. Y., Nov. 21. – People that know them well tell me that the Coolidges are more interested in getting that $2,000,000 fund raised for that deaf and dumb school than they are in getting a job for themselves. It would be a mighty fine tribute to this gracious and charming woman for her to hand her old school that on March 4.

And this new Governor Roosevelt. Did you know what that guy has been doing for years at Warm Springs, Ga., for infantile paralysis victims? No, you didn't, for nothing has been said about it. Well, look it up. It's a real charity.

Yours,
*Will Rogers.*

## 725 HOOVER ALREADY MAKING GOOD HIS PROMISES, SAYS MR. ROGERS

NEW YORK, N. Y., Nov. 22. – Hoover is the first elected candidate I ever saw that kept his promises. He said he would follow out

Coolidge's policies, and I see where he is fishing already. I see where he caught a "dolphin." I suppose the Senate will hold an investigation now to find out what a "dolphin" is.

Hoover is putting in at Nicaragua. He wants to see some of our marines. He hasn't seen any since the old days in China. If it wasn't for the movie weeklies picturing them going from one country to another, we would never know what they looked like.

Yours,
*Will Rogers.*

P. S. – New York's got a new one, a "free lance model."

## 726 Will Rogers Thinks Football A Nuisance Like Politics

NEW YORK, N. Y., Nov. 23. – Today, Saturday, minds are not on politics, they are not on national affairs, they are on football. Did you know that football is becoming about as big a nusiance as politics? Millions of football fans are going to football games this afternoon. Mind you, I think it's a great thing. You spend all these years playing football and then you go through life waiting for somebody to give you a signal.

Harvard and Yale have been beaten by everything but the pages in Congress. They play today, to determine which is the worst team in America. I think it will be a tie.

Yours,
*Will Rogers.*

## 727 Will Rogers Discusses Football And College Success

NEW YORK, N. Y., Nov. 25. – The football season is closing and college life is about over for the year. A few students will stay out the season for the dances, and some of the players may take up a couple of pipe courses and hang around till Spring practice starts, but most of the good ones will go home for the Winter to show the clippings.

The college president will be looking over the gate receipts to see if he stays another year. Cheer leaders will go back to train calling. The alumni will start arguing over a new coach.

It's no trouble to tell the successful educational institution these days. It's the one that can afford a new stadium next year.

An old Yale man that is disappointed with life,
*Will Rogers.*

## 728 WILL ROGERS SAYS VICTIMS OF HIS JOKES DON'T SEEM HURT

NEW YORK, N. Y., Nov. 26. – An old friend of mine, Mr. Paul Block, hopped on me for joking prominent men. Well, they all come back in the dressing room afterwards and don't seem much hurt. Among the insulted last week was General Pershing, Barney Baruch, Herbert Swope and Charley Schwab.

He says I kidded Yale's football team. I did that up in New Haven with our show and the boys all took it good-naturedly. He says I owe Hearst five grand. That I admit. I have been waiting, hoping that Coolidge would veto the election and save me the five.

Now, Paul, don't take these big men so serious. When you meet 'em and know 'em they are as human as anybody. So the next time you come I will introduce you and you will come back and we will finally decide that most people need kidding.

Yours,
*Will Rogers.*

## 729 WILL ROGERS WRITES OF DEMOCRATS AND THANKSGIVING

NEW YORK, N. Y., Nov. 27. – Tomorrow is Thanksgiving. Mr. Coolidge asked us to thank the Lord, but to kinder let a hint fall to Him also that we are aware that a Republican administration had assisted Him in providing this plentiful bounty. But the poor Democrat, I don't mean him as an individual, I mean just as a democrat, the President could have just as well set by a minute as a whole day for him to offer gratitude for what's been coming to him. He wouldn't have known what to have done with the other thirty seconds anyway.

But all these storms and wrecks, is that a Republican visitation? But like my two Black Crow friends, "Maybe I shouldn't have brought that up."

Yours,
*Will Rogers.*

## 730 WILL ROGERS EXPLAINS NICARAGUAN ENTHUSIASM

NEW YORK, N. Y., Nov. 28. – I see where Mr. Hoover got a great welcome in Nicaragua. No wonder. I guess he and Lindbergh were about the only Americans they ever saw that weren't marines.

I see where The New York World suggests barring The Literary Digest from announcing the results of the election beforehand. They claim it takes all the life and pep out of the minority party. I would think the election four years previous would do the same thing, so why not bar it too?

Yours,
*Will Rogers.*

## 731 This Is The Country Boy's Year, Mr. Rogers Is Forced To Decide

NEW YORK, N. Y., Nov. 29. – Say, our champion New York University team looked like Man o' War till that bunch of Oregon apple knockers got a hold of 'em this afternoon.

It was no place for a raccoon coat athlete, up against an old bunch of wheat shockers whose college emblem is a pair of overalls. These old salmon giggers from the mouth of the Columbia had the city slickers strewn from goal to goal.

With Yale, Harvard, Princeton, Columbia and Al Smith going down, all in succession, it just looks like it's the country boy's year.

Yours,
*Will Rogers.*

## 732 Will Rogers Giving Warning, Congress Is To Meet Again

NEW YORK, N. Y., Nov. 30. – Well, Mr. Coolidge went down South in old Virginia and spent Thanksgiving, but you notice he didn't go there till after it had gone Republican. He used to spend his Thanksgiving in Massachusetts, but not lately.

With all our boasted prosperity, I don't see that we are any better off. The old turkey hash showed up as usual today and will be with us the next few days, just the same as it did when we was poor.

Yours,
*Will Rogers.*

P. S. – I am warning you now, that if something is not done to prevent it, Congress is going to meet right away, so come on, good patriots, and help protect your country.

## 733 Will Rogers Sees Cruelty By Western Football Teams

NEW YORK, N. Y., Dec. 2. – The Humane Society stops all cruelty to animals. Why don't they do something in this football situation by making it an unlawful offense for a Western college to assault, maim and disfigure the inmates of Eastern infirmaries?

After meeting Stanford yesterday the cadets said: "Who took the Navy away from us and brought these instead? It's more government inefficiency." And the Notre Dame-Southern California game demonstrated again that after all this is a Protestant country.

Yours,

*Will Rogers.*

P. S. – The people went Republican in Virginia, but the quail stayed Democratic. Calvin couldn't come home with them in the bag.

## 734 Will Rogers Explains The Lame Duck Session

NEW YORK, N. Y., Dec. 3. – Congress opened today. It's called the lame duck session. A lame duck is a politician who is still alive, but the government paymaster has been notified that he will become totally disabled on March 4.

Today's session was very congenial. They met, prayed, and adjourned. But wait till the Boulder Dam bill comes up. Then the City of Washington will get a shock to its national pride. They will find that the power lobby didn't just settle there on account of the beauty of that charming city. We shall soon discover the susceptible.

Yours,

*Will Rogers.*

## 735 Will Rogers Suggests A 1932 Job For The Marines

NEW YORK, N. Y., Dec. 4. – I like this part of Mr. Coolidge's message best: "Both parties in Nicaragua were pleased with the outcome of their election and have asked for the marines again next time. But I did not commit myself." Yes, I think I would let Hoover contract 'em for that one.

The marines will certainly be tickled to know they can get booking four years ahead. They have always just had to pick up little wars from day to day. Now they can kinda look ahead and plan, and have a permanent address.

If they satisfied both parties after election, I believe the Democrats will sign 'em up right here at home, for the November, 1932, follies.

I will get deeper into the message tomorrow.

Yours,
*Will Rogers.*

## 736 WILL ROGERS'S OWN REPORT ON THE STATE OF THE NATION

NEW YORK, N. Y., Dec. 5. – My November message on the "State of the Nation": The nation never looked like it was facing a worse Winter—birds, geese, Democrats and all perishable animals are already huddled up in three or four States down South. We are at peace with the world because the world is waiting to get another gun and get it loaded. Wall Street is in good shape, but Eighth Avenue never was as bad off. The farmers are going into the Winter with pretty good radios, but not much feed for their stock.

Yours,
*Will Rogers.*

P. S. – I don't want you to think this message is pessimistic. Mr. Coolidge is an optimist, and will be till March 4.

## 737 EVEN MR. ROGERS IS DEALING THROUGH THE STOCK EXCHANGE

NEW YORK, N. Y., Dec. 6. – If the Democrats had had the party incorporated and listed on the Exchange as "Democratic Hopes and Aspirations, Inc.," then let somebody buy ten shares to get it started, millions would have bought it on the Exchange that wouldn't think of taking it at the polls. They buy anything there worse than Democrats.

You can't sell a pair of shoes in New York without it's done through the Stock Exchange. I got an order in with a broker for ten subway tickets.

Yours,
*Will Rogers.*

## 738 Will Rogers Adds His Finding To The Report On The Vestris

NEW YORK, N. Y., Dec. 7. – Hoover is going in and out of those South American countries so fast they must be equipped with revolving doors.

That Vestris investigation certainly turned in a thorough report. They said the ship was wrong, the crew was wrong, the captain was wrong, the inspectors were wrong, England was wrong, America was wrong, the ocean was wrong.

The only thing they failed to criticize was the thing that caused it all, that was the weather.

Yours,
*Will Rogers.*

## 739 Will Rogers Picks His Team, Only Five, To Run The Nation

NEW YORK, N. Y., Dec. 9. – Everybody is picking an all American team. Here is mine: Edison, Ford, Hoover, Rockefeller Jr., Lindbergh. They will have to play basketball as there is only five.

But you let that bunch act as a board of directors and run this whole country. Take the whole thing out of politics. In ten years we wouldn't have a cent of debt, and would move Thanksgiving Day up to where we now hold elections, then we would have a real cause for giving thanks.

Yours,
*Will Rogers.*

## 740 Will Rogers Interested In Second White House Plan

NEW YORK, N. Y., Dec. 10. – I told you Mr. Coolidge would run again some day. Didn't you see where he asked the St. Louis Post-Dispatch to get another White House where you could escape the asphyxiation of the other end of Pennsylvania Avenue? That request couldn't have been made for Hoover, for it will take eight years to get it through Congress. I think that trip to Virginia the other day did it, when for the first time he saw Washington's and Jefferson's old week-end hideaways.

But he can acquire the same results by just shutting the gate on the house he is in. It's not the humidity in Washington, it's the humility in having to meet who you do. Every Senator with a hill east of the Rocky Mountains will start trying to peddle it to us now.

Yours,
*Will Rogers.*

## 741 Will Rogers Thinks Prince Would Have Been Safe In Air

NEW YORK, N. Y., Dec. 11. – With planes equipped with three motors, equipped to light on land or water, with pilots as fine as any country possesses, why did their Cabinet make the Prince spend two and a half weeks of antiquated travel? It wasn't fair to him or his sick father. They knew planes are safe. Why, in five years we will look back on this incident as almost unbelievable. We will wonder why his advisers didn't make him walk across Europe for fear the train might wreck.

Well, the whole world knows that had it been left to him he would have gone to that bedside the same as you or I would go to our father's—the quickest way. Because that's a game kid. You got to trust aviation in war. Why can't you trust it in peace?

Yours,
*Will Rogers.*

## 742 Will Rogers's Suggestion To The State Of Michigan

NEW YORK, N. Y., Dec. 12. – For her fourth offense selling liquor the great State of Michigan sends the mother of ten children to the penitentiary for life. I guess that will just about blot out the liquor business in the State. I suppose she was the last one selling. Any woman that tries to raise ten orphan kids in that cold State not only ought to be allowed to sell booze, but the State should furnish it to her to sell, and guarantee that it was pure. That would make her the greatest life saver in Michigan.

It certainly ought to be a lesson to people with ten children to never move to Michigan.

Yours,
*Will Rogers.*

## 743 ROGERS DISCOVERS A JOB FOR HOOVER IN SOUTH AMERICA

NEW YORK, N. Y., Dec. 13. – Didn't I tell you those Latin races are the most hospitable people in the world? Look, they are putting on a war just for Mr. Hoover's benefit. He can start right in taking over their war relief.

The Argentine Socialists are blaming Mr. Hoover for the execution of Sacco and Vanzetti. That gives you about the best line on the intelligence of the "Reds" that you could have.

New York has just appointed a new police chief. The murderers just wouldn't surrender to the other one. But this new one, he is just as high toned as they are. So we ought to get some results, now.

Yours,
*Will Rogers.*

## 744 WILL ROGERS HAS HIS OWN IDEA ABOUT BOUNDARY DISPUTES

NEW YORK, N. Y., Dec. 14. – Say, didn't I always tell you that Prince of Wales was quite a boy? He can do a whole lot besides look good and dance. He stood responsible for that operation that his own younger doctor performed. If he had been allowed to come in an airplane he would have saved his father two weeks earlier.

I do hope we are smart enough to stay out of this boundary dispute between Bolivia and Paraguay. Any nation that will argue over land as cheap as land is today ain't in their right mind anyhow. Oklahoma and Texas been arguing over a boundary and Oklahoma won. We made Texas take the land. I wish my neighbor would want my farm. He would certainly get it.

Yours,
*Will Rogers.*

## 745 WILL ROGERS WANTS DEMOCRATS TO PICK NEW WHITE HOUSE SITE

NEW YORK, N. Y., Dec. 16. – Didn't I tell you we would have nothing but arguments as to where this miniature White House is to be located? We will perhaps have another civil war to see which side of the Montgomery Ward line it's located on. I don't think it should be a partisan question at all. As the Republican party is the one that have to continuously live in it, I think they ought to at least let the Democrats locate it anyhow.

Just think, one of those filibusters have held up Boulder Dam for seven years, and when it came to a vote only eleven men were against it. Maybe one man is holding up the Kellogg peace treaty.

Yours,
*Will Rogers.*

## 746 Will Rogers Still In Debate Over Prince Of Wale's Trip

NEW YORK, N. Y., Dec. 17. – The best informed man in America wrote me this today in a letter, so I get paid for it. Mr. Brisbane says: "Will, the Prince obeyed orders in not taking a plane. The King is a link to the past, and must stick to the past. The aeroplane is a link to the future. He still drives to Parliament in a carriage. Once the duty of every Britisher was to obey the King. Now it's the King's business to obey the Prime Minister, who represents every Britisher and improvements."

I don't care how right you are, Arthur, and I don't care how careful Premier Baldwin was. I still claim he should have flew, or flown (whatever it is in English) and I bet the Prince will tell you so, too.

Yours,
*Will Rogers.*

## 747 Will Rogers Compares War To A Hockey Game He Saw

NEW YORK, N. Y., Dec. 18. – I saw the picture of the Paraguayan and Bolivian Army. Tex Rickard used to be down in those two countries. Why don't they let him put on that fight for them? I saw a hockey game he put on here Sunday night and war is kinder effeminate after it. He would build a grandstand, charge admission, and the peanut and hot dog and movie privileges would put even the losers on velvet. Let the winner meet Peru in the semi-finals and that winner meet Dempsey in the finals.

Yours,
*Will Rogers.*

## 748 Will Rogers Interested In Afghanistan's Affairs

NEW YORK, N. Y., Dec. 19. – Well, they finally stopped us from sending marines to every war we could hear of. They are having one in Afghanistan. The thing will be over before Congress can pronounce it, much less find out where it is located.

It seems the King over there thought he was adopting modern ideas by limiting his subjects to one wife per each. No wonder they threw him out. He was just old-fashioned and didn't know it. He wasn't modern. He was just queer.

Yours,
*Will Rogers.*

## 749 Mr. Rogers Has His Own Idea Of What A Man Should Wear

NEW YORK, N. Y., Dec. 20. – There is some nuts got a habit here in New York–I doubt if it has reached your town, for most of your States have asylums–it's to go bareheaded on the street.

Now, he has worn something on his head ever since his mother tied a hood under his chin, but he has never attracted any attention; so he lets it rain down his neck to show people that he bathes.

If your head hasn't got enough in it to carry a hat, why all the sunshine on it in the world won't do it any good.

We have a scene in our show where another comedian and myself come out with dress suits and barefooted, no difference from being bareheaded on the street. Only we get paid for attracting attention and being funny.

Let women leave off something, they do it much better than men. Every time a woman leaves off something she looks better, but every time a man leaves off something he looks worse.

Yours,
*Will Rogers.*

## 750 Suggestions By Will Rogers As To Cruisers And Peace

NEW YORK, N. Y., Dec. 21. – When the Senate can't think of anything else to argue over, they argue over "Which bill will we pass first?" Some think they should pass the cruiser appropriation bill first, and some think they should pass the treaty between France and America where they say "it's wrong to fight each other."

Being only a taxpayer and having no legal right, might I just suggest that the reason France says it's wrong to fight us is because we have more cruisers than they do? Now, this is only a suggestion and it may not be based on facts, but perhaps if we had more cruisers than England they, too, might sign a treaty saying "War is wrong with you people."

Yours,
*Will Rogers.*

## 751 Will Rogers Discovers Some Christmas Thoughts

NEW YORK, N. Y., Dec. 23. – Christmas finds the following watching to see if there really is a Santa Claus.

Kellogg is looking for some Senators' autographs in his sock.

Bolivia is trying to set Paraguay's whiskers on fire and burn up the tree.

Arizona is so sore at California over Boulder Dam that they have turned atheist and won't celebrate Xmas.

Ten thousand Republican candidates for Cabinet jobs are beginning to have grave doubts.

And 14,000,000 Democrats say it may be Christmas to some people, but it's just the 25th of some month for them.

Yours,
*Will Rogers.*

## 752 Will Rogers Sends Out Several Christmas Greetings

NEW YORK, N. Y., Dec. 24. – Merry Xmas to you, President and Mrs. Coolidge. Only two more months and then breakfast without a Senatorial committee. There ought to be time off for good behavior for a President.

Merry Xmas to you and Mrs. Hoover, Herbert. You are away on the ocean on a battleship, out of reach of Xmas postcards. That ain't Xmas, that's Heaven.

And Merry Xmas to you, Mr. and Mrs. Charley Dawes. Charley, lots of 'em have forgotten you after four years of solitary confinement, but not me.

And a last Merry Xmas to Charley Curtis before he leaves public life, and to the Senate and the House a Merry Xmas. May the literacy test never be applied to your constituents.

Yours,
*Will Rogers.*

## 753 Will Rogers Ruminates On The Christmas Spirit

NEW YORK, N. Y., Dec. 25. – Well, the Xmas spirit is over now. Everybody can get back to their natural dispositions. If there had been as many good wishes in the heart as there was on paper the devil would have to dig up some new clients.

Christmas will never be a real charity benefit till we learn to eat those Xmas cards. If we spent as much with the Salvation Army as we do with the telegraph companies every Xmas, why the poor would be fat all Winter.

But we can all go back to work with a clear conscience. We fed 'em Xmas and New Year's; now all the poor have to do is just to fill in the few meals till next Xmas.

Yours,
*Will Rogers.*

## 754 Will Rogers Tells Of Penalty Of Cabinet Picking

NEW YORK, N. Y., Dec. 26. – Mr. Hoover changed his mind and is going to Washington and break the news to the officeseekers, instead of having them come down to Florida and him have to feed 'em while there. That will knock those two railroads out of the biggest business they would have all year.

A President-elect's popularity is the shortest lived of any public man. It only lasts till he picks his Cabinet.

Say, this police commissioner has rounded so many crooks up and put 'em in jail that it's interfering with the theatre attendance.

Yours,
*Will Rogers.*

## 755 Will Rogers Sees A Flaw In Prize Prohibition Plan

NEW YORK, N. Y., Dec. 27. – This is a prosperous country without a doubt. Did you read where some fellow got $25,000 as a prize just for saying, "Make liquor so high that the bootlegger can't sell it at a profit"? Then the producer will sell direct to the consumer and it will only cut out the middleman, the same thing they have tried to do in every industry since the world began, and haven't succeeded.

Besides, where is your economic problem of finding work for your unemployed bootleggers? Now if a man got $25,000 for suggesting that, what ought some fellow get for suggesting one that would work?

A California boy suggested education, but it's the educated that's doing all the drinking.

Yours for bigger prizes and better suggestions,

*Will Rogers.*

## 756 Will Rogers Figures Out Another Republican Victory

NEW YORK, N. Y., Dec. 28. – Mr. Coolidge couldn't hit a quail in the old Republican State of Virginia, but he ruined those Democratic turkeys in Georgia. Another Republican, an old colored fellow, called the turkeys up to where he could shoot 'em. So it was really another 100 per cent Republican victory over Democratic trustfulness.

Coolidge calling Hoover to Washington now makes me believe he will turn the thing over to him now and not wait till March, saying: "Here is this Senate. You take 'em and wrestle with 'em. Me for the rod and gun."

Yours,

*Will Rogers.*

## 757 Will Rogers Sends Some Different New Year Messages

NEW YORK, N. Y., Dec. 30. – Before our usual list of millionaires issue their yearly optimistic New Year's statement, please publish the following statements by men who are not connected with Wall Street:

Percival Proud, an actor: "It's absolutely the worst season our profession has ever witnessed, and I see no chance for the better."

James Swap, second-hand car dealer: "You can't sell a second-handed car unless you take in a third-handed one. It's a tough year."

Jim Goodview, suburban real estate: "They are building the houses up, instead of out, so who wants any more ground?"

Sam Wildoats, farmer: "1929 just brings on 365 more days to pay interest to the people who are prosperous."

Yours,
*Will Rogers.*

758

## Will Rogers Has His Say About Theatre Seat Prices

NEW YORK, N. Y., Dec. 31. – The old year went out tonight through the necks of millions of bottles. It's a good thing the drys won at the last election. New York couldn't a carried any more. There's not an idle flask in the city tonight. If they would just give the poor the empty bottles and let 'em sell 'em there would be no poverty for a year.

Our musical shows are getting $11 a seat tonight. That's box office prices, and one patron was able to get one at that price at the box office, and dropped dead with amazement before he could get to it. It would take Coolidge, Smith and Hoover playing the Three Musketeers in Yiddish to be worth $11.

Yours,
*Will Rogers.*

P. S. – If the Democrats had listened to me and not entered a ticket at all this year, they would have been celebrating too tonight.

## 759 Will Rogers's Own Summary Of The New Year Predictions

NEW YORK, N. Y., Jan. 1. – Nothing much in papers today but just what I predicted to you the other day would be on New Year's Day—optimistic predictions by all prominent men who are doing well.

Mr. Coolidge: "I look for nothing but prosperity through January and February."

Mr. Hoover says: "I look for things to kinder drag along in a haphazard way till about March, then real prosperity will start and continue for four to perhaps eight years. After that there may be depression."

Mellon says: "The country is prosperous if they just let well enough alone."

Yours,
*Will Rogers.*

## 760 Rogers Sees Dry Law With Us While There's A Bottle Left

NEW YORK, N. Y., Jan. 2. – See where Mr. Hearst has offered $25,000 now for some plan to get the Eighteenth Amendment out of the Constitution and into effect. This twenty-five is being thrown away on a lost cause, the same as Durant's twenty-five on the plan to enforce prohibition. It's not going to be enforced, and it's not going to be taken out of the Constitution, and there is where I will win my five back on W. R. if he will bet me. But he is too smart to think either one of these will happen. It's in our Constitution and will stay as long as there is a battle left.

Yours,
*Will Rogers.*

## 761 Will Rogers Defends Boy Who Ran The Wrong Way

NEW YORK, N. Y., Jan. 3. – Everybody is a-picking on that poor boy out there in California that run the wrong way with that football. If I was an editorial writer like Mr. Hearst, Mr. Brisbane, Bruce Barton, Glenn Frank and all of those, I would ask how many out of the hundred and ten million of the rest of us are headed the wrong way? How many out of us have even had presence of mind enough to pick up a fumble? How many grabbed out of the scramble what they think is success and don't know till they reach the goal line whether it's the right one or not.

So come on, preachers, hop on this as your text. All I want is 10 per cent of that Sunday's collection to get this boy a medal for at least doing something different from one million other college boys. Even if it was wrong, his mind wasn't standardized.

Yours,
*Will Rogers.*

## 762 WILL ROGERS SEES NO COMFORT AHEAD FOR MR. HOOVER

NEW YORK, N. Y., Jan. 4. – Mr. Hoover lands at Old Point Comfort tomorrow. That's about the last comfort he will get for the next four years.

If his proposed Cabinet meet him at the train in Washington it should be a greater reception than Lindbergh's.

Mr. Coolidge also just got back off a trip away down in Georgia. That's as far for him as Chile and Peru was for Hoover. Mr. Coolidge took passports down there with him.

We are loaning Europe two financiers to show 'em how to pay each other off without any money, by just reorganizing and issuing more stock like we do.

Yours,
*Will Rogers.*

## 763 WILL ROGERS PAYS A TRIBUTE TO PERSONALITY OF RICKARD

NEW YORK, N. Y., Jan. 6. – The world is full of men who do big things, but when you meet 'em they are not outstanding personalities. Pretty near everybody is almost alike.

Tex Rickard was one of the very few outstanding personalities of our time. It's a loss that we didn't have his autobiography written by himself. He was a character. I wouldn't a missed knowing him for anything.

Yours,
*Will Rogers.*

## 764 Will Rogers Sees New Test Ahead For The Airplane

NEW YORK, N. Y., Jan. 7. – Say, it looked like we would have to shoot those aeroplane endurance guys to get 'em to come down. They beat all airship records and are going after the record the Arizona Senator talking against Boulder Dam made. When motors function that long, how could there be any safer transportation in the world than a three-motored ship with a good pilot?

I see where Mr. Coolidge reported to Mr. Hoover about how things were on his trip to Georgia.

Yours,
*Will Rogers.*

## 765 Rogers Sees Peace Treaties As Mere Writing Tests

NEW YORK, N. Y., Jan. 8. – These so-called peace treaties are a funny thing. The Democrats had one years ago, but nobody wanted peace just because the Democrats suggested it. We have had ten years of peace without any treaty but now the Republicans want to make it even more peaceful.

You ask 'em, "Does it prevent war?" "No." "Does it prevent peace?" "No." "Is it for anything?" "No." "Is it against anything?" "No."

I think the whole thing is just to find out if we can write.

Yours,
*Will Rogers.*

## 766 Will Rogers Discovers What The World Waits For

NEW YORK, N. Y., Jan. 9. – The big automobile show is on here in New York this week and the only change in a whole two billion dollar industry is they have all stolen the same low flat radiator cap.

If I was them I would advertise, "My car stands well in traffic." There is millions standing, to where there is not dozens moving.

One-half the world has no excuse for not knowing what the other half is doing, nowadays. They are sitting in a taxicab waiting for a green light, the most looked forward to thing in the world today.

Yours,

*Will Rogers.*

## 767 Thoughts On Cabinet-Making From Ex-Candidate Rogers

NEW YORK, N. Y., Jan. 10. – I see where Mr. Coolidge keeps conferring with Mr. Hoover. Looks like he might get in the Cabinet himself. Mr. Kellogg wants to get out after his treaty is signed. So why not let Mr. Coolidge go Secretary of State and keep the same old gang.

That Postmaster General has been a great booster for aviation, so keep him, and if he wants Bill Donovan in there as Attorney General, I hope there won't be any gathering or united bunch that will try and tell Mr. Hoover not to appoint him.

We have had enough of that for one year.

Yours,

*Will Rogers.*

## 768 Will Rogers Has His Own Idea About Witchcraft Murder

NEW YORK, N. Y., Jan. 11. – I see by tonight's papers the Pennsylvania jury sentenced that 14-year-old boy to life imprisonment because he believed in witchcraft, for that's all he had ever been raised up to be. Like sentencing one of our children for acting according to their religious beliefs.

No doubt about there being witchcraft in that county. The jury's verdict shows that plainer than the boy's deed.

What's become of an old-fashioned law they called "change of venue"? I think it's still in vogue, among the rich at any rate. The Lord certainly had that dozen in mind when he said, "Father, forgive them; they know not what they do."

Andy, your State's gone haywire.

Yours,

*Will Rogers.*

## 769 WILL ROGERS SUGGESTS NEED FOR US TO JOIN THE LEAGUE

NEW YORK, N. Y., Jan. 13. – I see where we sent a delegation up to Canada to ask them if they wouldn't prohibit liquor from being sent out of their country, but our committee is coming back empty-handed with the exception of just what little they can carry. Canada told them: "If it is against your law to bring it in and then you can't stop it from coming in, how are we going to keep it from going out when it's not even against our law?"

We will have to get into the League of Nations after a while, just to get other nations to help us take care of our own business.

Yours,
*Will Rogers.*

## 770 WILL ROGERS PRESENTS VIEW OF WETS ON THAT $25,000,000

NEW YORK, N. Y., Jan. 14. – The Senate is fighting over a bill providing for $25,000,000 more to add to the prohibition enforcement. The drys claim they need the extra money to get more evidence. The wets claim: "Why should we furnish the drys money for evidence? We have to buy our evidence ourselves."

Since Morrow did some real good for his country and received such praise, our rich men are beginning to realize that you got to be something besides rich, to be favorably known nowadays. J. P. Morgan is the latest recruit.

Yours,
*Will Rogers.*

## 771 PEACE TREATY SIGNED BLIND, ROGERS SAYS, TO HURRY CRUISERS

NEW YORK, N. Y., Jan. 15. – Borah and Kellogg wanted peace without explanation. Jim Reed and Moses (imagine these two wanting same things), they wanted peace including explanation. They all compromised with the following footnote to Europe:

"We had the treaty explained (but don't let that mislead you), we learned no more from the explanation than we did from the treaty. So we hereby sign blind, in order to hurry on with the cruiser bill, and trust and pray that there is nothing in the treaty that interferes with the Monroe Doctrine, farm relief, prohibition or birth control."

Yours,
*Will Rogers.*

## 772 WILL ROGERS GIVES HIS IDEA OF MR. HOOVER'S CABINET

NEW YORK, N. Y., Jan. 16. – The favorite sport now of all newspapers and politicians is picking Mr. Hoover's Cabinet out for him.

Anybody that has ever endorsed a cigarette has been named to be on it. I don't care how many of these "write-up" cabinets you have been picked on. The only one that is going to draw any salary is the one Mr. Hoover picks himself. He is going to fool you when he picks his "all American."

He is going to have so many business men on there that he will make politicians wish they had taken up some other life.

Yours,
*Will Rogers.*

## 773 WILL ROGERS CITES A REASON FOR KEEPING DEMOCRACY ALIVE

NEW YORK, N. Y., Jan. 17. – Al Smith made a mighty nice, straightforward speech last night over the radio. And it's a good idea to not let the party die down, for you got to watch. You let the Democrats not be looking for just a minute and one of them Republicans will grab that Washington Monument and light out with it.

I hated to see Al passing the hat for the rich Democrats. He is too big a man to be handed a tin cup and sent out on the highways.

Yours,
*Will Rogers.*

## 774 AS TO JOBS AND VACATIONS: A FEW NOTES BY WILL ROGERS

NEW YORK, N. Y., Jan. 18. – Say, Al Smith landed a job in a bank here yesterday. Leaves on his vacation to Florida Sunday.

Mr. Hoover has conferred with about everybody there is in regard to work but Sandino and Peggy Joyce. He leaves for Florida Monday to draw straws for his Cabinet.

If California can't land Mr. Coolidge after March 4, why we will just have to console ourselves with Aimee and Ben Turpin.

Yours,
*Will Rogers.*

## 775 WILL ROGERS ANNOUNCES MR. HOOVER'S DEPARTURE

NEW YORK, N. Y., Jan. 20. – Mr. Hoover leaves the Employment Bureau today for a much-needed vacation, this time on a goodwill mission to Florida to personally thank them for their excellent judgment shown in the Republican primaries on Nov. 6 last.

Train stops are only scheduled through the old rock-ribbed Republican States of Virginia and North Carolina, where they will take on enough provisions to carry them through rebel territory.

Any applicant from Pennsylvania that don't receive a Cabinet appointment will know that they have been "hexed."

Yours,
*Will Rogers.*

## 776 MR. ROGERS'S OBSERVATIONS ON THE NEW TRAFFIC PLAN

NEW YORK, N. Y., Jan. 21. – This fellow Whalen is really trying his best to do something with this traffic situation in New York, and everybody is hoping he gets away with it.

For the first time in New York, he is making pedestrians act like an automobile. Now, whether they know that much depends on the people. Pedestrians must hold out their hand when getting ready to turn. Continually doing this is going to be hard for just a few of us here in New York.

Taxicabs must go over to New Jersey to turn right, and to Long Island to turn left.

Your theatre ticket is good for any theatre you happen to pass by.

Yours,
*Will Rogers.*

## 777 Mr. Rogers Recalls That He Was Original Morrow Man

NEW YORK, N. Y., Jan. 22. — I only got one distinction. I was the original Morrow for Secretary of State man. It will be offered to him. Hope he takes it. He is a great fellow. Our present friendly relations with Mexico are due to nothing in the world but the sheer personality of that man. A trained diplomat would never have adopted his plan, and it was the only one that would have worked. It would have been mighty easy to spoil things down there.

Yours,

*Will Rogers.*

P. S. — California had rain. You give us plenty of moisture in the ground and Florida can have all your Hoovers, Morrows, Works, Striblings and Dempseys.

## 778 Mr. Rogers On That Fund For Enforcing Prohibition

NEW YORK, N. Y., Jan. 23. — It's hard to get money out of the Senate for anything but for politics.

Yesterday the Democrats bet Mr. Hoover $24,000,000 (of the people's money) that he couldn't enforce prohibition. They are going to put the whole thing up to him by saying, "We give you plenty of money to do it."

That would be just like asking these Senators why they are not all great statesmen. We pay 'em enough money to be statesmen on.

Watch Coolidge veto it.

Yours,

*Will Rogers.*

P. S. — Some woman here in court yesterday said she had forgot whether she shot her husband or not. Suppose she intended to but just got busy on something important and forgot it.

## 779 Will Rogers's Idea Of Uses For That Twenty-four Million

NEW YORK, N. Y., Jan. 24. — The Democrats are having a tough time finding somebody to give the $24,000,000 to. Mellon says: "I don't need it." Coolidge says: "Don't leave it on my doorstep."

Hoover says: "My charity distributing days are over. Don't sic it on to me."

What they should do with it is take $1,500,000 and pay off Raskob, Kenny and Lehmann, get Bishop Cannon a new typewriter and take the other $22,000,000 and establish an endowment fund to take care of Senators whose political schemes backfire.

Yours,
*Will Rogers.*

## 780 Mr. Rogers Has His Own Views On Stock Exchange Seats

NEW YORK, N. Y., Jan. 25. – Certainly a great business opportunity showed up in the papers today–"No training, no conscience necessary; all you need is six hundred thousand dollars, but you get it back the first good day."

Wall Street is dividing the kitty with 275 more members. The eleven hundred they did have could take care of Mr. Sap but when Mrs. Sap started playing they just had to go out and get more help to take in the dough.

The farmers ought to go in together and buy one seat. That would relieve the whole bunch.

Yours,
*Will Rogers.*

P. S. – Didn't we used to have a word during the war called non-essential?

## 781 Mr. Rogers Has Phone Number Of The Life-Saving Capt. Fried

NEW YORK, N. Y., Jan. 27. – New York gives its annual reception again to Captain Fried of the America.

First Officer Manning and his men are just starting in on their life-saving careers. They are practically amateurs yet. But, this Fried–it's getting so a boat won't make up its mind to sink till they know he is out on the ocean some place. He takes on more passengers in the middle of the ocean than most ships do at port. If Hoover don't put him on his Cabinet, why Mussolini will on his. An S O S is that bird's telephone number.

So, viva the whole America crew and the generous passengers on board!

Yours,
*Will Rogers.*

## 782 Mr. Rogers On Getting Along Well With One's Neighbors

NEW YORK, N. Y., Jan. 28. – Just had a long visit and lunch with Ambassador Morrow. He is tickled to get back to Mexico, as he feels that there is where he can do the most good to his country. He told me of many helpful changes going on there now.

Coolidge will have no brighter accomplishment to look back on than his judgment in sending Morrow to that post, for after all, peace and good-will with your neighbor is a nation's greatest recommendation. You show me a man that gets on fine with his neighbors–no matter how often he beats his wife–and he must be a man with some good in him, even if it's just good judgment.

Morrow changed the whole system of diplomacy, from a drawing room to a pencil and some figures.

Yours,
*Will Rogers.*

## 783 If You Would Be President Rise Early, Mr. Rogers Warns

NEW YORK, N. Y., Jan. 29. – Al said he didn't know Hoover was in Florida. Yes, he has been in there since November.

Hoover invited him over at 9 o'clock, and Al said, "I am a big town boy, I don't get out that early."

Then, even at 11, Al had to go without his breakfast.

That's a tip to you, Al. All the boys we are electing President nowadays are early risers.

Kenny went along to referee, Raskob to try and pick up a contribution to the Democratic deficit.

Yours,
*Will Rogers.*

## 784 Will Rogers Discusses Cruisers And Rights At Sea

NEW YORK, N. Y., Jan. 30. – President Coolidge wants the cruisers voted for during his administration and paid for out of Hoover's budget.

Mr. Coolidge is going to have his budget balanced when he goes out, if he has to give out some I O U's.

Senator Borah wants a conference to decide "your rights on the seas, during a war which you haven't yet been able to get into."

That is just like holding a convention to discuss "the rights of innocent bystanders during a fight between police and bandits."

He only has one right and that's the right of a decent burial.

Yours,

*Will Rogers.*

## 785 Will Rogers Takes A Look At The Einstein Theory

NEW YORK, N. Y., Jan. 31. – This Einstein has proven a great comfort to us that always knew we didn't know much. He has shown us that the fellows that we thought was smart is just as dumb as we are.

The Senate investigates everything. It would be worth the money to see 'em light on this, still I guess they would do about as well as they do on some other things.

It's printed in the papers here after coming over by radiograph. It's either a laundry slip or a night club bill. I think this Dutchman is just having a quiet laugh at the world's expense.

Yours,

*Will Rogers.*

## 786 Will Rogers Suggests A Way To Use That $24,000,000

NEW YORK, N. Y., Feb. 1. – The drys are still trying to figure out some way of making Mellon take that twenty-four million for prohibition enforcement. Be a good joke on 'em if Mellon used it trying to enforce prohibition in one wing of the Capital.

I see some of the Senators are not for building the cruisers till we get a war booked. So we will have to figure out some kind of guarantee to those fellows that we will scare 'em up a war.

The Democrats are so used to running second in everything, they are satisfied with the second best navy.

Yours,

*Will Rogers.*

## 787 WILL ROGERS FINDS THE NEWS OF FISH AND GAME VARIETY

NEW YORK, N. Y., Feb. 3. – This week-end news comes under the Fish and Game Department. Our two leading actors left the humans flat last week.

Taking them up alphabetically, Mr. Coolidge went clear to Florida to speak to the birds and casually remind them that their luxury was directly traceable to a Republican Administration, that under a Democratic regime they would no doubt revert to slavery.

While Mr. Coolidge was orating to the jaybird, the woodpecker, and the robin red breast on the advantages of prosperity, why Mr. Hoover fought off and defeated single-handed a 45-pound sailfish that was trying to get into his Cabinet.

Yours,

*Will Rogers.*

P. S. – The Virginia quail are wondering when Carter Glass will build a sanctuary for them, as they can't continually rely on poor marksmanship.

## 788 WILL ROGERS ASKED, HE SAYS, TO BE TOASTMASTER AT A FIGHT

NEW YORK, N. Y., Feb. 4. – Jack Dempsey invited me to Miami to be master of ceremonies at the Stribling-Sharkey fight to see who will be Secretary of War. I felt it an honor when you know that Hoover, Coolidge and Smith are all available.

I don't know what the duties of a toastmaster at a fight are, but I would like to tell 'em the advantages of California under a Hoover administration. We have imported silk worms in California that are working twelve months a year, where in Japan they only worked three. They ain't organized yet.

Let's see. Tomorrow is Tuesday. Donovan is out of the Cabinet on Tuesdays.

Yours,

*Will Rogers.*

P. S. – Watch your tariff, Republicans. Grundy is loose again.

## 789 MR. ROGERS SEES SUGAR WITCHES PLAGUING REED SMOOT AGAIN

NEW YORK, N. Y., Feb. 5. – Reed Smoot is being "hexed" again with his cheap foreign sugar. To Smoot the Spanish-American

War was our greatest blunder, for both countries we freed grew sugar.

Kellogg can make peace or war, the Mississippi States can wash to the sea, liquors from the four corners of the earth can arrive untariffed, hides and T-bone steaks from the Argentine, wheat from Russia, but Reed Smoot prowls the docks at night to see that no "sweetening" is smuggled in.

When Smoot gets through raising the tariff on sugar, Lindbergh couldn't fly over it with a box of chocolates.

Where Brigham Young's monument was erected from old marriage certificates, Smoot's will be made entirely of sugar beets.

Yours,

*Will Rogers.*

P. S. – Watch 'em pay off Grundy at the first session of the new Congress.

## 790 Will Rogers Assured Now Of Peace Treaty's Value

NEW YORK, N. Y., Feb. 6. – People that had a doubt about that peace treaty amounting to much can rest more assured now. They voted the cruisers.

Heflin found a cross on one of the flags used in the navy. He wants to make it null and void to have anything to do with any flag that Betsy Ross was not the architect of. He has traced the hemstitching on this one right to the Vatican.

Tom will be wanting to abolish boulevards that make direct right angle crossings (claiming that it was some sort of papal sign), and make 'em cross each other slant-wise.

Yours,

*Will Rogers.*

P. S. – Grundy is bringing the new tariff bill down for the boys to sign.

## 791 Will Rogers Sees Airships In General Use Next Year

NEW YORK, N. Y., Feb. 7. – Just been all day over at the airplane show here in New York. It's been put on by the aero branch of the American Legion, and they have done a real job. Don't miss it.

It's not like a motor car show, with every car copying the other.

If they get a new type cigar lighter, it's the outstanding feature of a whole automobile show, but these airplane guys are all thinking for themselves. They have hundreds of different shapes, makes and models.

Why, I don't think the Eighteenth Amendment spurred on drinking any faster than Lindbergh's trip has aviation. The man that travels on the ground next Summer, he just don't deserve to get nowhere.

Yours,

*Will Rogers.*

P. S. – Keep your eye on Grundy. Being right, and a Rockefeller both, is a tough proposition to beat.

## 792 Will Rogers Tries To Explain 'Flu's' Effect On Stocks

NEW YORK, N. Y., Feb. 8. – Every day now stock market "faw down go boom," so tomorrow no session. Called off on account of the "flu." And a funny thing it was on account of the "flu." If it had "flu" up they wouldn't have had to call it off on account of the "flu," but as it "flu" downward, why everybody has to "flu" around Saturday and get ready for not only the "flu" Monday but maybe pneumonia.

I see where Heflin asked for a Senate investigation. This crash coming on the same day as the Pope becoming free don't look good to Tom.

Yours,

*Will Rogers.*

P. S. – Won't be long now till Grundy will start drawing dividends.

## 793 Will Rogers Thinks Edison Might Invent A Cabinet

NEW YORK, N. Y., Feb. 10. – See where Mr. Hoover has gone over to see Inventor Edison, to see if he can't invent a Cabinet that will please just even 5 per cent of the people that wasn't named on it. If he can, then he will be a real inventor.

New York can't sleep tonight wondering what the stock market will open at tomorrow. Radio just had its usual amount of static over the week-end, Steel turned out no product or received any new orders during Sunday, Montgomery Ward peddled nothing since Saturday, yet they will all change prices tomorrow.

"Why does this have to happen?" They say, "It's for the good of the country." Now you tell one.

Yours,
*Will Rogers.*

## 794 WILL ROGERS DISCUSSES INVENTOR IN A LIGHT VEIN

NEW YORK, N. Y., Feb. 11. – That Hoover is a mighty human guy at that. Just today he went away out of his own to encourage some old fellow, 82 years old, that had been working for years on some sort of a scheme he wanted to get patented and didn't know how. It was to make synthetic rubber boots out of nothing but just soil and oxygen from a real estate sales talk. With Hoover's influence chances are he will get it patented. (Shows you what a pull will do in this country.)

And Hoover wears rubber boots in fishing. Seems Henry Ford and Firestone dug this old crank up somewhere. They wear rubber boots, too.

Yours,
*Will Rogers.*

## 795 MR. ROGERS FINDS HUMAN ITEM IN THE NEWS FROM NEW JERSEY

NEW YORK, N. Y., Feb. 12. – The most human thing I read in the papers today, or this month.

The reform school in New Jersey gave a home coming and alumni meeting where over two hundred men who had been there as boys, lots of them now prominent, came back and told what they were doing. Some brought their wives and families with 'em. One told that he served five years there for larceny, and was now a big contractor installing burglar alarms in banks, and was bonded for $150,000.

It didn't give their names, but it ought to, for I believe it would endear every one of their standing in their home communities. It would at least be a change from that old success formula, "I started as a newsboy."

Bravo, New Jersey!

Yours,
*Will Rogers.*

## 796 Will Rogers Is Stirred By Lindbergh's Romance

NEW YORK, N. Y., Feb. 13. – Who cares about inauguration? One of those every four years. Who cares whether we voted sixteen new cruisers, or just a row-boat? What do we care what J. P. Morgan and Young decide the indemnity shall be? What do we care about an extra session? The Pope and Mussolini can't make the front page. Prohibition? Enforced or not enforced, who cares?

All those are a lot of applesauce.

The world's mind is on romance. It's Annie and Lindy that our minds are on today.

What do we care if Hoover catches a whale? Or Coolidge shoots a bear? It's our boy and that fine girl we are thinking of tonight—a great girl from a fine, wholesome family. That boy Lindbergh was just born to use good judgment.

Yours,
*Will Rogers.*

## 797 Will Rogers Says Hoover Can't Keep Fishing Till March

NEW YORK, N. Y., Feb. 14. – They are already claiming it's against "precedent" and that Hoover shouldn't enter Washington while Coolidge is "head man." Well, I am with Hoover. He fished all the way to South America and all the way back. Now they want him to fish till March. Any guy that can fish over a week and be satisfied is not the one we want for President.

This busy man's vacation is a lot of "baloney" anyhow. The bigger he is the less he enjoys a vacation. It's always a bird that never does anything that enjoys a vacation. There is nothing in the world as hard as playing when you don't want to.

Yours,
*Will Rogers.*

## 798 Will Rogers Discourses On Yale's New Study Course

NEW YORK, N. Y., Feb. 15. – Somebody just left Yale eight million as an endowment to study humans, including senior classmen. They want to figure out what kind of a heart beats under a raccoon coat; Yale wants to know why Notre Dame can throw a forward pass further than they can a green apple.

It's to study "group conduct" and human behavior. Chicago is the place for that.

All this stuff would have been a kick to Abe Lincoln, wouldn't it? A college president's work nowadays consists of thinking up new things for the students to play with that looks like studying. A kindergarten teacher ain't in it with schemes in trying to amuse.

Yours,
*Will Rogers.*

## 799 WILL ROGERS GETS LIGHT ON WHY FLORIDA WENT REPUBLICAN

NEW YORK, N. Y., Feb. 17. – There has been quite an argument over whose budget will pay for the new cruisers just voted. Coolidge has offered to split the cost 50-50. He will pay for the blue prints if Hoover will pay for the cruisers.

Greece owed us $17,850,000 on a war debt, so Saturday Congress passed a bill to loan 'em $12,150,000 so it would make it an even $30,000,000. We don't like to be bothered with being owed small uneven sums.

Truth comes out mighty slow. Florida wants the Federal Government to pay all the expenses of putting a windbreak around Lake Okeechobee, so the water won't all blow out. Religion didn't drive that State Republican.

Yours,
*Will Rogers.*

## 800 WILL ROGERS SAYS REED WILL BE MISSED IN THE SENATE

NEW YORK, N. Y., Feb. 18. – The war didn't scare the Senate as bad as Jim Reed's joke that he was going to tell who voted dry and drank not only wet, but anything (whether it was wet or not). Some haven't slept since he threatened to do it. No man that has left that Senate in many a day will be missed like Jim.

Ain't it funny how many hundreds of thousands of soldiers we can recruit with nerve. But we just can't find one politician in a million with backbone.

We got a new cure for the flu here in New York, Mayor Walker's doctor prescribed the Stribling-Sharkey fight.

Yours,
*Will Rogers.*

## 801 Uncertainty Over Cabinet Is Troubling Will Rogers

NEW YORK, N. Y., Feb. 19. — How do we stand all this uncertainty? Here it is only ten days till inauguration time and we don't know what Mr. Hoover is going to do and we don't know what Mr. Coolidge is going to do. Lindbergh is the one of our three prominent men who is not ashamed to have it known in advance what he is going to do.

Mr. Hoover ought to, out of courtesy to its members, announce his Cabinet at once, for just lots of times a Cabinet attracts more attention between the time they are announced, and the time they take seats, than they ever do afterward.

Yours,
*Will Rogers.*

## 802 Will Rogers Ready To Welcome Coolidge To Writers' Fold

NEW YORK, N. Y., Feb. 20. — It seems to be the nation's pastime now to offer Mr. Coolidge a job. I see today where the Denver Post offered him $75,000. I wonder if Mr. Coolidge wired back, "Is that to read it?" It looks like he will become a syndicate writer. Then all he will know is just what he reads in the papers. He will then become a "trained seal." That's what they call a special writer covering an event.

Well, us old-time newspaper men will give him a great welcome among us, Dempsey, Babe Ruth and myself. I would like to sit in the press stand by Mr. Coolidge's side, covering this next farm-relief session of Congress. I bet he would get more laughs out of it than anybody there.

Yours,
*Will Rogers.*

## 803 Will Rogers Muses On Life In The Time Of Washington

NEW YORK, N. Y., Feb. 21. – Washington's Birthday–Hear the political speeches delivered under the guise of being addresses on Washington! They will start out by saying that, "It's the birthday of our first President. Had he lived to see the fruits of the great Republican Party–"

As a matter of fact, there wasn't any Republicans in Washington's day. No Republicans, no boweevil, no income tax, no cover charge, no disarmament conferences, no luncheon clubs, no stop lights, no static, no head winds. Liquor was a companion, and not a problem. No margins, no ticket speculators, no golf pants or Scotch jokes, and Tom hadn't yet read about the iniquities of Rome.

My Lord, living in those times, who wouldn't be great?

Yours,
*Will Rogers.*

## 804 Will Rogers Sees Novelty In Lindbergh's New Job

NEW YORK, N. Y., Feb. 22. – Glad to see Lindbergh kinder settling down since his engagement. He only flew from Kansas City to Wichita yesterday. Certainly going back in his flying, and say, this marriage has made him hustle out and get him a job. He is to work for the government "on days when he has nothing else to do and is flying over Washington." But after all, that's not an odd arrangement, for everybody that works for the government "just works for it when they have nothing else to do." But this is the first time that's ever been stipulated in a contract.

New York gave Washington a great birthday today. If he had been here it would have reminded him of Valley Forge.

Yours,
*Will Rogers.*

## 805 Will Rogers Decides Washington Was A Diplomat

NEW YORK, N. Y., Feb. 24. – All we seem to celebrate Washington's Birthday for is so we can revive the argument as to "what he had to say about entanglements with Europe." Every speaker makes him say just what that speaker wants him to say. Coolidge says it was Jefferson that made the "wise crack" about not messing with outsiders.

So it looks like added to all his other accomplishments Washington was a diplomat. A diplomat is one that says something that is equally misunderstood by both sides, and never clear to either.

By the way, did you notice that everybody that spoke on the Father of Our Country's Birthday was a Republican? You would think the Democrats were a stepson.

Yours,
*Will Rogers.*

## 806 WILL ROGERS SEES LINDBERGH SHOWING UP OTHER FIANCES

NEW YORK, N. Y., Feb. 25. — Say, what do you know about Lindy? What a sucker he is making out of these other fiances who go to see their girls on a train or a bicycle. What a boost for aviation! The modern girl is going to say, "Fly to see me, kid; don't come creeping up here in a Buick."

You will find that the Dempsey shooting was financed by the Los Angeles Chamber of Commerce for him giving so much publicity to Florida.

Hoover's only got six more days to draw names out of the hat.

Yours,
*Will Rogers.*

## 807 WILL ROGERS DISCUSSES TROUBLES OF CABINET MAKING

NEW YORK, N. Y., Feb. 26. — No wonder Hoover can't get a Cabinet. Big men won't take it, for they won't take a chance on a Senate insult. If he has ever earned more than a Senator, he is in league with big business. If he ever drove a Standard Oil truck, or was a bookkeeper in a Morgan bank, he is in league with monopolies. If he is independently rich, he is in league with the devil.

But if he has never done anything, and been a financial failure at that, he will pass the Senate as a brother, and every time Hoover finds a man of that type he is a Democrat. And that's another stanch rule. You can't use even an able man from the other party. That would revert to democracy, and not politics.

Yours,
*Will Rogers.*

## 808 WILL ROGERS THINKS COOLIDGE WILL SPEND 4 YEARS UNPACKING

NEW YORK, N. Y., Feb. 27. – Mr. Arthur Brisbane and wife were to see our show this afternoon and around to the dressing room, where we settled the Cabinet to our satisfaction. We hope they will put a Postmaster General in there that is as strong for aviation as Mr. New was.

If this Mitchell is a Democrat and if they are going to transfer prohibition enforcement over to his department, that's a pretty slick trick of appointing a Democrat to enforce it. If you got something that can't be done, appoint your enemy to do it.

Everybody is wondering what Mr. Coolidge is going to do. What can he do? It will take him four years to unpack.

Yours,

*Will Rogers.*

## 809 WILL ROGERS TELLS THE WORLD HIS VIEW OF LINDBERGH'S FLYING ACCIDENT

NEW YORK, N. Y., Feb. 28. – I was just sitting down to write to you saying that I bet the minute Lindbergh's arm was able he would take Miss Morrow and fly again and here is the paper saying he did that very thing today. I knew he would and that's great, just another example of that boy doing the right thing.

Flying is Lindbergh's business. He spent years perfecting himself at it. Because he tips over on his nose once out of a million miles, a lot of editorial writers start howling about it.

This thing of talking about "somebody's life being too valuable to risk in an airplane" is not only the bunk, but it's an insult to the men we ask to do our flying. Where does anybody's life come in to be any more valuable than anybody else's? Ain't life just as precious to one as to another?

We have heard that "can't spare you" attitude till we got a lot of men in this country believing it now. Say, get over that old ego. This country will replace you before your folks get home from the funeral.

So bravo, Lindy. You are bigger tonight than you ever was before, and that's saying a lot. And bravo, little Miss Anne, you have helped aviation more today than you will ever know. And Mr. and Mrs. Morrow, bless your hearts for your splendid help. That's why you gave your daughter to him, because you knew he could take care of her.

If flying is dangerous pass a law and stop it. But don't divide our nation between a class that should fly and one that shouldn't. Aviation is not a fad, it's a necessity and will be our mode of travel long after all the people who are too valuable to fly have met their desired deaths by the roadsides on Sunday afternoons.

Yours,
*Will Rogers.*

## 810 Will Rogers Says Good-Bye To President And Mrs. Coolidge

NEW YORK, N. Y., March 1. – Mr. Coolidge, you are leaving us, and this is only a comedian's eulogy. But I will never forget what your bosom friend, Dwight Morrow, told me that you said to him on being suddenly sworn in an office that wasn't yours. "Dwight, I am not going to try and be a great President." That's all you said. That will stand in my memory as the greatest remark any officeholder ever made. For no man is great if he thinks he is.

You should be leaving without a single regret. I have told many jokes about you, and this don't mean I am going to quit, for we love jokes about those we like. And Mrs. Coolidge, any one who ever heard me mention your name on a public stage, knows what I think of you. I am only sorry I was too masculine to contribute to the beautiful gift of the ladies of Washington.

So good luck, Cal, you and Grace.

*Will Rogers.*

## 811 Will Rogers Remarks:

NEW YORK, N. Y., March 3. – I thought when we read that Mexico had ordered the pictures of the Lindbergh accident destroyed they did one of the nicest things that was ever done. But leave it to us to steal out some and go to any expense and means to get them before the public. Mexico knew what harm it would do aviation, and they also didn't want to see such a hero's picture with a smashed plane. We all know he would much rather have not had them used. If newspapers ever owed anybody in the world anything they owe it to that boy. He has furnished them with the only hundred percent clean topic they have had in two years.

Yours,
*Will Rogers.*

## 812 Hoover's Prohibition Talk Impresses Will Rogers

NEW YORK, N. Y., March 4. – It sure did seem strange to hear a Presidential speech on something besides prosperity. Mr. Hoover hadn't been sworn in three minutes before he waded into a topic that Mr. Coolidge had never mentioned in six years. That was prohibition. And judges, Senators, Governors, Congressmen and party leaders hadn't been to their homes, or hotels, three minutes till they waded into some old corn, (pre war), to kinder keep the chill off them after that rain. And over many a clinking glass the general comment was: "That was a fine speech of Hoover's, and right to the point, too."

Yours,

*Will Rogers.*

P. S. – Mr. Coolidge passed through here this evening and I believe I know what that quiet grin was about.

# NOTES

[1] *New York Times* (hereafter cited as *NYT*), Friday, July 30, 1926, 19:7. Between July 29 and September 26, 1926, the Daily Telegrams (DT) appeared only in *NYT;* the text is from there. Datelines given in the telegrams are the dates on which Rogers sent them; dates given in notes indicate time of publication, usually the next day.

Nancy Astor, one of the beautiful Langhorne sisters from Virginia, wife of Lord Waldorf Astor and as a British subject the first woman to sit in the House of Commons, serving from 1920 to 1944. Sharp-tongued and quick-witted, Lady Astor's career in Parliament was marked by her opposition to the liquor interests and her concern for social issues.

James J. "Jimmie" Walker, the dapper and flamboyant mayor of New York City from 1925 to 1932, was famous for his elaborate civic welcomes for visiting dignitaries. He had invited Lady Astor to visit his city, but she declined.

[2] *NYT,* Saturday, July 31, 1926, 13:7.

Andrew Mellon, secretary of the treasury of the United States from 1921 to 1932, traveled through Europe from July to September of 1926 to discuss war debts with European leaders.

Benito Mussolini, founder and leader of the Fascist movement, was dictator of Italy from 1922 to 1943.

No DT is available for Sunday, August 1, 1926.

[3] *NYT,* Monday, August 2, 1926, 19:7.

Tammany Hall, a powerful Democratic political organization in New York City, was an important source of appointees for civic jobs.

[4] *NYT,* Tuesday, August 3, 1926, 23:2.

[5] *NYT,* Wednesday, August 4, 1926, 21:7.

William E. Borah, Republican United States senator from Idaho from 1907 until his death in 1940; chairman of the Committee on Foreign Relations for seventeen years. Borah continued to press for the disposition of 4,207,392 square miles of territory taken from the defeated powers after World War I and distributed among other national groups.

Suzanne Lenglen, French tennis champion, turned professional in 1926 at the urging of C. C. "Cash and Carry" Pyle, sports promoter; she retired a year later.

George Bernard Shaw, British playwright, novelist, and literary critic.

[6] *NYT,* Thursday, August 5, 1926, 23:2.

Twenty-two swimmers, including eight women, attempted to swim the English Channel during July, August, and September of 1926.

Winston Churchill, chancellor of the exchequer of England from 1924 to 1929 and prime minister from 1940 to 1945 and from 1951 to 1955.

[7] *NYT,* Friday, August 6, 1926, 17:2.

[8] *NYT,* Saturday, August 7, 1926, 13:7.

Lincoln Andrews, assistant secretary of the treasury from 1925 to 1927, was the chief enforcer of prohibition laws.

[9] *NYT,* Sunday, August 8, 1926, II:1:2.

[10] *NYT,* Monday, August 9, 1926, 17:7.

Two days earlier American swimming champion Gertrude Ederle had become the first woman and sixth individual to swim the English Channel.

[11] *NYT,* Tuesday, August 10, 1926, 23:2.

Georges Clemenceau, premier of France during World War I. In an open letter to President Coolidge, the eighty-five-year-old Clemenceau admitted that France was a debtor nation but one that would remain totally independent.

[12] *NYT,* Wednesday, August 11, 1926, 23:2.

[13] *NYT,* Thursday, August 12, 1926, 21:7.

American tourists had been behaving obnoxiously in France. President Coolidge asked Americans who traveled abroad to be considerate and to remember that they were guests in other countries.

[14] *NYT,* Friday, August 13, 1926, 19:2.

Bernard Baruch, successful American businessman who officially advised several presidents, was active in Democratic politics. The financier told reporters that Clemenceau's letter was "food for thought."

No DTs are available for Saturday, August 14; Sunday, August 15; and Monday, August 16, 1926.

[15] *NYT,* Tuesday, August 17, 1926, 23:2.

A championship cricket series between Australian and English teams had begun June 12, 1926, and had produced no decision through four matches. The fifth and deciding match began on August 15 and was held on the Kensington Oval in London. England was the eventual winner.

[16] *NYT,* Wednesday, August 18, 1926, 23:2.

King George V was not in Scotland when Rogers and the newspapers believed he was but was grouse hunting elsewhere in Great Britain.

[17] *NYT,* Thursday, August 19, 1926, 21:2.

Frank B Kellogg, United States secretary of state from 1925 to 1929. Kellogg spoke in Plattsburgh, New York, on August 18 at the dedication of a memorial to Thomas Macdonough, early-day American naval commander.

The Preliminary Disarmament Conference was established by the League of Nations in 1925. The conference, held in Geneva, Switzerland, in the summer of 1926, ended when the United States, Britain, and other conferring nations could not agree on significant points.

[18] *NYT,* Friday, August 20, 1926, 19:2.

[19] *NYT,* Saturday, August 21, 1926, 13:2.

The Philippine Islands were transferred from Spain to the United States by the Treaty of Paris of 1898, which ended the Spanish-American War. By the Jones Act of 1916, the United States promised eventual independence for the islands, but subsequent Republican administrations, including that of President Coolidge, opposed self-government. Independence finally was granted in 1946.

The Irish Free State was accepted by the London Imperial Conference in October and November as a self-governing member of the British Commonwealth of Nations, but Northern Ireland remained under British rule.

[20] *NYT,* Sunday, August 22, 1926, I:5:3.

The Treaty of Versailles, which ended World War I, limited the size of the German army.

[21] *NYT,* Monday, August 23, 1926, 17:2.

Several European dictators, including Mussolini, were targets of unsuccessful assassination plots during 1926. One former official of the Ukranian Republic and the vice president of the Georgian Republic were assassinated.

[22] *NYT,* Tuesday, August 24, 1926, 23:7.

A military coup had overthrown Greek dictator Theodoros Pangalos on August 22. Pangalos tried to escape the country by hiding in a wireless turret of a ship, but he was caught and returned to Athens.

The hippopotamus was the first born in captivity since 1922.

George M. Cohan, American actor, playwright, and producer; composer of many popular, patriotic tunes.

[23] *NYT,* Wednesday, August 25, 1926, 23:7.

Parliament was recalled to deal with a continuing coal strike.

[24] *NYT,* Thursday, August 26, 1926, 21:7.

The French Parliament had passed a revenue bill in early August of 1926, and rumors indicated another tax increase was imminent.

[25] *NYT,* Friday, August 27, 1926, 19:7.

[26] *NYT,* Saturday, August 28, 1926, 13:7.

[27] *NYT,* Sunday, August 29, 1926, I:3:5.

Mrs. Amelia Corson of New York City swam the English Channel from Cape Grisnez, France, to Dover, England, in fifteen hours and twenty-eight minutes on August 29. Mrs. Corson, a mother of two children, was only the second woman and seventh individual to accomplish the feat.

[28] *NYT,* Monday, August 30, 1926, 3:4.

[29] *NYT,* Tuesday, August 31, 1926, 21:7.

A Labor party member interrupted debate in the House of Commons and was suspended from the "service of the House." A similar outburst had occurred in Washington during the previous session of Congress.

Newton Baker, secretary of war in President Woodrow Wilson's administration. On August 29 Baker called for mutual cancellation of all war debts.

John Hobbs, generally regarded as the greatest batsman in cricket, was the English hero of the recent test matches with Australia (see DT 15).

George Herman "Babe" Ruth, popular American baseball player and renowned home run hitter; played for the New York Yankees from 1920 to 1935.

Ernst Vierkoetter, a German, broke all previous marks for swimming the English channel. Vierkoetter rested on an English beach for twenty mintues following his swim and then immediately returned by tug to France.

[30] *NYT,* Wednesday, September 1, 1926, 2:4.

[31] *NYT,* Thursday, September 2, 1926, 23:7.

Charles Evans Hughes, United States secretary of state from 1921 to 1925. In 1930 Hughes was appointed chief justice of the Supreme Court, a post which he held until 1941.

Aristide Briand, recipient of the Nobel Peace Prize in 1926, served as prime minister of France intermittently from 1909 to 1929.

For Newton Baker see DT 29.

[32] *NYT,* Friday, September 3, 1926, 19:7.

In 1919 French hotel owner Raymond Orteig offered an award of $25,000 for the first successful nonstop flight between New York City and Paris. By 1926 several such flights had been proposed, and discussion about them dominated the news for several weeks.

Brigadier General William "Billy" Mitchell, assistant air chief and foremost champion of air power, had resigned his commission in the United States Army in February of 1926 after facing temporary suspension from duty for criticizing his superiors' refusal to support aviation. Rogers voiced strong support for Mitchell throughout the airman's court-martial in 1926.

[33] *NYT,* Saturday, September 4, 1926, 15:7.

Spain, a charter member of the League of Nations and a permanent member of its General Council, was assigned nonpermanent status when Germany was granted membership in the League in 1926 and given a permanent seat on the council. The realignment generated considerable controversy and prompted Spain to withdraw temporarily from the League.

No DT is available for Sunday, September 5, 1926.

[34] *NYT,* Monday, September 6, 1926, 17:7.

President Coolidge issued an executive statement on September 4, assuring other countries that the proposed five-year aviation expansion program of the United States did not violate the Washington naval armaments treaty of 1922.

Coolidge, who previously had been reluctant to support a strong national defense program, announced the new aviation proposal while on a fishing vacation at his summer home in the Adirondack Mountains.

[35] *NYT,* Tuesday, September 7, 1926, 23:7.

Harry Thaw, a wealthy American playboy, had married Evelyn Nesbit, an artist's model and actress, in 1905. A year later, Thaw shot and killed one of his wife's former suitors, Standord White, a prominent New York architect. Thaw was institutionalized until 1906 as criminally insane. The couple divorced in 1916, but rumors prevailed in 1926 that they had reconciled. They never remarried.

William T. Cosgrave, president of the Irish Free State from 1922 to 1932 and one of the leading figures of the Irish Revolution. President Cosgrave requested international assistance after a fire swept a packed movie theater in Dromcolliher, County Limerick, on September 6, killing forty-six persons. Rogers staged a benefit show for the victims and their families.

No DT is available for Wednesday, September 8, 1926.

36 *NYT,* Thursday, September 9, 1926, 25:7.

Civil war had disrupted Ireland since the creation of the Irish Free State in 1922. President Cosgrave had brought a measure of stability to the country, and the new nation had been admitted to the League of Nations.

Alfred E. Smith, governor of New York from 1919 to 1921 and from 1923 to 1929. Smith, an Irish Catholic and adamant antiprohibitionist, had sought the Democratic presidential nomination in 1920 and 1924 and finally became the nominee in 1928.

37 *NYT,* Friday, September 10, 1926, 23:7.

Irish-Americans dominated police departments in many American cities, particularly New York City. In 1930 the New York "force" was still more than one-third Irish.

No DT is available for Saturday, September 11, 1926.

38 *NYT,* Sunday, September 12, 1926, I:13:2.

Frenchman Georges Michel swam the English Channel on September 10 and beat Ernst Vierkoetter's record by one hour and thirty-eight minutes (see DT 29).

Dr. Otto Peltzer, a German school teacher, defeated Swedish athlete Edwin Wide and famed Finnish runner Paavo Nurmi by less than three meters in a 1,500-meter race at a track meet in Berlin on September 11.

39 *NYT,* Monday, September 13, 1926, 23:7.

Wide had edged Nurmi the previous day in the 1,500-meter race (see DT 38) and defeated him again in a record setting two-mile race on September 12. Nurmi established a new two-mile record in 1931.

No DTs are available for Tuesday, September 14; Wednesday, September 15; Thursday, September 16; and Friday, September 17, 1926.

40 *NYT,* Saturday, September 18, 1926, 19:4.

The Treaty of Versailles provided for Allied occupation of the Rhineland in Germany for fifteen years. The Allied forces were withdrawn in June of 1930.

René Fonck, French air ace of World War I. A group of Americans contracted with Captain Fonck in early 1926 to compete for Raymond Orteig's prize of $25,000 for the first nonstop New York to Paris flight. On September 21, after numerous delays and false starts, Fonck and three crew members took off from an airfield on Long Island, New York, but soon crashed. Two of the crew members were killed, but Fonck and his navigator escaped serious injury.

41 *NYT,* Sunday, September 19, 1926, II:1:7.

For René Fonck see DT 40; for Gertrude Ederle see DT 10; for Amelia Corson see DT 27.

[42] *NYT,* Monday, September 20, 1926, 25:7.

Sandy Hook, a peninsula of New Jersey, located fifteen miles south of Manhattan Island, was the point at which Europe-bound ocean liners dropped their coastal pilots.

[43] *NYT,* Tuesday, September 21, 1926, 32:7.

A devastating hurricane struck Florida on September 18, killing 372 persons and injuring 6,000 others. Property damage was estimated at more than $80,000,000.

No DT is available for Wednesday, September 22, 1926.

[44] *NYT,* Thursday, September 23, 1926, 27:7.

The *Leviathan,* one of the premier luxury liners of the 1920s, was operated by the United States Shipping Board.

[45] *NYT,* Friday, September 24, 1926, 25:7.

[46] *NYT,* Saturday, September 25, 1926, 8:3.

The owners of the *Leviathan* arranged for Will Rogers, former Secretary of State Charles Evans Hughes (see DT 31), and actor-author James Gleason to stage a benefit for victims of the Florida hurricane. The performers collected $40,600 for two shows.

Jack "Doc" Kearns, manager of Jack Dempsey and five other world champion boxers. Kearns and Dempsey had parted company earlier, but the former manager recently had brought suit against the boxer for contractural violations. On September 23, while the case still was undecided, Dempsey lost a title bout to Gene Tunney, prompting Rogers to label Dempsey's loss a moral victory for Kearns.

No DT is available for Sunday, September 26, 1926.

[47] *NYT,* Monday, September 27, 1926, 7:2.

Milton Hershey, millionaire chocolate manufacturer and noted philanthropist. Hershey gave $8,000 to see Rogers repeat the benefit performance.

[48] *Los Angeles Times* (hereinafter cited as *LAT*), Monday, October 11, 1926, I:1:4-5. Variant: *Boston Daily Globe* (hereinafter cited as *BDG*), gives dateline "Oct 11." After his return from Europe, Rogers began a lecture tour of the United States and Canada while McNaught prepared and sold syndication rights to the Daily Telegrams; no telegrams appeared for two weeks. Rogers resumed writing the daily dispatches on October 10 while in Canada, but newspaper datelines for the telegrams of October 10-13 conflict significantly with Rogers' lecture itinerary. Rogers possibly wrote several post-dated telegrams at one sitting and released them, without revision as to time and place, as his tour progressed.

The World Court, the Permanent Court of International Justice, was established to supplement the machinery of the League of Nations. Several prominent Americans, including President Coolidge, favored joining it, but Senate approval of United States membership was accompanied by reservations which clouded chances for American participation.

Fifteen-year-old Frances "Peaches" Browning had married fifty-year-old Edward "Daddy" Browning, a wealthy New York City realtor, in April of 1926. On October 2 Peaches left Browning and later filed for divorce. Litigation of the suit continued for several months and filled the pages of sensational tabloids. Eventually the couple legally separated.

Haiti had been occupied by American forces since 1915. A ten-year treaty between the United States and Haiti, originally signed in 1916, was renegotiated in 1926. The troops were withdrawn in 1934.

The Mason and Dixon Line, originally the southern boundary line of Pennsylvania, still was regarded in the 1920s as the sentimental border between the North and the South.

[49] *LAT,* Tuesday, October 12, 1926, I:1:2-3. Variants: *BDG* gives dateline "Oct 12"/*BDG* inserts "that" at end of fifth sentence.

The Eighteenth Amendment was ratified in 1919 and established prohibition of intoxicating liquors as a national policy. The Volstead Act of 1919 provided the machinery for enforcement. It defined as intoxicating liquor any beverage containing more than .5 percent alcohol.

[50] *LAT,* Wednesday, October 13, 1926, I:1:2. Variant: *BDG* gives dateline "Oct 12."

In Canada, a coalition of anti-administration farmers concerned about declining farm prices had recorded gains in parliamentary elections. Similar hardships in the United States prompted American farmers to pressure for changes in governmental policy.

[51] *LAT,* Thursday, October 14, 1926, I:1:4-5. Variant: *LAT* gives "on" for *BDG* "of" in second sentence.

Nicholas Longworth, Speaker of the United States House of Representatives from 1925 to 1931. Longworth, who was bald and played the violin, was married to Theodore Roosevelt's vibrant daughter Alice.

For Jack Dempsey see DT 46.

Harry Wills, black championship boxer from New Orleans who had sought to fight Dempsey for the world title. Promoters who opposed a racially mixed title bout had blocked the move. On October 12 young contender Jack Sharkey decisively beat aging Wills.

[52] *NYT,* Friday, October 15, 1926, 25:7. Variant: *LAT* gives heading "BULLETIN FROM WILL ROGERS."

Queen Marie, queen consort of Rumania from 1914 to 1927. With two of her children and a retinue of seventeen, the queen arrived on October 18 ostensibly for a good will tour of the United States. It quickly became clear that business considerations were paramount, and long before her departure on November 24 a tone of displeasure crept into newspaper accounts.

Charles Darwin, British naturalist who suggested evolutionary theory of man. His revolutionary ideas met with extreme opposition in some parts of the United States, including in Tennessee where a statute of March 23, 1925, forbade any publicly funded educational institution "to teach the theory that denies the story of the divine creation of man as taught in the Bible."

[53] *NYT,* Saturday, October 16, 1926, 19:7. Variants: *NYT* gives "He got in here this morning, took one look at Birmingham, and left" in second sentence, but *BDG* and *LAT* have it as here.

Jeddu Krishnamurti, an Indian Hindu, hailed in the 1920s as the reincarnated Messiah. Krishnamurti and his sponsor, Annie Besant, world president of the Theosophical Society, began a lecture tour of the United States in August of 1926. The couple left the country the following April gently criticizing American materialism.

Elbert Gary, a lawyer and chairman of the board of United States Steel Corporation from 1903 to 1927. United States Steel owned considerable property in the steel producing cities of Birmingham, Alabama, and Youngstown, Ohio.

[54] *NYT,* Sunday, October 17, 1926, I:24:3-4. *BDG* and *LAT* did not print the DT.

[55] *NYT,* Monday, October 18, 1926, 23:7. Variants: *LAT* gives heading "ROGERS SEEKS QUEEN'S AID"/*BDG* and *LAT* give, while *NYT* omits, "the rambling Rumanian" in first sentence / *BDG* gives "Louis Fuller" in second sentence.

Loie Fuller, American actress and dancer. Miss Fuller had befriended Queen Marie of Rumania during World War I and accompanied the monarch on her American tour. She emerged as a controversial power behind the scenes, although she denied that she had made the arrangements for the queen's activities.

[56] *NYT,* Tuesday, October 19, 1926, 4:6. Variants: *LAT* gives heading "WILL ROGERS THANKS QUEEN"/*NYT* begins third sentence "Americans," but *BDG* and *LAT* have it as here/*LAT* omits P.S.

Aimee Semple McPherson, colorful evangelist and faith healer of the 1920s and 1930s. In 1926 Miss McPherson claimed that she had been kidnapped and held captive for five weeks. An investigation indicated that she had spent part of the time in the company of Kenneth Ormiston, an associate, at Carmel-by-the-Sea, California. On September 27 she was indicted for conspiracy to obstruct justice and on other charges. The case was dismissed in January of 1927.

The Twenty-seventh Infantry Division of the United States Army, composed mainly of men from New York, had trained at Camp Wadsworth, near Spartanburg, before departing for France during World War I.

[57] *NYT,* Wednesday, October 20, 1926, 27:7. Variants: *NYT* gives "for separation." in first sentence, but *BDG* and *LAT* have it as here/*BDG* ends second sentence "Happy now."

[58] *NYT,* Thursday, October 21, 1926, 27:7. Variants: *LAT* gives heading "COMMENT BY WILL ROGERS" / *BDG* gives "like a flivver" in second sentence.

Byron Patton "Pat" Harrison, Democratic United States senator from Mississippi from 1919 to 1941. Witty and unpretentious, Harrison was a favorite among his colleagues in Congress.

[59] *NYT,* Friday, October 22, 1926, 23:7. Variants: *LAT* gives heading "ROGERS MUSE WAKED BY NEWS" / *BDG* gives "Claremore, Oklahoma," in close.

No new facts had enlivened the Browning case (see DTs 48, 56, and 57).

Henry Ford, founder of Ford Motor Company. Ford had announced on September 25, 1926, that his company was instituting a five-day work week, simultaneously adjusting wages so that workers would not lose in the process.

Queen Marie's personal accounts of her travels began appearing in newspapers on October 15 under the sponsorship of the North American Newspaper Alliance, a syndicate of sixty journals.

Aimee McPherson seemed to be subject to several illnesses, one of which had delayed her arrest in late September. She was not too ill, however, to appear daily in court during her trial.

[60] *NYT,* Saturday, October 23, 1926, 19:7. Variants: *LAT* gives heading "DIARY OF WILL ROGERS"/*BDG* and *LAT* add "the ballyhooing Balkan" and omit "Queen" in first sentence/*NYT* omits, while *BDG* and *LAT* add, entire second paragraph (*LAT* gives "Salt Lake City" as location).

Grover Cleveland Alexander, hard throwing pitcher and hero of the world champion St. Louis Cardinals of 1926. In October Alexander returned to his hometown of St. Paul, Nebraska, where he was accorded a rousing welcome.

While Aimee McPherson's trial continued, engineer Thomas Towne revealed in Salt Lake City that he had witnessed a red haired lady change clothes in a car near Los Angeles on May 18 and then drive off with a man. He identified the pair as McPherson and Kenneth Ormiston (see DT 56). Towne's testimony later was discredited.

[61] *NYT,* Sunday, October 24, 1926, I:23:2. *BDG* and *LAT* did not print the DT.

A worldwide slump in cotton prices had occurred in 1926.

Queen Marie had been guest of honor on October 22 at a private luncheon at the Bankers Club in New York City. The dinner lent weight to the widespread suspicion that the queen's visit involved a potential private loan for Rumania to be floated in the United States.

[62] *NYT,* Monday, October 25, 1926, 21:7. Variants: *LAT* gives heading "WILL ROGER'S DAILY DIARY"/*LAT* gives dateline "Joplin, (O.)."

The bodies of the Reverend Edward Hall and Mrs. Eleanor Mills were discovered in September of 1922 in a lovers' lane near New Brunswick, New Jersey. Hall's widow and her brothers were arrested and brought to trial in one of the most sensational murder cases of the 1920s. A number of individuals allegedly had witnessed the killings on the lonely rural road, but the defendants were acquitted in December of 1926 on the failure of the state to prove its case.

The first title bout between champion Jack Dempsey and challenger Gene Tunney was witnessed by more than 100,000 spectators in Philadelphia on September 23, 1926. Dempsey lost the world championship in the fight, which drew a gate of more than $1,000,000.

[63] *NYT,* Tuesday, October 26, 1926, 29:7. Variants: *LAT* gives heading "WILL ROGERS'S TRAVEL DIARY"/*NYT* spells out name of ranch in first sentence/*BDG* gives "round-up limousines" in fifth sentence/*NYT* omits sixth and following sentences.

The 101 Ranch, owned by the Miller brothers, Joe, Zack, and George, encompassed 110,000 acres in north central Oklahoma. The enterprise included a model farm, circus animals, petroleum deposits, experimental crops, and prize livestock. The brothers' 101 Ranch Real Wild West Show traveled throughout the United States and Europe from 1906 to 1931.

[64] *NYT,* Wednesday, October 27, 1926, 29:7. Variant: *LAT* gives heading "ROGERS LISTENS TO CANDIDATES."

Queen Marie's tour had taken the monarch in one week from New York to Washington and back, via Baltimore, Annapolis, and Philadelphia, then to West Point and Buffalo en route to Canada.

[65] *NYT,* Thursday, October 28, 1926, 27:7. Variants: *BDG* and *LAT* omit postscript.

Mary Garden, Scottish-born opera star who made her debut in the United States in 1907. Rogers, a friend of Miss Garden's, referred here to an incident in Paris during his recent European tour.

[66] *NYT,* Friday, October 29, 1926, 25:7. Variants: *LAT* gives heading "WANDERINGS OF WILL ROGERS"/*NYT* gives "How's Aimee and Al Smith and Pomerene making out?" in last sentence, but *BDG* and *LAT* have it as here.

Atlee Pomerene, Democratic United States senator from Ohio from 1911 to 1923. In 1926 Pomerene made an unsuccessful bid to return to the United States Senate.

[67] *BDG* (AM), Saturday, October 30, 1926, 1:6. *NYT* and *LAT* did not print the DT.

On July 17, 1926, the Reverend Frank Norris, fundamentalist minister of the First Baptist Church in Fort Worth, Texas, allegedly shot and killed Dexter Chipps, a businessman who was visiting in Norris' office. Chipps supposedly had protested the minister's radio denunciation of various civic and business leaders. The trial for murder opened on November 1 and resulted in Norris' acquittal on January 25, 1927.

[68] *NYT,* Sunday, October 31, 1926, I:18:2. *BDG* and *LAT* did not print the DT.

In the congressional elections of 1918, President Woodrow Wilson had asked American voters to approve his leadership by returning a Democratic majority to both houses of Congress. The Republicans, instead, won majorities in both the House and the Senate.

[69] *NYT,* Monday, November 1, 1926, 23:7. Variants: *BDG* gives "They don't" to begin second sentence.

Political observers believed that two newly-elected senators would face challenges to their being seated. Since May a Senate committee had publicized allegations that Republicans William Vare of Pennsylvania and Frank Smith of Illinois had spent far more than the legal limit for campaigning.

[70] *NYT,* Tuesday, November 2, 1926, 4:3.

[71] *LAT,* Wednesday, November 3, 1926, I:1:4-5. *NYT* did not print the DT.

Miriam "Ma" and James "Pa" Ferguson. James Ferguson served as governor of Texas from 1915 until his impeachment and removal from office in 1917 for various reasons, including misappropriation of state funds. He attempted to run again in 1924, but a court ruled he could not be a candidate. His wife Miriam promptly entered the race and won with the open support of her husband; she served from 1925 to 1927 and 1933 to 1935.

Dan Moody, attorney general of Texas from 1925 to 1927. Moody, thirty-three years old and an ardent prohibitionist, earlier had defeated Governor Miriam Ferguson in the Democratic primary of 1926. He was elected governor in that year and served from 1927 to 1931.

"Colonel" Edward M. House, Houston-born business and political leader and an adviser to several Texas governors. He was a well-known confidant of President Woodrow Wilson.

[72] *NYT,* Thursday, November 4, 1926, 19:3.

William M. Butler, chairman of the Republican National Committee in 1924 and an adviser to President Coolidge. Butler was appointed from Massachusetts in 1924 to fill a vacancy in the United States Senate. Despite Coolidge's public endorsement, he was defeated in the General Election on November 2, 1926; he resigned from the Senate one month later.

James Wadsworth, Jr., Republican United States senator from New York from 1915 to 1927. Despite much pressure, President Coolidge had not indicated a favorite between Wadsworth or Democrat Robert Wagner in the General Election. Later, Wadsworth served in the United States House of Representatives from 1933 to 1951.

After all votes were counted, including those of a special election in Maine on November 29, 1926, to fill a vacancy, Republicans held forty-eight seats in the Senate and Democrats held forty-seven, with one Farmer-Labor member.

73 *NYT,* Friday, November 5, 1926, 23:7.

Democratic candidates in Oklahoma captured a seat in the United States Senate and the governorship in the General Election.

74 *NYT,* Saturday, November 6, 1926, 19:7.

75 *NYT,* Sunday, November 7, 1926, I:28:2. *BDG* and *LAT* did not print the DT.

The "new referee" was John Carroll who was assigned to Queen Marie's tour by officials of the three railroads which had arranged the journey. His job was to resolve the friction between the monarch's aides and some Americans accompanying the party.

Gene Tunney's opponent in the first defense of his new heavyweight crown was uncertain. Jack Sharkey, who had turned professional in 1924, had issued a challenge, but the two men never met in the ring.

76 *NYT,* Monday, November 8, 1926, 21:7. Variants: *BDG, LAT, Kansas City Times* (hereinafter cited as *KCT)* omit "Coolidge" in first sentence/*BDG, LAT,* and *KCT* give "will have the" in first sentence.

77 *NYT,* Tuesday, November 9, 1926, 29:7. Variant: *LAT* gives "'a Spearmint man" in second sentence.

Rogers' parenthetical heading echoed that used by the *New York Times* on this day: "ON BOARD THE QUEEN OF RUMANIA'S TRAIN AT SEATTLE, Wash., Nov. 6."

A member of the queen's party disclosed that Ford Motor Company had furnished without charge the automobiles used by the royal party; the service cost Ford more than $250,000. The informant, J. B. Ayres, a Ford representative, was dismissed from the queen's train.

78 *NYT,* Wednesday, November 10, 1926, 29:7. Variants: *NYT* gives "sort of a tour" in second sentence, but *LAT* has it as here/*BDG* omits "tour" in second sentence.

79 *BDG* (AM), Thursday, November 11, 1926, 1:8. Variants: *LAT* gives "is in Kansas City today" in first sentence/*LAT* gives "Vare" for "war" in third sentence/*NYT* did not print the DT.

The Liberty Memorial, 360 feet high, was erected near downtown Kansas City, Missouri, in honor of soldiers from the city killed during World War I. The structure includes a masonry shaft thirty-five feet in diameter which rises 217 feet above a broad platform.

James A. Reed, Democratic United States senator from Missouri from 1911 to 1929. Reed, combative and sharp-tongued, was a prominent isolationist and anti-prohibitionist and was chairman of a Senate inquiry into campaign expenditures.

William Vare, United States representative from 1912 to 1923 and from 1923 to 1927. Vare, a powerful Republican politican from Philadelphia, was a successful candidate for the United States Senate in 1926. The Senate, however, voided the election due to excessive expenditures. Vare served as senator from 1927 until his unseating on December 6, 1929.

Frank Smith, Republican United States representative from Illinois from 1919 to 1921. Smith was elected to the United States Senate in the General Election of 1926. The Senate, however, refused to seat him because Smith, while serving as chairman of the Illinois Commerce Commission, had received $158,000 for his campaign from Samuel Insull, Chicago utilities magnate.

80 *LAT,* Friday, November 12, 1926, I:1:3-4. Variants: *KCT* gives first sentence "This is Armistice day."/*NYT* did not print the DT.

During the current football season, nine college and high school football players had died of injuries received in practices or games, while fifty other major injuries to players had occurred.

81 *NYT,* Saturday, November 13, 1926, 19:7. Variants: *NYT* gives "in speech. . . one of all, Jim Reed, raised" in first, second, and third sentences, but *BDG* and *LAT* have it as here.

At the dedication of the Library Memorial in Kansas City, President Coolidge paid tribute to the service in World War I of predominantly Kansas and Missouri units and to the role of a regiment of Missouri volunteers in the Mexican war.

Frank and Jesse James, outlaw brothers from Missouri who terrorized much of the Middle West before Jesse's death in 1882 and Frank's reformation.

Reed, born in Ohio and reared in Iowa, moved to Kansas City at age twenty-six. He gained local prominence as county prosecuting atorney from 1898 to 1900, securing 285 convictions in 287 cases. He also served two terms as mayor of Kansas City (see DT 79).

82 *NYT,* Sunday, November 14, 1926, I:5:3-4. *BDG* and *LAT* did not print the DT.

Warren G. Harding, president of the United States from 1921 to 1923; died in office. Harding once had proposed that in the event of another war the United States should not only draft its manhood but also its industrial, agricultural, and capital wealth to wage the conflict. Coolidge had reiterated this position in Kansas City.

83 *NYT,* Monday, November 15, 1926, 23:7. Variants: *NYT* omits second and third sentences, but *BDG* and *LAT* have it as here.

Princeton University defeated Harvard, 12 to 0, in a football game on November 6. During the following week, the *Harvard Lampoon,* a student humor magazine, strained relations between the two private eastern colleges when it published an article which satirized and denounced Princeton. The next Saturday Harvard lost to Brown University, 21 to 0.

Knute Rockne, Norwegian-born football coach at Notre Dame University from 1914 until his death in an airplane accident in 1931. While head coach from 1920 to 1930, Rockne directed his team to a record of ninety-six wins, twelve losses, and three ties. Notre Dame defeated the United States Military Academy, 7 to 0, on November 13.

84 *NYT,* Tuesday, November 16, 1926, 29:7.

King Ferdinand I, king of Rumania from 1914 to 1927 and husband of Queen Marie (see DT 52). According to published reports on November 15, the queen intended to curtail her American visit at the ailing king's request, with the promise that she would be home by Christmas. A day later she issued a formal denial that she had received any messages calling her home.

Wishing to have Lincoln limousines available at each stop, John Carroll, American coordinator of Queen Marie's tour, had informed the Ford Motor Company of his willingness to allow Ford representative J. B. Ayers to rejoin the queen's party.

85 *NYT,* Wednesday, November 17, 1926, 27:7. Variants: *NYT* omits "wake of" in first sentence/*BDG* begins sixth sentence "Auto dealer"/*NYT* ends seventh sentence after "way" and begins new paragraph at "Grand"/*BDG* adds to signature "Royal Joker Tours."

Kansas City had been the home since 1899 of the American Royal Livestock Show. Judging prize stock was a prominent feature of the event. Rogers was the scheduled banquet speaker for the Junior Farmers that evening.

86 *NYT,* Thursday, November 18, 1926, 25:7.

87 *NYT,* Friday, November 19, 1926, 27:7. Variant: *BDG* gives "barn" for "harem" in second sentence.

Benjamin Purnell, leader of the House of David, a religious cult which flourished in Benton Harbor, Michigan, during the first quarter of the twentieth century. Purnell claimed immortality, prohibited the cutting of hair or beard, and forbade his members to have sexual relations. He disappeared in 1922 when warrants were issued for his arrest on morality charges. He was arrested on November 19, 1926, but died in early 1927.

88 *NYT,* Saturday, November 20, 1926, 19:7.

A number of national and regional farmers conferences were meeting at this time, including conventions in St. Louis, Missouri; Portland, Maine; and Indianapolis, Indiana.

Voters in Colorado and other western states on November 2 defeated referendum proposals to repeal state dry laws passed in compliance with the Volstead Act.

No DT is available for Sunday, November 21, 1926.

89 *NYT,* Monday, November 22, 1926, 25:7. Variant: *NYT* gives "which was the worst team." to end first sentence, but *BDG* and *LAT* have it as here.

90 *NYT,* Tuesday, November 23, 1926, 31:7.

91 *NYT,* Wednesday, November 24, 1926, 25:7.

Mussolini had survived at least three attempts on his life since Rogers interviewed him during the Oklahoman's summer tour of Europe (see DT 2).

92 *NYT,* Thursday, November 25, 1926, 27:7. Variant: *BDG* omits "turkey" in second sentence.

Queen Marie boarded the S.S. *Berengaria* on November 24 to sail for Cherbourg, France, thus ending her visit to the United States at least a month earlier than first indicated.

93 *NYT,* Friday, November 26, 1926, 21:7. Variants: *LAT* gives "station" for "depot" in fifth sentence/*LAT* gives "as one of those America's solo tourists" in fifth and sixth sentences.

Samuel Hill, wealthy railroad executive, lawyer, and roadway builder. Hill had been instrumental in arranging Queen Marie's American visit and had accompanied the monarch during much of her tour.

William Brandon, governor of Alabama from 1923 to 1927. At the Democratic National Convention in 1924, each of the 103 nominating ballots for president had opened with Brandon intoning, "Alabama casts twenty-four votes for Oscar W. Underwood." Brandon, a prohibitionist, recently had been arrested while on a fishing trip and charged with illegal possession of liquor.

[94] *NYT,* Saturday, November 27, 1926, 19:7.

Several congressmen and senators had received free tickets to the Army-Navy football game in Chicago; paying customers understandably protested. Scheduled for Soldier Field, which had a seating capacity of 110,000, the game atracted more than 600,000 inquiries for tickets.

[95] *NYT,* Sunday, November 28, 1926, I:20:2-3. *BDG* and *LAT* did not print the DT.

Carnegie Tech of Pittsburgh, Pennsylvania—nick-named "Andy's Boys" for Secretary of the Treasury and Pittsburgh native Andrew Mellon—defeated Notre Dame, 19 to 0. Carnegie football fans performed a figurative victory dance in the shape of the "black bottom," one of the popular dance steps of the decade.

James Watson, Democratic United States senator from Indiana from 1916 to 1933. Watson narrowly won reelection after a term which included allegations of corruption and Ku Klux Klan support.

Frank McKinney "Kin" Hubbard, humorist and cartoonist for the *Indianapolis News* from 1891 to 1930. Hubbard created Abe Martin, a rustic character who appeared in daily syndicated line drawings, each with two sentences of current, universal comment.

George Ade, Indiana humorist and newspaperman. An earnest advocate of golf, Ade wrote a magazine article, the title of which warned wives, "Look Out for Your Husbands! Golf is Coming!"

The Ku Klux Klan of the post-Civil War period was revived in 1915 and gathered thousands of converts in both the North and the South during the 1920s through intensive promotional efforts. The activities of the extremely nationalistic and racist Klan, 5,000,000 strong, was a major issue in the nation. Indiana, a state politically dominated by the Klan, was shaking off its influence by late 1926.

Charles G. Dawes, vice president of the United States from 1925 to 1929. Dawes, presiding officer of the Senate, had slipped off to a hotel for a nap when President Coolidge's nominee for attorney general was up for Senate confirmation. After approval failed by one vote, Dawes never completely overcame the suspicion that he deliberately had been absent.

For Nicholas Longworth see DT 51.

Albert Ritchie, governor of Maryland from 1920 to 1935. Ritchie was a frequent candidate for the Democratic presidential nomination.

Frank Lowden, governor of Illinois from 1917 to 1921. Lowden was an active but unsuccessful candidate for the Republican presidential nomination in 1920. After a respite from public office, Lowden recently had announced his candidacy for the presidential nomination in 1928.

[96] *NYT,* Monday, November 29, 1926, 21:7. Variants: *BDG* and *LAT* give "aviation. Both" in first sentence.

[97] *NYT,* Tuesday, November 30, 1926, 31:7.

South Bend, Indiana, a city of 70,000 in 1920, was noted as a diversified manufacturing center and as the home of Notre Dame University.

98 *NYT,* Wednesday, December 1, 1926, 29:7.

Rudolph Valentino, popular Italian-born star of the American cinema during the 1920s. He rocketed to fame in *The Shiek* in 1921, and was the romantic hero of the era. He was declining in popularity, however, when he died suddenly in August of 1926. On November 25 Natacha Rambova, Valentino's second wife, professed to have established spiritual communication with him.

In a special election in Maine on November 29 to fill a vacancy in the United States Senate, Republican Arthur Gould defeated Democrat Fulton Reitman.

99 *NYT,* Thursday, December 2, 1926, 29:7.

In China, unstable since a revolution in 1911, American and other foreign nations had treaty rights allowing them to patrol Chinese waters to protect lives and property of their nationals. On November 30 two United States destroyers were ordered to the river city of Hankow to augment a force of American marines who reportedly had landed there earlier.

Nicaragua had two rival governments, with Mexico aiding the liberal and the United States the conservative. American marines landed in August of 1926 after the conservative president had requested their intervention.

American relations with Mexico deteriorated during 1926 as the United States renewed pressure concerning property rights of foreigners under the Mexican constitution. Secretary of State Kellogg issued several notes on these questions amid predictions of a break in diplomatic relations in 1927 when new, stricter laws were to become effective.

Tacna and Arica, border provinces between Chile and Peru, had been occupied by Chile for more than forty years. President Harding, acting as arbitrator, had failed in 1922 to settle the problem through a plebiscite. On November 30, 1926, Kellogg proposed that both provinces be demilitarized and given to Bolivia. The provinces were partitioned in 1929.

100 *NYT,* Friday, December 3, 1926, 25:7. Variant: *BDG* gives "Roumania" in fourth sentence.

101 *BDG* (AM), Saturday, December 4, 1926, 1:7. Variants: *KCT* gives "The Hall-Mills jury ended by turning in the verdict it had . . . let the jury render its verdict when it's sworn in instead of when it's worn out."/ *NYT* and *LAT* did not print the DT.

No DT is available for Sunday, December 5, 1926.

102 *LAT,* Monday, December 6, 1926, I:1:3-4; heading as in *NYT,* 2:3. Variants: *NYT* gives "pray to the Lord to give" in second sentence and omits third sentence entirely.

103 *NYT,* Tuesday, December 7, 1926, 2:2.

104 *NYT,* Wednesday, December 8, 1926, 29:7. Variants: *BDG* gives "Roumania" in first sentence/*LAT* did not print the DT.

Considerable speculation arose regarding a successor to ailing King Ferdinand of Rumania. A struggle was expected between factions which supported former Crown Prince Carol, who earlier had renounced his right to the throne, and his son, six-year-old Prince Michael. The health of Ferdinand improved during December, prompting the king to affirm his intention to fulfill his duties.

[105] *NYT,* Thursday, December 9, 1926, 29:7. *BDG* and *LAT* did not print the DT.

[106] *NYT,* Friday, December 10, 1926, 27:7.

Installment purchases, especially of automobiles and household appliances, expanded to 15 percent of retail sales in the 1920s. Government officials noted their concern but held that such purchases aided business and did not interfere with the prudent savings of the American people

[107] *NYT,* Saturday, December 11, 1926, 19:6.

For Governor Albert Ritchie see DT 95.

[108] *NYT,* Sunday, December 12, 1926, I:2:6. *BDG* and *LAT* did not print the DT.

President Coolidge in his budget message on December 9 predicted a treasury surplus of $383,079,095 for the fiscal year which had begun on July 1. Secretary of the Treasury Mellon suggested rebates to taxpayers, while Democratic Representative John Garner of Texas proposed a tax reduction.

Sol Bloom, Democratic United States representative from New York from 1923 to 1949. Bloom made a fortune in real estate, entertainment, and construction before entering politics.

Royal S. Copeland, Democratic United States senator from New York from 1923 to 1938. A physician, Copeland became dean of a New York City medical college in 1908 and entered political life ten years later as the municipal health commissioner.

[109] *NYT,* Monday, December 13, 1926, 23:7. Variants: *NYT* gives "Count Salm is . . . talent, husbands" in first and second sentences, but *BDG* and *LAT* have it as here.

Count Ludwig Salm von Hoogstraeten, Austrian nobleman, actor and tennis player. Salm married American heiress Millicent Rogers in 1924, but after many well-publicized marital stresses he filed a suit for separation; receiving an out-of-court settlement of more than $300,000, he dropped the suit in March of 1927. Countess Salm later obtained a divorce in Paris.

[110] *NYT,* Tuesday, December 14, 1926, 29:7. Variants: *NYT* omits "A. and M." and "Yours" in second paragraph, but *BDG* and *LAT* have it as here.

Rebecca Rogers, a graduate of the University of Texas and a secretary for Governor-elect Moody (see DT 71), robbed a bank in Buda, Texas, on December 11. Despite a plea that she needed the money to pay debts, she was tried and convicted for the crime.

Governor Ma Ferguson of Texas (see DT 71), had pardoned more than 3,200 convicted criminals by the end of her two-year term in January of 1927.

[111] *NYT,* Wednesday, December 15, 1926, 29:7.

[112] *NYT,* Thursday, December 16, 1926, 29:7.

Marion Talley, opera singer from Kansas City who became a minor celebrity in February of 1926 by being selected to sing a soprano role for the New York Metropolitan Opera. Miss Talley refused to perform at a concert in New Rochelle, New York, when advanced payment of a guaranteed $3,000 fee was not available.

A breach of promise settlement of $50,000 from a "wealthy shovel manufacturer" was awarded in Pittsburgh to a woman whom the *New York Times* described as "an actress and modiste."

113 *NYT,* Friday, December 17, 1926, 25:7.

Lennington "Len" Small, Republican governor of Illinois from 1921 to 1929. Small acquired his nickname "Hard Surface Road" for sponsoring an ambitious highway building program in Illinois. On December 15 Small appointed Frank Smith (see DT 79) to the United States Senate to fill a recent vacancy.

114 *NYT,* Saturday, December 18, 1926, 19:7.

During the early 1930s, the *Dearborn* (Michigan) *Independent,* a magazine owned by Henry Ford, repeated as fact anti-Semitic statements and allegations. Representative Sol Bloom introduced a resolution in December of 1926 calling for a congressional investigation of "Jewish" domination of the Federal Reserve System, a charge which stemmed from an article in the *Independent.*

115 *NYT,* Sunday, December 19, 1926, I:2:2. *BDG* and *LAT* did not print the DT.

Chicago city officials, concerned about insufficient water and sewage disposal systems, had completed a canal in 1900 to connect Lake Michigan, the Illinois River, and the Mississippi River. Other Great Lake cities threatened suit to halt further diversion of water, while several states actually sued. Eventually the United States Supreme Court and Congress became involved in an attempt to end the controversy.

116 *NYT,* Monday, December 20, 1926, 23:7. Variants: *NYT* gives "three—Senator Capper" in first sentence, but *BDG* and *LAT* have it as here/*NYT* and *LAT* give "William Allen White" in second sentence, but *BDG* has it as here.

Arthur Capper, United States senator from 1919 to 1949. Capper, a Republican and former governor, was an important member of the farm bloc in the Senate.

Charles Curtis, United States senator from 1907 to 1913 and from 1915 to 1929. Curtis, majority leader of the Republicans in the Senate, was a consistent supporter of President Coolidge. He left the Senate in 1929 to serve a term as vice president of the United States.

William Allen White, liberal Republican publisher and editor of the *Emporia* (Kansas) *Gazette* from 1895 until his retirement in 1943. White, winner of a Pulitzer Prize in 1923, was noted widely for his crusading and hard-hitting editorials. "Randolph" was the middle name of another well-known publisher, William Randolph Hearst (see DT 379).

The board of trustees of exclusive Beverly Hills, California, Rogers' residence, elected Rogers "mayor" of the city on December 12, partly as a joke and also for the publicity it would generate. He was scheduled to be sworn in during elaborate ceremonies on December 21.

117 *NYT,* Tuesday, December 21, 1926, 25:7. Variants: *BDG* gives "for speakers" in second sentence /*BDG* and *KCT* give "ever barked for" in eighth sentence/*LAT* did not print the DT.

The serious rivalry between California, Arizona, and other states of the Colorado River basin for control of water in the Southwest was a major news item in the 1920s.

Douglas Fairbanks, swashbuckling American actor and hero of numerous silent spectaculars; co-founder with wife Mary Pickford, Charlie Chaplin, and

D. W. Griffith of United Artists Film Corporation in 1919. Fairbanks chaired Rogers' welcoming committee in Beverly Hills.

[118] *NYT,* Wednesday, December 22, 1926, 24:6. Variants: *LAT* gives "arrived here today and had big reception." in first sentence/*NYT* gives "offer to let me preach, with Doug" in third sentence, but *BDG* and *LAT* have it as here/*LAT* gives fourth and fifth sentences "Seriously speaking, however, they gave me a great reception . . . Coolidge for sending me nice message. Also Gov. Al Smith and Mayor Jimmy Walker of New York, my only opposition. Also Hiram Johnson and Shortridge."/*NYT* gives "Shortridge, the" in fifth and sixth sentences, but *BDG* and *LAT* have it as here/*NYT* omits "his honor of" and gives "Beverly Hills is the best town west of Nantucket Lightship." in sixth and seventh sentences, but *BDG* and *LAT* have it as here/*KCT* did not print the DT.

Kenneth Ormiston, radio engineer who directed broadcasting at evangelist Aimee McPherson's Four Square Gospel Temple in Los Angeles. When law officers sought Ormiston in connection with McPherson's disappearance the previous spring, he dropped from sight until his arrest in Harrisburg, Pennsylvania, in December (see DT 56).

Tom Mix, famous cowboy film star and one of the most popular box office attractions in the history of the screen. Before entering motion pictures, Mix worked at the Miller Brothers' 101 Ranch in Oklahoma and appeared in wild west shows with Rogers.

William S. Hart, solemn-faced western hero of the silent screen who began his acting career on the stage in 1889, entered movies in 1914; he retired in 1926.

Bernard "Ben" Turpin, slapstick comedian best known for his cross-eyes and large toothbrush mustache.

Hiram Johnson, United States senator from California from 1917 until his death in 1945. Johnson, a Republican and former governor, earned a reputation in the Senate as an isolationist, opposing such measures as United States membership in the League of Nations.

Samuel Shortridge, United States senator from California from 1921 to 1933. An amiable conservative Republican, Shortridge was respected widely as an orator on political topics.

[119] *NYT,* Thursday, December 23, 1926, 14:3.

Henry Reilly, West Point graduate who served with the Forty-second Division in France during World War I. In a recent magazine article, Brigadier General Reilly had claimed that economic cutbacks in 1926 had caused nearly 14,000 desertions out of a regular army of 130,000.

[120] *NYT,* Friday, December 24, 1926, 12:5.

Tristram "Tris" Speaker, major league outfielder for twenty-two seasons, most notably with the Cleveland Indians from 1916 to 1926. As player-manager at Cleveland, he led his team to a World Series championship in 1920.

Tyrus 'Ty" Cobb, veteran outfielder and manager of the Detroit Tigers; considered one of the greatest baseball players of all times. Cobb and Speaker were dismissed by their respective clubs in the fall of 1926 after former Detroit pitcher Dutch Leonard accused both men of involvement in alleged betting and game fixing. They later were exonerated of any wrongdoing.

[121] *NYT,* Saturday, December 25, 1926, 2:8.

No DT is available for Sunday, December 26, 1926.

[122] *NYT,* Monday, December 27, 1926, 17:7. Variant: *LAT* gives origin "BEVERLY HILLS."

President Adolfo Díaz of Nicaragua, after an attempt on his life on December 23, welcomed the landing of additional United States marines to protect American lives and property (see DT 99). Meanwhile in China, American naval units were positioned at Foochow as well as Hankow (see DT 99).

While vacationing in Maine, heavyweight champion Gene Tunney attempted to walk across a frozen lake in order to reach a nearby Catholic church for mass. He broke through the ice but was rescued by a human chain.

123 *NYT,* Tuesday, December 28, 1926, 21:7. Variants: *BDG* and *LAT* give "it is preparing" in fifth sentence.

124 *NYT,* Wednesday, December 29, 1926, 23:7.

The American Legion, the principal organization of World War I veterans, recently had announced that its next convention would be held in Paris in September of 1927, raising the humorous possibility that a future Legion convention would be held in Nicaragua because of the recent landing of American troops in that country.

125 *NYT,* Thursday, December 30, 1926, 21:7. Variant: *LAT* gives origin "BEVERLY HILLS."

126 *NYT,* Friday, December 31, 1926, 15:7.

For William Butler see DT 72; for William Vare and Frank Smith see DT 79.

127 *NYT,* Saturday, January 1, 1927, 5:4. Variant: *LAT* gives "on optimism tomorrow. It's in every New Year's." in P. S.

A number of deaths during the holidays had been attributed to poisonous bootlegged alcohol. Treasury Secretary Mellon announced that the government was searching for non-lethal adulterants of denatured alcohol that would not alter its distastefulness.

Judge Elbert Gary (see DT 53) proclaimed in his annual New Year prediction that "any well-posted man" would consider 1927 a year of "extraordinarily good" business conditions.

No DT is available for Sunday, January 2, 19277.

128 *NYT,* Monday, January 3, 1927, 21:7. Variant: *LAT* gives origin "BEVERLY HILLS."

An earthquake struck the twin border towns of Calexico, California, and Mexicali, Baja California, Mexico, on January 1; no fatalities were reported. Joint rescue operations served to improve Mexican-American relations.

Secretary of State Kellogg recently had hinted that an investigation should be conducted into "Bolshevik" influence in the Mexican government. Despite public pressure, Kellogg refused to offer facts to support his allegations.

129 *NYT,* Tuesday, January 4, 1927, 27:7. Variants: *LAT* gives "his late honor" in close/only *LAT* gives the P. S.

Charles "Charlie" Chaplin, legendary English-born comedian who starred in several classic American and British films. He was known widely for his fiim portrayal of the little tramp. Chaplin's wife, Lita Grey, had left him, threatening to sue for divorce, alimony, a property settlement, and custody of the couple's two children.

District Attorney Asa Keyes of Los Angeles reluctantly dropped the prosecution of Aimee McPherson and Kenneth Ormiston on January 10 (see DTs 56 and 118.) Witnesses upon whose testimony the prosecutor's case depended had been accused in the press of perjury or had been revealed as recent inmates of mental institutions.

[130] *NYT,* Wednesday, January 5, 1927, 2:6. Variants: *LAT* gives "government-made" in third sentence/*BDG* and *LAT* omit first three words of fourth sentence.

An international compact outlawing the use of poison gases in warfare was signed at the Washington Arms Conference of 1921-1922; a protocol to extend it to other nations was finalized at Geneva, Switzerland, in June of 1925.

[131] *NYT,* Thursday, January 6, 1927, 29:7. Variants: *LAT* gives "swears Germany was" in second sentence/*BDG* gives "series of Marne" in second sentence/*BDG* and *LAT* give "War being on the level" in third sentence.

Baseball Commissioner Kenesaw Mountain Landis held hearings beginning on January 5 into new allegations of scandal in the sport (see DT 120). Landis' action was prompted by belated charges that games between the Chicago White Sox and the Detroit Tigers in 1917 and 1919 had been "fixed."

John "Black Jack" Pershing, United States Army Chief of Staff from 1921 to 1924; commander of the Allied Expeditionary Force in Europe during World War I. Marne was the scene of a crucial, devastating battle in France during the war.

[132] *NYT,* Friday, January 7, 1927, 21:7. Variants: *LAT* gives "refusing to loan cash to soldiers on their adjusted compensation on account of it being too much red tape." in first sentence/*LAT* gives "was for the boys when they were earning it. There is" in second sentence.

Veterans of the First World War were granted federal, interest-bearing certificates, redeemable in 1945, in which the principal amount varied with the number of days served. The certificates were not direct pensions and were not negotiable but could be used as collateral for commercial loans.

[133] *NYT,* Saturday, January 8, 1927, 19:7.

Clarence Little, noted biologist and geneticist who served as president of the University of Maine from 1922 to 1925 and of the University of Michigan from 1925 to 1929.

Benjamin "Benny" Friedman, all-American quarterback at the University of Michigan from 1924 to 1926.

Benjamin "Benny" Oosterbaan, all-American end at Michigan from 1925 to 1927; teamed with Friedman to form one of the most succesful passing duos in collegiate football history. The new stadium at the University of Michigan was dedicated in 1927 and had a seating capacity of 85,753.

No DT is available for Sunday, January 9, 1927.

[134] *NYT*, Monday, January 10, 1927, 25:7.

United States marines were ordered to enter the Nicaraguan capital of Managua on January 5 at the request of President Díaz. The troops, reinforced by American naval vessels, helped to supervise local elections.

[135] *LAT,* Tuesday, January 11, 1927, I:1:3. Variants: *BDG* gives "the doctor is the properly" in first sentence/*BDG* gives "that ever get" in second sentence/*NYT* did not print the DT.

Adolfo Díaz, president of Nicaragua from 1913 to 1916; seized power in 1925 and again became president in 1926, serving until 1928. Díaz sought American aid in order to repulse challenges to his rule.

Technically, only Mexico had recognized liberal Juan Sacasa as the legitimate president of Nicaragua.

[136] *NYT,* Wednesday, January 12, 1927, 27:7.

President Coolidge sent a formal message to Congress on January 10 which strongly defended his Nicaragua policy. On the same day Mrs. Lita Chaplin filed her long-expected suit for divorce, alleging infidelity and assorted other cruelties.

[137] *NYT,* Thursday, January 13, 1927, 27:7. Variants: *NYT* omits second sentence, but *BDG, LAT,* and *KCT* have it as here/*LAT* gives "you can jar" in sixth sentence.

[138] *NYT,* Friday, January 14, 1927, 21:7.

A trial involving a federal suit to recover $30,000,000 in delinquent taxes allegedly owed by Senator James Couzens and eight other original investors in the Ford Motor Company opened in Detroit in early 1927. Couzens, a former Ford executive, and other non-family stockholders had sold their shares in 1919, this sale being the basis for the government action. The court proceedings revealed many details of internal corporation management which fascinated the general public.

[139] *NYT,* Saturday, January 15, 1927, 17:7. Variants: *BDG* gives "goals: a product" in fourth and fifth sentences/*LAT* omits fifth sentence.

John "Jack" Wilce, head football coach at Ohio State University from 1913 to 1928; professor of clinical and preventive medicine and director of the university health service from 1924 to 1958. A non-university corporation constructed a new stadium at Ohio State with a seating capacity of 62,000.

The University of Michigan edged Ohio State, 17 to 16, in a football game on November 13. A late Buckeye touchdown had brought Ohio State to within reach of a tie, but the kick for point-after-touchdown sailed under the crossbar.

[140] *NYT,* Sunday, January 16, 1927, I:13:4. *BDG* and *LAT* did not print the DT.

[141] *BDG* (AM), Monday, January 17, 1927, 1:7. *NYT* and *LAT* did not print the DT.

Secretary of State Kellogg testified before the Senate Foreign Affairs Committee on January 15. He attempted to link Moscow to the deteriorating American relations with Mexico.

[142] *NYT,* Tuesday, January 18, 1927, 27:7.

On January 15 the Tennessee Supreme Court upheld the constitutionality of a state law which forbade the teaching of evolution in public schools. At the same time the court overruled on a technicality a lower court conviction of John Scopes, a biology teacher who had taught evolution, and ordered that there be no further prosecution of Scopes. The state law was repealed in 1967.

[143] *NYT,* Wednesday, January 19, 1927, 25:7. Variants: *NYT* gives "chewing gum" in third sentence/*BDG* gives signature "WILL ROGERS, The Mayor."

William Wrigley, Jr., manufacturer and distributor of chewing gum. Owner of Santa Catalina Island off the coast of California, Wrigley offered a prize of $25,000 for the first person to swim the previously unconquered twenty-two-mile channel between the island and the mainland. The competition attracted 153 contestants, but only one swimmer completed the course.

144 *NYT,* Thursday, January 20, 1927, 25:7. Variant: *BDG* adds "WILL ROGERS" to signature.

The Senate Committee on Naval Affairs voted on January 18 to appropriate $1,200,000 for the construction of three previously authorized cruisers.

145 *NYT,* Friday, January 21, 1927, 19:7. Variant: *BDG* gives "Nicaragua's, elected" in second and third sentences.

146 *NYT,* Saturday, January 22, 1927, 15:7. Variant: *LAT* omits P. S.

147 *NYT,* Sunday, January 23, 1927, I:2:4. *BDG* and *LAT* did not print the DT.

Alvin Victor "Vic" Donahey, governor of Ohio from 1923 to 1929; United States senator from 1925 to 1941. Donahey, a prohibitionist and a Protestant, was viewed as a potential Democratic presidential candidate because of his ability to attract Republican votes.

Austin Peay, governor of Tennessee from 1923 to 1927. Peay's death in office later in 1927 deprived Tennessee of a favorite son candidate for the Democratic presidential nomination.

Howard Gore, United States secretary of agriculture from 1924 to 1925; Republican governor of West Virginia from 1925 to 1929.

For Frank Lowden see DT 95; for Al Smith see DT 36.

William G. McAdoo, United States secretary of the treasury from 1913 to 1918; United States senator from California from 1933 to 1939. McAdoo, married to President Wilson's only daughter, was a prominent candidate for the Democratic presidential nomination in 1920 and 1924.

148 *NYT,* Monday, January 24, 1927, 19:7. *LAT* did not print the DT.

Arbitration with Mexico was requested by the Senate Foreign Affairs Committee in a special resolution on January 22. President Coolidge rejected the resolution later that same day, although he later reconsidered his action.

149 *NYT,* Tuesday, January 25, 1927, 25:7. Variant: *LAT* gives signature "The Prowling Mayor" after P. S.

The prosecution in the Norris trial rested on January 22 (see DT 67). Three days later, the case went to the jury which returned a verdict of acquittal after only two ballots. Meanwhile the separation suit between Edward and Peaches Browning opened as scheduled on January 24 in Carmel, New York.

Relations between Princeton and Harvard received another jolt when a former Harvard football player charged in a magazine article that for several years Princeton deliberately had played "dirty football" against Harvard. Officials at Princeton denied the allegations (see DT 83).

150 *BDG* (AM), Wednesday, January 26, 1927, 1:7. *NYT* did not print the DT.

The Browning trial included revelations of sexual abnormality and other testimony which presumably outraged the public. The presiding justice of the

New York Supreme Court defended his decision for open proceedings: "The policy of our law is against secrecy, except in such cases as are definitely set forth in the law."

[151] *NYT,* Thursday, January 27, 1927, 21:7.

Carolyn Heenan, mother of Peaches Browning, admitted in court that Edward Browning had paid her an allowance from the time of the wedding to the separation. The *New York Times* noted that Mrs. Heenan "stumbled and faltered through her story and at times her answers caused laughter."

[152] *NYT,* Friday, January 28, 1927, 21:7. Variants: *BDG* and *LAT* give "prove to China" in first sentence/*BDG* and *LAT* give signature "WILL ROGERS."/*BDG* omits "P. S. S."

American missionaries fled several provinces of China in January when mobs began attacking foreign residents and visitors.

Rolling chairs, which attendants pushed for a fee, were favorite conveyances for tourists along the famed "boardwalk" in Atlantic City, New Jersey.

Kenesaw Mountain Landis, prominent American jurist who served as major league baseball commissioner from 1920 until his death in 1944. On January 27 Landis exonerated Ty Cobb and Tris Speaker of charges brought against them by Dutch Leonard (see DT 120).

[153] *NYT,* Saturday, January 29, 1927, 17:7. Variant: *BDG* gives signature "WILL ROGERS."

[154] *NYT,* Sunday, January 30, 1927, I:3:6. *BDG* and *LAT* did not print the DT.

Philadelphia hosted the Sesqui-Centennial International Exposition of 1926, celebrating 150 years of progress since the Declaration of Independence. Internal division and wholesale public apathy frustrated the sponsors of the show; $5,000,000 in debts faced the Philadelphia city council as the gates closed.

As a youngster Rogers had attended the World Columbian Exposition at Chicago, probably in 1894. In 1904 he participated in the Louisiana Purchase Exposition at St. Louis as a member of the Cummins Wild West Show.

[155] *NYT,* Monday, January 31, 1927, 19:7. *LAT* did not print the DT.

Mayor Walker of New York visited Cuba as an official guest of the mayor of Havana. He attended horse races, delivered speeches, and received the traditional gold key to the city. Meanwhile, teachers' salaries, theatrical censorship, water pollution, rapid transit, and housing vied for his attention at home.

[156] *NYT,* Tuesday, February 1, 1927, 29:7. Variants: *BDG* omits fourth sentence/*LAT* gives "prohibition is another, Claremore's radium water another and last, the greatest, Democratic" in sixth sentence/*BDG* gives "another, then come Claremore, radium, water, and—last and greatest—Democratic" in sixth sentence.

[157] *NYT,* Wednesday, February 2, 1927, 27:7.

Josephus Daniels, editor and publisher of the *Raleigh* (North Carolina) *News and Observer* from 1894 to 1933; secretary of the navy from 1913 to 1921.

[158] *NYT,* Thursday, February 3, 1927, 23:7. Variants: *LAT* gives "Florida and like Dempsey they . . . same thing" in second and third sentences/*BDG* begins fifth sentence "It's a pleasure"/*BDG* and *LAT* give "A Mayor from" to

begin seventh sentence/*BDG* gives "Will Rogers" as signature after seventh sentence and *LAT* omits signature.

Florida land sales boomed during the early 1920s as a flood of tourists and new winter residents spurred construction of subdivisions, resorts, and golf courses. Subsequent transportation problems, housing shortages, and unfavorable publicity contributed to an economic decline in 1925. A devastating hurricane which struck the Miami area in September of 1926 ended any hope for revival. Despite the optimistic reports of Florida civic leaders, the recession in the state continued throughout the decade.

[159] *NYT,* Friday, February 4, 1927, 21:7. Variant: *LAT* gives "morning in Ormond" in first sentence.

John D. Rockefeller, founder of Standard Oil Company and at one point considered the wealthiest man in the world. As a philanthropist he donated an estimated $530,000,000 to various educational, scientific, and religious institutions. Eighty-seven-year-old Rockefeller also was known for handing shiny new dimes to friends and strangers.

[160] *NYT,* Saturday, February 5, 1927, 2:2. Variant: *BDG* gives signature "WILL ROGERS." after close.

In China General Chiang Kai-shek defeated opposing military and civil leaders and moved toward the partial unification of the country in the spring of 1927. Several foreign nations, including the United States, maintained forces in China to protect their citizens and property.

[161] *NYT,* Sunday, February 6, 1927, 21:2. *BDG* and *LAT* did not print the DT.

Residents of Los Angeles and its suburbs reported a slight earth tremor on February 4; no injuries or property damage occurred.

[162] *NYT,* Monday, February 7, 1927, 21:7. Variants: *LAT* gives "it up we . . . today out there, and . . . paper. So" in third sentence/*LAT* gives "a shakeless" in close.

[163] *NYT,* Tuesday, February 8, 1927, 25:7. Variants: *BDG* gives "I have to" and *LAT* gives "I got to" to begin sixth sentence/*LAT* gives "while we are" in seventh sentence.

[164] *LAT,* Wednesday, February 9, 1927, 1:2. Variants: *BDG* gives "haven't got enough" in third sentence/*BDG* gives P.S. as "Flew three hundred commercial aviation."/*NYT* did not print the DT.

Portuguese dissidents, disturbed by pressing domestic problems, led civil riots in Oporto and Lisbon in early 1927. The military-dominated government crushed the uprising after a great loss of lives.

[165] *NYT,* Thursday, February 10, 1927, 25:7.

King George V opened the British Parliament on February 3 with the traditional pomp and pageantry and then informed the assembled members that although he still desired a peaceful remedy of the difficulties in China, he had ordered a fleet to the Far East to protect British citizens and property there.

Edward, Prince of Wales, reigned for eleven months as King Edward VIII until his abdication in December of 1936. During the procession at the opening ceremonies of Parliament, Prince Edward somewhat relieved the seriousness of the occasion when he stumbled over his sword and long red gown.

[166] *NYT,* Friday, February 11, 1927, 23:7. Variants: *BDG* gives "Joe Leblanc" and *LAT* gives "Joe LeBlang," in second sentence/*BDG* gives signature "WILL ROGERS" before close.

Edward Franklin Albee, wealthy theatrical businessman and co-founder in 1928 of the Radio-Keith-Orpheum (RKO) Corporation. Albee owned a winter residence in Palm Beach.

Lee Shubert, with his brother Jacob, owned and operated numerous theaters throughout the United States from 1900 until his death in 1953; also produced several plays and shows.

Marcus Loew, Austrian-American exhibitor and distributor of films, owner of vaudeville and motion picture theaters, and co-founder and controller of Metro-Goldwyn-Mayer Corporation; died in September of 1927.

Adolph Zukor, pioneer American movie producer. By the mid-1920s Zukor had become president of the movie production and distribution firm Famous Players-Lasky Corporation, later known as Paramount Pictures.

Edgar Selwyn, successful actor, play broker, playwright, manager, and producer. From 1914 to 1924 he was president of Selwyn & Company, producers of plays; he later joined Metro-Goldwyn-Mayer as a writer and director, remaining with that firm until his death in 1944.

Arthur Hammerstein, flamboyant producer who made and lost fortunes in show business; son of operatic impresario Oscar Hammerstein and uncle of lyricist Oscar Hammerstein II. Among his most noted successful productions were *Rose-Marie* and *Naughty Marietta.*

Joe Leblang, considered the "King of Cutthroats," the name which embittered theater managers gave to those who sold cut-rate tickets to Broadway shows.

Eva Roberts Stotesbury, wife of a prominent Philadelphia banker and financier. The couple, owners of a winter home in Palm Beach, were regarded as the social leaders of the winter resort for many years.

Ben Bernie, known as the "Old Maestro;" one of the highest paid performers in the United States during the 1920s. Bernie's dance band created a popular, informal style, with the Old Maestro bantering with the audience and dancers.

[167] *NYT,* Saturday, February 12, 1927, 5:2. Variant: *BDG* gives signature "WILL ROGERS."

[168] *NYT,* Sunday, February 13, 1927, 6:2. *BDG* and *LAT* did not print the DT.

Ty Cobb (see DT 120), nicknamed the "Georgia Peach," was born in Narrows, Georgia.

[169] *NYT,* Monday, February 14, 1927, 19:7.

The McNary-Haugen farm relief bill was designed to ease a post-World War I depression in agriculture by providing such basic federal assistance as the control of surpluses and the stablization of prices. Coolidge twice vetoed the measure.

[170] *NYT,* Tuesday, February 15, 1927, 2:2. Variants: *BDG* and *LAT* give "are supposed" in first sentence.

John Richards, Democratic governor of South Carolina from 1927 to 1931.

[171] *NYT,* Wednesday, February 16, 1927, 25:7. Variants: *BDG* gives "Pres Nicholas Butler" in first sentence/*BDG* begins second sentence "He says the" and *LAT* begins it "Butler says the"/*BDG* and *LAT* give "Nick may" to begin third sentence.

William Upshaw, United States representative from Georgia from 1919 to 1927. An extremely religious man, Upshaw believed in the total abstinence from alcoholic beverages for all government officials as an example for American youth. He quit the Democratic party because of its liberal position on the liquor issue and ran for president in 1932 on the Prohibition ticket.

Nicholas Murray Butler, professor of philosophy at Columbia University and president of the institution from 1902 to 1945. Butler, a Republican, advocated repeal of the Eighteenth Amendment.

[172] *NYT,* Thursday, February 17, 1927, 3:5. Variant: *LAT* gives "My personal congressional" in first sentence.

Thomas Blanton, Democratic United States representative from Texas from 1917 to 1929 and from 1930 to 1937. Blanton and Bloom (see DT 108) sparred during a congressional committee hearing of a proposed Sunday closing law for the District of Columbia. Bloom, an opponent of the bill, objected to Blanton's treatment of a witness also opposing the measure. The men exchanged heated words and finally punches. Fisticuffs between other members of Congress had occurred earlier in the week.

[173] *NYT,* Friday, February 18, 1927, 23:7. Variants: *BDG* gives "about plans to" in first sentence/*BDG* and *LAT* give "foundations" in fifth sentence/*BDG* gives signature "WILL ROGERS." after close/*BDG* and *LAT* give "Will Hayes" in P. S.

Residents of Beverly Hills held an "indignation" meeting on February 13 where they jestingly demanded the resignation of Mayor Rogers because of his prolonged absences from the city. Eddie Cantor, chairman of the gathering, humorously declared that his friend Rogers should be recalled either from his travels or from his position as mayor.

Will H. Hays, president of the Motion Picture Producers and Distributors Association of America from 1922 to 1945. As "czar" of the film industry, Hays labored to improve the medium and to create a new image of the industry after various scandals of the early 1920s.

[174] *NYT,* Saturday, February 19, 1927, 17:7. Variants: *BDG* and *KCT* give origin "PINEHURST, N. C."/*BDG, LAT,* and *KCT* give "not totally exterminate" in third sentence/*BDG* and *LAT* omit "A MISSIONARY" in close.

J. Thomas "Tom" Heflin, Democratic United States senator from Alabama from 1920 to 1931. Heflin attacked the Catholic church three times in two days in speeches before the Senate. He criticized several Catholics and friends of Catholics, including Governor Al Smith and Senator James Wadsworth of New York.

[175] *NYT,* Sunday, February 20, 1927, 2:7. *BDG* and *LAT* did not print the DT.

[176] *NYT,* Monday, February 21, 1927, 8:3. Variants: *LAT* ends third sentence "Ferguson." omitting last four words/*KCT* gives "Hon. G. Carter" in third sentence/*BDG, LAT,* and *KCT* give "Mayor Jimmy Walker." in fourth sentence.

Amon G. Carter, publisher of the *Fort Worth* (Texas) *Star-Telegram* from 1909 until his death in 1955. Carter was known as the one-man chamber of commerce for Fort Worth and West Texas and was a long-time friend of the Rogers family.

Mary "Texas" Guinan, Texas-born actress who left the stage in the 1920s to own and operate a night club in New York; renowned for her conflicts with prohibition agents and her brash greeting to each customer: "Hello sucker."

Byron Bancroft "Ban" Johnson, baseball executive; first president of the American League, serving from 1900 to 1927. Johnson upgraded many aspects of professional baseball and gave the new league respectability nearly equaling that of the National League. He had opposed the election of Landis (see DT 152) as commissioner and clashed with him in the Cobb-Speaker controversy (see DT 120).

For boxer Harry Wills see DT 51; for Jack Sharkey see DT 75.

177 *NYT,* Tuesday, February 22, 1927, 2:3. Variants: *LAT* gives "test last week" in first sentence/*LAT* gives "did pass." in second sentence/*BDG* gives "somewhere outside . . . action. Old" in fifth and sixth sentences/*BDG* omits eighth sentence/*LAT* ends eighth sentence "Hotel as the sole surviving gentile."

The Arkansas state senate moved to table the Rotenberry antievolution bill which would prohibit the teaching of evolution in tax-supported schools in the state. Arkansas legislators enacted an antievolution law in 1928.

178 *NYT,* Wednesday, February 23, 1927, 25:7. Variant: *LAT* begins second sentence of P. S. "This is where . . . ."

An auction of the personal effects of Rudolph Valentino (see DT 98), including antiques, horses, motor cars, and costumes, netted $96,654 for the film star's heirs.

Rogers' wife, Betty Blake Rogers, was a native of Rogers, Arkansas, an Ozark mountain resort community located twenty miles north of Fayetteville in the northwestern corner of the state. The couple had married on November 25, 1908, in the Blake home in Rogers.

179 *NYT,* Thursday, February 24, 1927, 25:7. Variants: *LAT* gives "and about all' in second sentence/*LAT* gives "Know, but" in fourth sentence.

President Coolidge saluted George Washington in a speech before a joint session of Congress. Coolidge dwelled on the first president's personal life as he praised his diligent industry as a surveyor, farmer, and businessman.

180 *BDG* (AM), Friday, February 25, 1927, 1:7; heading from *KCT,* 15:4. *NYT* and *LAT* did not print the DT.

181 *NYT,* Saturday, February 26, 1927, 17:7. Variants: *LAT* gives "Mc-Nary-Haugen" in first sentence/*KCT* gives "of is being" in second sentence/*KCT* ends close "A Dirt Farmer." omiting last four words.

President Coolidge returned the McNary-Haugen farm relief bill to Congress without his signature; he considered the measure harmful, unfair, and illegal. His action prompted farm bloc leaders to declare their open opposition to Coolidge's renomination in 1928 and the candidacy of any easterner opposed to the farm bill.

No DT is available for Sunday, February 27, 1927.

182 *NYT,* Monday, February 28, 1927, 10:5. Variants: *KCT* gives "farm bill" in first sentence/*BDG* gives close "An Atwater Kent Farmer,"/*KCT* gives signature "WILL ROGERS."/second P. S. only printed in *LAT*.

The radio control law authorized a federal commission to regulate the rapidly expanding radio broadcasting industry.

183 *NYT,* Tuesday, March 1, 1927, 29:7. Variant: *LAT* omits fifth sentence.

[184] *NYT,* Wednesday, March 2, 1927, 27:7. Variants: *LAT* and *KCT* give "I hate to" in fourth sentence/*KCT* gives "bolshevist" in fourth sentence.

The American State Department dispatched another note to the Mexican government on February 28, but administration officials refused to divulge its contents.

[185] *KCT,* Thursday, March 3, 1927, 15:2. Variants: *BDG* gives "but Arizona will be dammed if . . . split a dam with a lot of dam real estate boosters. If they want a dam so dammed bad, let 'em dam their climate" in first sentence/ *BDG* gives "or Arizona's river at" in fourth sentence/*NYT* and *LAT* did not print the DT.

Arizonians maintained that construction of Boulder Dam (later known as Hoover Dam) on the Colorado River would limit water for irrigation. Senators Ashurst and Cameron of Arizona and Senators Smoot and King of Utah led opposition to the dam, delaying the start of construction until 1931. When completed in 1936, it became the primary supplier of hydroelectric power for southern California.

[186] *NYT,* Friday, March 4, 1927, 23:7. Variants: *LAT* gives origin "Phoenix,"/*LAT* adds close "Headed for Beverly Hills to take up Mayor's job."

Chinese troops had seized a United States commercial vessel, but American marines recaptured it on March 2. Meanwhile, President Coolidge dispatched additional marines to Nicaragua to stabilize conditions in that country. No diplomatic notes were sent to Mexico on March 3.

[187] *NYT,* Saturday, March 5, 1927, 2:2. Variants: *BDG* and *KCT* omit close, but add signature "WILL ROGERS"/*LAT* adds signature "WILL." after close.

[188] *NYT,* Sunday, March 6, 1927, 19:2. *BDG, LAT,* and *KCT* did not print the DT.

Four men named Reed served in the Sixty-ninth Congress. Rogers probably referred to Democratic Senator James Reed of Missouri (see DT 79) and Republican Senator David Reed of Pennsylvania who often disagreed and debated, especially regarding Republican campaign corruption in Illinois and Pennsylvania.

[189] *NYT,* Monday, March 7, 1927, 21:7. Variants: *LAT* gives origin "BEVERLY HILLS"/*BDG* ends third sentence "gave out." and *KCT* ends it "gave in."/LAT gives "misfortune, and we thought that wind had done us about all the damage that it would in one year. But the big" in fourth sentence/ *BDG* begins fourth sentence "The big blow in the Senate" omitting first ten words/*KCT* gives "repair the damage they did." in fifth sentence/*LAT* gives "got us some" in eighth sentence/*LAT* gives "they are coming in" in ninth sentence/ *BDG* and *KCT* add signature "WILL ROGERS." after close.

Rogers referred to the hurricane which struck Florida the previous fall (see DT 43) and the subsequent Red Cross aid for the victims.

[190] *NYT,* Tuesday, March 8, 1927, 27:7. Variants: *KCT* gives "for business" in second sentence/*LAT* gives "but I realize I" in second sentence/*BDG* and *KCT* give "business. I must realize I" in second sentence/*NYT* gives "heart-down-heartedly," in close, but *BDG, LAT,* and *KCT* have it as here.

William Penn Adair Rogers was Will's full name.

[191] *NYT,* Wednesday, March 9, 1927, 27:7. *KCT* did not print the DT.

The United States Supreme Court in a landmark decision on March 7 ruled a Texas statute unconstitutional which barred Negroes from voting in primary elections. The case in question involved Dr. L. A. Nixon, a black from El Paso, who had sought to vote in a statewide Democratic primary in July of 1924 but was denied because of his color.

192 *NYT,* Thursday, March 10, 1927, 27:7. Variant: *BDG* gives signature "WILL ROGERS."

President Coolidge's advisers had suggested that he spend the summer in the West for no previous chief executive had vacationed west of the Mississippi River while still in office. The president received offers of a number of western White Houses, including estates in Utah, Wyoming, Colorado, and California.

193 *NYT,* Friday, March 11, 1927, 23:7. Variants: *LAT* gives origin "STOCKTON"/*LAT* gives "instead of just" in third sentence/P. S. only printed in *LAT*.

The California state senate passed the Jones bill on March 10, making possession of a distillery for unlawful purposes a felony.

194 *NYT,* Saturday, March 12, 1927, 3:2. Variants: *BDG* gives "even then they" in third sentence/*KCT* did not print the DT/*LAT* did not print the DT but printed the following for March 12:

*Will Rogers Remarks:*

*SAN FRANCISCO, March 11. — [To the Editor of The Times:] This town is all excited about a bridge over the bay to Oakland. If Arizona hears about it they will talk it to death. What you need in San Francisco is not a bridge; it's an overcoat. There is no jealousy now between here and down there. They have become reconciled. Well it isn't bad to be second in a big State like this.*
*Saw Fanny Ward here today. She is entered in a baby show.*
*Regards.*

*Will.*

Curtis D. Wilbur, United States secretary of the navy from 1924 to 1929. Wilbur claimed that European aircraft did not have the range capability to attack the United States. He also asserted that enemy aircraft carriers could not penetrate American naval defenses.

The San Francisco-Oakland Bay Bridge, first proposed in 1927, was opened to the public in 1936.

Fannie Ward, American stage actress of the 1890s and the early 1900s, was famous for looking perpetually young.

195 *NYT,* Sunday, March 13, 1927, 5:2. *BDG, LAT,* and *KCT* did not print the DT.

Henry F. Ashurst, Democratic United States senator from Arizona from 1912 to 1941.

Ralph H. Cameron, Republican United States senator from Arizona from 1921 to 1927. Ashurst and Cameron filibustered for two days in a successful effort to block passage of the Boulder Dam bill (see DT 185).

For Vice President Charles Dawes see DT 95.

196 *NYT,* Monday, March 14, 1927, 4:3.

Great Britain, the United States, and other foreign powers assumed administration of the custom houses in China to insure an uninterrupted flow of revenue in the wake of the Chinese civil war. After payments for the foreign debt were deducted, the remainder of the customs receipts went to national and local authorities.

[197] *NYT,* Tuesday, March 15, 1927, 27:7. Variant: *LAT* gives "rains have" in P. S.

William King, Democratic United States senator from Utah from 1917 to 1941. The Haitian government barred King from entering the island nation because of his criticism of Haitian politics and the president.

[198] *NYT,* Wednesday, March 16, 1927, 27:7. Variants: *KCT* gives "may go to" in P. S./*LAT* omits P. S.

The California state assembly passed a bill on March 15, establishing a board of governors to supervise the 8,000 lawyers in the state. Rogers addressed the legislature after debate and vote on the bill.

Clement C. Young, Republican governor of California from 1927 to 1930.

Gold was discovered in early March near Weepah, a community in western Nevada.

[199] *NYT,* Thursday, March 17, 1927, 25:7. Variants: *LAT* gives origin "RENO"/*LAT* gives "Just advised publicly and free the . . . and House of Representatives of the State of Nevada at Carson City." for first sentence/*LAT* gives "bill there today." in second sentence/*LAT* gives "The gamblers killed" in third sentence/*LAT* omits fourth and fifth sentences and instead gives "They said, why should gambling be permitted all over America and not have to pay any license? It was almost like asking a bootlegger to pay a license. After people have gambled for years for nothing it's hard to get them to pay a license for it."/ *LAT* omits P. S.

Frederick Balzar, Republican governor of Nevada from 1927 to 1934.

The Nevada state house of representatives passed an open gambling bill in early 1927, but the measure failed in the state senate. The state finally legalized gambling in 1931.

James "Gentleman Jim" Corbett, considered the first scientific boxer. Corbett defeated John L. Sullivan for the world heavyweight championship in 1892 but lost the title to Robert Fitzsimmons by a knockout in Carson City, Nevada, in 1897.

Samuel Langhorn Clemens, "Mark Twain," American author and humorist, resided in Virginia City, Nevada, from 1861 to 1862, during which time he prospected for gold and wrote humorous articles for the *Territorial Enterprise,* a local newspaper.

[200] *NYT,* Friday, March 18, 1927, 8:2. Variants: *LAT* gives "answering the" in first sentence/*LAT* begins fourth sentence "Notre Dame" omitting first two words/*BDG* and *LAT* omit close and give signature "WILL ROGERS."/ *LAT* omits P. S.

Treasury Secretary Mellon responded publicly to a letter from the faculty of Princeton University which had endorsed a similar letter from Columbia University. The professors urged that the debt of American allies be refunded or cancelled. Mellon defended administration policy as sufficiently lenient and opposed refunding the debt.

[201] *NYT,* Saturday, March 19, 1927, 19:7. Variant: *LAT* omits fourth, fifth, and sixth sentences.

[202] *NYT,* Sunday, March 20, 1927, 12:2. *BDG, LAT,* and *KCT* did not print the DT.

Alice Roosevelt Longworth, daughter of President Theodore Roosevelt, wife of Speaker of the House Nicholas Longworth, and famous Washington hostess.

Mrs. Longworth, a close friend of Rogers, was renowned for her influence and bluntness in politics and current affairs.

[203] *NYT,* Monday, March 21, 1927, 21:7. Variants: *KCT* begins second sentence "Later he came"/*BDG* gives "jokes I can't" in fourth and fifth sentences/ *KCT* gives "just plain" in ninth sentence/*LAT* did not print the DT.

Henry L. Whitfield, Democratic governor of Mississippi from 1924 to 1927.

[204] *LAT,* Tuesday, March 22, 1927, 1:4. Variants: *BDG* gives "a marriage contract clause." in fifth sentence/*NYT* and *KCT* did not print the DT.

Arthur Brisbane, nationally syndicated newspaper columnist and editor. Brisbane began his editorial column "Today" in 1917; it eventually was syndicated to 200 daily and 1,200 weekly newspapers. He long had stressed the value of commercial and military aviation.

Edward Browning won his separation suit from his young wife Peaches on March 22 (see DT 48). The court dismissed Mrs. Browning's own suit for separation and disallowed her $300-a-week allowance.

[205] *NYT,* Wednesday, March 23, 1927, 2:2. Variant: *KCT* gives "Chinese" in first sentence.

British troops killed twenty-four Chinese soldiers on March 21 from among a large force attempting to penetrate British defenses to take refuge in the international settlement in Shanghai.

[206] *NYT,* Thursday, March 24, 1927, 16:3.

Criticisms of Jews, published in Henry Ford's *Dearborn Independent* (see DT 114), resulted in a libel suit against Ford. The auto maker hired Senator James Reed to defend his non-involvment in the matter. Ford settled the case out of court on July 27, 1927, with a public apology and a plea for forgiveness.

[207] *NYT,* Friday, March 24, 1927, 2:5. Variants: *BDG* gives "embarkation" and *LAT* gives "to our" in third sentence/*LAT* gives "that business." in sixth sentence/*BDG* and *KCT* give signature "WILL ROGERS." after close/*LAT* omits P. S.

Bertha Knight Landes, mayor of Seattle from 1926 to 1928. Mrs. Landes was the first woman mayor of a large American city.

Italy and Yugoslavia accused each other of interference in neighboring Albania and reportedly ordered troops to their borders in case of war; however, no armed conflict occurred.

[208] *NYT,* Saturday, March 26, 1927, 18:2. *LAT* and *KCT* did not print the DT.

A disarmament commission convened in Geneva on March 21 to prepare an agenda and propose a date for a general international arms limitation conference. Such preliminary meetings culminated in the Kellogg-Briand antiwar pact in 1928.

[209] *NYT,* Sunday, March 27, 1927, 15:2. *BDG, LAT,* and *KCT* did not print the DT.

Clarence Dill, Democratic United States senator from Washington from 1923 to 1935. Dill recently had married Rosalie Jones, a wealthy suffragette leader from New York City; they were divorced in 1936.

Louis Davenport owned and operated the Davenport Hotel and Restaurant, one of the most famous inns in the Northwest and a favorite of Rogers since his days in vaudeville.

Robert T. "Bobby" Jones, Georgia-born amateur golfer; one of the greatest players of the sport of all times; winner of four United States open championships, three British open crowns, and five United States amateur titles; retired in 1930 at age twenty-eight.

Burton K. Wheeler, Democratic United States senator from Montana from 1923 to 1947. Wheeler gained national attention for pressing the investigation of the Teapot Dome scandal during the 1920s.

Thomas J. Walsh, Democratic United States senator from Montana from 1913 to 1933. Walsh served as chairman of the committee investigating Teapot Dome.

210 *NYT,* Monday, March 28, 1927, 2:5. *KCT* did not print the DT.

Smedley Butler, Major General of the United States Marine Corps who served with distinction in Mexico in 1914 and in Haiti in 1917. From 1924 to 1925 he served as director of the Department of Safety in Philadelphia, but he failed to halt the liquor traffic in that city. In 1927 he was appointed commander of the American marine detachment in China.

211 *NYT,* Tuesday, March 29, 1927, 27:7. Variants: *BDG* and *LAT* give "the town" in third sentence/*KCT* did not print the DT.

Foreign missionaries in China resisted orders to vacate their posts or send their families to safety despite the rising fury of the civil war. Many refused to flee in the belief that a new government would restore peace and order.

212 *NYT,* Wednesday, March 30, 1927, 27:7.

213 *NYT,* Thursday, March 31, 1927, 25:7. Variants: *LAT* gives "alone if . . . us. We will" in second and third sentences.

214 *NYT,* Friday, April 1, 1927, 25:7.

Charles M. Russell, famous western painter known as the "cowboy artist." Rogers, a close friend of Russell, wrote the introduction to Russell's *Trails Plowed Under,* a collection of cowboy yarns of the western range published in 1927, shortly after the artist's death.

215 *NYT,* Saturday, April 2, 1927, 19:7. *BDG* and *LAT* did not print the DT.

A heavy touring car with two male occupants smashed a Ford coupé carrying Henry Ford and two associates. The incident, which occurred on the night of March 27 near Dearborn, Michigan, raised speculation that the two men had attempted to assassinate the automobile manufacturer. Ford's injuries were not serious, however, and authorities later termed the whole affair an accident.

Kellogg, Wrigley, Gillette, Mennen, B. V. D., and Hart, Schaffner and Marx were name brands of popular consumer items.

216 *NYT,* Monday, April 4, 1927, 25:7. Variants: *LAT* gives origin "RAVENNA, Neb."/*LAT* gives "educational tour" in first sentence/*LAT* gives "there to spoil it." in second sentence/*LAT* gives "not even a political speaker has publicly insulted their intelligence . . . . Their only interest in any foreign affairs is in the Ford and Chaplin Trials." in fourth and sixth sentences/*LAT* gives "They are too near Canada for prohibition to be an issue, and so far away from Washington that they wouldn't care" in seventh sentence.

For William Upshaw, prohibitionist congressman from Georgia, see DT 172.

217 *NYT,* Tuesday, April 5, 1927, 29:7.

218 *NYT,* Wednesday, April 6, 1927, 29:7. Variants: *BDG* gives "Everybody sitting" in P. S./*LAT* omits P. S.

Fort Riley, established in 1853 and located fourteen miles west of Manhattan, Kansas, boasted the only cavalry school maintained by the United States Army.

219 *NYT,* Thursday, April 7, 1927, 27:7. Variants: *LAT* gives "vote, but the trouble with Chicago is they are scarce on better elements." in second and third sentences/*LAT* gives "will get back" in fifth sentence.

William "Big Bill" Thompson. In 1927 Thompson, a Republican, former cattle rancher, and one time mayor of Chicago, had attacked his mayoral opponent, incumbent William Dever, for permitting the use in the public schools of history textbooks favorable to George III of England. Dever generally had the support of "good government" advocates, but Thompson won the election and served as mayor of Chicago from 1927 to 1931.

John W. Davis, ambassador to Great Britain from 1918 to 1921. Davis, a former congressman from West Virginia, was the Democratic presidential nominee in 1924.

220 *NYT,* Friday, April 8, 1927, 25:7. *LAT* did not print the DT.

221 *NYT,* Saturday, April 9, 1927, 21:7. Variant: *LAT* gives "where you were phoning." in seventh sentence.

The first thoroughly publicized demonstration of television occurred on April 7. The new medium, still in experimental stages of development, produced signals synchronized with a telephone message and transmitted by wire from Washington, D. C., to New York.

Wayne B. Wheeler, general counsel of the Anti-Saloon League of America. Wheeler prosecuted more than 2,000 saloon cases, coauthored state and national prohibition legislation, and defended such laws in state and federal courts.

222 *NYT,* Sunday, April 10, 1927, I:21:2. *BDG* and *LAT* did not print the DT.

Thomas D. Schall, Republican United States senator from Minnesota from 1925 to 1935. Schall defeated incumbent Magnus Johnson for the Senate in 1924 but subsequently was charged with violating the state corrupt practices law. A state senate investigating committee absolved Schall of the allegations in April of 1927.

Magnus Johnson, United States senator from Minnesota from 1923 to 1925. Swedish-born, Johnson actively participated in the Populist movement of the 1890s, farmers' cooperatives, and the Minnesota Farmer-Labor party of the 1920s. He later served in Congress from 1933 to 1935.

223 *NYT,* Monday, April 11, 1927, 23:7. Variants: *BDG* gives "Congress and Senate ought to can 'em that quick." in fifth sentence/*LAT* omits P. S.

224 *NYT,* Tuesday, April 12, 1927, 29:7.

225 *NYT,* Wednesday, April 13, 1927, 27:7. Variants: *LAT* gives "talk and argument for and against prohibition is worse on the morals of the public than" in third sentence/*LAT* gives "this right away . . . Aurora." in first sentence of P. S.

William "Billy" Sunday, popular evangelist and former professional baseball player who reached the height of his ministerial career in the 1920s.

226 *NYT,* Thursday, April 14, 1927, 29:7. Variant: *LAT* omits close.

Charles McNary, Republican United States senator from Oregon from 1928 until his death in 1944. McNary agreed, after several conferences with President Coolidge, to sound out farm leaders about a possible compromise agricultural relief measure (see DT 7).

227 *NYT,* Friday, April 15, 1927, 23:7. Variants: *KCT* gives "no contribution like" in fourth sentence/*KCT* gives "just tribute" in fifth sentence/*LAT* gives "fifty-one" in sixth sentence/*KCT* gives "are practicable" in eighth sentence /*KCT* gives "send 'em from" in tenth sentence/*KCT* omits "Purdue." in close.

Pilot Clarence D. Chamberlin and copilot Bert Acosta flew fifty-one hours, eleven minutes, and twenty-five seconds over Long Island on April 12 to 14 in preparation for a nonstop flight from New York to Paris.

228 *NYT,* Saturday, April 16, 1927, 17:7. Variants: *LAT* gives "for the way . . . farmers is to" in fourth sentence/*LAT* omits close.

The Cleveland Union Terminal, which included a railroad depot, hotel, offices, and the fifty-two-story Terminal Tower, officially opened in June of 1930, although construction began in 1925. Railroad connections reached the depot only after workmen blasted tunnels out of solid rock.

229 *NYT,* Monday, April 18, 1927, 23:7. Variant: *LAT* gives signature "the war correspondent of Cleveland, O."

230 *NYT,* Tuesday, April 19, 1927, 29:7. Variants: *LAT* ends first sentence with "Smith's."/*KCT* gives "morning; that those fortunate" in second sentence/*BDG* did not print the DT.

Charles Marshall, a Protestant lawyer from New York, wrote an open letter to Governor Smith questioning the desirability of a Roman Catholic becoming president. Smith, in a carefully written reply, expounded the principle of "religious freedom and equality."

231 *NYT,* Wednesday, April 20, 1927, 27:7. Variants: *KCT* gives "Politicians believe an" in fifth sentence/*KCT* omits close/*LAT* did not print the DT.

Carmi Thompson, a Cleveland attorney and former treasurer of the United States. Coolidge appointed Thompson in 1926 to study the economic and internal conditions of the Philippines. In a report published on December 22, 1926, Thompson recommended an extension of internal autonomy for the Philippines, although not immediate, absolute independence.

Theodore E. Burton, Republican United States representative from Ohio from 1889 to 1891, 1895 to 1909, and 1921 to 1928; United States senator from 1909 to 1915 and from 1928 until his death in 1929.

232 *NYT,* Thursday, April 21, 1927, 29:7. Variant: *LAT* gives "today is by . . . daytime. The" in first sentence.

The Snyder trial opened April 18 in New York City and concluded on May 9 with the conviction of Ruth Brown Snyder and her corset-salesman friend Henry Gray for the murder of Mrs. Snyder's husband, magazine editor Albert Snyder. Defense and prosecution attorneys had rejected sixty-one prospective jurors before they accepted a New York hotel press agent on April 20.

Herbert Hoover, United States secretary of commerce from 1921 to 1928. A White House spokesman commented at a press conference that President

Coolidge viewed Secretary Hoover as "competent to fill any position in the Cabinet." Some reporters considered the statement a slap at Hoover for permitting his presidential candidacy to grow before Coolidge had withdrawn from the race.

Movie czar Will Hays (see DT 173) was expected to cringe at news reports of a fight between two minor actors over the wife of one of them. Beaten and knocked unconscious, the husband died of cerebral hemorrhage.

233 *NYT,* Friday, April 22, 1927, 23:7. Variants: *BDG* throughout gives "Shakspere"/*NYT* gives "he is not the only" and *KCT* gives "call the bard's name" in fourth sentence/*KCT* omits close.

For John W. Davis, Democratic presidential candidate in 1924, see DT 219. The problem of "no policy to run on" was more the fault of a deeply divided convention than of its eventual nominee.

234 *NYT,* Saturday, April 23, 1927, 19:7. Variants: *KCT* gives "it is ink" in second sentence/*KCT* gives "The foregoing" in P. S./*LAT* and *KCT* give "because editors are" in P. S.

Henry Leach, editor of *The Forum* magazine, published an open letter to Coolidge, with a courtesy copy sent to the White House, inquiring about the president's intentions for another term. Newspapers indicated that Coolidge did not respond.

235 *NYT,* Monday, April 25, 1927, 25:7. Variants: *LAT* omits third and fourth sentences/*BDG* omits second paragraph/*LAT* gives "better picture . . . better subject . . . greater subject" in eighth sentence/*LAT* and *KCT* omit "The Burgomaster" in close.

Clarence Darrow, renowned labor and civil liberties attorney. Darrow and prohibitionist Wayne Wheeler (see DT 221) debated at Carnegie Hall in New York City on April 23. No decision in the debate was announced, although Darrow's frank hostility to Prohibition received the greater applause.

*King of Kings,* a Cecil B. De Mille production, premiered at the Gaiety Theatre in New York City on April 19. Hailed for its direction, acting, and costumes, the motion picture was considered the most impressive film of its time.

236 *NYT,* Tuesday, April 26, 1927, 29:7. Variants: *LAT* gives "these people" and *KCT* gives "of them need" in sixth sentence/*BDG* and *LAT* omit eighth sentence/*BDG* gives "The sufferers" and *LAT* gives "in even if" in ninth sentence/*LAT* and *KCT* omit close.

The Mississippi River, swollen by unusually heavy spring rains in many of its tributary areas, began to flood early in April. Each day brought news of the crest moving downstream, with new inundations as sodden levees collapsed or had to be dynamited to save river front cities.

Florenz "Flo" Ziegfeld, theatrical producer whose musical revue, the *Follies,* noted for its lavish settings and attractive chorus girls, opened in the United States in 1907 and remained highly successful for the next twenty years. Rogers, W. C. Fields, Eddie Cantor, and hundreds of other entertainers performed for Ziegfeld.

237 *NYT,* Wednesday, April 27, 1927, 27:7. Variants: *LAT* omits third and fourth sentences/*BDG* begins fourth sentence "So McCormack and."

John McCormack, Irish-born operatic and concert tenor who made his American debut in 1909 and achieved wide recognition thereafter.

238 *NYT,* Thursday, April 28, 1927, 25:7. Variants: *LAT* gives "differed in Nicaragua" in second sentence/*KCT* did not print the DT.

President Coolidge defended his foreign policy and his recent criticism of newspapers in a speech before members of United Press news service in New York City on April 25. Coolidge described his foreign policy as one "of peace and good will based on a better understanding through justice and fair dealing."

[239] *NYT,* Friday, April 29, 1927, 23:7. Variants: *LAT* gives "people never" in second sentence/*BDG* gives "in the papers" in third sentence/*LAT* gives "for dramatic description" in fifth sentence/*LAT* gives "house top floating down the river with its little human family on it than all" in sixth sentence.

[240] *NYT,* Saturday, April 30, 1927, 21:7. Variants: *LAT* omits last seven words in first sentence/*LAT* gives "are growing for Presidential purposes eight" in third sentence/*LAT* ends fourth sentence at "meantime'" omitting last fourteen words/*LAT* gives "nothing till Coolidge is overtaken by old age" in fifth sentence.

President Woodrow Wilson was born in Staunton, Virginia, raised in Georgia, and elected to the presidency from New Jersey.

Harry F. Byrd, governor of Virginia from 1926 to 1930; United States senator from 1933 to 1965. Byrd received several votes for the Democratic presidential nomination in 1932 and 1944, and in 1960 he garnered fifteen electoral votes for president from unpledged electors from the South.

[241] *NYT,* Monday, May 2, 1927, 23:7. Variants: *BDG* gives "Va. Casey" and *LAT* gives "Va. When Casey" and *KCT* gives "from Washington." in first sentence.

Charles "Casey" Jones, president of the Curtiss Flying Company and vice president of the Curtiss-Reed Metal Propeller Company. Jones, an early-day sponsor of air races and events, founded a civilian school for mechanics and aviation engineers in 1932.

Chamberlin (see DT 227), pilot of the first nonstop United States to Europe flight with a passenger. Chamberlin completed the historic flight on June 6, 1927, one week after Charles Lindbergh flew the Atlantic (see DT 273).

Rogers' benefit for victims of the Mississippi River flood was a sellout.

President Coolidge appointed Secretary of Commerce Hoover to head a cabinet committee to assist the Red Cross. The flood emergency continued to worsen, with 200,000 homeless by early May. After inspecting the situation in the lower valley, Hoover issued a plea for more funds.

[242] *NYT,* Tuesday, May 3, 1927, 29:7. Variant: *KCT* ends DT at end of fifth sentence.

As the flood crest approached New Orleans, rescue workers dynamited the levees below the city to relieve pressure; the water level subsequently stopped rising and on May 1 newspapers carried stories that the danger had passed.

Ringgold "Ring" Lardner, sports and general writer for newspapers, chiefly midwestern; wrote a syndicated humorous column, short stories, plays, and books. He occasionally contributed sketches and lyrics for the Ziegfeld *Follies.*

[243] *NYT,* Wednesday, May 4, 1927, 27:7. Variants: *LAT* gives "happens in this country." in third sentence/*LAT* gives close "Yours, the old."

[244] *NYT,* Thursday, May 5, 1927, 29:7. Variant: *NYT* omits the fifth sentence.

Al Smith, a potential presidential candidate, was identified with Tammany Hall, a Democratic faction in New York City.

Forty suicides and attempted suicides, usually by male high school and college students, had captured the attention of the American public during the first five months of 1927.

[245] *NYT,* Friday, May 6, 1927, 25:7. Variants: *KCT* omits first sentence/ *KCT* gives "more than to mail" and *BDG* and *LAT* omit "sufferers" in third sentence/*LAT* ends sixth sentence with "done."/*NYT* omits seventh sentence.

[246] *NYT,* Saturday, May 7, 1927, 19:7. Variants: *KCT* ends fourth sentence with "power"/*LAT* omits last two words of fourth paragraph, and *BDG* and *KCT* omit entire paragraph/*LAT* omits P. S.

Rogers' disgust at the Snyder-Gray murder trial reflected a ripening national mood. Mrs. Snyder testified for three days; the jury delivered a verdict of guilty on May 9.

Frieda Hempel, concert and operatic soprano. Mme. Hempel sued industrialist and philanthropist August Heckscher for allegedly breaching an agreement concluded the preceding year by which she retired from the stage in return for an annual payment of $48,000. The two parties settled the suit out of court, with Mme. Hempel agreeing to accept $15,000 annually.

[247] *NYT,* Sunday, May 8, 1927, I:27:4. *BDG, LAT,* and *KCT* did not print the DT.

President Coolidge, born and reared in Plymouth Notch, Windsor County, Vermont, attended college at Amherst in Massachusetts and remained in that state to practice law and to enter public service.

[248] *NYT,* Monday, May 9, 1927, 23:7. Variants: *KCT* gives "William M. Butler" and *LAT* gives "Coolidge's 'Man Friday,' just came back from the west end of the island and reported to Crusoe that" in first sentence/*LAT* gives "started everybody is pulling for them to make it." in P. S.

William M. Butler, chairman of the Republican National Committee, returned from a three-week western tour during which he sounded out public sentiment about the administration. He gave a favorable report to President Coolidge, the cabinet, and congressional leaders.

French war heroes Captains Charles Nungesser and Francois Coli, in a single engine biplane, departed Paris at dawn on May 8, bound for New York. Clarence Chamberlin planned to meet them, Boston officials readied an escort, and New York prepared a civic welcome, but the fliers disappeared beyond Ireland.

[249] This DT is taken from the records of the Will Rogers Memorial. *NYT, BDG, LAT,* and *KCT* did not print it, possibly because officials still had not heard from Nungesser and Coli. No other DT received such a general rejection by editors.

Italian aviator Francesco de Pinedo with two aides departed Italy in February on a four-continent flight in a "hydroairplane." After negotiating Africa and South America, the plane was destroyed by fire in Arizona in early April. Premier Mussolini sent another plane which arrived on May 1 and was assembled and flown on May 8. Pinedo eventually reached Rome in mid-June.

[250] *NYT,* Wednesday, May 11, 1927, 27:7. Variants: *KCT* omits "and the town . . . Claremore," in third sentence/*LAT* omits P. S.

Coolidge moved to Northampton, 100 miles west of Boston, after he graduated from Amherst College in 1895. Ten years later he married Grace Goodhue, a gifted teacher in a local school for the deaf. He served as mayor of Northampton from 1909 to 1911.

Harvard was scheduled to play the University of Pennsylvania instead of Princeton in 1927, while the football schedule for 1928, announced about a week later, added the United States Military Academy for the first time since 1910. Smith College is a private, nondenominational school for women.

The fate of Nungesser and Coli remained in doubt. Meanwhile, Hoover continued his relief work for victims of the Mississippi River flood. During previous days he had inspected inundated areas and had conferred with state and local authorities and with bankers about relief and rehabilitation measures.

251 *LAT,* Thursday, May 12, 1927, I:1:8; heading from *KCT,* 15:3. Variants: *KCT* gives "farmer's bill not" in third sentence/*NYT* did not print the DT.

French citizens, deeply disappointed at the increasingly certain loss of their heroes Nungesser and Coli, resumed their bitterness of the previous summer toward Americans. Allegations were made, and quickly denied, that the United States government deliberately had withheld weather reports which might have aided the French fliers.

252 *NYT,* Friday, May 13, 1927, 25:7. Variants: *KCT* begins close "In" and *LAT* omits close.

Nicola Sacco and Bartolomeo Vanzetti were arrested in April of 1920 for a payroll robbery in South Braintree, Massachusetts, and for murders of a paymaster and a guard. They were tried and convicted in 1921 on evidence which left many doubts. Appeals and requests for new trials followed, while many people believed that the convictions resulted more from the men's Italian birth, philosophical atheism, and political radicalism than from proven guilt. A special state commission continued to study the convictions in May of 1927.

253 *NYT,* Saturday, May 14, 1927, 21:7. Variant: *KCT* gives "are some of" in fourth sentence.

Secretary of the Treasury Mellon believed that British receipts in loan payments from its allies plus reparations from Germany more than balanced British debt remittances to the United States. The British government asked the United States to correct Mellon's "inaccurate and misleading statement," but the secretary only admitted that a minor "typographical error" had been made.

After this date Rogers dropped the Sunday telegram—which had appeared with some regularity since August of 1926 and exclusively in *NYT*—and began a six-telegram-a-week routine. He continued to write a "weekly article," a feature-length discourse on current events, for publication on Sunday.

254 *NYT,* Monday, May 16, 1927, 23:7. Variants: *LAT* gives "them what is the matter and what has caused" in first sentence/*LAT* gives "mind us eating it, but when we tried" in third sentence.

The Democratic minority in the Rhode Island legislature filibustered in 1924, blocking passage of the annual appropriation bills in an effort to force constitutional change. The state house soon ceased to meet, and after highly unparliamentary behavior senate Republicans fled to Massachusetts, preventing action through absence of a quorum. Banks, however, salvaged state finances with short-term loans.

255 *NYT,* Tuesday, May 17, 1927, 31:7. Variant: *LAT* gives " 'Gantry.' The Baptist shriek" in first sentence.

*Elmer Gantry,* a novel written by Sinclair Lewis in 1927, concerned the life of a sometime Baptist evangelist and charlatan, and a lover of whiskey, women, and himself. It combined the worst qualities of American Christianity of the 1920s. Reviewers fumed and the sale of the book was banned in Boston.

"It," a slang word popularized during the 1920s by the British novelist Elinor Glyn. Mrs. Glyn achieved such success in Hollywood in the art of personal advertisement that Paramount studios invented for her a motion picture entitled *It,* in which leading lady Clara Bow personified playful feminine allure.

256 *NYT,* Wednesday, May 18, 1927, 27:7. Variants: *BDG, LAT,* and *KCT* give "financial condition of" in first sentence/*LAT* gives "in a short time now." in second sentence/*BDG* gives $2000 for his wife" and *LAT* gives $2500 for his wife and $400 for" in third sentence/*LAT* gives "off all payments to" in fourth sentence.

A lower federal court ruled that the Fifth Amendment protection against self-incrimination automatically exempted a bootlegger from filing an income tax return. The Supreme Court in a unanimous opinion held that the individual should have filed a return, specifically taking exception to the portions of required information which might prove incriminating.

257 *BDG* (AM), Thursday, May 19, 1927, 1:8; heading from *KCT,* 15:5. Variants: *LAT* omits sixth sentence/*NYT* did not print the DT.

President Coolidge addressed the annual convention of the American Medical Association in Washington, D. C., on May 17.

258 *NYT,* Friday, May 20, 1927, 21:7.

259 *BDG* (PM), Saturday, May 21, 1927, 5:5; heading from *KCT,* 17:3. Variants: *LAT* gives "An odd, tall, slim, smiling, bashful American" in second sentence/*LAT* gives "life's work." in fifth sentence/*LAT* gives "of that old Mississippi" in seventh sentence/*NYT* and *BDG* (AM) did not print the DT.

Charles Lindbergh, American aviator who made the first solo, nonstop transatlantic flight. On May 20 he departed for Paris in a Ryan monoplane and completed the epic flight thirty-three and one half hours later.

260 *NYT,* Monday, May 23, 1927, 23:7. Variants: *LAT* gives "do but he has been invited to speak at the regular" and *BDG* gives "has an invitation" in second sentence/*LAT* gives "The Prince . . . appear in a town with that bird if he wants anybody" in third sentence/*LAT* gives "of Lindbergh's ardent" in close.

261 *NYT,* Tuesday, May 24, 1927, 27:7. Variants: *LAT* gives "first time now. I . . . year even including" in first and second sentences/*LAT* gives "town with a great harbor which in the old days not only harbored some great fleets," in third and fourth sentences/*KCT* gives "state. Being in the . . . law, this" in sixth and seventh sentences/*LAT* omits third paragraph.

Maine passed the first state prohibition law in 1846.

Theodore Roosevelt, president of the United States from 1901 to 1909.

262 *NYT,* Wednesday, May 25, 1927, 25:7. Variants: *KCT* gives "There are 125 million" in first sentence/*LAT* and *KCT* end second sentence "hero." and omit next seven words/*LAT* ends third sentence "one." and omits next sixteen words/*LAT* omits four words in parentheses and gives "provide a big sum for him and" in fifth sentence/*LAT* omits sixth sentence/*LAT* omits "and . . . did" in seventh sentence/*LAT* omits eleventh sentence/*LAT* gives "hundred and twenty million" in close/*LAT* gives "flood fund." in P. S., omitting next three sentences.

263 *NYT,* Thursday, May 26, 1927, 27:7. *LAT* did not print the DT.

264 *NYT,* Friday, May 27, 1927, 25:7. Variant: *BDG* and *KCT* give "we were really honest" in second sentence.

When Lindbergh arrived in Paris, 100,000 Frenchmen crowded Le Bourget Airport to greet him. The flier received the French Cross of the Legion of Honor and the ceremonial key to the city and was toasted at numerous banquets.

[265] *NYT,* Saturday, May 28, 1927, 19:7. Variants: *LAT* and *KCT* give "Lindbergh" and *NYT* gives "meets his own President" in first sentence/*NYT* omits fourth sentence/*LAT* gives "night to give . . . any benefits given in any city." in sixth sentence.

[266] *NYT,* Monday, May 30, 1927, 17:7. Variants: *BDG, LAT,* and *KCT* give close and signature "yours, WILL ROGERS."

Secretary Hoover broadcasted nationally from New Orleans on May 28. He reported that there were 700,000 victims of the flood of whom 600,000 depended on private aid. Receipts from the Red Cross drive totaled $14,000,000 with $2,000,000 more needed. The government had spent more than $5,000,000 while corporations had contributed several million.

On his return from France, Lindbergh visited Belgium where he was feted lavishly by King Albert and the royal family.

[267] *NYT,* Tuesday, May 31, 1927, clipping marked "Killed first Edition" in Rogers Family Collection. Variant: First sentence as in *KCT.*

For Milton Hershey see DT 47.

Two burglars entered the home of stockbroker Jesse Livermore of Kings Point, Long Island, in the predawn hours of May 29, robbing the Livermores and their guests of $100,000 in jewelry. Because the thieves addressed the victims by their first names, police theorized that it was an "inside job."

[268] *NYT,* Wednesday, June 1, 1927, 29:7. Variants: *LAT* gives "Memorial Day" in first sentence/*LAT* begins fourth sentence "Lincoln"/*LAT* gives "him nice will" in P. S.

President Coolidge's Memorial Day message dealt at length with foreign policy. Delivered at ceremonies at Arlington National Cemetery, the address was more than five times as long as Lincoln's speech at Gettysburg.

When Lindbergh arrived in London on May 9, he discovered a number of cabled messages requesting his early return to the United States Although he did not reveal the exact nature of the telegrams from the government, he announced the next day that his European tour had been curtailed.

[269] *NYT,* Thursday, June 2, 1927, 27:7. Variant: *BDG* gives "this it would" in ninth sentence.

[270] *NYT,* Friday, June 3, 1927, 23:7. Variants: *LAT* gives "night for $8,000." in second and third sentences/*LAT* gives "that's double" in fourth sentence/*LAT* omits sixth sentence/*NYT* gives surnames only in P. S.

President Coolidge offered Lindbergh a navy cruiser on which to return to the United States with the landing to be made at Washington, D.C. Lindbergh's acceptance disappointed Mayor Walker of New York City who had hoped that the American hero would visit his city first. Lindbergh already had accepted the New York State Medal of Valor from Governor Smith.

[271] *NYT,* Saturday, June 4, 1927, 19:7. Variants: *LAT* gives "returning to their old homes." in third sentence/*LAT* omits "no seed" in sixth sentence/*LAT* gives "(America's greatest single possession)" in eighth sentence/*LAT* gives close "Yours,"/*LAT* inserts "Editor's Note" correcting total in DT, June 2, to $48,000 —"an error on the part of the telegraph company."

John Barton Payne, chairman of the American Red Cross from 1921 to 1935 and former secretary of the interior of the United States.

272 *NYT,* Monday, June 6, 1927, 23:7. Variants: *BDG* gives "figures, some papers" in second P. S./*LAT* omits second P. S./*KCT* did not print the DT.

273 *NYT,* Tuesday, June 7, 1927, 31:7. Variants: *LAT* gives "about him going to take passengers I would have signed on. Then" in second and third sentences/*LAT* gives "man just like Lindbergh, and" in fourth sentence/*LAT* gives "It wasn't his fault that he didn't jump off weeks ago. He . . . innocent victim of rows and squabbles of which" in fifth and sixth sentences/*LAT* ends eighth sentence "as easy as any."/*LAT* gives "Well, I will . . . over when they get a bridge." in ninth sentence/*LAT* gives "the Chief going in the right direction." in P. S./*LAT* gives "that remind me of Chamberlin." in second sentence of P. S.

Chamberlin (see DT 214) with a single passenger, financial backer Charles Levine, flew from Long Island, New York, to Eisleben, Germany, in forty-six hours and thirty minutes from June 4 to 6, marking the first transatlantic flight with a passenger.

Rogers probably referred to the *Chief,* the sleek and fast luxury passenger train of the Atchison, Topeka, & Santa Fe Railway Company.

274 *NYT,* Wednesday, June 8, 1927, 27:7. Variants: *LAT* gives second sentence as "Now that the flood has passed its danger mark and is going down, the politicians are coming up."/*LAT* gives "Back to Beverly" in P. S.

President Coolidge, who earlier in the year had vetoed a farm relief bill, announced on May 31 that he would spend his summer vacation at a South Dakota state game lodge in the Black Hills.

Democrats criticized President Coolidge for refusing to call a special session of Congress to consider flood relief for the Mississippi Valley. Speaker of the House Nicholas Longworth, a Republican, promised high priority for the matter at the next regular session in December.

Pola Negri, Polish-born actress who arrived in Hollywood in 1923 after a brief career in German motion pictures. Once married to a Polish nobleman, she had been linked romantically with Rudolph Valentino. On May 14 she married Prince Serge Mdivani, a native of the Caucasian state of Georgia.

275 *NYT,* Thursday, June 9, 1927, 29:7.

William McAdoo (see DT 147) spoke at graduation ceremonies at Tusculum College, Greenville, Tennessee.

276 *NYT,* Friday, June 10, 1927, 25:7. Variant: *KCT* gives "Bolsheviki" in third sentence.

Internal strife in the Soviet Union had increased recently. Sources had revealed numerous counterrevolutionary activities for which several dissidents were executed.

For Will Hays, czar of the movie industry, see DT 173.

277 *NYT,* Saturday, June 11, 1927, 21:7. Variant: *BDG* gives close and signature "(Signed)./MAYOR."

278 *NYT,* Monday, June 13, 1927, 21:7. Variant: *LAT* gives "these flights" in first sentence.

Mary Pickford, actress who in the heyday of silent film was known as "the world's sweetheart." She married actor Douglas Fairbanks, Sr., in 1920 but divorced him in 1935. Their palatial home "Pickfair" remains a major attraction in Beverly Hills.

[279] *NYT,* Tuesday, June 14, 1927, 29:7. Variant: *KCT* gives signature "WILL ROGERS."

A successor to the popular Ford Model T had been rumored for several months. Ford Motor Company finally indicated on June 8 that an extensive advertising campaign soon would be launched to promote the new car, details of which remained vague.

[280] *NYT,* Wednesday, June 15, 1927, 29:7. Variants: *LAT* and *KCT* give "miss many" in fifth sentence/*BDG* adds to signature "WILL ROGERS."

Although a naval limitations conference was not scheduled to convene until June 20 in Geneva, rumors already prevailed that Japan would request a larger ratio of ships and neutralization of the Panama Canal, the United States would again attempt to limit naval craft other than previously limited capital ships, and Great Britain would propose cuts in cruiser and submarine construction.

[281] *NYT,* Thursday, June 16, 1927, 29:7. Variants: *BDG* ends second sentence "in a Ford."/*LAT* omits the fourth sentence of P. S.

President Coolidge and entourage left Washington on June 13 for a three-month vacation in the Black Hills. The eighty-member presidential party traveled in a nine-car special train.

This is Rogers' first reference to the illness which led to major surgery on June 17. He had suffered severe stomach cramps on three separate occasions during his recent cross-country tour. His physicians in Los Angeles concluded that he should enter California Lutheran Hospital for surgery to correct cholelithiasis, or gallstones. Rogers recorded his surgical experiences in *Ether and Me, or Just Relax.*

[282] *NYT,* Friday, June 17, 1927, 25:7. Variant: *KCT* gives "in a hospital" in third sentence.

[283] *NYT,* Saturday, June 18, 1927, 19:7. Variant: *BDG, LAT,* and *KCT* give "in a hospital you" in first sentence.

President Coolidge's pet raccoon, Rebecca, along with Mrs. Coolidge's five canaries and the family's collies, had accompanied the presidential party to the Black Hills.

[284] *NYT,* Monday, June 20, 1927, 21:7. Variant: Only *NYT* printed the NOTE.

Rogers' operation had been successful. Doctors removed two stones of significant size but not the gall bladder itself. A complication arose when the accumulated poison did not drain properly. Rogers' condition became so serious that his physicians, in addition to Mrs. Rogers, remained at the hospital overnight.

No DT is available for Tuesday, June 21, 1927.

[285] *NYT,* Wednesday, June 22, 1927, 29:7. Variants: *BDG, LAT,* and *KCT* omit first four words/*LAT* begins: "Mr. Coolidge sent me a nice message and I certainly do appreciate it." but does not quote it/*KCT* begins "Well, I certainly do appreciate the wire the President sent me today." but does not quote it/*BDG* gives "got love wires" in fifth sentence.

The crisis in Rogers' illness came on June 19 and 20 when the accumulation of poison could not be relieved. Mrs. Rogers later noted that most people "did not know how grave" the situation was. In time, however, the poison began to drain, and Rogers fully recovered. During his hospital stay, he received encouraging messages from theatrical figures, chambers of commerce, the New Orleans Red Cross, senators, governors, relatives, and many others.

286 *NYT,* Thursday, June 23, 1927, 27:7. Variants: *LAT* gives "officially invite Colonel" in third sentence/*BDG* and *KCT* give "(Signed)" before title and signature/*LAT* omits title/only *LAT* gives second P. S.

Sawtelle is a village in western Los Angeles, adjoining Santa Monica. It is the site of a Veterans' Administration facility, the largest soldiers' home in the country.

Harry Carr, correspondent, editor, and executive for the *Los Angeles Times* from 1897 until his death in 1936. Writing in his local affairs column "The Lancer" on June 21, Carr hailed Rogers as "The Brave Jester" and called him "one game guy" for writing copy almost to the operating table.

287 *NYT*, Friday, June 24, 1927, 25:7. Variant: *BDG* gives "tamed the . . . Worms. Won't" in the first and second sentences.

President Coolidge used worms as bait to catch seven trout. Secretary Hoover decried his technique as "the horror of all fly fishermen," and Senators Borah and Reed denounced the misuse of worms. But the public outcry was largely in good fun and helped Coolidge reap political benefit from his vacation.

288 *NYT,* Saturday, June 25, 1927, 19:7. Variant: Only *LAT* gives the P. S.

A scandal arose involving the receivership of the Julian Petroleum Company, a Southern California firm which had collapsed financially in May. Several indictments charging embezzlement and usury resulted, including allegations against fifty-five Los Angeles business leaders and motion picture executives. Within a year seven principals had been acquitted of conspiracy and the prosecution characterized as a failure.

289 *NYT,* Monday, June 27, 1927, 21:7.

At the Washington Armament Conference in 1922, the United States, Great Britain, France, Japan, and Italy established a ten-year "holiday" during which time no new capital ships were to be built. They also set the ratio of capital ships already constructed at five each for the United States and Britain, three for Japan, and 1.67 each for France and Italy. As a result the United States scrapped twenty-six vessels totaling 694,000 tons, Britain twenty-four ships totaling 589,000 tons, and Japan sixteen ships totaling 427,000 tons. At the latest disarmament conference in Geneva, the United States failed in efforts to extend the "5-5-3" ratio to cruisers, destroyers, submarines, and other craft.

290 *NYT,* Tuesday, June 28, 1927, 27:7. Variant: *LAT* omits "the popular movie stars" in first sentence.

Rod La Rocque, popular American leading man of the silent screen who successfully made the transition to "talkies."

Vilma Banky, blonde, Austro-Hungarian star of American silent films. The couple celebrated their forty-second anniversary a few months before La Rocque's death in 1969.

Samuel Goldwyn, a Polish-American who arrived in Hollywood in 1910 and quickly became one of the top motion picture producers. Goldwyn planned and supervised the La Rocque and Banky wedding which was held at the Church of the Good Shepherd in Beverly Hills. Six hundred guests attended, while 400 policemen were needed to control thousands of spectators.

Richard Evelyn Byrd, polar explorer and member of the distinguished Byrd family of Virginia. Commander Byrd and three companions flew nonstop from New York to France in forty-two hours from June 29 to July 1. Byrd informed the nation of his progress through radio reports.

[291] *NYT,* Wednesday, June 29, 1927, 27:7. Variants: *BDG, LAT,* and *KCT* give "my ever entering" in P. S.

[292] *NYT,* Thursday, June 30, 1927, 29:7.

For Governor Harry Byrd of Virginia see DT 240.

[293] *NYT,* Friday, July 1, 1927, 23:7.

[294] *NYT,* Saturday, July 2, 1927, 19:7. Variant: *LAT* gives origin "CALIFORNIA LUTHERAN HOSPITAL."

Commander Byrd and his companions had intended to land at Le Bourget Airfield in Paris, but dense fog and sudden radio failure caused the fliers to pass over Paris and return toward the English Channel. The flight ended at dawn on July 1 when Byrd's plane fell into the sea near Ver Sur Mer, France, 120 miles from Paris. The four fliers swam ashore unhurt. The cause of the radio failure could not be pinpointed.

[295] *NYT,* Monday, July 4, 1927, 17:7. Variants: *LAT* gives origin "BEVERLY HILLS"/*KCT* gives "lose-armed" in second sentence/*KCT* gives "but for the" in fifth sentence.

Rogers intended this telegram to be a good-natured spoof of the numerous air races being held in the United States. Many of his readers, however, eagerly accepted his challenge of a "non-stop" automobile race from Oklahoma to California. At 4:00 a.m. on July 13, Mr. and Mrs. John Collins of Tulsa, Oklahoma, aroused the Rogers family to claim first prize. Numerous other competitors soon followed. Rogers' "joke" cost the comedian $840 in prize money, the goodwill of the Beverly Hills police department, and a night's sleep.

[296] *NYT,* Tuesday, July 5, 1927, 23:7. Variants: *BDG* gives "popping their" in first sentence/*KCT* gives "you farther." in fifth sentence.

George M. Cohan (see DT 22) actually was born on July 3, 1878, but celebrated his birthday on July 4. Coolidge was born on July 4, 1872.

[297] *NYT,* Wednesday, July 6, 1927, 27:7. Variants: *BDG* and *KCT* give "trouble is since" in fourth sentence/*BDG* gives "of telephone" in sixth sentence.

For an account of the Julian oil scandal see DT 288.

[298] *NYT,* Thursday, July 7, 1927, 27:7. Variants: *KCT* gives "seems about" in first sentence/*KCT* gives "you read" in third sentence/*KCT* gives "they'll want" and LAT gives "they all will want" in P. S.

[299] *NYT,* Friday, July 8, 1927, 21:7. Variant: *BDG* gives "cap and that . . . time; that" in second and third sentences.

A nationally-distributed news photograph showed President Coolidge dressed in a cowboy outfit which the Boy Scouts of Custer County, South Dakota, had presented to him on the occasion of his fifty-fifth birthday. The western attire included chaps inscribed with "CAL."

300 *NYT,* Saturday, July 9, 1927, 15:7.

Henry Ford issued a public apology on July 8 for anti-Semitic remarks published in his magazine the *Dearborn Independent* (see DT 114).

301 *NYT,* Monday, July 11, 1927, 21:7. Variants: *LAT* gives origin "BEVERLY HILLS"/*LAT* gives "his old" in third sentence/*BDG* omits first three sentences and only prints P. S./*KCT* did not print the DT.

Jesse Lasky, United States motion picture producer and theater owner. In May of 1927 Adolph Zukor (see DT 166) and Lasky, partners in Famous Players-Lasky Corporation, announced across-the-board payroll cuts for all their employees. On July 10 in an unrelated incident, the two men were cited for conspiracy to control the distribution of films and ownership of movie theaters. The Federal Trade Commission temporarily restrained Lasky and Zukor from building and buying additional theaters.

302 *NYT,* Tuesday, July 12, 1927, 27:7. Variants: *KCT* gives "were coming" in fourth sentence/*BDG* gives "out one" in P. S .

Kevin O'Higgins, vice president of the Irish Free State from 1923 to 1927 and minister for home affairs and justice. O'Higgins was assassinated near Dublin on July 10 during a period of extreme controversy regarding the taking of an oath of allegiance by members of the lower house of the Irish legislature.

Newspapers reported that the executive committee of the Anti-Saloon League of America had called for the impeachment of President Coolidge and the removal of Secretary Mellon for failure to enforce Prohibition. The League denied the news stories.

303 *NYT,* Wednesday, July 13, 1927, 25:7. Variant: *KCT* gives "is likely to" in second sentence.

Coolidge turned to fly fishing after worm lovers protested his earlier choice of bait (see DT 287). He quickly adapted to the new technique and proved skillful at the sport.

Benjamin B. Lindsey, judge of the juvenile court in Denver from 1901 to 1927 and noted social reformer. Lindsey drafted numerous legislative proposals and lectured widely for the juvenile court movement. His most controversial stance, however, was his advocacy of "companionate marriage," which called for easier divorces and birth control.

304 *NYT,* Thursday, July 14, 1927, 25:7. *KCT* did not print the DT.

305 *NYT,* Friday, July 15, 1927, 19:7.

John Barton Payne, national chairman of the American Red Cross (see DT 271), honored Rogers with a life membership in the organization in appreciation of Rogers' work in behalf of the victims of the Mississippi River flood.

306 *NYT,* Saturday, July 16, 1927, 13:7. Variants: *LAT* gives "lots of . . . prospect of disastrous" and *KCT* gives "the possible disastrous" in first sentence/*KCT* gives "it is" in third sentence/*KCT* gives "we have lost" in fourth sentence/*LAT* ends fourth sentence "lost nothing." omitting last five words/*KCT* gives "we can come" in fifth sentence/*LAT* omits fifth sentence/*KCT* gives "they wouldn't" and *LAT* gives "them—wouldn't" in sixth sentence/*KCT* gives "nations found . . . we had . . . they gradually would" in seventh sentence/*KCT* gives "we may come back" in ninth sentence/*LAT* omits eighth, ninth, and tenth sentences.

Negotiators ended the naval conference at Geneva without substantial agreement as to further disarmament. An impasse occurred when Great Britain insisted that it needed seventy cruisers to maintain adequate security while the United States and Japan held to a smaller figure.

307 *NYT,* Monday, July 18, 1927, 19:7. Variants: *LAT* gives origin "BEVERLY HILLS"/*LAT* gives " 'Films . . . nations.' " in first sentence/*LAT* and *KCT* give "Democrat and . . . elected president." in third sentence/*LAT* gives "If you are" and *BDG* gives "If you people" and *KCT* gives "is nobody" in P. S.

Louis "Bull" Montana, Italian-born professional wrestler; introduced into American motion pictures by Douglas Fairbanks, Sr., as a fierce-faced character actor. For Ben Turpin see DT 118.

308 *NYT,* Tuesday, July 19, 1927, 25:7. Variants: *LAT* gives "300 natives" in first sentence/*KCT* did not print the DT.

United States marines and Nicaraguan loyalist troops, aided by American bombing planes, repulsed an attack by liberal forces on a conservative stronghold. The rebel army suffered more than fifty dead.

309 *LAT,* Wednesday, July 20, 1927, 1:3. Variants: *BDG* gives "big raids" in first sentence/*BDG* gives "Cal himself" in second sentence/*NYT* and *KCT* did not print the DT.

Federal prohibition agents in South Dakota staged one of their frequent weekend raids on the bootlegging trade in the Black Hills, they arrested eleven alleged offenders in Rapid City.

310 *NYT,* Thursday, July 21, 1927, 23:7. Variants: *KCT* gives "Sporting experts" in first sentence/*KCT* gives " 'If' they don't win they will all be wrong again. They are . . . wrong." and *BDG* gives " 'If' don't win . . . again. They are . . . trust to . . . wrong." in second and third sentences/LAT gives "judgment even" in second sentence.

Arenas in a number of cities had been mentioned as possible sites of a rematch bout between heavyweight champion Gene Tunney and former title holder Jack Dempsey (see DT 62). Soldier Field in Chicago ultimately was selected because of its seating capacity of 110,000.

George "Tex" Rickard, sports promoter who staged several championship boxing matches during the 1920s. He is credited with the first "million dollar gate" in boxing, the Jack Dempsey-George Carpentier fight on July 2, 1921. Rickard's bouts grossed more than $15,000,000.

311 *NYT,* Friday, July 22, 1927, 21:7.

Michael I, king of Rumania from 1927 to 1930 and from 1940 to 1947. Six-year-old Michael became king under a regency upon the death of his grandfather, Ferdinand I. His father, Prince Carol, who had renounced his rights to the throne in 1925, returned from exile in 1930 and seized the crown. In 1940 pro-German Rumanians forced Carol to abdicate and restored Michael to the throne.

Grace Goodhue Coolidge, wife of President Coolidge. Rogers once referred to Mrs. Coolidge as "Public Female Favorite No. 1." She was a gracious and popular first lady and increased the number of entertainers invited to the White House, including Rogers who spent a night there following his trip abroad in 1926.

312 *NYT,* Saturday, July 23, 1927, 15:7. Variants: *LAT* gives "This proves" in first sentence/*NYT* gives "lawsuit that" in second sentence, but *BDG, LAT,* and *KCT* have it as here/only *LAT* printed the P. S.

Dempsey won a controversial heavyweight bout with Jack Sharkey (see DT 75) on July 22. Sharkey cried foul, alleging the knockout punch came when he turned his head toward the ring referee to protest Dempsey's below-the-belt hits. A few days earlier, Dempsey's attorneys had failed to prevent Dempsey's former manager, Jack Kearns, from instigating suits to collect past earnings (see DT 47).

[313] *NYT,* Monday, July 25, 1927, 21:7. Variants: *LAT* gives origin "BEVERLY HILLS"/*BDG* gives "Lindsay's" and *LAT* gives "matrimonial upheaval" in first sentence.

For Judge Benjamin Lindsey see DT 303.

[314] *NYT,* Tuesday, July 26, 1927, 23:7. Variants: *LAT* gives "boy's sweetheart," and *KCT* gives "girls sweetheart's" in first sentence/*BDG* gives "girl's family" and *KCT* gives "Canadian family . . . are wary of" in third sentence/ *KCT* gives "won't call" in fourth sentence.

Amidst widespread publicity, Lena Wilson, described by newspapers as a "child of the Canadian woods," and James "Bud" Stillman, Jr., son of a socially prominent New York City banker, announced their engagement on July 26. Stillman met Miss Wilson, daughter of a Canadian farmer, while vacationing with his family near the Wilson home. Rumors prevailed that the Stillman family disapproved of the union.

Thick fog prevented Lindbergh from landing in Portland, Maine, where he was scheduled for an appearance. He circled the city for ninety minutes before proceeding to Concord, New Hampshire, to await better weather. He completed his flight to Portland the next day, July 25.

[315] *NYT,* Wednesday, July 27, 1927, 25:7. Variants: *KCT* omits second and third sentences and last six words of first sentence/*LAT* gives "if Nick finds out, he will" in third sentence/*LAT* gives "are set" in fourth sentence/*LAT* gives "talking you have fouled him." in seventh sentence.

[316] *NYT,* Thursday, July 28, 1927, 21:7.

[317] *NYT,* Friday, July 29, 1927, 21:7. Variants: *KCT* gives "team put" in second sentence/*BDG* gives "and soothing syrup" in third sentence/*BDG* and *KCT* give "speech yesterday" in fifth sentence.

For Michael I, King of Rumania, see DT 311; for Congressman Nicholas Longworth see DT 51.

[318] *NYT,* Saturday, July 30, 1927, 17:7. Variants: *BDG* gives "idea three" in fourth sentence/*KCT* gives "Washington." in first sentence of P. S./*KCT* gives "copies" in second sentence of P. S./*KCT* gives "has stayed" in fourth sentence of P. S.

Walter Johnson, probably the fastest pitcher in professional baseball history. On August 2, 1927, Johnson's teammates from the Washington Senators, fans, and friends honored the exceptional player upon his twentieth and final season in baseball.

[319] *NYT,* Monday, August 1, 1927, 21:7.

John Roach Straton, pastor of Calvary Baptist Church in New York City from 1918 to 1929. Straton attracted national fame as a fundamentalist leader, active foe of Darwinism, prohibitionist, and strident opponent of the presidential candidacy of Governor Al Smith, a Catholic.

Minnie "Ma" Kennedy, evangelist and mother of Aimee McPherson (see DT 56). Credited with much influence in the development of her daughter's early career, Ma Kennedy broke with Aimee over control of their Angelus Temple in

Los Angeles. The long smoldering row erupted on July 27 when they publicly accused each other of harassment.

Impetus for construction of Yankee Stadium, which Rogers called "Ruth's tabernacle," had been credited to the drawing power of premier Yankee slugger Babe Ruth (see DT 29).

Edward, Prince of Wales (see DT 165), arrived in Canada on July 30 to visit his ranch in Alberta and perform some official duties. Charles Lindbergh recently had left a Canadian retreat where he had been resting after a tour of the United States.

A massive earthquake struck Kansu, a remote province in western China, on May 23. The quake killed an estimated 100,000 people and devastated a 20,000-square-mile area.

[320] *NYT,* Tuesday, August 2, 1927, 23:7.

[321] *LAT,* Wednesday, August 3, 1927, I:1:4; heading from *KCT,* 13:4. Variants: *BDG* and *KCT* did not print the P. S./*NYT* did not print the DT.

Chamberlin (see DT 241), in a demonstration of the feasibility of ship-to-shore airplane communications, took off from a special runway on the deck of the luxury liner S. S. *Leviathan* as it lay at anchor eighty miles off the eastern coast of the United States. He landed at Teterboro Field in New Jersey less than three hours later.

The postscript appeared exclusively in the *Los Angeles Times;* the streets Rogers mentioned are near Hollywood.

[322] *NYT,* Thursday, August 4, 1927, 23:7.

At noon on August 2, Coolidge presented reporters at the summer White House with a written statement that he did not "choose to run" for president in 1928. Some people interpreted the president's message as a willingness to accept a draft.

[323] *LAT,* Friday, August 5, 1927, I:1:3; heading from *KCT,* 13:4. Variants: *KCT* gives "he doesn't faint." in second sentence/*BDG* and *KCT* give P. S.: "The deer season opened out here yesterday and a deer hunter brought in his first man before noon."/*NYT* did not print the DT.

[324] *BDG* (AM), Saturday, August 6, 1927, 1:8; heading from *NYT,* 15:7. Variants: *KCT* gives "ended with us" in first sentence/*LAT* gives "be big chief" in second sentence of P. S./*NYT* printed only the P. S. as the body of the DT.

The arms limitation conference at Geneva held its final session on August 4, with British, United States, and Japanese representatives restating their respective cases as the unproductive meeting adjourned.

The Sioux tribe adopted Coolidge and gave him the Indian name "Leading Eagle" during an impressive ceremony on August 4.

[325] *NYT,* Monday, August 8, 1927, 19:7. Variants: *LAT* gives origin "BEVERLY HILLS"/*LAT* gives "the ones that are expressing an" in first sentence/*NYT* and *KCT* omit third sentence/*BDG, LAT,* and *KCT* give signature "WILL ROGERS."/*LAT* omits close and title and *BDG* omits title.

The drama of the Sacco-Vanzetti case intensified as the two men went on a hunger strike. Radicals and many moderates in the United States and abroad protested the sentence of execution and called for clemency (see DT 252).

Alvin Fuller, Republican governor of Massachusetts from 1925 to 1929. Fuller set the executions of Sacco and Vanzetti for August 10; he later postponed the sentences to August 22 to allow a final round of appeals. Sacco and Vanzetti were executed on August 23.

326 *NYT,* Tuesday, August 9, 1927, 25:7. Variant: *LAT* omits fourth sentence.

Vice President Dawes, the Prince of Wales, Secretary of State Kellogg, and other dignitaries attended the dedication at Buffalo of the International Peace Bridge which connected New York and Ontario. Dawes, a potential presidential candidate, chose the occasion to criticize British attitudes toward naval limitation.

327 *NYT,* Wednesday, August 10, 1927, 25:7. Variants: *KCT* gives "premier, who really is their president," in first sentence/*LAT* did not print the DT.

Stanley Baldwin, conservative prime minister of Great Britain from 1923 to 1924, 1924 to 1929, and 1935 to 1937. Baldwin spoke at the dedication of the International Peace Bridge (see DT 326).

328 *NYT,* Thursday, August 11, 1927, 23:7. Variants: *NYT* omits "secret" in second sentence/*BDG* gives "to return" and *KCT* gives "and a start on building" in third sentence/*NYT* and *LAT* omit fifth sentence.

President Coolidge revealed on August 9 that the United States would continue its "moderate naval building program," one which American public opinion could support.

329 *NYT,* Friday, August 12, 1927, 19:7. Variant: *BDG* gives "California. Fords" in first paragraph.

Santa Barbara annually held a three-day fiesta called "Old Spanish Days." Celebrated in August during the full moon, the observance recalled the founding of the presidio in 1782, its years as a Franciscan mission, its conquest by Americans in 1847, and its prosperous cattle period.

330 *BDG* (AM), Saturday, August 13, 1927, 1:6; heading from *KCT,* 13:2. Variants: *LAT* omits first and second sentences/*KCT* gives "Ten planes" in third sentence/*NYT* did not print the DT.

Hawaiian industrialist James Dole offered $35,000 in prizes—$25,000 for first and $10,000 for second—for a nonstop flight from California to Hawaii. By August 3 fifteen aircraft had been entered in the competition, but a series of crashes reduced the field. On August 12 race officials announced a four-day postponement to check the condition of the planes.

331 *NYT,* Monday, August 15, 1927, 19:7. Variants: *LAT* gives origin "BEVERLY HILLS"/*NYT* gives "with Providence to" in second sentence.

Eugene Meyer, chairman of the Federal Farm Loan Board, visited President Coolidge on August 13 and predicted a $1,000,000,000 gain in agricultural income in 1927, the best outlook since the postwar drop in prices.

332 *NYT,* Tuesday, August 16, 1927, 27:7. Variants: *KCT* gives "Fairbanks said yesterday" in first sentence/*KCT* ends second sentence with "tie."

333 *NYT,* Wednesday, August 17, 1927, 25:7.

Here Rogers explained his signature to DT 325. A new California state law declared that in cities of the sixth class, which Beverly Hills recently had become, the chairman of the Board of Trustees automatically would become mayor;

thus, Sil Spaulding, chairman of the Beverly Hills Board of Trustees, replaced Rogers as mayor. In recognition of Rogers' service, the board honored him with the title of "Mayor Emeritus."

[334] *NYT,* Thursday, August 18, 1927, 23:7. Variant: *KCT* gives "is an awful lonesome place this" in first sentence.

The Dole race to Hawaii began on the morning of August 16. Only nine aircraft remained of the fifteen which had qualified on August 3. Four of the nine planes took off without mishap on August 16, two others crashed at takeoff, two returned to San Francisco shortly after passing the Golden Gate, and one was denied permission to leave.

[335] *NYT,* Friday, August 19, 1927, 19:7. Variants: *KCT* gives "or injured we" in third sentence/*BDG* and *KCT* omit second paragraph/*LAT* gives "Just a plain citizen" for close.

Two groups of Germans in twin Junkers planes, departed Dessau, Germany, on August 14, bound for New York City. One plane turned back within six hours and crashed on landing with slight damage. The other aircraft reached Western Ireland before fog and gale-blown rain forced it to return to Dessau. No fliers were injured.

[336] *LAT,* Saturday, August 20, 1927, I:1:6; heading from *KCT,* 13:6. Variants: *BDG* and *KCT* give "are not Lindberghs." in fourth sentence/*NYT* did not print the DT.

Movie stunt flier Art Goebel won the Hawaiian derby, completing the flight in slightly more than twenty-six hours. Of the participating planes, only Goebel's aircraft carried radio-sending equipment. Only one other plane finished, and the fact that a woman passenger on one aircraft had been lost intensified public criticism of the race. The sponsoring committee in San Francisco had attempted to approve genuinely safe planes and competent pilots, but the relative smallness of Hawaii compounded navigation error.

[337] *NYT,* Monday, August 22, 1927, 19:7. Variants: *BDG* gives "Just across Arizona" in first sentence/*BDG* omits sixth sentence and *KCT* ends it after "Moody."/*LAT* omits P. S./*BDG* gives "All that I can" and *KCT* gives "for one, is that . . . down there will be two lost" in P. S.

For Governor Dan Moody see DT 71; for publisher Amon G. Carter see DT 176.

Criticism of the disastrous Hawaiian air derby continued (see DT 336). One of the original contestants, delayed at the start, had taken off on August 19 and had flown along the route of the competition. Radio signals indicated that he apparently had crashed 600 miles west of San Francisco. The race had claimed three lives with seven persons missing.

[338] *NYT,* Tuesday, August 23, 1927, 27:7. Variant: *LAT* gives "been desecrated to" and *BDG* gives "Curtis' to the" and *LAT* gives "Curtis's to the" in second sentence/*KCT* did not print the DT.

Senator Arthur Capper, long-time friend of farmers and editor of various publications, including *Capper's Farmer* magazine, visited Coolidge at the time of the president's announcement of withdrawal as a candidate (see DT 322). Senator Charles Curtis, a potential presidential candidate, was one-eighth Kaw Indian.

[339] *NYT,* Wednesday, August 24, 1927, 25:7. Variants: *LAT* gives origin "Crestland"/*LAT* gives "raining and bad" in second sentence/*BDG* gives "for the powder makers." in third sentence.

E. I. Du Pont de Nemours & Company manufactured chemicals used in ammunition.

For evangelist Billy Sunday see DT 225.

340 *NYT,* Thursday, August 25, 1927, 23:7. Variants: *LAT* omits eighth sentence/*NYT* gives "Your official" to begin close.

Coolidge had requested vital repairs for the White House, including work on the roof; Congress responded with an appropriation of $375,000. Workmen finished their tasks in time for Rogers to use the White House to film some scenes of his new motion picture, *A Texas Steer.*

341 *NYT,* Friday, August 26, 1927, 19:7.

Lita Chaplin received a divorce from actor Charlie Chaplin, plus custody of their two sons and a property settlement of $625,000 for herself and $200,000 in trust for the children (see DT 129).

Frank W. Stearns, Boston merchant who supported and promoted Coolidge's election as lieutenant governor and governor of Massachusetts and later as vice president; Coolidge's closest associate and confidant. From August 23 to 28 Coolidge toured Yellowstone National Park, visiting "Old Faithful" geyser and other favorite sightseeing spots.

342 *NYT,* Saturday, August 27, 1927, 15:7. Variants: *KCT* gives "get the capital moved" in fifth sentence/*NYT* omits P. S.

343 *NYT,* Monday, August 29, 1927, 19:7. Variants: *BDG* gives close and signature "Yours, WILL ROGERS." and *LAT* gives signature "HON. WILL ROGERS."

Bobby Jones of Atlanta won his third United States amateur golfing title in four years on August 27; earlier that month he had captured his second consecutive British open championship.

The title of "Congressman-at-Large for the United States" was bestowed on Rogers by the National Press Club at a special reception in Washington, D. C., on August 27. As bearer of the honor, the Oklahoman had to "roam over the country, pry into the state of the Union, check up on prohibition enforcement, and report at regular intervals" to the club.

344 *NYT,* Tuesday, August 30, 1927, 25:7.

Pilot William Brock and Detroit businessman Edward Schlee began a round-the-world flight in August in a Stinson-Detroiter monoplane. They hoped to break the existing record of twenty-eight and one half days. They reached London on August 28, but upon arriving in Tokyo on September 13, they abandoned the adventure and returned to the United States abroad a surface vessel.

For swimmer Gertrude Ederle see DT 10.

Charles Levine, passenger on Chamberlin's epic flight of June 6, 1927 (see DT 273), generated considerable publicity in Europe for his reckless flying and numerous fist fights. In contrast Lindbergh visited eastern and midwestern cities to promote aviation, published his story of the Paris flight, *We,* and with his mother announced plans to purchase the old family home in Minnesota.

345 *NYT,* Wednesday, August 31, 1927, 23:7. Variant: *LAT* gives "fellow men" in seventh sentence.

346 McNaught Syndicate; heading from *KCT,* Thursday, September 1, 1927, 13:2. Variants: *LAT* gives "movie of Hoyt's old stage play, 'A Texas Steer.' " and *KCT* gives "play, 'A Texas Steer.' " in first sentence/*BDG* omits

sixth and seventh sentences/*KCT* gives "was drinking" in eighth sentence/*BDG* omits title before signature/*NYT* did not print the DT.

Charles Hoyt, American playwright of popular comedies, including *The Texas Steer; or, Money Makes the Mare Go* (1890) and *A Trip to Chinatown* (1891).

347 *LAT,* Friday, September 2, 1927, I:1:3; heading from *KCT,* 13:5. Variants: *LAT* gives origin "WASHINGTON, D. C.," *BDG* and *KCT* as here/ *BDG* gives "that old lady" in first sentence/*BDG* gives "If an old lady of 63 can . . . her to look" and *KCT* gives "If a woman of 63 can" in fourth sentence/*NYT* did not print the DT.

Princess Loewenstein-Wertheim, sixty-two-year-old British widow of a German prince and first woman to fly the English Channel, and two commercial airways pilots departed England on August 31, bound for Ottawa, Canada. Their plane disappeared over the Atlantic.

348 *NYT,* Saturday, September 3, 1927, 17:7. Variant: *KCT* gives "his manager, went" in fifth sentence.

Dempsey trained at Lincoln Fields race track in Crete, Illinois, thirty miles from Chicago.

Leo Flynn, boxing trainer, manager, and promoter. Flynn served as adviser and trainer for Jack Dempsey's bouts with Jack Sharkey and Gene Tunney in 1927.

349 *NYT,* Monday, September 5, 1927, 17:7. Variants: *KCT* gives "from the City of Mexico" in second sentence/*KCT* gives "put out the fire." in fourth sentence/*BDG* omits title in close and *LAT* omits close.

Emilio Carranza, known as "Mexico's Lindy," flew nonstop from Mexico City to Juarez on September 2 in ten hours and forty-nine minutes. Newspaper reports mentioned the wing fire and the unique extinguishing method.

350 *NYT,* Tuesday, September 6, 1927, 27:7. Variants: *KCT* gives "There is raving . . . in motor car deaths." in first sentence/*KCT* gives "never hear about relief" in second sentence.

According to news sources, at least fifteen fliers had disappeared while attempting to cross the Pacific and Atlantic oceans. On September 2 the American Bar Association adopted a resolution calling for federal regulation of transoceanic flights. A *New York Times* editorial acknowledged that "there is something to be said" for regulation.

351 *NYT,* Wednesday, Seeptember 7, 1927, 31:7. Variants: *BDG* gives "movies on whom all" in third sentence/*BDG* gives "in any other business." in fifth sentence/*KCT* gives "the Anti-Saloon League" in eighth sentence/*NYT* and *LAT* omit last nine words of eighth sentence, but *BDG* and *KCT* have it as here (*BDG* giving it "Mrs. Coolidge")/*KCT* gives "The best proof a man is good is to have" in ninth sentence/*LAT* omits close, and *BDG* and *LAT* omit title/*KCT* omits signature.

For prohibitionist Wayne Wheeler see DT 221; for film producer Marcus Loew see DT 166.

352 *NYT,* Thursday, September 8, 1927, 29:7. Variants: *NYT* inserts "Coolidge in first sentence, but *BDG, LAT,* and *KCT* omit surname/*KCT* gives title and signature "CONGRESSMAN-AT-LARGE ROGERS."

President Coolidge addressed a number of farmers during a tour of an experimental farm in South Dakota on September 2. The secretary of the group offered Coolidge a standard 160-acre project farm as a retirement home. The president merely smiled.

353 *NYT,* Friday, September 9, 1927, 27:7. Variant: First sentence punctuation is as in *BDG.*

The Dempsey-Tunney rematch scheduled for 110,000-seat Soldier Field in Chicago, was expected to draw a total "gate" of $3,000,000 and to require 6,500 police and ushers to manage the crowd.

354 *NYT,* Saturday, September 10, 1927, 19:7. Variants: *NYT* gives "get answered" in second sentence/*BDG* and *LAT* give "Frisco" in third sentence/*KCT* gives "overland, he never would do it with a hydroplane." in third sentence.

Two more planes disappeared during transatlantic crossings. On September 3 an editor for the *New York Daily Mirror* and two other men departed New York for Rome on a promotional flight for the newspaper. Four days later a pair of Canadian aviators , competing for a $25,000 prize, left Newfoundland for London. By September 10 both planes were listed as lost.

355 *NYT,* Monday, September 12, 1927, 25:7. Variant: *LAT* gives origin "BEVERLY HILLS."

Although Governor Al Smith appeared to be the leading candidate for the Democratic nomination, William McAdoo remained a possibility. Others under consideration included Senators James Reed, Pat Harrison, and Joseph Robinson; Governor Albert Ritchie; Indianapolis banker Evans Woollen; and former Secretary of War Newton Baker.

356 *NYT,* Tuesday, September 13, 1927, 33:7. Variant: *BDG* omits "Walter" in second sentence.

For golfer Bobby Jones see DTs 209 and 343.

Walter Hagen, foremost professional golfer of the 1910s and 1920s. On September 10 Hagen won the Western Open in Chicago, while pre-fight publicity revealed that Dempsey was playing golf, rather than sparring.

357 *NYT,* Wednesday, September 14, 1927, 33:7. Variants: *BDG, LAT,* and *KCT* omit "FIRST . . . STUDIO" in heading/*LAT* gives close and signature but not title.

President and Mrs. Coolidge had ended their summer vacation in South Dakota by September 11 and had returned to Washington. Rogers remained confident that Coolidge would be president when the next summer arrived and thus offered the old Rogers ranch home near Claremore as a vacation retreat.

358 *NYT,* Thursday, September 15, 1927, 31:7. Variant: *BDG, LAT,* and *KCT* omit "FIRST. . . STUDIO" in heading/*LAT* gives "Mayor Thompson" in fourth sentence/*KCT* gives "opposite from" in sixth sentence.

359 *NYT,* Friday, September 16, 1927, 25:7. Variants: *BDG, LAT,* and *KCT* omit "FIRST . . . STUDIO" in heading/*LAT* gives "Mayor Thompson" in fourth sentence/*KCT* gives "opposite from" in sixth sentence.

360 *NYT,* Saturday, September 17, 1927, 19:7.

Screen comedian Charlie Chaplin's divorce settlement totaled $1,025,000 (see DT 341). The "new picture" which Rogers mentioned probably was the award-winning *The Circus* (1928), which Chaplin wrote and directed and in which he starred.

[361] *NYT,* Monday, September 19, 1927, 27:7. Variants: *LAT* gives origin "BEVERLY HILLS"/*KCT* presented this DT and #362 as parts of the same, with dateline "Sept. 18" and portion of #362 as P. S.; the whole was published on September 20, 15:3.

Former Secretary of the Treasury William McAdoo (see DT 147) withdrew his candidacy for the Democratic presidential nomination on September 17. In a prepared statement he reviewed his long public career and then rhetorically asked, "Do you not think that I have earned at least an 'honorable discharge'?" Some former McAdoo supporters subsequently suggested that Governor Smith follow suit in withdrawing.

[362] *NYT,* Tuesday, September 20, 1927, 31:7. Variant: *KCT* presents this and the previous DT as a single one in issue of September 20.

[363] *NYT,* Wednesday, September 21, 1927, 31:7. Variants: *BDG, LAT,* and *KCT* omit "FIRST . . . STUDIO" in heading/*LAT* gives "Another P. S." for second one/*BDG* inserts close and signature after postscripts, which it treats as second and third paragraphs of text proper.

Lindbergh had departed San Diego nineteen week earlier in *The Spirit of St. Louis,* bound for Paris and fame. On September 20 he returned to San Diego where he was honored at a civic banquet at which Will Rogers spoke, and, with Rogers, initiated into a local fraternal group.

In a publicity stunt for the motion picture company Metro-Goldwyn-Meyer, Martin Jensen, who placed second in the Hawaiian air derby in August, took off on September 16 from San Diego with a lion named Leo. Bound for New York City, Jensen crash-landed that afternoon in Arizona without injury to himself or the lion.

For aviation promoter Charles Levine see DT 344.

Abe Attell, world featherweight boxing champion from 1901 to 1912. Attell had been implicated in the gambling scandal surrounding the baseball World Series of 1919.

[364] *NYT,* Thursday, September 22, 1927, 31:7. Variants: *KCT* gives "the pig the ham" in sixth sentence/*BDG* and *LAT* give "The pigs" in seventh sentence/*LAT* gives "Toplitzky" and *KCT* gives "Toplisky" in seventh sentence/*BDG* and *LAT* give "Tia Juana" in P. S./*KCT* gives "Can it rightfully . . . America?" in P. S.

*The Spirit of St. Louis,* which Lindbergh commemorated in his autobiographical book *We* (1927), was constructed in San Diego at the Ryan Airlines factory. Workmen put the finishing touches on the plane only six weeks before Lindbergh flew it to Paris.

Lindbergh purchased five sandwiches—two ham, two beef, and one egg—"to go" at a drugstore in Queensboro Plaza in New York City on the evening before his departure for Paris.

Rogers probably referred to Marco H. Hellman, Los Angeles banker and prominent land owner.

Joe Toplitsky, Los Angeles realtor and insurance executive.

[365] *NYT,* Friday, September 23, 1927, 29:7. Variant: *KCT* inserts in origin: "FIRST NATIONAL STUDIOS."

Rogers enjoyed one of his greatest thrills on September 21. An airline president chose that day to announce the commencement of regular passenger service between San Diego and Los Angeles. Lindbergh consented, in the interest of commercial aviation, to pilot the inaugural flight. Rogers shared the cockpit with Lindbergh, and various dignitaries, including Mrs. Rogers, comprised the remainder of the planeload.

[366] *NYT*, Saturday, September 24, 1927, 19:7.

Dwight Morrow, United States ambassador to Mexico from 1927 to 1930. As a partner in the banking firm of J. P. Morgan and Company, Morrow had shown his diplomatic skills during and after World War I. Under his tactful guidance as ambassador, relations with Mexico improved as a number of disputes were adjusted.

In the Dempsey-Tunney rematch, defending champion Tunney heavily outpointed Dempsey through the first six rounds. Then in the seventh round, Dempsey managed a rush of blows which knocked Tunney down for the first time in his carer. Dempsey, who was nearly as confused as Tunney, stayed in his corner: however, the referee waited until Dempsey went to a neutral corner before he began the count. Thus, Tunney gained five valuable seconds and went on to win the match on points.

[367] *BDG* (AM), Monday, September 26, 1927, 1:5; heading from *KCT*, 13:2. Variants: *LAT* and *KCT* begin first sentence "Eleven people died"/*KCT* gives "announcer to tell them who" in second sentence/*KCT* gives "Fewer diplomats . . . fewer arms." and *LAT* gives "not fewer wars" in ninth sentence/ *NYT* did not print the DT.

The fatal heart attacks generally were blamed on the excitement of the seventh round.

Radio announcers, then as later, had to read long lists of credits and recite sponsors' commercial messages.

German Foreign Secretary Gustav Stresseman, in a speech on September 24, pleaded for international arms limitation. Armaments give no real security, he claimed, because other nations see them only as threats. The Allies had forced Germany to disarm following World War I.

[368] *NYT*, Tuesday, September 27, 1927, 29:7. Variants: *LAT* gives "they got it." and *KCT* gives "they can get it." in fourth sentence.

Various potential presidential candidates recently had voiced their opinions about Prohibition in speeches and newspaper interviews. Democratic Senator Reed of Missouri was interested more in establishing himself as favoring farm relief, rather than in emphasizing his well-known "wet" sentiments.

[369] *NYT*, Wednesday, September 28, 1927, 27:7. Variant: *LAT* omits sixth sentence.

[370] *NYT*, Thursday, September 29, 1927, 29:7. Variants: *BDG* and *LAT* give signature after third sentence/*BDG*, *LAT*, and *KCT* insert "P. S." before fourth and fifth sentences/*LAT* inserts "P. S. S." before the sixth and seventh sentences.

In Cleveland the Court of Common Pleas affirmed the right of a recently married couple to sit in a parked car and engage in public embraces. The arresting officer, against whom $3,675 in damages were assessed, had contended that the couple were guilty of disorderly conduct

The American Legion held its annual convention in Paris in 1927. Twenty-seven thousand Legionaires attended the festive gathering which began on September 20 and ended two days later. Soldiers returning from abroad during World War I often were welcomed with doughnuts, coffee, and other rewards.

Governors of the seven states drained by the Colorado River held a three-week meeting in Denver to discuss the proposed Boulder Dam. Arizona withdrew its objections to the dam, and California agreed that Arizona and Nevada might share in revenue from power sold by the project; thus, only division of the lower river remained for major discussion.

[371] *NYT,* Friday, September 30, 1927, 27:7.

Theaters in Los Angeles advertised films of the Dempsey-Tunney fight only five days after the match, although federal laws prohibited the interstate transportation of such films.

[372] *NYT,* Saturday, October 1, 1927, 21:7. Variant: *LAT* gives origin "BEVERLY HILLS."

Plutarco Calles, president of Mexico from 1924 to 1928. The exchange of telephone messages was staged elaborately in Washington and Mexico City.

A tornado swept through residential areas of St. Louis on the afternoon of September 29; it killed ninety persons and caused $50,000,000 property damage. The Red Cross lent immediate aid to the victims.

[373] *NYT,* Monday, October 3, 1927, 27:7. Variants: *BDG* gives "does seem good" and *KCT* gives "does feel good" in third sentence/*KCT* gives "they may beat" in fourth sentence.

For sports promoter Tex Rickard see DT 310.

Henry Louis "Lou" Gehrig, first baseman and home run slugger who starred with the New York Yankees from 1925 to 1939. The Yankees were favored to defeat the Pittsburgh Pirates in the World Series, scheduled to start on October 5.

[374] *NYT,* Tuesday, October 4, 1927, 31:7. Variants: *BDG* inserts "FIRST NATIONAL STUDIOS" in heading/*KCT* begins first sentence "See quoted a"/ *BDG, LAT,* and *KCT* give "government is all" and *LAT* gives "they read" and *KCT* gives "read where I" in third sentence.

British and American relations had deteriorated since the three-power naval conference in August. Rogers referred to an editorial in the *Manchester* (England) *Sunday Chronicle* which was quoted in the *Chicago Tribune.*

Governor Austin Peay of Tennessee (see DT 147) died suddenly on October 2 of a cerebral hemorrhage. Although he was governor at the time of the Scopes trial, he did not enter into the attendant controversy regarding evolution.

[375] *NYT,* Wednesday, October 5, 1927, 29:7. Variant: *KCT* gives "I unintentionally broke" to begin DT.

[376] *NYT,* Thursday, October 6, 1927, 27:7. Variants: *LAT* gives "fellow Babe Ruth and his home runs that" and *KCT* gives "his homer that" and *LAT* gives "on the radio today" in first sentence/*BDG* and *KCT* give "singles and a sacrifice fly. I" and *LAT* gives "singles in the whole game. I" in second sentence/ *KCT* gives "for it would have" and *BDG* gives "broken a record" in P. S.

Paul "Big Poison" Waner and Lloyd "Little Poison" Waner. Natives of Ada, Oklahoma, the Waner brothers played in right and center fields, respectively, for the Pittsburgh Pirates during the 1920s and 1930s. In the first game of the World Series which the Yankees won, 5 to 4, Paul had three hits, including a double, while Lloyd hit a double and scored twice.

[377] *NYT,* Friday, October 7, 1927, 29:7. Variants: *BDG* inserts "FIRST NATIONAL STUDIOS" in heading/*BDG* gives "to Borah" and *LAT* gives "marines will do a litle voting themselves." in first sentence/*BDG* ends second sentence "today." and *LAT* ends second sentence "Wednesday."/*KCT* gives "he couldn't find" in third sentence.

Senator Borah had expressed concern to Secretary Kellogg over the lack of current registration lists in Nicaragua. Kellogg agreed that registration was vital and that supervision of elections involved necessary control over preliminary steps, including registration. He asured Borah that the United States would guarantee Nicaraguans their rights.

James Davis, United States secretary of labor from 1921 to 1930. After inspecting the First National Studios with Rogers, Davis concluded that motion pictures were the most representative American indusry.

378 *NYT,* Saturday, October 8, 1927, 19:7.

Anthony "Tony" Lazzeri, second baseman and shortstop for the New York Yankees from 1925 to 1937. Lazzeri amassed a .292 batting average in the major leagues.

Bernard "Benny" Bengough, catcher for the New York Yankees from 1923 to 1930; later played for the St. Louis Browns; retired in 1932. Bengough had a lifetime major league batting average of .255.

George Pipgras, pitcher for the Yankees from 1923 to 1933; later with the Boston Red Sox from 1933 to 1935. Pipgras started, finished, and won three World Series games for the Yankees during his thirteen-year career.

Michael "Mike" Cvengros, pitcher for several major league clubs from 1922 to 1929, including Pittsburgh in 1927. Primarily a relief pitcher, Cvengros appeared in two World Series games in 1927.

New York swept the series in four games.

379 *NYT,* Monday, October 10, 1927, 23:7. Variants: *LAT* gives origin "BEVERLY HILLS"/only *LAT* gives first P. S./*LAT* gives second postscript "Another P. S."/*KCT* combines first three sentences: "Arthur Brisbane says Coolidge won't run." and gives fourth as here, omits fifth through seventh sentences, and gives eighth: "I will bet $5,000 he runs. No ifs about it. I bet he runs, the winner . . . knowledge." and uses second P. S.

Brisbane, an editor and columnist for Hearst newspapers (see DT 204), insisted that President Coolidge's statement of withdrawal issued in August was genuine. The president declined to clarify his remarks, but it increasingly was taken as an absolute refusal of further nomination.

William Randolph Hearst, powerful and controversial editor, publisher, and political figure; a dominant figure in American journalism.

380 *LAT,* Tuesday, October 11, 1927, I:1:3; heading from *KCT,* 15:2. Variants: *KCT* gives "there is something to be" in second sentence/*KCT* omits second P. S./*NYT* did not print the DT.

Secretary of the Treasury Andrew Mellon had reported a government surplus of $400,000,000, which prompted the administration to call for a tax reduction of no more than $300,000,000. A special committee on taxation of the United States Chamber of Commerce recommended that the reduction be at least $400,000,000, that corporation taxes be cut, and that federal estate and war excises be repealed.

381 *NYT,* Wednesday, October 12, 1927, 29:7. Variants: *KCT* omits fourth, fifth, and sixth sentences, and *LAT* omits fourth through eighth sentences/*KCT* gives seventh and eighth sentences as P. S.

French and American relations were strained somewhat over negotiations of a new trade treaty which included French tariffs on American manufactured goods. Announced on October 5, the rates were suspended in November.

Hazen "Kiki" Cuyler, outfielder for the Pittsburgh Pirates from 1921 to 1927; later played with three other major league teams before retiring in 1938.

Cuyler led the Pirates to a world championship in 1925. The Pittsburgh club owner, dissatisfied with his efforts in 1927, benched him for much of the season. After the team's poor showing in the World Series, Cuyler broke his self-imposed silence to criticize the front office; he soon was traded.

[382] *NYT*, Thursday, October 13, 1927, 27:4-5. Variants: *BDG, LAT,* and *KCT* omit introductory sentence/*BDG* gives "WILL NOT RUN" in Hearst's first sentence/*KCT* gives "public official who" in Hearst's third sentence/only *LAT* gives "it wasn't . . . for." in Rogers fourteenth and fifteenth sentences/*KCT* gives "the progressive offsprings, so" in Rogers' eighteenth sentence/*KCT* gives "Arthur B. got" in Rogers' nineteenth sentence.

The proposed Brisbane-Rogers bet on a third term for Coolidge (see DT 379) suddenly became a Hearst-Rogers wager, with different odds and more at stake. The publisher's communication resembled the editorials which he often sent his newspapers for obligatory front page space.

[383] *NYT*, Friday, October 14, 1927, 27:7. *LAT* did not print the DT.

Senator James Reed of Missouri (see DT 79)) virtually declared his candidacy in a major speech on October 12 at Sedalia, Missouri. After assailing the Harding and Coolidge administrations, particularly concerning the naval oil scandals and a recent war debt controversy, Reed criticized the McNary-Haugen farm relief plan; thus he seemed opposed to all Republicans.

Senator Reed caused a breach in the Democratic party in Missouri in 1919 when he denounced President Wilson's peace policy. The next year the state party repudiated Reed's remarks and rejected him as a delegate to the national convention.

[384] *NYT*, Saturday, October 15, 1927, 21:7. Variants: *BDG* and *LAT* omit P. S.

Twenty-three-year-old Ruth Elder and a male pilot attempted a New York-to-Paris flight in a Stinson-Detroiter monoplane. They departed on October 11, but engine trouble two days later forced them to ditch their plane in the Atlantic. Crewmen of a nearby Dutch tanker rescued them.

Three females reportedly swam the English Channel in October, but their feats virtually went unnoticed. One of the women subsequently confessed that she had faked her claim in order to expose the absence of safeguards for swimmers who attempted the crossing.

Princess Ileana, the youngest daughter of King Ferdinand and Queen Marie of Rumania, reportedly eloped with a Rumanian naval lieutenant. Her mother denied the rumor, which was followed by a story that the princess had become a virtual prisoner in the royal palace, but that rumor also was denied. In 1931 the princess married Archduke Anton of Austria-Tuscany.

President Coolidge and Secretary Mellon attended a ceremony at the Carnegie Institute Museum on October 13 to honor business leaders of Pittsburgh for their cultural endeavors. Coolidge praised American contributions to international art, and Mellon extolled the work of industrialist and philanthropist Andrew Carnegie for supporting art and the city of Pittsburgh.

[385] *NYT*, Monday, October 17, 1927, 25:7. Variants: *BDG, LAT,* and *KCT* give "Kemal" in second sentence.

Notre Dame defeated the United States Naval Academy on October 15 by a score of 19 to 6.

Mustafa Kemal Pasha, president of the Turkish Republic from 1923 to 1938. On October 14 Kemal began a 400,000-word speech in the Turkish national assembly. The six-day oration reviewed the history of the republic in considerable detail.

Ruth Elder's rescuers, the crew of a Dutch tanker, attempted to raise her plane onto the deck of the ship, but the aircraft had to be cut loose when a fire started in an engine. When Miss Elder boarded the rescue ship, she shook hands with the captain and thanked him. She then turned aside and applied fresh lipstick. Her husband, advertiser Lyle Womack, completely approved of her flying, she reported.

386 *LAT,* Tuesday, October 18, 1927, I:1:6; heading from *KCT,* 15:3. Variants: *BDG* begins ninth sentence "Mr. Brisbane is"/*KCT* omits ninth sentence/*NYT* did not print the DT.

Arthur Brisbane was well-known for his profitable real estate operations which included apartments, hotels, and the new Ziegfeld Theater in New York City (see DT 204).

387 *NYT,* Wednesday, October 19, 1927, 29:2. Variants: *LAT* and *KCT* give "progress in aviation" in first sentence.

Western Air Express Company, organized by Harris "Pop" Hanshue with the financial assistance of publisher Harry Chandler and others, held one of the original air mail contracts. Between October 18 and 21 Rogers twice crossed the United States on regularly scheduled airmail-passenger flights, including a Western Air Express flight from Los Angeles to Salt Lake City.

Brigham Young, organized and guided the mass migration of Mormans to the Great Salt Lake Valley in Utah in 1848. Young adopted polygamy, had about twenty wives, and fathered fifty-six children.

388 *NYT,* Thursday, October 20, 1927, 31:7. Variants: *LAT* and *KCT* omit "(Tuesday)" and *BDG, LAT,* and *KCT* omit "(Wednesday)" in first sentence.

389 *NYT,* Friday, October 21, 1927, 25:7. Variants: *BDG* and *LAT* give "Beverly Hills" in first sentence/*KCT* gives "you'd just" in fourth sentence.

390 *NYT,* Saturday, October 22, 1927, 19:7. Variants: *LAT* gives origin "BEVERLY HILLS"/*LAT* gives third sentence "Got home in time for dinner."/ *LAT* and *KCT* give "Beverly this afternoon" in fourth sentence/*LAT* gives "arrive in New York till" and *KCT* gives "there until tomorow morning" in sixth sentence/*LAT* omits first sentence of P. S./*BDG* gives second sentence of P. S. "We flew all over it." and *LAT* gives "We flew all over and around the Boulder Dam site." and *KCT* gives "over around it'" in same sentence.

By the time Rogers landed at Vail Field in Los Angeles, he had completed the first regularly-scheduled passenger flight between New York and Los Angeles; actual flying time totaled eighty-one hours. Lindbergh flew air mail service before he embarked on his epic transatlantic flight.

391 *NYT,* Monday, October 24, 1927, 23:7. Variants: *LAT* gives origin "BEVERLY HILLS"/*LAT* gives "Morrow has arrived in Mexico to" in first sentence/*LAT* omits second paragraph/*BDG* gives "anxious days for" in seventh sentence.

Ambassador Morrow (see DT 366) entered Mexico under guard on October 22 and reached the capital city the next day. He presented his credentials to President Calles on October 29 with mutual expressions of amity and good will. His service as ambassador was one of the most successful of the decade.

Morrow and Coolidge were members of the class of 1895 at Amherst College in Massachusetts.

The United States refused to recognize the Soviet Union following the Bolshevik Revolution in 1917. Mutual recognition finally came in November of 1931.

[392] *NYT,* Tuesday, October 25, 1927, 31:7. Variants: *BDG* omits third paragraph/*KCT* omits fifth sentence.

Morrow arrived safely in Mexico City despite an undercurrent of revolutionary activity. Several of the insurrectionist leaders, some of whom were presidential candidates, reportedly had been executed.

Frances Grayson, a Long Island realtor, had intended to fly to Denmark with a three-man crew, but three attempts between October 17 and 23 ended in failure. She then hired a male pilot who had experience flying in winter. On Christmas Eve they left Roosevelt Field, Long Island, for Newfoundland but disappeared en route.

Prince Carol of Rumania reportedly had abandoned his mistress, Madame Magda Lepescu, in an effort to win favor among opponents of the regency government of King Michael (see DT 311).

The Mann Act of 1910 prohibited the interstate transportation of women for immoral purposes.

[393] *LAT,* Wednesday, October 26, 1927, I:1:6; heading from *KCT,* 13:2. Variants: *KCT* gives "holding its benefit" in first sentence/only *KCT* gives P. S./*NYT* did not print the DT.

The annual meeting of the American Bankers' Association convened in Houston on October 24. The members principally were concerned about the 3,800 bank suspensions during the previous six years; suggested remedies included closer federal supervision. New legislation passed in February of 1927 had taken effect, resulting in many mergers and the growth of branch banking.

[394] *NYT,* Thursday, October 27, 1927, 31:7. Variants: *BDG* gives "cut down expenditures" in third sentence/*NYT* omits third paragraph, but *BDG, LAT,* and *KCT* have it as here.

Thomas Magruder, rear admiral in the United States Navy. In an article for the *Saturday Evening Post,* September 24, 1927, Magruder suggested that the Navy should economize by reducing the number of installations and officers. Secretary of the Navy Curtis Wilbur criticized the admiral for his remarks and subsequently relieved him of his command on October 25.

A leader of the nudist, communal cult discovered on the French Riviera claimed that members had no money, no property, no marriage, and no nationality.

[395] *NYT,* Friday, October 28, 1927, 25:7.

Senator Charles Curtis of Kansas (see DT 116) announced his candidacy for the Republican presidential nomination on October 26 and thus became the first official entry in the campaign of 1928. He insisted that he would not be merely a favorite son candidate.

[396] *NYT,* Saturday, October 29, 1927, 19:7. Variants: *NYT* omits first paragraph, but *BDG, LAT,* and *KCT* have it as here/*BDG* and *KCT* give second paragraph as P. S.

T. Coleman du Pont, Republican United States senator from Delaware from 1921 to 1922 and 1925 to 1928. Du Pont resigned from the Senate in 1928 because of cancer of the larnyx.

Simeon Fess, Republican United States senator from Ohio from 1923 to 1935. Coolidge mildly reprimanded Fess for promoting Coolidge for a third term. The president continued to maintain that he would refuse the nomination.

Admiral Magruder, commandant of the Philadelphia naval yard (see DT 394), wrote President Coolidge to protest his removal from command and to seek revocation of the orders. He also requested an interview with the president. Secretary of the Navy Wilbur emphasized to the press that the reassignment order was "not punitive[;] it is administrative."

397 *NYT,* Monday, October 31, 1927, 21:7. Variants: *BDG* and *LAT* omit time in heading/*LAT* gives "they would call" in second sentence/*LAT* uses P. S. as close.

San Simeon Ranch, the most fabulous of all the holdings of publisher William Randolph Hearst, consisted of 270,000 acres straddling the Santa Lucia mountains and stretching for approximately fifty miles along the central California coast.

398 *NYT,* Tuesday, November 1, 1927, 29:7. Variants: *BDG* gives "Four people" in first sentence/*BDG* and *KCT* give "six injured" in second sentence.

The *Los Angeles Times* for October 29 and 30 listed the names of those who were killed and injured in the collision, but it gave more prominent space to the aviation accident in New Jersey which killed four persons.

399 *NYT,* Wednesday, November 2, 1927, 29:7. Variant: *KCT* gives "will not revert" in ninth sentence.

Mayor Thompson, who had campaigned against "treason-tainted school textbooks" and had caused the suspension and trial of the superintendent of schools in Chicago (see DT 219), launched an America First Foundation with a $10 membership fee required.

400 *NYT,* Thursday, November 3, 1927, 29:7. Variants: *BDG, LAT,* and *KCT* omit "FIRST NATIONAL STUDIOS" in heading.

Jurors in the trial of former Secretary of the Interior Albert Fall and oil company executive Harry Sinclair allegedly had been shadowed by a detective agency hired by the defense. The government had brought Fall and Sinclair to trial for alleged leasing of naval oil reserves, especially property at Teapot Dome, Wyoming. The trial opened on October 16 and ended suddenly on November 2 in a mistrial because of attempted tampering with the jury.

401 *NYT,* Friday, November 4, 1927, 23:7. Variant: *KCT* gives "ask the hardworking" in third sentence.

The Bureau of Internal Revenue issued a report on November 3 which revealed the rise in Americans' standard of living.

The first Ford Model A rolled off the assembly line in Detroit on November 1.

402 *NYT,* Saturday, November 5, 1927, 21:7.

Rumor prevailed that Ford would offer the new Model A on a "club plan." The user would make a small down payment and pay a monthly fee. At the end of a year he could have the car overhauled for a slight charge or exchange it for a new one Title would remain with the company, though the user would have the option to purchase. Such an arrangement never materialized.

403 *NYT,* Monday, November 7, 1927, 25:7.

The *Los Angeles Times* reported on November 6 that Rogers had left Saturday night, November 5, by train "for the East to attend the premiere of his new picture, *The Texas Steer.*" But Rogers, who disliked premieres, apparently decided to take his wife on an auto tour of the Southwest.

404 *NYT,* Tuesday, November 8, 1927, 29:7. Variants: *BDG* gives "the Navajoes over three" and *LAT* gives "on Navajo lands more than three" and *KCT* gives "on the Navajos' land over three" in first sentence/*LAT* gives "hadn't had any yet" in third sentence/*BDG* and *KCT* give "Poor Lo! I suppose" in seventh sentence.

The Navajo Bridge, completed in 1929, spanned the Colorado River near Lee Ferry, Arizona. Navajos claimed that the birdge did not benefit them and that their oil revenues were appropriated unfairly for its construction.

For Rear Admiral Thomas Magruder see DT 394.

Charles Summerall, major general; Chief of Staff of the United States Army from 1926 to 1930. In October Secretary of War Dwight Davis recalled Summerall from a speaking tour in the West because he had criticized army economy, especially expenses on housing arrangements for personnel. After consultation with President Coolidge and Secretary Davis, Summerall resumed duty.

405 *NYT,* Wednesday, November 9, 1927, 27:7.

Voters in New York and New Mexico considered constitutional amendments in 1927 which would provide four-year terms for governors. Both amendments failed.

406 *NYT,* Thursday, November 10, 1927, 27:7. Variants: *KCT* begins fifth sentence "New Mexico," omitting first eight words/*LAT* omits sixth sentence /*LAT* omits close and signature.

New York voters adopted eight constitutional amendments and defeated one in elections on November 8; the results precisely reflected Governor Smith's desires.

In Philadelphia candidates supported by the political machine of Republican William Vare (see DT 69) won the mayoral post and positions on the city council but charges of fraud clouded the election results.

Cleveland voters defeated a proposal to repeal the city manager form of municipal government and return to the mayor-council plan.

New Mexico voters rejected a four-year term for state officials (see DT 405).

In Kentucky Republican Flem Sampson defeated favored Democrat J. C. W. Beckham in the gubernatorial election. Observers believed that Beckham's proposed repeal of pari-mutuel betting led to his defeat.

No DT is available for Friday, November 11, 1927.

407 *NYT,* Saturday, November 12, 1927, 19:7. Variants: *BDG* and *KCT* give "through Kansas cornfields" in first sentence.

The boll weevil and the Mississippi River flood combined to reduce cotton production in 1927, resulting in an 80 percent increase in the price of cotton above that of a year earlier. Despite a late start because of cold weather, corn producers raised slightly more than in the previous year, with the price approximately 12 percent higher. Beef cattle sold at the highest prices since 1920.

Fundamentalist minister John Roach Straton (see DT 319) ignored the objections of his congregation and held a faith healing service on Sunday, November 10. Within a month Dr. Straton had published a book on faith healing.

408 *NYT,* Monday, November 14, 1927, 23:7. Variant: *LAT* gives "King George he knows is" in third sentence.

Rogers visited Mayor Thompson (see DT 219) soon after the mayor returned from Washington, D. C., where he had testified before the House Flood Control Committee.

Notre Dame University lost to the United States Military Academy, 18 to 0, in a football game on November 12, marking the only defeat for the Fighting Irish in 1927.

Governor Al Smith of New York, an Irish-American Catholic, had enjoyed recent success at the polls (see DT 407).

For Notre Dame football coach Knute Rockne see DT 83.

No DT is available for Monday, November 14, 1927.

409 *NYT,* Tuesday, November 15, 1927, 31:7. Variants: *LAT* and *KCT* give "composed and can" in eighth and ninth sentences/*LAT* gives "Your old sleuth," in close/ *BDG* did not print the DT.

Henry Ford invited Will and Betty Rogers to Detroit for a special unveiling of the long-awaited Model A. The new automobile made its public debut on December 1, 1927.

Old Sleuth, a fictional detective created in the 1870s by Harlan Halsey for the popular magazine *The Fireside Companion.* After 1882 Halsey's mysteries were reprinted in *The Old Sleuth Library.*

410 *NYT,* Wednesday, November 16, 1927, 27:7. *BDG, LAT,* and *KCT* did not print the DT.

411 *NYT,* Thursday, November 17, 1927, 27:7. Variants: *BDG* and *LAT* give "papers today" in first sentence.

Aviator Ruth Elder (see DTs 384 and 385) arrived in the United States from Paris on November 11. Her husband appeared at ceremonies in New York and Washington but then departed for Panama amid rumors that the couple had separated.

George Remus, lawyer and convicted bootlegger, was arrested in early October for the murder of his wife. Under special accelerated conditions his trial opened in Cincinnati on November 12 with Remus conducting his own defense, alleging insanity and a conspiracy to kill him. The court acquitted him on grounds of insanity.

412 *NYT,* Friday, November 18, 1927, 25:7. Variants: *KCT* gives "I get that the wheat . . . Hoover because he" in third and fourth sentences/*LAT* omits second and third paragraphs and *KCT* omits sixth sentence and P. S./*BDG* omits P. S.

Heavy rains in early November caused flooding in northern and western New England; damage was especially severe in Vermont. The Red Cross, army engineers, and Secretary Hoover soon arrived to inspect and assess damage and plan rehabilitation. Officials estimated losses at $30,000,000 in Vermont alone with more than 100 dead and 6,000 persons homeless.

Since early October the farm bloc in Congress had criticized Secretary Hoover for opposing high fixed wheat prices during World War I. The National Farmers' Union joined the denunciation on November 16.

413 *NYT,* Saturday, November 19, 1927, 19:7. Variant: *NYT* gives "prosperous even if" in fourth sentence, but *BDG, LAT,* and *KCT* have it as here.

Many political observers viewed President Coolidge's speech on November 17 to the Philadelphia Union League Club as a campaign document. The league honored Coolidge with its distinguished service medal. Coolidge responded with a long speech praising the past accomplishments and prosperous condition of the United States, but his remarks gave no hint of his electoral intentions in 1928.

[414] *NYT,* Monday, November 21, 1927, 25:7. Variants: *KCT* gives "luncheons or hog-calling" in fourth sentence/*NYT* omits sixth sentence, but *BDG, LAT,* and *KCT* have it as here.

[415] *NYT,* Tuesday, November 22, 1927, 31:7.

Rupert Hughes, writer, poet, and novelist. In writing *George Washington, the Rebel and the Patriot, 1762-1777* (1927), the second of a multi-volume biography, Hughes used a variety of primary sources, including Washington's diary. He described Washington as a vigorous Virginia aristrocrat who avoided neither alcohol nor women but who used his considerable talents to lead the revolutionary army and the United States to victory.

[416] *NYT,* Wednesday, November 23, 1927, 27:7. Variants: *BDG* gives "owe billions of dollars" in fourth sentence/*BDG* and *LAT* give "could go back to work with nothing" and *KCT* gives "could go back to bed. Nothing in view," in ninth sentence/*BDG, LAT,* and *KCT* give signature "WILL ROGERS."

The House Ways and Means Committee opened hearings on the proposed taxation bill on October 31 (see DT 380). Secretary of the Treasury Mellon suggested several reductions in taxes but insisted that the toal cut should not exceed $225,000,000 in order to permit some reduction of the national debt. The committee voted on November 21 for reductions of $250,000,000.

[417] *NYT,* Thursday, November 24, 1927, 25:7. Variants: *LAT* begins first sentence "Thanksgiving was started by the Pilgrims who"/*KCT* gives "the last year" in fourth sentence/*BDG* gives "promise of lower taxes." in sixth sentence.

Coal miners in Pennsylvania, West Virginia, and Ohio had been on strike since early April of 1927, because of alleged violations of a minimum wage agreement negotiated in 1924 between operators and the miners' union. Another coal strike, begun in September in Colorado by the radical Industrial Workers of the World, erupted into violence on November 21. Neither strike was settled by the end of the year.

[418] *NYT,* Friday, November 25, 1927, 23:7. Variants: *BDG* omits sixth sentence/*LAT* gives "Kentucky may prohibit" in seventh sentence.

The price of a seat on the New York Stock Exchange more than doubled to $625,000 in January of 1929.

Official returns in the Kentucky gubernatorial election gave Republican Flem Sampson 58 percent of the vote, insuring the continuation of legal betting on horse races (see DT 406).

[419] *NYT,* Saturday, November 26, 1927, 17:7. Variants: *LAT* omits first sentence/*LAT* gives "Carol's cause" in third sentence/*BDG* gives "One headline says 'One . . . 1914;' another, 'England' " in fifth and sixth sentences.

Premier Ion Bratianu, whose family and an aristocratic faction had ruled Rumania for much of its history since 1848, died on November 25. His brother, Vintila, succeeded, but Prince Carol's faction still challenged. The two wives referred to are Princess Helen, mother of King Michael (see DT 311), and Madame Magda Lupescu, Carol's mistress.

Balkan rivalries stirred Italian public opinion against Yugoslavia, which had responded to French overtures for a treaty of friendship (see DT 207). Britain hoped to preserve a balance of power in the Balkans.

420 *NYT,* Monday, November 28, 1927, 23:7. Variants: *LAT* gives origin "BEVERLY HILLS"/*KCT* omits "ball on Rumania's" in second sentence.

Bulgaria, one of the defeated nations in World War I, and Yugoslavia, which sought an alliance with France, held rival claims to Macedonia. Rumania had opposed Bulgaria in the Balkan War of 1913 and in World War I. Another potential French ally, Poland, threatened its smaller neighbor Lithuania, prompting a note from Russia which warned of the danger of war. Rogers expected Italian dictator Mussolini to reap whatever benefits that arose from the unsettled conditions.

421 *NYT,* Tuesday, November 29, 1927, 29:7.

The Anti-Saloon League of America opened its biennial convention on December 5 in Washington, D.C. Some members openly urged Democrats to support Prohibition or face overwhelming defeat in 1928.

422 *BDG* (PM), Wednesday, November 30, 1927, 19:1. Variants: *BDG* gives dateline "Nov 30" *LAT* has it as here/*LAT* gives "set, so I want" in first sentence/*BDG* omits fifth, sixth, and seventh sentences, but *LAT* gives them as here/*BDG* (AM) and *KCT* did not print the DT; *NYT* combines this and the next DT, November 30, under dateline "LAREDO, Texas, Nov. 30."

For Governor Dan Moody see DT 71.

Dr. A. William Lilliendahl, seventy-two-year-old lawyer and physician, was slain on a country lane in New Jersey on the night of September 15. His wife and her friend, a chicken dealer, were arrested, tried and convicted for the murder; they received ten-year prison terms. The case attracted the usual intense press coverage.

423 *BDG* (AM), Thursday, December 1, 1927, 1:5; heading from *KCT,* 15:2. Variants: *NYT* combines previous DT, dateline "SAN ANTONIO, Texas, Nov. 29" and this one under dateline as above; heading: "Mr. Rogers, Going Into Mexico, Has a Nomination to Suggest." *BDG, LAT,* and *KCT* present the two separately.

Rogers visited Mexico at the invitation of Dwight Morrow, the newly appointed American ambassador. The *KCT* heading gives prominence to General Alvaro Obregón, former Mexican president (see DT 430).

424 *NYT,* Friday, December 2, 1927, 25:7. Variants: *KCT* gives origin "THE CITY OF MEXICO"/*BDG* omits third, fourth, and fifth sentences, and *LAT* omits fourth and fifth sentences/*KCT* gives "The whole nation has been waiting like America to see" in fourth sentence/*KCT* gives "If it's decided they're cheap enough tomorrow" in fifth sentence/*LAT* omits close and title.

While traveling on the presidential train in remote rural Mexico, Rogers missed publication deadlines for Saturday, December 3, and Monday, December 5. DTs intended for publication on those days appeared in print one day later.

425 *NYT,* Sunday, December 4, 1927, I:3:2. Variants: *BDG* and *KCT* give origin and date "ON MEXICAN PRESIDENTIAL TRAIN, Dec. 4." and *LAT* gives "ON BOARD PRESIDENTIAL TRAIN (Mexico)"/*BDG* gives "With Ambassador Morrow have" and *LAT* gives "President Calles and Ambassador Morow have" and *KCT* gives "Have just inspected" in first sentence/*BDG, LAT,* and *KCT* omit sixth sentence and close.

For President Plutarco Calles see DT 372.

[426] *NYT,* Tuesday, December 6, 1927, 31:7. Variants: *BDG, LAT,* and *KCT* gives origin "ON BOARD PRESIDENTIAL TRAIN" omitting "via Laredo, Texas" (*LAT* omits "BOARD")/*BDG* and *KCT* give "Sunday, the President" and *LAT* give "Out on one . . . entertained the President went" in second sentence/*BDG, LAT,* and *KCT* give "They had no" in third sentence.

Rogers performed rope tricks for the presidential party and mingled with the Mexican cowboys at a ranch near Aguascalientes. He disliked bullfights—the violence, especially to horses, bothered him.

[427] *NYT,* Wednesday, December 7, 1927, 31:7. Variants: *LAT* omits "via Laredo, Texas" in origin/*BDG, LAT,* and *KCT* give date "Dec. 6."

On this date *NYT* corrected its dateline to allow for a two-day delay in DTs from the presidential train; thus two DTs appear with a date of December 5.

[428] *NYT,* Thursday, December 8, 1927, 31:7. Variants: *BDG, LAT,* and *KCT* give date "'Dec. 7."/*BDG* begins origin "Mexico City, (date), On Board" and *KCT* ends origin "INTO THE CITY OF MEXICO"/*LAT* gives "open Monday and" in third sentence.

[429] *NYT,* Friday, December 9, 1927, 27:7. Variants: *KCT* gives origin "THE CITY OF MEXICO"/*BDG* gives "in Mexico and" and *KCT* gives "Arrived here and" in first sentence/*BDG, LAT,* and *KCT* omit second and third sentences.

President Coolidge addressed the Republican National Committee on December 7. He read an optimistic review of his administration and then added a brief comment that his decision in August held firm—he did not choose to run for a third term (see DT 322). Some political observers remained uncertain as to his actual intent.

Senator-elect Frank Smith (see DT 69) was denied his seat in the Senate on December 7 by a vote of 53 to 28, with insurgent Republicans joining most Democrats in the majority. Two days later, William Vare was ousted from the Senate by a vote of 56 to 30.

The Republican National Committee chose Kansas City, Missouri, as the site of the Republican National Convention in 1928, but twenty ballots were necessary before a consensus was reached.

[430] *NYT,* Saturday, December 10, 1927, 19:7. Variant: *KCT* gives origin "THE CITY OF MEXICO."

Alvaro Obregón, Mexican military leader and politician. General Obregón, a former president of Mexico, was the prospective candidate of the largest political faction in Mexico for the presidential election in 1928.

No DT is available for Monday, December 12, 1927.

[431] *NYT,* Tuesday, December 13, 1927, 31:7. Variants: *KCT* gives origin "THE CITY OF MEXICO"/*BDG* and *KCT* give "It will take more" in third sentence/*LAT* gives "Lindbergh is coming! Got to" in fourth sentence.

Guadalupe Day, celebrated annually on December 12, commemorated the appearance in 1531 of Our Lady of Guadalupe, the patroness of Mexico. Despite antireligious laws enacted in the 1920s, thousands of Mexican pilgrims continued to travel to the principal shrine of Our Lady in Guadalupe Hidalgo, a suburb of Mexico City.

Lindbergh flew *The Spirit of St. Louis* from Washington, D.C., to Mexico City at the invitation of President Calles. He arrived in the Mexican capital on December 14.

[432] *NYT,* Wednesday, December 14, 1927, 31:7. Variants: *KCT* gives origin "THE CITY OF MEXICO"/*KCT* gives "Popocatepetl" in first sentence/*LAT* ends second sentence "pronounce or spell."/*KCT* ends sixth sentence "reception."

Popocatépetl, a dormant volcano forty miles southeast of Mexico City, is the second highest peak in the country (17,883 feet).

[433] *NYT,* Thursday, December 15, 1927, 1:5, 3:4. Variants: *KCT* gives origin "THE CITY OF MEXICO"/*LAT* gives "I saw 200,000" and *KCT* gives "even his own country" in tenth sentence/*LAT* and *KCT* give "hotel on a building" in twelfth sentence/*LAT* gives "he is the most" in twenty-second sentence/*KCT* gives "ones that he will" and *LAT* gives "ones he will" in twenty-third sentence/*LAT* gives "he is eating now" in twenty-fourth sentence/*LAT* and *KCT* add close and signature, but *NYT* gives it as regular by-lined article/*BDG* did not print the DT.

Lindbergh encountered fog throughout much of his twenty-seven-hour flight to Mexico City, but he eventually landed safely, three hours overdue.

The dinner honoring Rogers was part of Ambassador Morow's carefully planned campaign for better relations between Mexico and the United States.

[434] *NYT,* Friday, December 16, 1927, 27:7. Variants: *KCT* gives origin "THE CITY OF MEXICO"/*LAT* and *KCT* give "it. While he . . . Mexico they . . . they were President." in first and second sentences/*KCT* omits fourth paragraph.

Four unnamed United States senators received money from Mexican sources, according to stories which appeared in various Hearst papers from December 6 to 9 The newspapers hinted that the Soviet Union was responsible for the bribes. A special Senate commitee revealed that Republicans William Borah, Robert La Follette, and George Norris and Democrat Thomas Heflin—all critics of a hard-line policy toward Mexico—were the senators alleged to have been bribed. Hearst later admitted his evidence was spurious, and the four were exonerated.

[435] *NYT,* Saturday, December 17, 1927, 21:7. Variants: *KCT* gives origin "THE CITY OF MEXICO"/*BDG, LAT,* and *KCT* give "take President" in third sentence/*LAT* gives "see the girls." in sixth sentence/*LAT* omits seventh sentence.

Senator Heflin (see DT 174) was the only Democrat among the four senators mentioned in the Hearst charges.

[436] *NYT,* Monday, December 19, 1927, 25:7. Variants: *KCT* gives "from the City of Mexico" in first sentence/*KCT* ends fourth sentence "fight."/*KCT* gives "staying away didn't do" in ninth sentence.

Lindbergh attended a bullfight in Mexico despite the protests of the American Humane Society.

[437] *NYT,* Tuesday, December 20, 1927, 31:7. Variants: *KCT* gives "Left the City of Mexico" and *LAT* gives "Tampico, land in Brownsville" in second sentence.

Evangeline Lindbergh, Charles Lindbergh's mother, visited Mexico to spend Christmas holidays with her son at the special invitation of Ambassador Morrow.

Morrow was confirmed by the Senate as ambassador to Mexico on December 17.

No DT is available for Wednesday, December 21, 1927.

[438] *NYT*, Thursday, December 22, 1927, 23:2.

In Oklahoma a number of state legislative leaders opposed to Governor Henry Johnston had requested a special session to institute impeachment proceedings, but the governor refused to comply. The legislators convened themselves on December 6 and ignored a state supreme court decision that they had acted illegally. When Johnston summoned the National Guard to prevent the lawmakers from meeting in the capitol, the assemblymen moved to a hotel where the state house voted impeachment charges against the governor on December 13. The state senate adjourned without considering the charges.

[439] *NYT*, Friday, December 23, 1927, 19:2. Variants: *LAT* omits second and third paragraphs/*KCT* gives "in the City of Mexico" in fourth sentence/*BDG* did not print the DT.

[440] *NYT*, Saturday, December 24, 1927, 15:2. Variants: *BDG*, *LAT*, and *KCT* give "I wanted to" in third sentence/*KCT* gives "That looks like" to begin fifth sentence.

Rogers parodied the Hearst documents investigation (see DT 434).

[441] *NYT*, Monday, December 26, 1927, 25:7. Variant: *LAT* omits P. S.

[442] *NYT*, Tuesday, December 27, 1927, 21:7. Variants: *LAT* and *KCT* give "leaving tomorrow" in first sentence/*BDG* gives "talking of the battle line" in second sentence/*LAT* omits fourth sentence.

[443] *NYT*, Wednesday, December 28, 1927, 25:7.

An earthquake struck near Rome on December 26 but caused no deaths, relatively few injuries, and only moderate property damage.

[444] *NYT*, Thursday, December 29, 1927, 25:7. Variant: *BDG* gives "Ginanini." in second sentence.

Amadeo Giannini, San Francisco civic leader and banker. In 1904 he formed the Bank of Italy, which survived the earthquake and fire of 1906 to become the nucleus of a system of 300 banks in California. Giannini consolidated his eastern holdings in 1919 and by February of 1928 had bought the Bank of America in New York City.

[445] *NYT*, Friday, December 30, 1927, 21:7. Variants: *LAT* gives "us. Viva airplanes." in sixth sentence and *KCT* ends sixth sentence "us." omitting last two words.

The airplane catapulting experiments were part of an effort by the Navy to adapt to conditions of aerial warfare.

[446] *NYT*, Saturday, December 31, 1927, 19:7. Variants: *KCT* gives "put in jail" in third sentence/*KCT* gives "murder trial." in fourth sentence, omitting remainder of DT, close, and signature/*LAT* omits fifth sentence/*BDG* did not print the DT.

A twelve-year-old Los Angeles girl was kidnapped on December 15 and subsequently murdered. Authorities arrested and charged William Hickman with the crime, but his plea of insanity promised a long trial with many headlines and pictures.

[447] *NYT*, Monday, January 2, 1928, 31:2.

Democrats in Congress urged a reduction in taxes of $300,000,000 while the administration continued to press for a cut of only $225,000,000 (see DT 416).

Senator Reed Smoot, chairman of the Senate Finance Committee, and Secretary Mellon agreed that Congress should postpone consideration of the tax reducing measure until after the first tax returns of the new year were received on March 15.

448 *NYT,* Tuesday, January 3, 1928, 27:7. Variants: *KCT* gives "optimism today" in first sentence/*BDG* gives "the one hundred and ten." and *KCT* gives "the hundred and ten." in fifth sentence/*LAT* did not print the DT.

449 *NYT,* Wednesday, January 4, 1928, 27:7. Variants: *NYT* gives "our State's lack" in fifth sentence, but *BDG, LAT,* and *KCT* have it as here/*BDG* gives "of discourtesy loses" in fifth sentence.

The highway measure was introduced into Congress in December by Representative Claude Hudspeth of Texas. It was referred to the House Committee on Roads, but no official action resulted.

450 *NYT,* Thursday, January 5, 1928, 31:7. Variants: *LAT* omits fifth sentence/*KCT* gives "the new canal." in fifth sentence.

451 *NYT,* Friday, January 6, 1928, 25:7. Variant: *KCT* ends tenth sentence "about."

The Coast Guard destroyer *Paulding* and the Navy submarine *S-4* collided off Provincetown, Massachusetts, on December 17. The *S-4* sank, killing forty persons. Six crew members survived in an undamaged compartment for at least six days, tapping Morse code signals while rescue workers futilely tried to raise the vessel. A naval court of inquiry divided responsibility between the two ships; a proposed investigation by Congress never materialized.

452 *NYT,* Saturday, January 7, 1928, 19:7. Variants: *KCT* gives "Jan. 5." in dateline/*LAT* and *KCT* give "Washington, where" in first sentence.

Rogers spoke at a Jackson Day banquet in Washington, D.C., an annual affair held in honor of the founder of the Democratic party, Andrew Jackson. Governor Smith excused himself from the affair because of state business, about which he had sent a 40,000-word message to the New York legislature on January 4.

453 *NYT,* Monday, January 9, 1928, 25:7. Variants: *KCT* gives "reading the papers." in first sentence/*KCT* begins second sentence "Kansas City is pretty"/ *NYT* gives "and messing the" and *KCT* gives "and mangling the" in second sentence.

Civic leaders from Boston, Miami, San Francisco, and Cleveland campaigned actively to host the Democratic National Convention in 1928.

454 *NYT,* Tuesday, January 10, 1928, 22:7. Variants: *KCT* gives "had an English breakfast for" in second sentence/*KCT* gives "kid Chicago" in third sentence/*LAT* omits fifth and sixth sentences/*LAT* gives "Yours," as close.

Mayor Thompson continued to be identified as anti-British because of his well-known campaign against various American history textbooks (see DT 219).

455 *NYT,* Wednesday, January 11, 1928, 31:7. Variants: *LAT* gives "I am here entirely in the interests of the Democrats." betweeen first and second sentences/*KCT* gives "inner is over and" in second sentence/*KCT* omits seventh and eighth sentences.

456 *NYT,* Thursday, January 12, 1928, 29:7. Variants: *LAT* gives "tie for" in eighth sentence/*LAT* gives "Well, we better" in ninth sentence/*NYT* gives "Doheny" and *BDG* gives "Donohey" in sixteenth sentence.

For Vice President Charles Dawes and Frank Lowden see DT 95; for Senator James Reed see DT 79; for Senator Thomas Heflin see DT 174.

Walter George, Democratic United States senator from Georgia from 1922 to 1957.

For Governor Vic Donahey of Ohio see DT 147.

[457] *NYT,* Friday, January 13, 1928, 25:7. Variants: *NYT* and *KCT* give "deal. You can" in sixth sentence/*KCT* begins seventh sentence "Save a"/*BDG* gives "the biggest hotel with" in seventh sentence.

Houston, with a population of more than 250,000 in 1928, promised to be unbearably humid in June, even at the convention headquarters, the Rice Hotel. A check for $200,000 from Houston businessman Jesse Jones helped to insure the selection of the city as the site of the convention.

[458] *NYT,* Saturday, January 14, 1928, 19:5-6. Variants: *BDG, LAT,* and *KCT* give "impression that" in first sentence/*BDG* gives "imagine him" in second sentence/*KCT* gives "that I was" in third sentence/*BDG* gives "and it did not give a" in fourth sentence.

Rogers hosted a nationwide radio program on January 4. After introductory remarks, he announced a switch to Washington for a special report from President Coolidge. Rogers then imitated Coolidge's voice and gave a humorous account of the state of the country.

[459] *NYT,* Monday, January 16, 1928, 23:7. Variant: *BDG* gives "flag draped" in first sentence.

Cuba hosted the Sixth International Conference of American States which convened in Havana on January 16. President Coolidge opened the conference at the special invitation of the president of Cuba.

[460] *NYT,* Tuesday, January 17, 1928, 31:7. Variants: *KCT* omits second and third sentences/*BDG* gives "3:30 or 3:29" in seventh sentence.

President Coolidge opened the Pan American Conference with a promise that the United States would send engineering advisers to Latin America to help build roads. He also complimented Cuba and Mexico on their progress and acknowledged the equality of the Western Hemisphere nations; he said nothing of intervention.

[461] *NYT,* Wednesday, January 18, 1928, 27:7. Variants: *BDG, LAT,* and *KCT* begin second sentence "He sneaked out"/*BDG* and *LAT* give "Hotel Bar." in seventh sentence.

For former Secretary of State Charles Evans Hughes see DT 31.

Morgan O'Brien, New York lawyer, jurist, and civic leader. O'Brien was active in the Democratic party and Irish-American organizations in New York.

Oscar W Underwood, Democratic United States senator from Alabama from 1915 to 1927.

Henry Fletcher, United States ambasador to Italy from 1924 to 1929.

[462] *NYT,* Thursday, January 19, 1928, 25:7. Variants: *LAT* ends third sentence "anthem." omitting fourth sentence/*BDG* gives "the Chinese, the 'Limy,' the Italian, the Zulu," and *NYT* and *KCT* give "all, even" in fourth sentence/*LAT* omits sixth and seventh sentences/*KCT* gives "anthems were" in sixth sentence/*BDG* gives "national anthems you" in eighth sentence.

Irving Berlin, American songwriter, noted as composer of popular tunes, including "Alexander's Ragtime Band" (1911).

463 *NYT,* Friday, January 20, 1928, 23:7 Variants: *BDG* gives "Jan. 10" in dateline/*LAT* gives "before he had a chance to become famous." in P. S./*KCT* did not print the DT.

A five-year-old girl from Mount Morris, Michigan, was kidnapped and murdered on January 12. Four days later a forty-seven-year-old carpenter confessed to the crime. Arraigned secretly on January 17, he pleaded guilty and was sentenced to life imprisonment. Newspaper editors generally approved the swift resolution of the case in view of threatened mob action.

464 *NYT,* Saturday, January 21, 1928, 19:7. Variants: *BDG, LAT,* and *KCT* give "be triumphal." in second sentence/*KCT* ends DT at "good time."

Senator Thomas Heflin of Alabama, an Irish-American (see DT 174), offered no real threat to the American visit of President William Cosgrave of Ireland although the trip aroused the ire of radical Irish Republicans in Ireland and the United States (see DT 35). Cosgrave visited New York City and Mayor Jimmie Walker (see DT 1), Washington, D. C., Philadelphia, and Chicago.

465 *NYT,* Monday, January 23, 1928, 23:7. Variants: *LAT* gives dateline "Jan. 21."/*KCT* gives "here, and" and *BDG* gives "sympathy goes back" in fourth sentence/*LAT* gives "6,000,000" in fifth sentence.

Florida slowly recovered from recent devastating hurricanes and tumbling property values (see DTs 43 and 158).

President Coolidge sailed from Cuba to Key West, Florida. There he boarded a special train which stopped in Jacksonville while enroute to Washington, D. C.

466 *NYT,* Tuesday, January 24, 1928, 31:7.

467 *NYT,* Wednesday, January 25, 1928, 25:7. Variant: *LAT* gives "the Episcopalians." in third sentence.

Roman Catholicism was attacked by Senator Heflin (see DT 174) in two speeches before the Senate in January. Because Governor Smith was a Catholic, Heflin declared, he could not and should not be nominated. The Senate later censured Heflin for threatening to tar and feather a fellow senator who had denounced his remarks.

468 *NYT,* Thursday, January 26, 1928, 25:7. Variants: *LAT* gives "murderer Hickman" in first sentence/*KCT* gives "alienists. American" in second and third sentences/*KCT* gives "enough you were too" in fourth sentence.

The Hickman murder case (see DT 446) ended in a conviction on February 9 following a two-week trial. After delays for appeal, William Hickman was executed on October 19.

469 *NYT,* Friday, January 27, 1928, 23:7. Variant: *KCT* gives "do it in" in second sentence.

Richard Loeb and Nathan Leopold, intellectual sons of wealthy Chicago parents; confessed in 1924 to the kidnapping and murder of Bobby Franks in a "thrill" slaying. Defended by Clarence Darrow (see DT 235), they pleaded guilty on grounds of mental illness and requested clemency. They were sentenced to life imprisonment plus ninety-nine years.

[470] *NYT,* Saturday, January 28, 1928, 17:7. Variants: *LAT* gives "of Nicaragua. Now" and *KCT* gives "Nicaraguan question. Now," in first sentence/ *BDG, LAT,* and *KCT* give "want out." in fifth sentence.

Hughes (see DT 31) spoke at a dinner for the American Chamber of Commerce of Cuba on January 21. He described the Latin American policy of the United States as a structure with four pillars: stability, respect for territorial integrity, mutual good will, and cooperation.

[471] *NYT,* Monday, January 30, 1928, 23:7. Variants: *LAT* gives origin "BEVERLY HILLS"/*NYT* gives "revolutions, which, when" in first sentence/ *KCT* omits seventh sentence/*LAT* ends seventh sentence "in revolutions."

Mexico proposed at the Pan American Conference that nations should pledge not to permit their residents to participate in revolutionary activities in other countries. After vigorous debate only Nicaragua and El Salvador joined Mexico in voting to consider the proposal.

[472] *NYT,* Tuesday, January 31, 1928, 27:7.

Marion S. Taylor, a Baptist preacher's son who parlayed his years as a church organist, school superintendent, and Chautauqua lecturer into a radio career during the 1930s as "The Voice of Experience."

For Judge Benjamin Lindsey see DT 303.

[473] *NYT,* Wednesday, February 1, 1928, 29:7. Variant: *NYT* omits first sentence, but *BDG, LAT,* and *KCT* have it as here.

President Coolidge addressed a semiannual meeting of chief government employees. He reported that budgetary savings had held federal expenditures near the $3,000,000,000 annual level.

Former heavyweight champion Jack Dempsey (see DT 46) claimed that pains in his left eye would prevent him from meeting Gene Tunney (see DT 62) in a proposed return bout in June.

The East Coast reporteed gales, snow, and intense cold, including unseasonable eighteen and twenty-degree readings in Miami, Florida.

[474] *NYT,* Thursday, February 2, 1928, 25:7. Variant: *LAT* gives "would only have" in second sentence.

[475] *NYT,* Friday, February 3, 1928, 25:4-5.

An Oklahoma congressman addressed the House of Representatives on January 9 and humorously urged the nomination of Rogers as president of the United States. On January 21 the Democratic convention of Rogers County, Oklahoma endorsed Will's "candidacy." On February 1 Charles Haskell, a former governor of Oklahoma, issued a serious declaration of support, prompting this reply from Rogers.

[476] *NYT,* Saturday, February 4, 1928, 17:7. Variants: *KCT* omits first and second sentences/*NYT* gives "was one testimony" in fourth sentence, but *BDG, LAT,* and *KCT* have it as here/*KCT* ends fourth sentence "yesterday in the Hickman case."

Two "alienists," or mental disease specialists, testified for the defense in the Hickman trial (see DTs 446 and 468). They concluded that Hickman suffered from "cirrus [serous?] miningitis," or inflammation of the brain covering and from a form of dementia praecox, as well as possessing "two gold teeth and sore tonsils."

[477] *NYT,* Monday, February 6, 1928, 21:7. Variants: *LAT* gives origin "BEVERLY HILLS"/*KCT* omits sixth and seventh sentences.

President Coolidge spoke at the dedication of the National Press Club Building on February 4. The press, he held, should be patriotic as well as cooperative and supportive of the national administration, yet it must be just and truthful.

[478] *LAT,* Tuesday, February 7, 1928, I:1:2; heading from *KCT,* 13:3. Variants: *LAT* and *KCT* end DT "remedied." and omit next nine words/*NYT* did not print the DT.

[479] *NYT,* Wednesday, February 8, 1928, 27:7. Variants: *BDG* and *LAT* give "This one is" and *KCT* gives "is one too" in third sentence/*KCT* gives "get on with" in fourth sentence.

The United States and France signed an arbitration treaty in Washington, D. C., on February 6 as part of the complicated negotiations which led to the signing of the Kellogg-Briand antiwar treaty in August of 1928.

[480] *NYT,* Thursday, February 9, 1928, 27:7. Variants: *KCT* gives "month and" in second sentence/*BDG* and *LAT* begin fifth sentence "Yours for"/*KCT* omits fifth sentence.

Lindbergh landed in Havana on the afternoon of February 8 after an 800-mile flight from Haiti. The large airport crowd included many delegates from the Pan American Conference. Lindbergh was driven from the airport to downtown Havana, where he was honored with a ceremonial welcome from the president of Cuba.

[481] *LAT,* Friday, February 10, 1928, I:1:2; heading from *KCT,* 13:3. Variants: *LAT* gives "John D. is" in third and fourth sentences, but *BDG* and *KCT* have it as here/*NYT* did not print the DT.

John D. Rockefeller, Jr., youngest son of the Standard Oil Company magnate; specialized in managing the family philanthropies. As chairman of the board of the Rockefeller Foundation, Rockefeller pressured Robert Stewart, Standard Oil board chairman, to testify before a Senate committee investigating the oil land scandals of the Harding administration. The committee also desired personal testimony from Rockefeller and issued him a subpoena which he stiffly accepted.

[482] *NYT,* Saturday, February 11, 1928, 19:7. Variants: *BDG* gives "sunstroked" in fourth sentence/*KCT* ends fourth sentence "before the conventions."

Senator Borah sent questionnaires in late January to prospective presidential candidates of both parties asking their opinions about prohibition. On February 9 Borah asked Secretary of Commerce Hoover for his sentiments; Hoover weighed the matter for two weeks (see DT 493).

[483] *NYT,* Monday, February 13, 1928, 21:7. Variants: *KCT* gives "President. Why here the" in first sentence/*KCT* ends second sentence "than the chamber of commerce."/*BDG* and *LAT* give "The Senate" in third sentence.

The Senate adopted a resolution on February 10 which declared that any departure from the two-term limit for presidents would be "unwise, unpatriotic and fraught with peril to our free institutions." Progressive and farm-bloc Republicans joined most Democrats in passing the resolution.

[484] *NYT,* Tuesday, February 14, 1928, 25:7. Variant: *KCT* ends second sentence "his gifts."

Young Rockefeller (see DT 481) appeared before the Senate Oil Inquiry Committee on February 11. He testified that since 1925, when the first hints of scandal became known, he had urged Stewart, head of Standard Oil (see DT 481), to reveal what he knew of the facts. He was disappointed at Stewart's hesitancy to do so.

485 *NYT,* Wednesday, February 15, 1928, 25:7. Variants: *BDG* gives "candidate spend too much" in third sentence/*KCT* omits third and fourth sentences.

Argentina criticized the United States for its refusal to import Argentine beef. The Argentine delegation to the Pan American Conference sought to lower trade barriers between member nations. The United States defended the right of each nation to regulate its domestic questions, including tariffs. The position of the United States prevailed.

In Nicaragua followers of the rebel general Augusto Sandino increased their revolutionary activities. The American carrier *Saratoga* responded to the new crisis, and 1,000 more marines were ordered to the republic.

486 *NYT,* Thursday, February 16, 1928, 25:7. Variants: *KCT* gives "It didn't" in third sentence/*KCT* gives "give in any" in fourth sentence/*LAT* and *KCT* end fifth sentence "the next conference."

No DT is available for Friday, February 17, 1928.

487 *LAT,* Saturday, February 18, 1928, I:1:3; heading from *KCT,* 17:6. Variants: *BDG* gives "nominations the next day. Mr. Adolph" in third and fourth sentences/*BDG* gives "us and took" in fourth and fifth sentences/*LAT* gives "Jessie" in sixth sentence/*LAT* gives "Your underpaid," at close/*NYT* did not print the DT.

George Lorimer, editor-in-chief of the *Saturday Evening Post* from 1899 to 1936. His editorials became increasingly pro-Republican in the 1920s. Rogers wrote approximately thirty articles for the *Post* between 1926 and 1935.

Adolph S. Ochs, publisher of the *New York Times* from 1896 until his death in 1935. Ochs, a Democrat, was an ardent admirer of Rogers' daily telegrams.

Jesse H. Jones, Houston civic leader, financier, and political figure; owner of the *Houston Chronicle,* chairman of the finance committee of the Democratic National Committee, and responsible for the selection of Houston as the site of the Democratic National Convention of 1928.

488 *NYT,* Monday, February 20, 1928, 23:7. Variants: *LAT* gives "The old Democrats are getting smarter." and *KCT* gives "The Democrats" in fourth sentence/*KCT* ends fifth sentence "campaign contributions."

The bill of Senator Walsh (see DT 209) called for a Senate investigation into monopolistic practices of private power companies. The Senate approved the inquiry on February 15 but shifted the responsibility to the Federal Trade Commission, of known conservative outlook. Twenty Democrats and eleven progressive Republicans voted for a Senate inquiry.

489 *NYT,* Tuesday, February 21, 1928, 27:7. Variants: *LAT* and *KCT* give "garage. With . . . course, good" in third and fourth sentences.

George W. Norris, United States senator from Nebraska from 1913 to 1943. Norris gained prominence as an unbending progressive Republican of immense integrity; he often opposed the administration on agricultural issues and other matters.

490 *NYT,* Wednesday, February 22, 1928, 23:7. Variants: *BDG, LAT,* and *KCT* begin first sentence "I am up here", but *NYT* has it as here.

William Bulow, Democratic governor of South Dakota from 1927 to 1931. Bulow's election as governor in 1926 broke a quarter-century of Republican rule in South Dakota. His rustic wit had impressed Rogers and others who heard him at the Jackson Day dinner in early January (see DT 452).

491 *NYT,* Thursday, February 23, 1928, 23:7. Variants: *KCT* ends first sentence "the Californians."/*KCT* gives "all go like" in third sentence/*KCT* gives "election law requires" in fifth sentence.

Persons born in Iowa comprised the third largest group of migrants in California, according to the United States Census of 1930.

Counties in Iowa traditionally retained responsibility for road construction. A major step was taken toward state responsibility when the state legislature referred a bond issue for $100,000,000 to the voters. Their approval in November of 1928 put Iowa on a par with other states.

492 *NYT*, Friday, February 24, 1928, 23:7.

Although Senator Reed's candidacy generated considerable support in Missouri, it produced few delegates in the rest of the country.

493 *NYT,* Saturday, February 25, 1928, 19:7. Variant: *KCT* gives "everybody gives him" in first sentence.

Hoover responded on February 23 to Senator Borah's inquiry about Prohibition (see DT 482). He stated his opposition to its repeal, citing Prohibition as a "great and economic experiment, noble in motive. . . . It must be worked out constructively."

Five bombs had exploded in Chicago in recent weeks, usually at the homes of lesser public officials. Three hundred policemen were assigned to guard threatened homes, including Mayor Thompson's. The mayor had gone to Washington to urge a vigorous flood control program and to attend a White House luncheon.

494 *NYT,* Monday, February 27, 1928, 21:7. Variant: *LAT* gives "Brooks is not" in P. S.

Harry Brooks, young test pilot for the Stout-Ford Airplane Company. Brooks attempted a distance flight from Detroit to Miami, but fuel line problems forced him to land 200 miles short of his goal. After repairs presumably had been made, he took off for Miami but crashed into the sea moments later and perished.

495 *NYT,* Tuesday, February 28, 1928, 27:7.

Joseph "Joe" Robinson, Democratic United States senator from Arkansas from 1913 until his death in 1937; unsuccessful Democratic nominee for vice president in 1928.

496 *NYT,* Wednesday, February 29, 1928, 27:7. Variants: *KCT* omits second sentence/*KCT* gives P. S. as a part of DT.

Coal mining operations and conditions in the two-year-old coal strike in Pennsylvania had been under investigation by a Senate subcommittee since February 24. The United Mine Workers of America insisted that the industry abide by the price and wage schedule negotiated in 1924. Mine owners said the proposed wages were too high and hired strikebreakers, which resulted in the expulsion of union miners from company towns, squalid living conditions, and violence.

The residents of Camden, Arkansas, donated land in 1927 for a forest products manufacturing plant. The factory issued a payroll of $15,000 a week.

For Betty Rogers see DT 178.

[497] *NYT,* Thursday, March 1, 1928, 27:7.

[498] *NYT,* Friday, March 2, 1928, 27:7. Variant: *KCT* gives "get, nobody" in eighth sentence.

Muscle Shoals, Alabama, was the site of a dam, hydroelectric power plant, and two nitrate manufacturing plants, constructed by the federal government during World War I. During the 1920s the government unsuccessfully attempted to sell the Tennessee River facilities to private interests.

The Madden Bill, introduced into Congress by Representative Martin Madden of Illinois, proposed that the Muscle Shoals nitrate plants be sold to the American Cyanamid Company. An Alabama power company and Henry Ford also had bid for the facilities.

For "Walsh's resolution," a bill to investigate power companies, see DTs 209 and 488.

For Senator Tom Heflin see DT 174; for Senator Walter George see DT 456.

[499] *NYT,* Saturday, March 3, 1928, 19:7. Variant: *LAT* gives "Will says" to begin third sentence.

Will Hays, chairman of the Republican National Committee from 1918 to 1921 (see DT 173), informed the Senate Oil Inquiry Committee on March 1 that oilman Harry Sinclair had given him $260,000 in bonds while he was party chairman, $75,000 of which was a personal contribution and the rest a "loan." Hays returned $100,000 of the bonds to Sinclair and later claimed he knew nothing of the bonds being part of the Teapot Dome payoff. Democratic party leaders denied charges that some Democrats also had received money from Sinclair.

[500] *NYT,* Monday, March 5, 1928, 25:7. Variants: *KCT* gives "those Negro pupils . . . white persons that" in eighth sentence/*KCT* gives "there isn't enough" in tenth sentence.

Auburn University was donated to the state of Alabama in 1872 as a land grant institution and renamed Alabama Polytechnic Institute. In 1960 it again took the name Auburn.

Booker T. Washington, organizer and director of Tuskegee Institute, a state supported black school which emphasized industrial education. Washington served as principal of the institution from its inception in 1884 until his death in 1915.

For Senator Thomas Heflin see DTs 174 and 498.

[501] *NYT,* Tuesday, March 6, 1928, 29:7. Variants: *LAT* gives "Cotea" in first sentence/*KCT* gives "to Paris ahead . . . but neglected it" in fifth sentence/*KCT* gives "to Europe." and *BDG* gives "when the Wright plane" in eighth sentence.

Major Walter Weaver and Second Lieutenants Narcisse Cote and Roderick Ott of the United States Army Air Service provided air transportation for Rogers from Montgomery to Albany.

Orville Wright, who with his late brother Wilbur made the first successful flight in an airplane, announced on February 3 that he had decided to send the famous first plane to a British museum because the Smithsonian Institution claimed that an aircraft invented by their former executive officer, Samuel Langley, had preceded the Wright's plane. On March 3 a Smithsonian official failed to placate Wright. In 1948, after a reevaluation by the Smithsonian and Wright's acceptance, the Wright airplane was transferred to the American institution.

502 *NYT,* Wednesday, March 7, 1928, 27:7. Variant: *KCT* gives origin "CHARLESTON."

William Green, Republican United States representative from Iowa from 1911 to 1928. While a member of Congress, Green opposed the Coolidge administration's attempts to repeal inheritance taxes. On February 20, 1928, he was appointed judge of the Court of Claims of the United States, serving until 1942.

503 *NYT,* Thursday, March 8, 1928, 27:7. Variants: *BDG* gives "to. Today it's" in third and fourth sentences/*LAT* gives "a success" in fifth sentence/*KCT* gives "roads to 'em." in seventh sentence.

President Jackson's Indian removal policy of the 1830s caused the relocation of most members of the Cherokee tribe, as well as other Indian groups, from their traditional homeland in the southeastern part of the United States to present-day Oklahoma. A number of Indians, including many Cherokee, avoided removal. Rogers' eastern Cherokee brothers—Rogers was 9/32 Cherokee—numbered more than 3,000 in 1930. They lived in primitive agricultural settlements.

John D. Rockefeller, Sr., announced on March 6 a gift of $5,000,000 to the Great Smoky Mountains National Park as a tribute to the memory of his late wife, Laura Spelman Rockefeller. The donation was to pay one half of the amount necessary to purchase land for the project.

504 *NYT,* Friday, March 9, 1928, 27:7. Variants: *LAT* gives "supervise the election" in first sentence/*LAT* gives "are few votes" in second sentence/*KCT* did not print the DT.

Senator Heflin (see DT 174) offered a resolution in the Senate in January that the United States marines be withdrawn from Nicaragua. On March 7, after weeks of hearings, the Senate Foreign Relations Committee rejected the resolution and voted to retain the marines to insure a fair election.

Augusto Sandino, Nicaraguan guerrilla leader who supported a liberal insurrection in 1926 and seized American property. Sandino waged guerrilla warfare against American marines from 1927 to 1932, claiming that his campaign was motivated solely by his desire to end the intervention. Sandino agreed to amnesty terms in 1933 when the marines were withdrawn; he was assassinated in 1934.

505 *NYT,* Saturday, March 10, 1928, 19:7. Variant: *KCT* gives " 'certain small car' out" in first sentence.

506 *NYT,* Monday, March 12, 1928, 23:7. Variant: *BDG* (PM) ends fifth sentence " 'till a year from the next December.' "

A constitutional amendment to eliminate "lame duck" sessions of Congress by changing the date for beginning congressional terms had passed the Senate earlier. On March 9 the proposal passed the House but did not receive the two-thirds majority necessary to send an amendment to the states. Resubmitted in 1932, the proposal was ratified as the Twentieth Amendment less than a year later.

507 *NYT,* Tuesday, March 13, 1928, 31:7. Variant: *KCT* gives "make Republicans" in second sentence.

Senator Borah considered it humiliating and indecent that Teapot Dome funds were contributed to the Republican party (see DT 499). He publicly suggested that each Republican contribute at least one dollar to remove the stigma of scandal from the party. Contributors had sent only $7,000 by early April.

508 *NYT,* Wednesday, March 14, 1928, 27:7. Variants: *BDG* gives "hats and thinks it's" and *LAT* gives "hats and thinks its" and *KCT* gives "hats, and think, it's" in fourth and fifth sentences.

George Sisler, star first baseman for three major league clubs from 1915 to 1930, including the Washington Senators in 1928. Named to the Baseball Hall of Fame in 1939, Sisler hit .340 in 2,055 games during his career and twice led the American League in hitting.

Rogers "Rajah" Hornsby, infielder and exceptional righthanded hitter for several major league clubs from 1915 to 1932, including one season with the Boston Braves in 1928. A member of the Baseball Hall of Fame, Hornsby won the National League batting title seven times and hit more than .400 three times.

509 *NYT,* Thursday, March 15, 1928, 27:7. Variant: *KCT* gives "knows which section" in second sentence.

In California the St. Francis Dam in the St. Fransquito Canyon, located within fifty miles of downtown Los Angeles, collapsed without warning during the night of March 12-13. More than 450 persons died, and $12,000,000 worth of property was destroyed.

Henry "Harry" Carey II, screen actor and leading man of silent movies; considered the epitome of the western hero. His ranch home was untouched by the St. Francis flood, but Carey's Trading Post, a tourist landmark, was swept away.

510 *NYT,* Friday, March 16, 1928, 25:7. Variant: *LAT* gives "exposing Republican" in first sentence.

511 *NYT,* Saturday, March 17, 1928, 17:7. Variants: *KCT* ends fourth sentence "customary dime."/*KCT* omits fifth and sixth sentences/*BDG* gives "only one I" in ninth sentence.

512 *NYT,* Monday, March 19, 1928, 23:7.

Mayor Walker of New York concentrated on the ceremonial role of his position which permitted prolonged absences from city hall.

Rogers appeared at a benefit for the Salvation Army Building Fund. The event, sponsored by the Kiwanis Club and the American Legion, was oversubscribed by $25,000.

The Prince of Wales (see DT 165) was an avid polo player, although he suffered numerous, widely-publicized spills while riding.

513 *NYT,* Tuesday, March 20, 1928, 29:7.

Senator Capper (see DT 116) lashed out in the Senate at Republican leadership. He assailed the leaders for allowing the party to be tainted by the corruption of the Teapot Dome scandal.

514 *NYT,* Wednesday, March 21, 1928, 29:7. Variant: *KCT* omits second sentence.

Lindbergh received the Woodrow Wilson Medal and Peace Prize on March 19 at a dinner of the Woodrow Wilson Foundation in New York City. The award included a twelve-inch bronze medal, a special citation, and $25,000.

Lindbergh flew eighty-eight sightseeing flights over Washington, D. C., in a period of several days, giving rides to more than 200 members of Congress, 600 of their relatives, and others. While in Washington Lindbergh urged Congress to enact higher pay for Army Air Corps fliers.

515 *NYT,* Thursday, March 22, 1928, 27:7. Variants: *LAT* gives "Caught a" in first sentence/*BDG* begins third sentence "We certainly."

Lloyd O. Yost, independent pilot from Pinehurst, North Carolina. An air-mail route from New York to Atlanta opened on April 1.

Josephus Daniels had served as editor of the *Raleigh News and Observer* for thirty-four years.

Governor Smith had been accused by Senator Arthur Robinson of Indiana of an alleged connection with the oil scandals because Smith had appointed oilman Harry Sinclair (see DT 499) to the New York State Racing Commission in 1920. The governor denied receiving any funds from Sinclair and denounced Robinson's allegations and conduct.

516 *NYT,* Friday, March 23, 1928, 23:7. Variants: *LAT* gives "do, all . . . us will have to go to work" and *KCT* gives "us have to go" in eighth sentence.

The Maryland Racing Commission banned Sinclair's horses from race tracks in the state because of adverse criticism from pending court decisions and the Senate investigation of Sinclair (see DT 400). The ban was lifted on April 23, following Sinclair's acquittal in the Teapot Dome conspiracy case.

For Governor Albert Ritchie see DT 95.

517 *NYT,* Saturday, March 24, 1928, 19:7. Variants: *BDG* gives "best offers from" in second sentence/*KCT* omits fifth sentence.

C. Bascom Slemp, former congressman from Virginia and secretary to President Coolidge from 1923 to 1925. Slemp, a personal manager of Coolidge's presidential campaign in 1924, recently had urged a draft of the president in 1928. On March 21 he announced his support for Secretary Hoover.

Frank Willis, Republican United States senator from Ohio from 1921 until his death in 1928.

Representatives Edith Rogers of Massachusetts and Katherine Langley of Kentucky accompanied Lindbergh during his first congressional sightseeing flight over Washington (see DT 514).

The Nicaraguan congress rejected a bill on March 14 which would have allowed United States supervision of the forthcoming presidential election. On March 22 President Díaz signed a decree permitting American supervision. He claimed that his country did not have enough experience to conduct such an election unassisted.

518 *NYT,* Monday, March 26, 1928, 23:7. Variants: *BDG* and *KCT* give "get disinfectant to" in fourth sentence.

For Senator Borah's campaign to improve the image of the Republican party , see DT 507.

For Alice Longworth, Washington hostess and political commentator, see DT 202.

519 *NYT,* Tuesday, March 27, 1928, 29:7. Variants: *BDG* begins third sentence "Congress spent"/*BDG* gives "politics; the House spent" and *KCT* gives "The house spent" in third and fourth sentences/*KCT* omits seventh and eighth sentences.

Ohio Congressman Charles Brand, angry with Hoover for entering the Ohio primary against favorite son candidate Senator Frank Willis, labeled Hoover a Democrat, a corrupt politician, and constitutionally ineligible to run for president. Representative Theodore Burton answered the charges with two letters in which Brand had urged the appointment of Hoover as secretary of agriculture.

520 *NYT,* Wednesday, March 28, 1928, 29:7. Variant: *LAT* gives "Mussolini that" in sixth sentence.

While Ford paid $8.00 per eight-hour day at his Kentucky and West Virginia mines, other independent coal companies paid $2.85 per day and union miners received $7.50. The Senate committee investigating the coal mining industry desired to subpoena Ford, but he was in Europe and was unable to testify.

Secretary Mellon's dominance of the Republican party in his native state of Pennslyvania was unchallenged; he also influenced state Democrats.

[521] *NYT,* Thursday, March 29, 1928, 29:7. Variant: *KCT* gives "Baptist I went" in second sentence.

A Cleveland grand jury subpoenaed Rogers to inspect the fifty-three-year-old Cuyahoga County jail. Rogers and several clergymen, one of several groups whose counsel was sought, toured the jail which Rogers described as "the worst in the country." A decade later the county boasted a modern, new facility.

[522] *NYT,* Friday, March 30, 1928, 27:7. Variants: *BDG* gives "in tires." and *KCT* gives "tires." in third sentence/*BDG* and *KCT* end fourth sentence "these blimps." and omit fifth and sixth sentences/*LAT* gives "blimps that reminded me of my operation." in fourth, fifth, and sixth sentences.

Charles Goodyear, American inventor and pioneer of the rubber industry, discovered the process of vulcanization in 1839. The Goodyear Tire and Rubber Company, founded in 1898 and named in honor of the inventor, first developed its famous airships, or blimps, in the early 1900s.

For Judge Benjamin Lindsey see DT 303.

[523] *NYT,* Saturday, March 31, 1928, 21:7. Variants: *BDG* and *LAT* give "why, pick out" and *KCT* gives "nothing . . . with. One like Dwight Morrow." in first sentence/*KCT* gives fourth sentence "He is Wall Street's biggest ad."/ *KCT* omits sixth sentence/*KCT* ends seventh sentence "Mexico myself."/*KCT* omits P. S.

[524] *NYT,* Monday, April 2, 1928, 23:7. Variants: *KCT* gives "Democratic opponent ran" and *LAT* gives "opponents run on" in seventh sentence/*BDG* gives "Nigger, put" and *LAT* gives "Rastus, put" in ninth sentence.

Flemon "Flem" Sampson, Republican governor of Kentucky from 1929 to 1931. For an account of Sampson's upset election for governor, see DT 406. Rogers' commission as a Kentucky Colonel was purely honorary.

[525] *NYT,* Tuesday, April 3, 1928, 31:7. Variants: *BDG* gives "and it may be on" in first sentence/*NYT* gives "$150,000" in first sentence, but *BDG, LAT,* and *KCT* have it as here/*LAT* ends fifth sentence "old stands."

[526] *NYT,* Wednesday, April 4, 1928, 31:7. Variant: *LAT* gives "but what went in them, so" in ninth sentence.

Battle Creek, Michigan, "the health city," with a population of 43,573 in 1930, included a world-renowned sanitarium and several breakfast cereal factories.

[527] *NYT,* Thursday, April 5, 1928, 29:7. Variants: *BDG, LAT,* and *KCT* begin second sentence "Indianans,"/*LAT* gives "redeem the State" in fifth sentence/*LAT* and *KCT* give "that can beat" in sixth sentence.

For humorists George Ade and Kin Hubbard, the latter known for his creation of rustic Abe Martin, see DT 95.

Indiana recently had been scandalized by political corruption and by Ku Klux Klan activities which had reached the highest circles of state government.

[528] *NYT*, Friday, April 6, 1928, 25:7. Variants: *BDG* ends third sentence "McCormack."/*KCT* gives "if they elect" in fourth sentence/*LAT* gives "women's angle" in fifth sentence.

For Alice Longworth see DT 202.

Ruth Hanna McCormick, Republican United States representative from Illinois from 1929 to 1931. Mrs. McCormick was the daughter of Ohio industrialist and political figure Mark Hanna and the widow of publisher and congressman Joseph Medill McCormick.

[529] *BDG* (AM), Saturday, April 7, 1928, 1:7; heading from *KCT*, 15:2. Variants: *KCT* omits first sentence/*KCT* gives "Timbucktoo" in third and fifth sentences/*NYT* did not print the DT.

For columnist Arthur Brisbane see DT 204.

Four French aviators flew a strenuous circuit of 6,250 miles between Paris and North Africa from April 3 to 7, stopping only briefly for refueling and rest. The fliers tested radio navigation techniques during their five-day flight.

[530] *NYT*, Monday, April 9, 1928, 23:7. Variants: *KCT* omits fourth sentence/*BDG* ends title "need aide."/*KCT* ends title "Kentucky." and gives P. S. "Should . . . aid."

[531] *NYT*, Tuesday, April 10, 1928, 31:7. Variants: *KCT* gives "here in an airplane." in first sentence/*BDG* gives "Kiwanis or Rotary clubs could" and *LAT* gives "Kiwanis could" in seventh sentence.

Rogers' proposal to paint town names on roofs had been recommended the preceding summer by Secretary Hoover and since had been urged by the Department of Commerce, the American Legion, and others.

[532] *NYT*, Wednesday, April 11, 1928, 31:7. Variants: *LAT* gives "they have here is" and *KCT* gives "they have there is" in second sentence/*BDG* gives close "Yours truly,"/*KCT* omits P. S./*LAT* gives second signature "BILL ROGERS." after P. S.

For Speaker of the House Nicholas Longworth see DT 51.

Ashland College of Kentucky won the National Interscholastic Tournament, a postseason collegiate basketball contest held annually in New York City.

[533] *NYT*, Thursday, April 12, 1928, 29:7. Variants: *LAT* gives "took the tariff" in first sentence/*BDG* and *KCT* give "Ireland—and he" in third and fourth sentences/*KCT* gives "billion, but" in fourth sentence/*KCT* gives "idea for his" in fifth sentence/*LAT* gives signature "WILL ROGERS."

Henry Ford had refused to enter the Irish Free State, the homeland of his ancestors, during his European tour, because it had imposed import duties on his automobiles and other products. Free State officials and Ford negotiated for several weeks, but Ford returned to the United States, having never entered free Ireland.

[534] *NYT*, Friday, April 13, 1928, 27:7. Variants: *BDG* and *LAT* give "flyers yet, but" in first sentence.

Two Germans, Captain Hermann Koehl and Baron Gunther von Huenefeld, and an Irishman, Commandant James Fitzmaurice, took off on April 11 from near Dublin, Ireland, in a German Junkers monoplane, bound for New York.

For aviator Casey Jones see DT 241.

[535] *KCT*, Saturday, April 14, 1928, 15:2. Variants: *BDG* ends first sentence "Irish."/*BDG* gives second sentence "It would have been a shame . . . that were lost."/*BDG* omits fifth sentence/*BDG* gives "Yours," for close/*NYT* and *LAT* did not print the DT.

Koehl, von Huenefeld, and Fitzmaurice encountered headwinds which forced them to land on April 13 on Greenely Island, a lighthouse station off the coast of Labrador. They had completed the first transatlantic flight from east to west.

Maxwell Balfour, first lieutenant in the United States Army Air Service.

[536] *NYT*, Monday, April 16, 1928, 25:7. Variants: *KCT* gives "they get Congress" in third sentence/*KCT* omits sixth and seventh sentences.

Governor Smith visited Asheville, North Carolina, for two weeks during April. He received warm welcomes during side stops and political forays in the area.

Andrew "Andy" Cohen, outfielder for the New York Giants from 1926 to 1929. Cohen signed with the Giants for $25,000 in 1926 at the age of twenty-three. Some experts considered him a potential rival of Babe Ruth, but the youngster hit poorly and after three years dropped to the minor leagues. But for much of 1928 his dazzling fielding and occasional hits made him a real drawing card.

[537] *NYT*, Tuesday, April 17, 1928, 31:7. Variant: *BDG* gives "cause, because you" in third and fourth sentences.

Vice President Dawes had attempted to reform Senate rules regarding filibusters.

[538] *BDG* (AM), Wednesday, April 18, 1928, 28:5; heading from *KCT*, 13:4. Variants: *KCT* gives fifth sentence "I used to write in the newspapers too."/*KCT* omits sixth, seventh, and eighth sentences/*LAT* gives "out of with Will" in seventh sentence/*LAT* omits "Yours," after ninth sentence/*KCT* gives "Isn't that nice?" after contribution by "Lardner "/*NYT* did not print the DT.

Ring Lardner (see DT 242) and George M. Cohan (see DT 296) collaborated in writing and producing *Elmer the Great*, a musical comedy about baseball, which opened on Broadway on September 24, 1928, and closed after only forty performances.

[539] *NYT*, Thursday, April 19, 1928, 27:7. Variants: *LAT* gives "Stone's, (the actor's)" in first sentence/*KCT* ends first sentence "new plane."

Fred Stone, vaudeville and musical comedy actor; close personal friend of Rogers. When Stone was disabled in an airplane accident in August of 1928 (see DT 632), Rogers cancelled his own engagements for several months and took over his friend's role in the play *Three Cheers*.

John "Johnny" Campion, aviator from St. Louis who served as private pilot and flying instructor for Stone.

Andrew "Andy" Payne, distance runner. Twenty-two-year-old Payne, a shy Oklahoma farmer, gained national prominence in winning the "bunion derby" of 1928, a transcontinental footrace sponsored by sports promoter C. C. Pyle (see DT 5). Payne later served for many years as clerk of the Oklahoma Supreme Court.

[540] *NYT*, Friday, April 20, 1928, 25:7. Variants: *LAT* gives "pulling a Jim" and *KCT* gives "pulling for Jim" in fourth sentence/*BDG* gives 'D. A. R." in seventh and eighth sentences.

Harry Sinclair's race horses (see DT 516) were readmitted to race tracks in Maryland after the oil man's acquittal.

Guy D. Goff, Republican United States senator from West Virginia from 1925 to 1931. Goff indeed shared presidential ambitions with Senator Watson (see DT 95).

The Daughters of the American Revolution had blacklisted certain speakers which the organization considered radical and pacifistic. Publisher William Allen White of Emporia, Kansas, led the list (see DT 116). Randolph was the middle name of publisher William Randolph Hearst (see DT 379).

President Coolidge addressed the national convention of the DAR in Washington, D. C., on April 18. He sternly told the group that "Government must be kept out of Business." Governor Ritchie (see DT 95) had spoken similarly of states' rights and had condemned Prohibition.

541 *NYT,* Saturday, April 21, 1928, 19:7. Variants: *LAT* gives "there as" in third sentence/*LAT* gives "up to show" in fourth sentence.

Clement "Clem" Shaver, chairman of the Democratic National Committee from 1924 to 1928.

542 *NYT,* Monday, April 23, 1928, 25:7. Variants: *BDG* gives "McCormack" in first sentence/*LAT* omits fifth and sixth sentences/*LAT* gives "Well, Sinclair, come clear." in seventh sentence.

For Ruth Hanna McCormick see DT 528.

Marcus "Mark" Hanna, railroad executive and politician; Republican United States senator from Ohio from 1897 to 1904. Hanna supported William McKinley for president in 1896 and became McKinley's closest adviser.

Ruth Bryan Owen, lecturer and educator; Democratic United States representative from Florida from 1929 to 1933.

William Jennings Bryan, political leader and orator. Bryan was the Democratic candidate for president in 1896, 1900, and 1908 and served as United States secretary of state from 1913 to 1915.

Sinclair was acquited on April 21 of the charge that he had conspired to defraud the government (see DT 400).

543 *NYT,* Tuesday, April 24, 1928, 27:7. Variants: *BDG* begins first sentence "Chicago is quiet" and *LAT* gives "is quiet" in first sentence/*BDG* and *LAT* give "murder headlined today" and *KCT* gives "murder today." in first sentence/*KCT* omits second and third sentences.

544 *NYT,* Wednesday, April 25, 1928, 29:7. Variant: *KCT* gives "before a Yale class" in first sentence.

Gene Tunney, world champion heavyweight boxer, lectured to an English literature class at Yale University on the occasion of the birthday of William Shakespeare. He explained to his audience that after some initial difficulty he eventually read and understood all the writings of Shakespeare.

545 *NYT,* Thursday, April 26, 1928, 29:7. Variants: *NYT* gives "a hen and" in third sentence and gives "eat 'em. If you" in sixth sentence, but *BDG, LAT,* and *KCT* have it as here.

The seventeen-story building housed the Chicago Mercantile Exchange, whose predecessor had been the Butter and Egg Board. Organized in 1919, the Exchange provided a nationwide open market with futures trading and hedging.

[546] *NYT,* Friday, April 27, 1928, 27:7. Variant: *LAT* omits P. S.

Secretary Hoover had captured enough delegates by April 25 to allow his friends to claim the Republican nomination for him.

[547] *NYT,* Saturday, April 28, 1928, 21:7. Variants: *LAT* gives "in a Ryan" and *KCT* gives "new monoplane" in first sentence/*BDG* gives "home of the Cherry" in seventh sentence/*KCT* gives "Tomorrow to Topeka," in tenth sentence.

J. N. "Ding" Darling, political cartoonist who illustrated for several newspapers but primarily for the *Des Moines Register* from 1906 to 1949; won Pulitzer prizes in 1924 and 1943.

The Cherry Sisters—Ella, Jessie, Addie, Lizzie, and Effie—made a small fortune from one of the worst vaudeville acts in the country. One critic described their act as "so very bad that it was good," and theater managers paid them as high as $1,000 a week. By 1928 only Addie and Effie continued to perform.

For Senator Charles Curtis see DT 116.

[548] *NYT,* Monday, April 30, 1928, 23:7. Variants: *NYT* gives "Presidential sons, Curtis" in first and second sentences, but *BDG* and *KCT* have it as here/*BDG* gives "Muelback" and *KCT* gives "Muehlebach" in fourth sentence/*LAT* did not print the DT.

The Muehlbach Hotel in Kansas City was headquarters for the Republican National Committee during the national convention.

[549] *NYT,* Tuesday, May 1, 1928, 31:7. Variants: *KCT* omits first, second and third sentences/*LAT* gives "in nearly every" in second sentence/*LAT* gives "didn't kill that" and *BDG* and *LAT* give "because they fell below their average." in third sentence.

For Tunney on Shakespeare see DT 544.

Tom Heeney, heavyweight boxer from New Zealand. Tunney knocked out Heeney in the eleventh round of their title bout on July 26, 1928.

Zane Grey, New York dentist who from 1904 until his death in 1939 devoted his life to writing adventure stories, most of which dealt with the American West.

Harold Bell Wright, painter, minister, and popular novelist, especially of stories set in the Ozarks, including *The Shepherd of the Hills* (1907).

[550] *NYT,* Wednesday, May 2, 1928, 27:7. Variants: *NYT* gives "raised, I" in fourth sentence, but *BDG, LAT,* and *KCT* have it as here/*LAT* gives "get in." in fourth sentence/*KCT* gives "of a building." in fifth sentence/*LAT* ends sixth sentence "paint."/*LAT* gives "Okla. They had" and *KCT* gives "Ok., which had its name" in seventh sentence.

[551] *NYT,* Thursday, May 3, 1928, 29:7.

Appropriations of $4,628,045,035, a peacetime record, were passed during the first session of the Seventieth Congress.

For the James brothers see DT 81; for Judd Gray and Ruth Snyder see DT 232.

[552] *NYT,* Friday, May 4, 1928, 27:7. Variants: *NYT* gives "as happened" in first sentence, but *BDG, LAT,* and *KCT* have it as here/*LAT* gives "Lake City, make" in second and third sentences/*BDG* gives "California—see" and *LAT* gives "California. See" in fifth sentence.

The California presidential primary election was held on May 1.

Charles Evans Hughes (see DT 31) and Woodrow Wilson ran a close race in six states, including California, in the presidential election of 1916. Late returns from the West gave Wilson an unexpected victory by an electoral margin of twenty-three and a popular plurality of 591,385 out of more than 18,000,000 votes cast.

553 *NYT,* Saturday, May 5, 1928, 19:7. Variants: *NYT* gives "salary in the" in second sentence, but *BDG, LAT,* and *KCT* have it as here/*LAT* gives "bar our pictures. . . retain our pictures" and *BDG* gives "bar our movies, but for . . . will export one" in fifth sentence/*NYT* did not print the P. S., but *BDG, LAT,* and *KCT* have it as here.

Hays, who earned $100,000 a year as the so-called movie czar, obtained the cooperation of the French government in revising a local statute which hampered distribution of American films in France.

554 *NYT,* Monday, May 7, 1928, 25:7. Variants: *NYT* gives "received the amount" in first sentence, but *BDG, LAT,* and *KCT* have it as here/*LAT* gives "Jim Reed is" in sixth sentence/*KCT* gives "with less than four" in P. S.

Senator Walsh (see DT 209) had sought the Democratic presidential nomination in a desire to stop Governor Smith. He viewed Smith's convincing victory in the California primary of May 1 as proof that the New York governor would not alienate western voters; he therefore withdrew on May 4.

For Senator James Watson see DT 95.

555 *NYT,* Tuesday, May 8, 1928, 29:7. Variants: *LAT* gives "wives, it" in first sentence/*BDG* ends P. S. "from the next township."

Prince Carol (see DT 392) acknowledged his willingness to assume power in Rumania if invited by the powerful Peasant party. He insisted that his companion, Madame Lupescu, had not caused his exile from Rumania and would not prevent his return.

556 *NYT,* Wednesday, May 9, 1928, 27:7. Variants: *KCT* gives "He has only . . . that advertising" in third sentence/*KCT* gives "William Allen White" in eighth sentence.

The Senate Campaign Funds Investigating Committee began hearings on May 7. Of the five senators Rogers mentioned, none were serious contenders, except possibly Curtis (see DT 116).

For George Norris see DT 489; for Guy D. Goff see DT 540; for Walter George see DT 456; for Thomas Walsh see DT 209; for William Allen White see DT 116.

557 *NYT,* Thursday, May 10, 1928, 29:7. Variant: *NYT* gives "food relief" in fourth sentence, but *BDG, LAT,* and *KCT* have it as here.

The Senate Campaign Funds Committee heard from Governor Ritchie of Maryland (see DT 95) and Senator Reed of Missouri (see DT 79) on the second day of hearings. Ritchie reported no disbursements, and Reed claimed that he knew of only $250 spent on his behalf.

Prince Carol announced that he would visit the United States, as his mother, Queen Marie, had done in the fall of 1926, should his plans to return to Rumania not materialize (see DT 555). The British Home Office had asked the prince to leave England, and the Rumanian Peasant party had renounced any interest in bringing him to power.

[558] *NYT,* Friday, May 11, 1928, 27:7. Variants: gives "Herbert Hoover" in first sentence, but *BDG, LAT,* and *KCT* have it as here/*LAT* and *KCT* give "old Purdue," in third sentence.

Senator Watson (see DT 95) defeated Secretary Hoover in the Indiana Republican primary on May 8. The victory reaffirmed the senator's political strength in his home state and gave him thirty-three convention votes.

For George Ade and Kin Hubbard see DT 95.

Booth Tarkington, American novelist and playwright whose most noted and characteristic works concerned stories set in small midwestern towns; won Pulitzer prizes in 1918 and 1921.

Jesse Andrews, gentleman farmer from Indiana.

Ade received a bachelor's degree from Purdue University—'Perdue"—in 1887. Tarkington briefly attended the same institution.

[559] *NYT,* Saturday, May 12, 1928, 19:7. Variants: *KCT* omits first, second, third, and fourth sentences/*KCT* gives "tell John" in fifth sentence/*LAT* ends seventh sentence "writing letters."

Japanese troops invaded the Chinese province of Shantung in April of 1928 in order to protect Japanese railroad investments there. Hostilities flared from May 3 to 11; Japanese intervention continued until the spring of 1929.

John D. Rockefeller, Jr., holder of 15 percent of the voting stock of Standard Oil Company, requested the resignation of Robert Stewart, chairman of the firm, because of contradictions in his testimony in the Teapot Dome inquiries (see DT 484). Stewart subsequently gained support among the directors of the company and retained his position.

[560] *NYT,* Monday, May 14, 1928, 23:7. Variants: *NYT* omits fourth sentence, but *BDG, LAT,* and *KCT* have it as here/*KCT* gives "nominating." in sixth sentence.

Although Mellon issued a public statement praising Secretary Hoover, he nevertheless recommended that the Pennsylvania delegation to the Republican National Convention remain unpledged.

[561] *NYT,* Tuesday, May 15, 1928, 29:7. Variants: *KCT* gives "to kid and . . . 'bunion,' " in second sentence/*BDG* gives "can fight . . . years, only." in fourth sentence.

Andy Payne continued to maintain his lead in C. C. Pyle's transcontinental footrace (see DT 539).

[562] *NYT,* Wednesday, May 16, 1928, 27:7.

Divorces in Nevada increased 91.3 percent from 1926 to 1927, according to a report released by the United States Department of Commerce. Washoe County, in which Reno is located, had 112 percent more divorces during the same period.

[563] *NYT,* Thursday, May 17, 1928, 27:7. Variants: *LAT* gives "made tonight here" and *KCT* gives "would ask civilization" in first sentence/*LAT* gives "Angeles (the . . . advance) with a dinner" in first and second sentences.

The Los Angeles Junior Chamber of Commerce held a fund-raising banquet on May 15 for which Rogers served as toastmaster. Receipts from the dinner were to be used for a winter sports program.

A third Dempsey-Tunney fight never materialized. For Tunney's attraction to Shakespearean studies, see DT 544.

[564] *NYT,* Friday, May 18, 1928, 25:7. Variants: *NYT* gives "for that" in third sentence, but *BDG, LAT,* and *KCT* have it as here/*KCT* gives "in a court" in third sentence/*LAT* gives "there's fist" and *KCT* gives "there is fist" in fourth sentence/*NYT* and *BDG* omit fifth sentence, but *LAT* and *KCT* have it as here/*KCT* gives "Dupont's powder" in fifth sentence/*BDG* gives advance flying field and" and *LAT* gives "advance airfields and" and *KCT* gives "advance aviation interest." in sixth sentence.

Former Governor of South Carolina John Evans and former Speaker of the State Assembly Edgar Brown disputed a recent action of the state Democratic convention which had affirmed a rule pledging support to the nominee of the Democratic National Convention. Brown held that opponents to the rule sought to destroy the state party. Evans shouted that Brown was already a Republican. After exchanging blows, the two were separated.

Oklahoma pilots and aviation officials crisscrossed the state from May 16 to May 20, visiting nineteen cities in an effort to promote the industry. Ten new landing fields were opened to attract the "air tourists."

Hoover vacationed for a few days near Williamsport, Pennsylvania. On May 16 he landed twenty-five of thirty-one convention delegates in New Jersey.

[565] *NYT,* Saturday, May 19, 1928, 17:7. Variants: *LAT* gives "article three" in first sentence/*KCT* omits second, third, fourth, and fifth sentences/*BDG* and *LAT* give "tell it." in fourth sentence/*BDG* and *KCT* give "never get off" in seventh sentence/*KCT* gives "town which painted name." in P. S.

Rogers had commented in a weekly article on February 12, 1928, that travel time from Chicago to the West Coast would be reduced considerably when airplanes began to compete with railroads for passengers. On May 14 a combine of passenger train and airplane companies announced forty-eight-hour transcontinental passenger service. Patrons would leave New York in the evening, spend two nights on railway "sleepers," fly during the day, and reach Los Angeles the evening of the second day.

[566] *NYT,* Monday, May 21, 1928, 23:7. Variants: *LAT* gives origin "BEVERLY HILLS"/*LAT* and *KCT* give "why your only" and *LAT* gives "he replies" in second sentence/*BDG* and *KCT* give "from tomorrow it" and *LAT* gives "from tomorrow we will" in fourth sentence/*KCT* gives "means 'will under pressure,' . . . argue for three" in fifth sentence.

Coolidge had said he did not "choose to run" (see DT 322), but Rogers and others believed he would accept the candidacy if drafted.

[567] *NYT,* Tuesday, May 22, 1928, 29:7. Variants: *LAT* gives "Wasn't it your" and *BDG* gives "Congress to be:" in first sentence/*LAT* gives "dam. In the Senate, in" in third sentence/*NYT, BDG,* and *KCT* omit P.S., but *LAT* has it as here.

The Boulder Dam bill continued to be opposed by a powerful bloc of senators from the Southwest (see DT 185).

Los Angeles police had arrested a blonde divorcee, Hertha "Babe" Murray, and committed her to a psychopathic ward of a local hospital. A week later Mrs. Murray publicly accused millionaire Claus Spreckles of arranging the arrest to "frame" her and destroy evidence of their relationship. Mrs. Murray's mother supported her story with letters revealing the love affair. The whole incident brought reprimands from a judge and a few days of lurid headlines but no litigation.

[568] *NYT,* Wednesday, May 23, 1928, 27:7. Variants: *LAT* begins first sentence "Headline in paper" and *KCT* gives " 'Three man' " in first sentence/*NYT* gives "column it says," in second sentence, but *BDG, LAT,* and *KCT* have it

as here/*LAT* and *KCT* give "foot-racers ran seventy-four miles . . . horse seventy-four miles" in P. S.

The stock market featured a long string of 4,000,000-share days during May. The New York Stock Exchange reduced the daily trading period from five to four hours beginning on May 21; sales subsequently dropped to 2,671,540 shares.

General Motors was one of the most glamorous and active stocks in 1928.

The runners in C. C. Pyle's "bunion derby" (see DTs 539 and 561) completed the longest lap of the race on May 21, 74.6 miles between Waverly and Deposit, New York. The distance was only a few miles short of three times the regulation marathon distance of twenty-six miles and 385 yards.

[569] *NYT,* Thursday, May 24, 1928, 31:7. Variants: *NYT* gives "fairly known" in first sentence, but *BDG, LAT,* and *KCT* have it as here/*NYT* gives "for his job?" in fifth sentence, but *BDG, LAT,* and *KCT* have it as here.

Lindbergh accepted a position as chairman of the technical committee of Transcontinental Air Transport, an airline-railway combination (see DT 565). Rogers had hinted about Lindbergh's involvement in the project in a weekly article on April 29, 1928.

Jason "Jay" Gould, American railway executive and financier. Gould partially succeeded in molding a central transcontinental route by consolidating the Union Pacific, Missouri Pacific, Kansas Pacific, and Texas and Pacific railroads during the 1870s and 1880s.

James "Jim" Hill, nineteenth century American businessman and financier, Hill personally supervised the selection of routes, improvement of terminal facilities, and construction and maintenance of the Great Northern Railway.

[570] *NYT,* Friday, May 25, 1928, 27:7. Variant: *LAT* gives "more pork-eating than" in fourth sentence.

A revised farm relief bill, which retained the basic elements of the one President Coolidge had vetoed the previous year (see DT 181), was submitted to Coolidge for his signature on May 16. Again Coolidge applied the argument of unconstitutionality as he vetoed the measure. He called the bill deceptive, intolerable, and futile.

Andy Payne appeared certain to win C. C. Pyle's "bunion derby," but doubts were raised about Pyle's financial solvency.

[571] *NYT,* Saturday, May 26, 1928, 19:7. Variants: *LAT* gives "News is that Congress" in first and second sentences/*LAT* gives "get its share" in seventh sentence.

The Senate passed a second deficiency appropriation bill on May 23. The measure amounted to $149,000,000, half again as high as the House bill, and included some flood relief appropriations.

Payne won the transcontinental footrace which was completed on May 27. Promoter Pyle assured Payne and other finishers that the $48,000 in prize money was deposited safely in a bank in New York. His associates, however, admitted that Pyle had lost $60,000 in the venture.

Henry Ford challenged one of his plant managers to a 100-yard footrace on a golf course at Wallingford, Pennsylvania. The employee, a much younger man, won by a narrow margin.

[572] *NYT,* Monday, May 28, 1928, 27:7. Variants: *LAT* gives origin "BEVERLY HILLS"/*BDG* and *KCT* give "farmer's" and *KCT* gives "compromise ready" and *BDG* gives "why don't they" in fourth sentence.

Supporters of the Boulder Dam bill continued to encounter opposition from Arizona congressmen, including Senator Carl Hayden, who successfully countered the efforts of Senator Hiram Johnson of California to have the measure brought to a vote.

Some observers accused supporters of the McNary-Haugen bill of forcing President Coolidge to veto the measure in order to inject farm relief into the presidential campaign. With Congress unable to override the veto, many Republicans predicted party doom unless they chose a candidate who could win the support of the farm community.

573 *NYT,* Tuesday, May 29, 1928, 27:7. Variant: *KCT* gives "maybe some 1,500" in seventh sentence.

Andy Payne's father, A. L. Payne, worked for Rogers' father, Clement Vann Rogers, on the home ranch near Oologah, Oklahoma, before settling on a nearby farm. The youngest of seven children was five-year-old Will Rogers Payne, named for the famous friend of the family.

Payne received his check for first prize at the end of an extra twenty-six hour marathon on June 2 in Madison Square Garden. Pyle expected to recoup his losses by managing Payne and other top runners in professional races and events.

574 *NYT,* Wednesday, May 30, 1928, 21:7. Variant: *KCT* ends first sentence "senate."

A filibuster to prevent action on the bill for Boulder Dam began at 2:30 p.m. on May 28 and lasted through the next day.

Payne flew to Washington, D. C., with some Oklahoma businessmen on May 28 after expressing confidence in Pyle's promise of prize money. Members of the House cheered Payne enthusiastically, but the filibuster prevented his introduction to the Senate.

Charles "Charley" Paddock, American journalist and track star. After Paddock won the 100-meter event in the Olympics of 1920, sports writers dubbed him "the world's fastest human." He interrupted his training for the Olympic Games of 1928 to return to his home state for the Southern Pacific tryouts.

575 *NYT,* Thursday, May 31, 1928, 25:7. Variants: *BDG* gives "California's" and *LAT* gives "and Arizonans" in second sentence/*KCT* gives "even in Pennsylvania" in sixth sentence.

Voters in Pennsylvania and Illinois elected William Vare and Frank Smith to the United States Senate in 1926, but the Senate refused to seat the men because of excessive campaign expenditures (see DT 79).

576 *NYT,* Friday, June 1, 1928, 27:7. Variants: *LAT* begins first sentence "Newspapers say 'Goff' "/*BDG* gives " 'Golf' " in first sentence/*LAT* begins second sentence "Another Memorial Day"/*BDG, LAT,* and *KCT* give "balloon races must" in fifth sentence.

Senator Goff (see DT 540) defeated Secretary Hoover in the Republican presidential preference primary in Goff's home state of West Virginia on May 30.

President Coolidge revealed on May 30 that Secretary of State Kellogg had succeeded in expanding bilateral French-American talks into multilateral negotiations (see DT 479). A preliminary draft of the Kellogg-Briand Peace Pact had been sent to Great Britain, Germany, Italy, and Japan.

Fourteen balloons, competing in the National Elimination Balloon Race, left Pittsburgh during generally rainy and threatening weather. A thunderstorm forced all but one of the crafts to quit the race. Lightning during the storm killed two crewmen, and falls and intense cold at high altitudes injured several others.

[577] *NYT,* Saturday, June 2, 1928, 19:7. Variant: *KCT* gives "the big" in second sentence.

President Coolidge announced on May 31 that he and his wife would spend the summer on Cedar Island in the Brulé River, twenty-nine miles from Superior, Wisconsin.

Wisconsin, home of the Progressive Republican La Follette family, was politically unpredictable throughout the 1910s and 1920s.

[578] *NYT,* Monday, June 4, 1928, 23:7. Variants: *LAT* gives origin "BEVERLY HILLS"/*LAT* gives "and was ready" in first sentence/*KCT* gives "he would be" in sixth sentence.

The complicated negotiations of the Kellogg-Briand Pact continued (see DT 576). Secretary Kellogg's proposed anti-war treaty, issued in April, prompted additional modifications, differing interpretations, and various considerations from the major powers.

[579] *NYT,* Tuesday, June 5, 1928, 31:7. Variants: *KCT* omits first and second sentences/*LAT* gives "his interests." in first sentence/*BDG* gives "convention I would" in second sentence/*LAT* and *KCT* give "else and Coolidge" in third sentence.

Likeliest emissary from Coolidge was William Butler, chairman of the Republican National Committee and an adviser to the president.

Coolidge used the veto twelve times during the Seventieth Congress, whereas he had used only five in the first three and one half years of his term.

[580] *NYT,* Wednesday, June 6, 1928, 27:7.

Captains Charles Kingsford-Smith and Charles Ulm, Australians with Royal Air Force experience, and two Americans, navigator Harry Lyon and radio operator James Warner, flew from Hawaii to Fiji, covering the 3,138 miles in thiry-four hours and setting a record for the longest flight over water.

Fiji islanders, once feared as cannibals, sacrificed a large tree-lined park so that the aviators could land safely at Suva, the island capital

[581] *NYT,* Thursday, June 7, 1928, 29:7. Variants: *LAT* gives "broke on plane, came down" in first sentence/*BDG* gives "back — the first" in first and second sentences/*KCT* begins second sentence "the first"/third sentence is from *LAT*/*NYT* gives "Lake, where these" and *BDG* and *KCT* end third sentence "into Salt Lake."/*KCT* gives "If I had . . . further would" and *LAT* gives "if had . . . further would" in fourth sentence/*BDG* gives "Kansas; draft" and *KCT* gives "Kansas City to" in fifth sentence.

Rogers received a jolt at Las Vegas, Nevada, when a Western Air Express mail plane in which he was riding upset while landing. He and another passenger were shaken, but Rogers insisted that the accident was harmless.

Rogers' humorous presidential candidacy was launched on May 24 by Robert Sherwood, editor of *Life* magazine.

[582] *NYT,* Friday, June 8, 1928, 27:7. Variants: *NYT* gives "On to the convention," as eighth sentence and places "Yours," as close before signature, but *BDG, LAT,* and *KCT* have it as here.

The American-Russian Eagle Club in Hollywood California, burned after an explosion during the early morning hours of June 7. Fifteen motion picture celebrities, including Charlie Chaplin, fled into the streets Eight injuries, one serious, were reported.

583 *NYT,* Saturday, June 9, 1928, 19:7. Variants: *BDG* gives "daylight for" and *BDG* and *KCT* give "Mellon who" and *LAT* gives "Mellon telling who" in second sentence.

Rogers pretended to represent the Anti-Bunk party as a candidate for president. Nominated by *Life* magazine on May 24, he delivered his "acceptance speech" in the next issue of the publication (see DT 581). Rogers wrote a series of "campaign" articles for *Life* during this period while also contributing lengthy daily newpaper articles as a syndicated correspondent at the Republican and Democratic national conventions.

The marathon dance contest began on June 2 with 137 couples and ended on June 13 after setting a reported world record of 259 hours and forty minutes.

584 *NYT,* Monday, June 11, 1928, 23:7. Variants: *NYT* gives "even delegates, was" in second sentence, but *BDG* and *LAT* give "delegates"/*KCT* did not print the DT.

585 *NYT,* Tuesday, June 12, 1928, 29:7. Variants: *KCT* gives "senators will draw" in third sentence/*LAT* omits seventh sentence.

Mrs. Coolidge (see DT 311) was a favorite of Rogers. In a longer syndicated dispatch the previous day, Rogers revealed his personal choice for Republican presidential nominee: "I am for Mrs. Coolidge I want her to run on a Vindication platform. And if the Republican Party paid its just debts she would be nominated."

586 *NYT,* Wednesday, June 13, 1928, 29:7. Variants: *LAT* gives "Andy came in" in second sentence/*KCT* did not print the DT.

Ernestine Schumann-Heink, Austrian-born concert and operatic contralto; appeared in 1926 at the age of sixty-four in the Metropolitan Opera Company production of *Das Reingold.*

Senator Fess of Ohio (see DT 396) was temporary chairman of the convention and keynote speaker. Many observers considered his speech dry and stiff.

587 *NYT,* Thursday, June 14, 1928, 29:7. *KCT* did not print the DT.

Carranza, hailed as "Mexico's Lindy" (see DT 349), departed Mexico City on June 12 and landed in Washington, D. C., twenty-four hours later. His flight helped to ameliorate relations between Mexico and the United States.

George H. Moses, United States senator from New Hampshire from 1918 to 1933. Moses acknowledged his election as permanent chairman of the convention with a burst of partisan oratory. He declared that the Republicans would "bury" whomever the Democratics nominate for president—"we care not whether his name be Brown, Jones, Robinson, or Smith."

588 *NYT,* Friday, June 15, 1928, 27:7. *KCT* did not print the DT.

Seven armed men seized $19,000 from a bank in downtown Kansas City, fatally wounded a traffic policeman, and fled in a getaway car. Two days later five suspects, all local residents, were in jail.

Chicago Mayor William Thompson, a delegate to the Republican convention, was accused of having underworld support. Several Indiana delegates had visited a former Republican state chairman in a nearby federal prison.

Robert M. La Follette, Jr., Republican United States senator from Wisconsin from 1925 to 1947. La Follette offered a minority platform which denounced corruption in government, United States action in Nicaragua, and an expanded navy and favored the McNary-Haugen farm relief bill, federal power projects, and a modified enforcement of Prohibition. By a voice vote, the convention rejected the platform.

For Senator Tom Heflin see DT 174.

[589] *NYT,* Saturday, June 16, 1928, 19:7. Variants: *BDG* gives "campaign—will it be" and *LAT* gives "campaign, be America" in sixth and seventh sentences/*LAT* gives "Come on in if" in tenth and eleventh sentences/*KCT* did not print the DT.

Convention delegates nominated Hoover on the first ballot on June 15. He received 837 votes out of 1,089 possible.

Curtis, who was one-eighth Indian, received 1,052 votes on the only ballot for vice president. Newspaper accounts mentioned his relatives who still lived on Kaw Indian tribal lands.

[590] *NYT,* Monday, June 18, 1928, 27:7. *KCT* did not print the DT.

[591] *NYT,* Tuesday, June 19, 1928, 29:7. Variants: *LAT* and *KCT* give "to thinking" in sixth sentence.

Gordon W. "Pawnee Bill" Lillie, Oklahoma rancher, wild west showman, and friend of the Pawnee Indians. His ranch near Pawnee included buffalo herds, Indian ponies, and frontier trading post.

Amelia Earhart, a social worker and flying enthusiast from Kansas, accompanied pilot Wilmer Stultz and mechanic Louis Gordon on a flight from Newfoundland to Burry Port, Wales. When she landed in Wales on June 18 she became the first woman to have flown the Atlantic.

[592] *NYT;* Wednesday, June 20, 1928, 27:7.

For Andy Payne see DTs 539 and 571.

For Governor Albert Ritchie see DT 95.

[593] *NYT,* Thursday, June 21, 1928, 27:7. Variants: *LAT* gives "now, just . . . on, sell" in third and fourth sentences/*BDG* and *LAT* begin sixth sentences "I had been"/*NYT* gives "Amos" and *KCT* gives "Almon" in eighth sentence, but *BDG* and *LAT* have it as here/*BDG* gives "Jessie Jones will get me a ticket" in ninth sentence.

For Amon G. Carter see DT 176; for Governor Dan Moody see DT 71; for Jesse Jones see DT 487.

[594] *NYT,* Friday, June 22, 1928, 25:7.

H(enry) L(ouis) Mencken, American editor, author, and publisher; social and political critic who was well-known for his acid pen. Rogers and Mencken shared correspondents' assignments at both national political conventions in 1924.

Shady Oaks Farm, owned by Amon G. Carter, was located ten miles from the center of Fort Worth.

[595] *NYT,* Saturday, June 23, 1928, 17:7. Variants: *LAT* gives "sound reason, and" in fourth sentence/*NYT* gives "for or against" in seventh sentence, but *BDG, LAT,* and *KCT* have it as here/*BDG* and *LAT* "Jessie" and *KCT* gives "Jess" in P. S.

Captain Tom Hickman, Texas Ranger and an internationally known judge of stock shows and rodeos.

[596] *NYT,* Monday, June 25, 1928, 23:7. Variant: *LAT* ends fourth sentence "the films."

For Senator Simeon Fess see DTs 396 and 586.

Mary Pickford (see DT 278) and her husband Douglas Fairbanks returned from a tour of Europe with twelve trunks of newly-purchased clothing and perfumes. They declared their value at $5,000, but customs appraisers assessed the real worth at $7,268 and accepted the Fairbanks' check for $3,900 for the duty.

Mae Murray, American leading lady of the silent screen. Miss Murray and her husband David Mdivani revealed on June 23 that they were parents of a sixteen-month-old son. They had attempted to keep the matter secret to protect the actress' career.

Senator Heflin (see DT 174) spoke to 10,000 Klansmen in an open field near Syracuse, New York, on June 16. The speakers' platform collapsed, but Heflin recovered from the incident and continued his two-hour speech.

[597] *NYT,* Tuesday, June 26, 1928, 27:7. Variants: *BDG* (PM) gives "radio tonight and" and *KCT* gives "this, run" in third sentence/*NYT* gives "run to the radio this evening and" in third sentence, but *BDG* (AM) and *KCT* have it as here/*BDG* gives 'Bowers." and *KCT* gives 'Tuesday night." to end fourth sentence/*LAT* did not print the DT.

Claude G. Bowers, author, journalist, and staunch Democrat. A popular orator, Bowers delivered the keynote addresses at the Democratic national conventions in 1920 and 1928.

[598] *NYT,* Wednesday, June 27, 1928, 27:7. Variant: *BDG* gives "its tribute" in first sentence.

Samuel J. Tilden, governor of New York from 1875 to 1876. As the Democratic presidential nominee in 1876, Tilden received more popular votes than the Republican candidate, Rutherford B. Hayes, but an electoral commission awarded Hayes enough contested electoral votes to give him the presidency.

Builders of the convention auditorium, a temporary wooden structure, attempted to lessen the heat with various cooling devices, but temperatures in Houston reached or surpassed 90° every day of the convention.

[599] *NYT,* Thursday, June 28, 1928, 27:7. Variants: *KCT* gives "never get" in second sentence/*KCT* ends fifth sentence "benediction, the platform." /*KCT* begins sixth sentence "It . . . adopt a wet one week."

For Senator Joe Robinson see DT 495.

[600] *NYT,* Friday, June 29, 1928, 27:7. Variants: *BDG* and *KCT* give "him we would" in second sentence.

Eighteen seconding speeches for Governor Smith were delivered at the convention.

[601] *NYT,* Saturday, June 30, 1928, 19:7. Variants: *KCT* omits fourth, fifth, and sixth sentences/*LAT* gives close "Yours harmoniously," before signature.

Governor Smith's nomination came late on June 28; the final tally showed that he received 849⅔ votes out of 1,000 possible.

Senator Robinson was nominated for vice president on June 29.

[602] *NYT,* Monday, July 2, 1928, 21:7. Variants: *KCT* gives "Kelley field," in first sentence/*KCT* gives "They kinda want a . . . all of the post-offices" in fourth sentence/*BDG* (AM) and *LAT* did not print the DT.

Kelly Field, located near San Antonio, Texas, was the site of the Army Air Corps Flying School, training ground for Charles Lindbergh and other military aviators.

The King Ranch, located southwest of Corpus Christi and with headquarters at Kingsville, was founded in 1853 by Richard King and later managed by King's son-in-law, Robert Kleberg. The million-acre ranch was a center of cattle breeding and irrigated farming.

[603] *NYT,* Tuesday, July 3, 1928, 23:7.

[604] *NYT,* Wednesday, July 4, 1928, 17:7. Variants: *KCT* gives "flew home." in first sentence/*KCT* gives "and then thousands of acres of" and *LAT* gives "the Salton Sea," in second sentence.

[605] *NYT,* Thursday, July 5, 1928, 21:7. Variants: *NYT* gives "how much five" in second sentence, but *BDG, LAT,* and *KCT* have it as here/*BDG* gives third sentence "He don't need the jokes."—omitting thirteen words/*NYT* gives "five by rights. Coolidge should" in fifth and sixth sentences, but *BDG, LAT,* and *KCT* have it as here/*BDG* gives "If he will pay half in money, or" in eighth sentence, omitting four words/*NYT* gives "they cracked" in ninth sentence, but *LAT* and *KCT* have it as here.

For the Hearst-Rogers bet see DT 382.

[606] *NYT,* Friday, July 6, 1928, 23:7. Variants: *BDG* gives dateline "June 5."/*LAT* gives "be. 'What has' " in eighth sentence.

Jean Lussier, a salesman from Springfield, Massachusetts, went over the Canadian side of Niagara Falls in a steel-reinforced rubber ball. He was dazed slightly but suffered only minor bruises.

[607] *NYT,* Saturday, July 7, 1928, 15:7. Variants: *KCT* gives "sure times" in first sentence/*BDG* gives "farmers got" in sixth sentence/*KCT* omits eighth sentence.

Belgian financier Alfred Loewenstein disappeared early on July 5 from his private plane while on a cross-channel flight from England to Belgium. Authorities recovered his body on July 19 and declared his death accidental.

Mayor Walker was on a month-long West Coast vacation, spending time at beaches and rodeos.

Hoover's campaign manager issued a clarifying statement to reassure farmers of the nominee's deep concern for their welfare. An earlier interview had been misinterpreted in the press and had given a different impression about his views on agriculture.

[608] *NYT,* Monday, July 9, 1928, 21:7. Variant: *NYT* gives "man, said that" in first sentence, but *BDG, LAT,* and *KCT* have it as here.

Hubert Work, United States secretary of the interior from 1923 to 1928; chairman of the Republican National Committee from 1928 to 1929; manager of Hoover's presidential campaign in 1928.

Mrs. Catherine Shaver, wife of Democratic National Chairman Clement Shaver, assailed the prohibition plank of the Democratic party and Governor Smith's stand on the issue in a speech to the National Women's Democratic Law Enforcement League on July 6.

609 *NYT*, Tuesday, July 10, 1928, 25:7. Variants: *KCT* gives "runner Charlie Paddock" in first sentence/*BDG* omits second, third, and fourth sentences /*LAT* begins second sentence "It come close to being unfortunate"/*LAT* ends third sentence "association wouldn't have thought of not letting him go over."

Paddock (see DT 574) had been omitted from the United States Olympic track team for alleged professionalism. After the Southern Pacific Association threatened to withdraw its athletes from the team, the Olympic selection committee reviewed the evidence and rescinded its earlier decision. Paddock was accepted on July 9.

610 *LAT,* Wednesday, July 11, 1928, I:1:2; heading from *KCT,* 13:4. Variants: *BDG* omits fifth sentence/*NYT* did not print the DT.

An Italian dirigible, the *Italia,* departed Norway on May 23 for a flight to the North Pole to collect scientific data. Two days later an Arctic gale caused the craft to crash on an ice floe in the North Atlantic. Eight crewmen survived, but seventeen persons died in the crash and during rescue missions.

611 *NYT,* Thursday, July 12, 1928, 25:7. Variants: *KCT* gives "I suggest" in second sentence/*LAT* gives "Mayor Walker" and *BDG* gives "Jimmie" in fourth sentence/*NYT* gives "give lot" in fourth sentence, but *BDG, LAT,* and *KCT* have it as here.

Walker addressed the Wampus Club, an organization of Hollywood publicity men, on July 9. He warned motion picture executives that they could expect detrimental government action against the industry if they entered partisan politics and ended on the losing side.

612 *NYT,* Friday, July 13, 1928, 19:7. Variant: *BDG* gives "somebody and something." in third sentence.

The Democratic National Committee named John Raskob, chairman of the finance committee of General Motors Corporation, as national chairman of the party. Through his efforts the national committee raised $5,342,000 for the campaign treasury.

613 *NYT,* Saturday, July 14, 1928, 15:7.

Tammany Hall continued to be associated with corruption despite Governor Smith's efforts to present the New York political organization as representative of American patriotism and liberalism.

Peggy Hopkins Joyce, Virginia-born dancer and actress noted for her six marriages and countless engagements. On July 13 she announced that she was to wed Lord Northesk of England, but the engagement later was broken.

614 *NYT,* Monday, July 16, 1928, 21:7. Variants: *LAT* gives origin "BEVERLY HILLS"/*BDG* gives "found a legitimate" in first sentence/*KCT* ends fourth sentence "in the City of Mexico."/*KCT* gives "were so proud" in seventh sentence.

Carranza (see DTs 349 and 587) took off secretly on a nonstop flight from New York City to Mexico City on July 12 but was killed when lightning struck his plane and caused it to crash in New Jersey.

615 *NYT,* Tuesday, July 17, 1928, 23:7. Variants: *KCT* gives "our respected" in second sentence/*NYT* gives "Charlie" in sixth sentence, but *BDG, LAT,* and *KCT* have it as here/*KCT* gives "Fish get" in ninth sentence.

For Fred Stone see DT 539.

616 *NYT,* Wednesday, July 18, 1928, 23:7.

Umberto Nobile, Italian engineer and commander of the ill-fated *Italia* expedition (see DT 610). Nobile was held responsible for the crash of the *Italia,* and in near disgrace he returned to Italy with the survivors.

Custom held that presidential and vice presidential nominees be notified personally of their selection.

617 *NYT,* Thursday, July 19, 1928, 23:7. Variants: *LAT* begins first sentence "Just"/*KCT* begins second sentence "No one who has a sense of humor" /*LAT* gives "met a human in" in third sentence/*NYT* gives "away as he." in third sentence, but *BDG* and *LAT* have it as here/*KCT* gives "he had after . . . there." in third and fourth sentences/*NYT* gives "escaping assassination" in fourth sentence, but *BDG, LAT,* and *KCT* have it as here.

Alvaro Obregón (see DT 430), who was elected president of Mexico on July 1, was shot and killed by a professed admirer on July 17. In November of 1927 he had escaped injury when a bomb was hurled at him.

618 *NYT,* Friday, July 20, 1928, 21:7. Variants: *KCT* ends sixth sentence "reading public."/*KCT* gives "cowboy pictures" in seventh sentence.

619 *NYT,* Saturday, July 21, 1928, 15:7. Variants: *KCT* gives "it's hard" in third sentence/*LAT* gives "endurance outside . . . track. I" in fourth and fifth sentences/*NYT* gives "horses from running" in fifth sentence, but *BDG, LAT,* and *KCT* have it as here.

William "Bill" Tilden, generally considered the foremost tennis player of the first half of the twentieth century. Officials had barred Tilden from Davis Cup competition because of alleged professionalism. They later relented and allowed him to play in the finals, but after France won the tourney he was suspended by the United States Lawn Tennis Association. He turned professional in 1931.

Aviatrix Amelia Earhart (see DT 591) was in Chicago as the "honorary maid of honor" at the wedding of her mechanic, Lou Gordon.

620 *NYT,* Monday, July 23, 1928, 19:7. Variants: *NYT* gives "down to Jersey today" in first sentence, but *BDG, LAT,* and *KCT* have it as here.

For boxer Tom Heeney see DT 549; for John Raskob see DT 612.

621 *NYT,* Tuesday, July 24, 1928, 23:7. Variants: *LAT* gives "Newport where they" in first and second sentences/*BDG* gives "flew over" in fifth sentence.

In Newport members of the cast of a local play were denied access to Bailey's Beach, an exclusive area near the millionaires' mansions on Ocean Avenue.

Montauk Point, the easternmost spot on Long Island, was a favorite vacation spot for many New Yorkers.

622 *NYT,* Wednesday, July 25, 1928, 23:7. Variants: BDG omits origin and dateline/*NYT* gives "captive ballon." to end tenth sentence, but *BDG, LAT,* and *KCT* have it as here.

Graham McNamee, a sports and general announcer for the National Broadcasting Company and one of the best known announcers in the industry. McNamee was the ringside commentator for the Tunney-Heeney championship bout.

[623] *NYT,* Thursday, July 26, 1928, 23:7. Variants: *NYT* gives "Heeney, and people" in third and fourth sentences, but *BDG, LAT,* and *KCT* have it as here/*LAT* gives "tournament people get" and *KCT* gives "tournament backers get" in fifth sentence.

Raskob, newly elected chairman of the Democratic National Committee (see DT 612), resigned as member of the finance committee of General Motors until after the election because he did not want the company to be associated with politics.

Dempsey was employed by promoter Tex Rickard as an assistant for the Tunney-Heeney bout in order to bolster public interest in the title match.

Bill Tilden was reinstated as an amateur on July 24 in order that he might compete in the Davis Cup tennis finals in France (see DT 619).

[624] *NYT,* Friday, July 27, 1928, 21:7. Variants: *KCT* begins third sentence "These met here"/*LAT* gives "only the evils" in sixth sentence/*KCT* ends P.S. "arrived at yet late."

Winona Lake, a religious resort founded by members of the Presbyterian church, was a frequent vacation spot for motion picture czar Will Hays, a Presbyterian, and was the home of evangelist and Presbyterian minister Billy Sunday.

[625] *NYT,* Saturday, July 28, 1928, 15:7.

Thompson had suffered recent political and financial reverses: The *Chicago Tribune* won a $2,000,000 law suit against him in June, and the city controller and the police commissioner of Chicago resigned in early June.

[626] *NYT,* Monday, July 30, 1928, 19:7. Variant: *NYT* begins third sentence "Still flying", but *BDG, LAT,* and *KCT* have it as here.

[627] *NYT,* Tuesday, July 31, 1928, 23:7. Variants: *LAT* ends fourth sentence "me confidentially, 'East.' "/*BDG* and *LAT* end fifth sentence "William Allen White?"

White opened the Republican campaign in Kansas with a speech on July 12 in which he praised Smith's courage but declared that "his election would menace the nation." He cited Smith's voting record as a New York assemblyman who allegedly favored gambling, prostitution, and the saloon. Smith denied the charges. On July 29 White promised more detail to support his statements but three days later withdrew the accusations

[628] *NYT,* Wednesday, August 1, 1928, 23:7. Variants: *LAT* ends first sentence "tickets."/*KCT* ends sixth sentence "we have."

This DT used a new point of origin, Santa Monica, which was the location of the Rogers family ranch. The family recently had moved there after a delay of nearly a year. The ranch is now a state park and popular tourist attraction in California.

The Olympic Games opened on July 29 in Amsterdam, Holland. A United States shot putter set a record on the first day of competition, but Great Britain, Ireland, and Canada scored successive victories in other track and field events. The United States improved thereafter and finished with fifty-four medals in track and field, the largest national total.

[629] *NYT,* Thursday, August 2, 1928, 23:7. Variants: *KCT* gives "this Mrs. Willebrandt" and *BDG* gives "Willerbrandt" in third sentence.

In New York City federal prohibition agents raided several night clubs on the evenings of July 30 and 31. The raids resulted in twenty-six indictments which named 139 defendants.

Mabel Walker Willebrandt, assistant United States attorney general from 1921 to 1929. Willebrandt's responsibilities included enforcement of the Eighteenth Amendment and federal tax laws and supervision of the Bureau of Federal Prisons She was credited with ordering the raids in New York City.

[630] *NYT,* Friday, August 3, 1928, 19:7. Variants: *KCT* ends second sentence "he is for Smith."/*BDG* and *LAT* begin fourth sentence "The effect"

For the Old Spanish Days Fiesta in Santa Barbara, see DT 329. The *Los Angeles Times* printed a picture of McAdoo, Democratic party leader (see DT 147), in fiesta garb astride a horse and Rogers afoot beside him.

The United States Olympic team led the competition in total points, although American men had failed to win a single track event and Canadians had placed first in the 100-meter and 200-meter dashes.

[631] *NYT,* Saturday, August 4, 1928, 15:7. Variants: *NYT* begins first sentence "Just flew up" but *BDG, LAT,* and *KCT* have it as here/*BDG* gives "McManus' Jiggs and Maggie, and" and *KCT* gives "McManus. Hoover" in fourth sentence.

The Bohemian Club of San Francisco was founded by artists and was open to persons interested in the arts. The group's most famous activity was the "High Jinks," an annual two-week encampment in a 2,437-acre redwood grove near Monte Rio, California.

Harrison Fisher, popularly known as the "King of the Magazine Cover Artists" who successfully depicted American female beauty in portraits which made the "Harrison Fisher girl" as well-known and influential as the earlier "Gibson girl."

James "Jimmy" Swinnerton, American cartoonist who began "The Little Bears and Tigers" with the Hearst papers in 1902 and later produced "Little Jimmy."

George McManus, creator of one of the most popular Hearst comic strips, "Bringing up Father." Rowdy, brow-beaten Jiggs and his social climbing wife Maggie delighted Americans for decades in stage, screen, and radio adaptations as well as in the original cartoon.

[632] *NYT,* Monday, August 6, 1928, 21:7. Variant: *KCT* gives dateline "Aug. 7."

Hoover, relaxing in Palo Alto, California, conferred with Republican congressional leader John Tilson, Iowa farm journal editor Dante Pierce, and campaign advisers Nathan McChesney and James Good.

Stone (see DT 539) was unable to pull his airplane out of a dive and crashed during a solo flight. Despite two broken legs, a fractured jaw, and other injuries, his condition was considered serious but not critical.

[633] *NYT,* Tuesday, August 7, 1928, 23:7. Variants: *KCT* gives "day or so who" and *BDG* gives " 'wonderful air trips.' " in first sentence/*NYT* gives "to San Francisco, where" in second sentence, but *BDG, LAT,* and *KCT* have it as here/*LAT* gives "seventeen-passenger planes" in second sentence/*KCT* gives "their countrymen" in fourth sentence/*LAT* gives "safer lines"' in seventh sentence.

Two airline services, Maddux Air Lines and Western Air Express Corporation, offered daily passenger flights between San Francisco and Los Angeles. Their service compared favorably with that of the leading European lines.

634 *NYT,* Wednesday, August 8, 1928, 23:7. Variant: *KCT* omits first and second sentences.

635 *NYT,* Thursday, August 9, 1928, 21:7. Variants: *LAT* gives "each successive edition . . . till this afternoon's extras had tornadoes sweeping" in first sentence/*LAT* gives "candidates after nominations, they" in fifth and sixth sentences.

A hurricane struck near Palm Beach, Florida, on August 7, causing considerable financial loss due to flooding and crop destruction. The storm eventually crossed to the Gulf of Mexico then turned north to ravage Georgia and the Carolinas.

Smith demanded an opportunity to respond publicly to fundamentalist John Roach Straton's scathing attack upon Smith from a New York pulpit the previous Sunday. Straton (see DT 319) offered to repeat the sermon for Smith at an appropriate place. The exchange continued, but the confrontation never materialized.

636 *LAT,* Friday, August 10, 1928, I:1:2; heading from *KCT,* 2:3. Variants: *KCT* omits fourth and fifth sentences/*NYT* did not print the DT.

A German scientist announced on August 8 that he had transmitted ten pictures per second of 8,000 light points each; however, the picture produced a slightly "jerky" motion. American technicians progressed more rapidly and broadcasted the first television drama in the General Electric laboratory at Schenectady, New York, later in the year.

Clara Bow, American actress who personified the "It" girl of the 1920s (see DT 255). She depicted in films the vibrant young generation of the period.

637 *NYT,* Saturday, August 11, 1928, 15:7. Variants: *KCT* gives "bullrushes, but" in first sentence/*KCT* begins third sentence "And save"/*NYT* omits "Amen" but *BDG, LAT,* and *KCT* have it as here.

Senator Moses of New Hampshire (see DT 587) traveled to California to advise Hoover of the political situation in the East and to deliver formal notification of the Republican nomination.

638 *NYT,* Monday, August 13, 1928, 19:7.

Hoover delivered his acceptance speech to a crowd of 70,000 at Stanford University Stadium and to millions more via radio.

Roy Gray of Fort Madison, Iowa, was named the "Average American" in an article in *American Magazine.* Chosen through a series of crude statistical maneuvers, Gray owned and operated a small clothing store and had served as president of the local chamber of commerce. Although he admired Lindbergh, he was skeptical of Prohibition, ignorant of foreign affairs, and interested in sports.

639 *NYT,* Tuesday, August 14, 1928, 25:7. Variants: *BDG* and *LAT* give "poverty, favored" in third sentence.

640 *NYT,* Wednesday, August 15, 1928, 23:7. Variants: *KCT* gives "trusts to get attention, then" in first sentence/*NYT* gives "either has to rob" in first sentence, but *BDG, LAT,* and *KCT* have it as here/*KCT* gives "generally consisting of'" in fourth sentence/*KCT* gives "coming its way." in fifth sentence.

A number of Democrats had announced or soon would announce that they had bolted party nominee Smith to support Hoover. Among the disenchanted were retired Oklahoma Senator Robert Owen, Alabama Senator Thomas Heflin, North Carolina Senator Furnifold Simmons, and Lieutenant Governor Thomas Love of Texas who boasted that he would take 400,000 voters into Hoover's camp.

641 *NYT,* Thursday, August 16, 1928, 23:7. Variants: *NYT* gives "Joseph Daniels" in first sentence, but *BDG, LAT,* and *KCT* have it as here/*KCT* gives "every voter will" in third sentence/*NYT* gives "candidate, he" in fourth sentence, but *BDG, LAT,* and *KCT* have it as here.

Lowden stopped short of endorsing Hoover but expressed appreciation that the candidate recognized agriculture as the most urgent economic problem in the nation.

Charles W. Bryan, governor of Nebraska from 1931 to 1935; Democratic candidate for vice president in 1924. Although his brother, William Jennings Bryan (see DT 542), had opposed Smith's nomination in 1924, Charles Bryan pledged his support to the entire Democratic slate in 1928

Daniels (see DT 157) had issued an order in 1914 while secretary of the navy which prohibited beer and wine on all naval vessels and installations; hard liquor had been banned since the Civil War.

642 *NYT,* Friday, August 17, 1928, 21:7. Variants: *LAT* and *KCT* give "to see his bunch" in fifth sentence.

Byrd (see DT 292) was in the midst of elaborate preparations for an $855,000 expedition to the Antarctic. He and seventy associates even had undergone dental examinations to forestall any loss of efficiency because of illness.

643 *NYT,* Saturday, August 18, 1928, 15:7. Variant: *NYT* gives "of all men who" in second sentence, but *BDG, LAT,* and *KCT* have it as here.

644 *NYT,* Monday, August 20, 1928, 19:7. Variants: *NYT* gives "Showing you . . . nowadays, they" in first and second sentence, but *BDG, LAT,* and *KCT* have it as here/*KCT* omits third sentence/*LAT* gives fourth sentence "I, like my Injun compatriot, Curtis, stand on farm relief."/*KCT* omits eighth sentence.

Curtis, part Kaw and Osage, was notified formally of his nomination for vice president during ceremonies on the steps of the Kansas state capitol on August 18.

645 *NYT,* Tuesday, August 21, 1928, 25:7. Variant: *NYT* gives "farmer and skin" in fifth sentence, but *BDG, LAT,* and *KCT* have it as here.

646 *NYT,* Wednesday, August 22, 1928, 23:7. Variants: *LAT* and *KCT* give "wonder if they are" in sixth sentence.

Art Goebel, winner of the Hawaiian air derby in 1927 (see DT 336), flew from Los Angeles to Long Island, New York on August 19 to 20 and set a nonstop transcontinental flying record of eighteen hours and fifty-eight minutes. It was the first continuous west-to-east transcontinental air crossing.

Smith issued a statement on August 20 in which he defended bill-by-bill his record as a member of the New York state assembly. Smith denounced White's accusations of July 29 as false and politically inspired (see DT 627). He also firmly rejected the challenges and charges of the Reverend Straton (see DT 635).

647 *NYT,* Thursday, August 23, 1928, 23:7. Variants: *KCT* gives "will go up" in first sentence/*NYT* gives "static won't grab you." in fifth sentence, but *BDG, LAT,* and *KCT* have it as here.

Rogers and sons Jimmy and Will, Jr. attended religious ceremonies held at Hotevilla, one of the five principal Hopi pueblos, located 100 miles northeast of Flagstaff, Arizona. The Snake Dance, performed by the Snake and Antelope societies of the Hopi, was held every other year.

Smith delivered his acceptance speech to a crowd of 2,000 in the chambers of the New York state legislature. His speech also was broadcasted over a radio network of 405 stations.

[648] *NYT,* Friday, August 24, 1928, 21:7. Variants: *KCT* gives "before they entered the den they could" in fourth sentence/*KCT* omits fifth and sixth sentences.

"The Varsity Drag," a popular song and dance during the late 1920s, first was performed in the musical *Good News* in 1927. Bud De Sylva and Lew Brown wrote the lyrics to the tune, and Ray Henderson composed the music.

[649] *NYT,* Saturday, August 25, 1928, 17:7. Variants: *BDG* begins first sentence "Haven't seen"/*KCT* omits first and second sentences/*KCT* gives "see the snake dances here would . . . types here." in third sentence/*NYT* gives "white man's shoulder" in third sentence, but *BDG, LAT,* and *KCT* have it as here.

[650] *NYT,* Monday, August 27, 1928, 21:7.

[651] *NYT,* Tuesday, August, 28, 1928, 25:7. Variants: *BDG* gives "so that would" in sixth sentence/*BDG* and *LAT* give "twice rather than do it." in seventh sentence/*BDG* and *KCT* omit eighth sentence.

William C. Durant, founder and president of General Motors Corporation from 1908 to 1920. Durant offered a prize of $25,000 for the best and most practical plan to make Prohibition effective. More than 23,000 proposals were submitted.

[652] *NYT,* Wednesday, August 29, 1928, 23:7. Variants: *LAT* gives "John may belong to" in second sentence and *KCT* ends second sentence "for him." omitting twelve words/*BDG* gives "my auto won't" in fourth sentence.

John Coolidge, the president's oldest son, "joined the orchestra" at a dance at a Wisconsin resort on August 27. He played jazz on the saxaphone and also sang. Coolidge was a member of a fraternity at Amherst College, his father's alma mater.

For John Raskob see DT 612.

[653] *NYT,* Thursday, August 30, 1928, 23:7. Variant: *LAT* gives "enter a new war" in third sentence.

The Kellogg-Briand Pact, an international treaty to outlaw war (see DT 479), was signed by representatives of fifteen nations on August 27 in Paris.

[654] *NYT,* Friday, August 31, 1928, 21:7. Variant: *NYT* gives "imagine that financial" in third sentence, but *BDG, LAT,* and *KCT* have it as here.

Tunney, who had announced his retirement from the ring on July 31, spoke at a dinner party given for him by an English boxing promoter on August 29. The world champion said he had quit boxing because he was past his prime, although he appreciated the financial rewards.

Early morning blasts occurred at the Paramount-Famous Players-Lasky movie lot and at a Hollywood battery service station. The motion picture industry had begun the conversion from silent to talking films. Rogers had yet to make the transition himself.

655 *NYT,* Saturday, September 1, 1928, 15:7. Variants: *LAT* gives "Candidate Robinson" and *KCT* gives "in Hot Springs yesterday" in third sentence.

Secretary of State Kellogg visited Ireland partly as a rebuke to Great Britain because of an Anglo-French naval alliance announced in July. Irish representatives were among the signers of the Kellogg-Briand antiwar treaty.

Robinson was the last major candidate to be notified officially of his nomination. He delivered his acceptance speech from the steps of a hotel in Hot Springs, Arkansas.

656 *NYT,* Monday, September 3, 1928, 15:7. Variants: *LAT* gives "that this Calles was . . . man, and that" in sixth sentence/*KCT* gives "us selecting by" in seventh sentence/*NYT* gives "and the United States electing" in seventh sentence, but *BDG, LAT,* and *KCT* have it as here.

For Plutarco Calles see DT 372.

657 *NYT,* Tuesday, September 4, 1928, 25:7. Variants: *NYT* gives "civilians" for "Civitans" in second sentence, but *BDG, LAT,* and *KCT* have it as here/*KCT* gives "Stratton" in fifth sentence.

The National Air Races for 1928 were to begin in Los Angeles on September 8 with numerous events planned, including a New York-to-Los Angeles free-for-all nonstop race for prizes aggregating $22,500 in cash.

Babe Ruth (see DT 29) refused to be photographed with Hoover prior to a baseball game in Washington, D.C. He later expressed his regrets about the incident and explained that it had resulted from a "misunderstanding."

The Reverend Straton renewed his attack on Smith on September 2 (see DT 635), labeling the Democratic presidential nominee America's "deadliest foe of moral progress and true political wisdom." Smith at once challenged Straton to a debate, but negotiation of time and place prolonged the event.

658 *NYT,* Wednesday, September 5, 1928, 29:7. Variants: *KCT* ends first sentence "Brisbane in his editorial."/*NYT* gives "Brisbane. He says" in first and second sentences, but *BDG* and *LAT* have it as here.

Brisbane (see DT 204), in quoting a phrase from DT 656, wrote in his weekly column: "Will Rogers, who once taught Sunday school, wishes Mexico would stop electing with bullets and that the United States would elect 'by the ballot instead of by the bullion.' He will have to wait."

659 *NYT,* Thursday, September 6, 1928, 27:7.

660 *NYT,* Friday, September 7, 1928, 25:7.

661 *NYT,* Saturday, September 8, 1928, 19:7. Variants: *BDG* gives "medium-priced two in" in second sentence/*NYT* ends eighth sentence "foreigners." but *BDG, LAT,* and *KCT* have it as here.

Promoter Rickard announced on September 6 the signing of Olympic marathon winner Abdel Baghinel, "El Ouafi," an Algerian whose time a month earlier had been two hours, thirty-two minutes, and fifty-seven seconds. Rickard staged a sixteen-mile race in Tulsa on October 7, which El Ouafi won when Payne withdrew because of muscle cramps.

662 *LAT,* Monday, September 10, 1928, I:1:6; heading from *KCT,* 2:3. Variants: *LAT* gives "goody" for "good year" in first sentence, but *BDG* and *KCT* have it as here/*NYT* did not print the DT.

Robert M. La Follette, Sr., Republican governor of Wisconsin from 1901 to 1906; United States senator from 1906 until his death in 1925. La Follette ran for president in 1924 on the Progressive party ticket. The total value of farm crops in 1924 exceeded $9,000,000,000 as compared to the low point of $5,600,-000,000 in 1921.

Although farm bloc leader George Peek and agricultural editor Henry Wallace, among others, supported Smith, most rural Republican spokesmen favored Hoover.

663 *NYT,* Tuesday, September 11, 1928, 29:7. Variant: *NYT* gives "Paris and he" in first sentence, but *BDG, LAT,* and *KCT* have it as here.

664 *NYT,* Wednesday, September 12, 1928, 29:7. Variants: *BDG* and *KCT* give "unlocked. 'Where' " and *BDG* gives "going between" in third sentence/*BDG* gives "Arkansas" in fourth sentence.

Ruth's home run on September 11 enabled the New York Yankees to edge the Philadelphia Athletics, 5 to 3.

The New York City nightclubs which had been raided in late July (see DT 629) had been ordered padlocked pending trial. On September 11 a federal court ordered the locks removed. A hint of politics appeared to surround the whole affair.

665 *NYT,* Thursday, September 13, 1928, 29:7. Variant: *KCT* gives "the new hospital" in first sentence.

Stone faced a long recuperation at home following his plane crash in early August (see DT 632), but he expressed gratitude to Rogers for agreeing to appear in his show, *Three Cheers,* which was due to open in New England in two weeks

Polo teams from the United States and Argentina were scheduled to meet in September in International Cup competition. The roster of the American contingent changed periodically as the United States Polo Association assessed potential members.

In early voting in Maine on September 10, Republicans swept a United States senate seat, four congressional posts, and the governorship.

666 *NYT,* Friday, September 14, 1928, 29:7. Variants: *LAT* gives "little film actress Bebe" in first sentence/*KCT* begins second sentence "On the evening of"/*LAT* gives "tennis matches she" in third sentence.

Virginia "Bebe" Daniels, popular American actress who made her film debut in 1908 at the age of seven. Frequently in the headlines, she was engaged for a brief time to track star Paddock (see DT 574). She married actor Ben Lyon in 1930.

Thomas Hitchcock, Jr., society figure and one of the leading polo players in the United States during the 1920s.

For Bill Tilden see DT 619.

The Mississippi Democratic primary customarily saw the party choosing the eventual winners because of the one-party nature of politics in the state.

667 *NYT,* Saturday, September 15, 1928, 21:7. Variants: *KCT* gives "the undertaking privilege" in third sentence/*BDG* gives "town, as the only" in seventh and eighth sentences.

Underworld figure Antonio Lombardo was slain on September 7 in Chicago and buried four days later with lavish floral offerings.

John Coolidge, the president's son (see DT 652), began work on September 10 as clerk for the general manager of the New York, New Haven, and Hartford Railroad Company.

Smith made extensive use of trains in his campaign travels.

[668] *NYT,* Monday, September 17, 1928, 25:7. Variants: *KCT* gives "which is not . . . brave expedition'" in second sentence/*KCT* gives "Paul Blocks, 15-year-old boy, gave" in fifth sentence.

The polo matches (see DT 665) were delayed because of illness to a number of the ponies.

Paul Block, publisher of the *Pittsburgh Post-Gazette, Toledo Blade,* and *Toledo Times.* His twelve-year-old-son, Billy, donated his savings of three years, $2,365, to Smith's campaign.

[669] *NYT,* Tuesday, September 18, 1928, 31:7. Variants: *NYT* and *LAT* give " 'seems as quiet.' " in sixth sentence, but *BDG* and *KCT* have it as here.

Thomas Edison, United States inventor best-known for the development of the phonograph and the improvement of the electric light bulb.

Harvey Firestone, founder in 1900 of Firestone Tire and Rubber Company; president of the firm from 1903 to 1932 and chairman of the board from 1932 until his death in 1938.

[670] *NYT,* Wednesday, September 19, 1928, 31:7. Variants: *KCT* gives "home state to treat" in first sentence/*KCT* gives "outlaws and comedians." in fourth sentence.

[671] *NYT,* Thursday, September 20, 1928, 31:7. Variant: *BDG* gives "profit to 'em" in third sentence.

Smith outlined his proposal for farm relief in a speech in Omaha on September 18. It included many of the same provisions as the McNary-Haugen bill.

Hoover had proposed an agriculture plan which depended on marketing through cooperatives.

[672] *NYT,* Friday, September 21, 1928, 31:7. Variant: *KCT* gives "taking as much interest" in second sentence.

A severe tropical hurricane devastated Puerto Rico and other West Indian islands and then struck Florida on September 16. The Everglades and Lake Okeechobee areas suffered heavy damage, with 1,500 fatalities, 15,000 persons homeless, and property damage of at least $50,000,000. Palm Beach, with its luxurious hotels and winter homes, also was hit hard.

[673] *NYT,* Saturday, September 22, 1928, 21:7. Variant: *KCT* gives "made fewer speeches . . . single man in" in third and fourth sentences.

For William Jennings Bryan see DT 542.

[674] *NYT,* Monday, September 24, 1928, 23:7. Variant: *KCT* gives "power magnates saying 'There is no' " in third sentence.

Smith in a speech in Oklahoma City on September 20 criticized Mabel Walker Willebrandt, assistant attorney general for the United States (see DT 629), for urging Methodist clergymen in Ohio to oppose him.

Speaking in Denver, Smith proposed government ownership of the principal power sites and generating plants but not government distribution of electricity.

[675] *NYT,* Tuesday, September 25, 1928, 33:7. Variant: *KCT* gives "going for the Yankees" in fourth sentence.

Albert Ottinger, Republican attorney general of New York from 1925 to 1926. Ottinger ran an unsuccessful race for governor in 1928 against Democrat Franklin D. Roosevelt.

676 *NYT,* Wednesday, September 26, 1928, 29:7. Variants: *KCT* gives "and fewer votes" in second sentence/*BDG* and *KCT* give "it, started practicing it." in third sentence/*BDG* and *KCT* give "we might just" in sixth sentence.

For Senator Thomas Walsh see DT 209.

677 *NYT,* Thursday, September 27, 1928, 31:7. Variants: *NYT* gives "today and carries New" in second sentence, but *BDG, LAT,* and *KCT* have it as here/*LAT* gives "Cleveland Indian vote" and *BDG* gives "runless and stopping all the whispering so that it looks" in second sentence.

In a mixture of items, Rogers here referred to the newly sharpened zeal of some publishers for polling voters. The *Literary Digest* published polls during the preceding week showed Hoover ahead. Seventy-five percent of those questioned however, had voted Republican in 1924, against 54 percent of the total electorate.

John "Little Napoleon" McGraw, major league infielder from 1892 to 1906 and controversial, but effective manager of the New York Giants from 1902 to 1932.

For Mabel Walker Willebrandt see DT 629.

678 *NYT,* Friday, September 28, 1928, 29:7.

Leona Curtis Knight, daughter of vice-presidential candidate Charles Curtis of Kansas and a delegate from Rhode Island to the Republican National Convention in 1928. Mrs. Knight had delivered a memorable seconding speech for her father's nomination.

679 *NYT,* Saturday, September 29, 1928, 21:7. Variants: *LAT* gives "the candidates" in first sentence/*LAT* gives "for 2300." in third sentence/*KCT* gives " 'whispering' " in fourth sentence.

For John Payne see DT 271.

Hoover already had issued statements of sympathy for the sufferers in Florida and had urged support of the Red Cross relief drive.

680 *NYT,* Monday, October 1, 1928, 25:7. Variants: *KCT* gives "Wow! That polo" in first sentence/*KCT* gives "in this prohibition" in fifth sentence.

The first polo match between Argentina and the United States was played on September 29. The United States team won in the final period, 7 to 6. Argentina won the second match game, but the United States took the third for the championship of the Americas.

Smith, speaking in Milwaukee, won partisan support with a specific proposal to modify Prohibition by including a "scientific" definition of the key word "intoxicating" in the Eighteenth Amendment and the Volstead Act and by returning the question to the states for their action. Dry forces redoubled their opposition to his candidacy.

681 *NYT,* Tuesday, October 2, 1928, 33:7. Variant: *LAT* gives "made any announcement" in first sentence.

Hoover delivered a highly effective pro-Coolidge speech during the presidential campaign of 1924.

[682] *NYT,* Wednesday, October 3, 1928, 33:7. Variants: *NYT* gives "convention, would" in second sentence, but *BDG, LAT,* and *KCT* have it as here/ *LAT* gives "would arrive and" in second sentence/*BDG* gives "to nominate Al" in third sentence/*KCT* gives "but not a namesake" in fifth sentence.

Franklin D. Roosevelt, wealthy New York attorney, former United States secretary of the navy, and distant relative of President Theodore Roosevelt. He served as governor of New York from 1929 to 1933 and as president of the United States from 1933 until his death in 1945. He had placed Al Smith's name in nomination at the Democratic national conventions of 1924 and 1928.

[683] *NYT,* Thursday, October 4, 1928, 31:7. Variants: *KCT* ends third sentence "around with them?"/*LAT* gives "stroll alone. Now my" in fourth and fifth sentences/*NYT* gives "when the world's" in fifth sntence, but *BDG, LAT,* and *KCT* have it as here.

Gene Tunney and Mary Lauder of Greenwich, Connecticut, heiress of a family related to Andrew Carnegie, were married on October 3 in Rome, Italy.

Thornton Wilder, Pultizer Prize winning novelist and playwright, had been a close companion of Tunney.

[684] *NYT,* Friday, October 5, 1928, 27:7.

Lindbergh flew to St. Louis where he registered as a Republican on October 3 and issued a public endorsement of Hoover.

[685] *NYT,* Saturday, October 6, 1928, 21:7. Variants: *KCT* gives "treasurers are asking" in second sentence/*NYT* gives "for the candidates." in second sentence, but *BDG, LAT,* and *KCT* have it as here

Democratic party treasurer Herbert Lehman made a radio appeal for funds on October 5.

[686] *NYT,* Monday, October 8, 1928, 25:7. Variants: *KCT* gives "answers the comedians." in third sentence/*BDG* gives "I'll look . . . for me'n the entire bunk" and *LAT* gives "they are in baseball . . . me and the entire bunk" and KCT gives "look for Missouri to go or me." in fifth sentence.

Hoover delivered a speech on October 6 in Elizabethtown, Tennessee, a Republican stronghold. Hoover objected to criticism of "middle America," wherein, he claimed, rested the strength of the national character.

The St. Louis Cardinals, champions of the National League and the favorites to win the World Series of 1928, had suffered two successive losses to the New York Yankees in the autumn classic.

[687] *NYT,* Tuesday, October 9, 1928, 33:7. Variants: *LAT* gives "Eight people" and *KCT* gives "airplanes, you would have thought that Nicaragua" in first sentence/*BDG* gives "than drink." in second sentence/*KCT* gives "doubt either" and *LAT* gives "elect him." in third sentence.

Six airplane crashes occurred during the weekend of October 6 to 7 with nine fatalities and ten injuries.

The Democratic and Republican parties had conducted an active money-raising drive for local, state, and national campaigns. Although they raised $4,-000,000 for the presidential campaign alone, congressional committees investigating campaign expenditures showed little concern.

[688] *NYT,* Wednesday, October 10, 1928, 31:7. Variant: *KCT* gives "over poison" in fourth sentence.

Ruth performed well with a series batting average of .636 as the New York Yankees won the first three games of the World Series. Injuries to New York players had made the St. Louis Cardinals the pre-series favorites.

New York officials blamed the consumption of wood alcohol for the deaths of thirty-three persons in two days. Federal prohibition agents claimed that current laws prevented them from moving against night clubs which sold the bad liquor. A special grand jury was called to consider indictments in the matter.

689 *NYT,* Thursday, October 11, 1928, 29:7. Variants: *LAT* gives "attended our" in first sentence/*KCT* gives "take up the case of" in third sentence.

Ruth hit three home runs in the fourth game of the World Series in St. Louis. The Yankees swept the series.

690 *NYT,* Friday, October 12, 1928, 27:7.

691 *NYT,* Saturday, October 13, 1928, 17:7. Variant: *NYT* gives "get sadly fooled," in fourth sentence, but *BDG, LAT,* and *KCT* have it as here.

The *Graf Zeppelin* departed its hanger in southern Germany on October 11, bound for New Jersey with sixty passengers and crew. The commander of the dirigible steered the ship southward because of inclement weather along a planned northern route.

Smith campaigned in two traditionally Democratic southern states, Tennessee and Kentucky, from October 9 to 12. At the same time Hoover appeared at rallies and dinners in usually rock-ribbed Republican New England.

No DT is available for Monday, October 15, 1928.

692 *NYT,* Tuesday, October 16, 1928, 33:7. Variant: *LAT* gives "air for four days" in fifth sentence.

The Naval Academy lost to Notre Dame, 7 to 0, at Soldier Field in Chicago on October 13.

The *Graf Zeppelin* (see DT 691) arrived in Lakehurst, New Jersey, on October 15, having flown 6,500 miles from Germany in 111 hours and thirty-eight minutes. It did not travel by way of Cape Horn, although it flew considerably south of a planned northern crossing of the Atlantic.

693 *NYT,* Wednesday, October 17, 1928, 31:7. Variants: *NYT* gives "We have opened up our show." for first sentence, but *BDG, LAT,* and *KCT* have it as here/*LAT* gives "sorry that elephants" and *KCT* gives "horses are not" in second sentence/*BDG* and *LAT* give "What's been . . . worry, was that" in fourth sentence.

*Three Cheers,* in which Rogers replaced injured Fred Stone (see DTs 539 and 632), ran in New York City through the entire season and closed in Pittsburgh in June of 1929. Rogers' scenes with Stone's daughter, Dorothy, were hailed as "a natural and pleasant reminder of Fred."

John Ringling, whose Ringling Brothers Barnum and Bailey Circus was one of the largest and most popular circus organizations in the United States.

694 *NYT,* Thursday, October 18, 1928, 31:7. Variants: *BDG* and *LAT* give "Agriculture has spent" in second sentence/*LAT* gives "that costs of 'promise of relief' have advanced" in third sentence/*NYT* gives "save than" in fourth sentence, but *BDG, LAT,* and *KCT* have it as here.

[695] *NYT,* Friday, October 19, 1928, 25:7. Variant: *LAT* ends P. S. "come out for—W.R."

Pollsters for the *Literary Digest* compiled their list of survey respondents from telephone books and other indices of relative wealth and education.

[696] *NYT,* Saturday, October 20, 1928, 19:7.

William "Wild Bill" Hopson, veteran air mail pilot for National Air Transport Company. Hopson crashed and died on October 19 during a flight from Clarion, Pennsylvania, to Cleveland, Ohio.

[697] *NYT,* Monday, October 22, 1928, 27:7. Variants: *KCT* gives "spoke last week at" in first sentence/*KCT* gives "Politics sneaked in" in seventh sentence/ *NYT* gives "the monuments possible" in seventh sentence, but *BDG, LAT,* and *KCT* have it as here/*LAT* ends eighth sentence "oil land corruption."

Coolidge delivered an address on October 20 at the dedication of the Fredericksburg and Spotsylvania County (Virginia) Battle Fields Memorial.

Smith's latest speech, in Chicago on October 19, concerned the recent cancellation of oil leases in the Salt Creek region of Wyoming, an action which echoed the Teapot Dome scandals of the Harding administration.

[698] *NYT,* Tuesday, October 23, 1928, 31:7.

For Senator George H. Moses see DT 587.

[699] *NYT,* Wednesday, October 24, 1928, 31:7. Variants: *BDG* and *LAT* give "Congress from" in second sentence/*KCT* gives "further come" and *LAT* gives "out for entire" in third sentence/*LAT* and *KCT* give "poorhouses is people" in fifth sentence/*KCT* gives "traffic here there" in sixth sntence.

[700] *NYT,* Thursday, October 25, 1928, 31:7. Variant: *NYT* gives "It is just" to begin .third sentence, but *BDG, LAT,* and *KCT* have it as here.

[701] *NYT,* Friday, October 26, 1928, 27:7. Variant: *LAT* begins fourth sentence "His last speech."

Smith spoke in Boston on October 24 before 31,000 partisans. He declared that the charge of "state socialism" raised against his policies by Hoover in a speech in New York City two days earlier was "subterfuge and camouflage."

[702] *NYT*, Saturday, October 27, 1928, 21:7.

For John Raskob see DT 612.

The Coolidges hosted movie stars Mary Pickford and Douglas Fairbanks at the White House on October 25. The film couple had had previous conversations about their income tax with officials in the Treasury Department.

[703] *NYT,* Monday, October 29, 1928, 25:7. Variant: *LAT* begins first sentence "Saturday some of the."

Smith made the statement, a hint at victory, in a speech in Philadelphia on October 28.

[704] *NYT,* Tuesday, October 30, 1928, 31:7. Variant: *BDG* gives "Of the all 'dumb' " to begin second sentence.

For Senator George H. Moses see DT 587.

[705] *NYT,* Wednesday, October 31, 1928, 33:7.

Smith's personality, religion, and ethnic background increasingly had become the major campaign issue.

[706] *NYT,* Thursday, November 1, 1928, 31:7. Variant: *KCT* gives "season next Tuesday, and about . . . 'the campaign is to' " in first and second sentences.

Both sides suffered in the campaign. Hoover was labeled a dangerous pacifist, an evolutionist, a "Negro-lover," and a "Negro-hater," while Smith faced the unproved charge of drunkenness, the alleged dangers of his Catholicism, and the backlash of sneers at his wife, Catherine.

[707] *NYT,* Friday, November 2, 1928, 27:7. Variants: *LAT* ends second sentence "sermons."/*NYT* gives "Those Nicaraguans" to begin third sentence, but *BDG, LAT,* and *KCT* have it as here.

The Nicaraguan government held a general election on October 28 with the assistance of the United States marines stationed in the country. United States and Nicaraguan officials lauded the work of the American troops.

[708] *NYT,* Saturday, November 3, 1928, 21:7. Variants: *KCT* omits fourth sentence/*NYT* gives "listen to the reason" in sixth sentence, but *BDG, LAT,* and *KCT* have it as here/*KCT* begins seventh sentence "I am for Curtis" omitting twelve preceding words/*BDG* gives "take turn about" in ninth sentence.

A seventeen-year-old stowaway had enlivened the return journey of the *Graf Zeppelin,* which landed in Germany on October 31.

Catherine "Katie" Smith, wife of Governor Smith. Many criticized the gracious and kind First Lady of New York for her lack of commitment to causes and to the rigid etiquette of social aspiration. She had been a chief target of a whispering campaign (see DT 706).

[709] *NYT,* Monday, November 5, 1928, 25:4-5. Variants: *BDG* gives "finally comes out" in first sentence/*NYT* ends third sentence "is the difference." and gives "have had any" in nineteenth sentence, but *BDG, LAT,* and *KCT* have it as here/*NYT* gives "have never lived off of tax payers," in twenty-second sentence, but *BDG, LAT,* and *KCT* have it as here/*NYT* gives "squawks, and alibies." in twenty-seventh sentence, but *BDG, LAT,* and *KCT* have it as here.

[710] *NYT,* Tuesday, November 6, 1928, 29:7. Variants: *KCT* gives "we fool" in second sentence/*LAT* begins fourth sentence "Vote for him" omitting first five words and omits fifth sentence/*BDG* gives "o'clock tomorrow night, but" in sixth sentence.

Norman Thomas, author, Socialist politician, and former Presbyterian minister; six-time Socialist party candidate for president, including in 1928.

[711] *NYT,* Wednesday, November 7, 1928, 27:7. Variants: *BDG* gives " 'Yom Kippur' " in first sentence/*BDG* ends eighth sentence "a woman's jury."

[712] *NYT,* Thursday, November 8, 1928, 31:7. Variants: *BDG* gives "right of franchise" in second sentence/*BDG* ends fifth sentence "back at work shop."

Hoover carried forty states, including five from the South, and won 444 electoral votes. His landslide carried for the Republicans both houses of Congress. The new Senate would have fifty-six Republicans, a net gain of seven, and the House of Representatives 267, an increase of thirty.

[713] *NYT*, Friday, November 9, 1928, 27:7. Variant: *LAT* gives "Offerings pouring" to begin first sentence.

In New York the race for governor was conceded on November 18 but was not official until December 11. The final count showed that Franklin D. Roosevelt, a Democrat (see DT 682), had edged Republican Albert Ottinger, 49.1 percent to 48.6 percent.

[714] *NYT*, Saturday, November 10, 1928, 19:7. Variants: *KCT* gives first sentence "When the politicians get . . . Tammany brown hats" and *BDG* gives "prosperity wisecracks, . . . hit on the reason" and *LAT* and *KCT* give "Raskob" in first sentence/*LAT* gives "been on the" in second sentence/*NYT* omits third and fourth sentences, but *BDG, LAT,* and *KCT* have them as here.

Coolidge's old duplex in Northampton, Massachusetts, was again available for rent. In 1906, when Coolidge first occupied it, he had paid $28 a month.

[715] *NYT*, Monday, November 12, 1928, 25:7. Variant: *NYT* gives date "Nov. 10."

Arkansas voters enacted the last antievolution statute in the nation in a referendum election on November 6. The United States Supreme Court declared the law unconstitutional in 1968. The Democratic ticket of Smith-Robinson carried the state with 60 percent of the vote.

Alanson Houghton, ambassador to Germany from 1922 to 1925 and to Great Britain from 1925 to 1929. Houghton had resigned his diplomatic post to run as a Republican for a United States Senate seat from New York. Coolidge permitted him to withdraw his resignation after the defeat.

[716] *NYT*, Tuesday, November 13, 1928, 33:7. Variants: *NYT* gives "And tonight when" to begin seventh sentence, but *BDG, LAT,* and *KCT* have it as here/*KCT* gives "of these three" in ninth sentence.

Coolidge addressed an Armistice Day service sponsored by the American Legion. In his speech he defended the United States foreign and military policies of the previous decade and the American record in World War I.

Hoover announced plans for a preinaugural good will tour of South America in late 1928.

Smith bid a formal farewell to active politics in a speech in New York City on November 13. In his message he urged his fellow Democrats to "carry on."

[717] *NYT*, Wednesday, November 14, 1928, 29:7. Variants: *LAT* gives "Coolidge's armament speech." in fourth sentence/*LAT* begins sixth sentence "In reply" omitting first three words.

Arnold Rothstein, a gambler and underworld figure, was shot in a New York hotel on November 14. He refused to name or describe his assailant and died two days later. No arrests had been made.

[718] *NYT*, Thursday, November 15, 1928, 31:7. Variants: *BDG* and *LAT* give "would like to" in fifth sentence/*NYT* gives "at night." to end ninth sentence, but *BDG, LAT,* and *KCT* have it as here.

Henry Fletcher (see DT 461)) returned to the United States after more than four years as ambassador to Italy. He attended a Latin American conference in Washington, D.C., and lent his assistance to the incoming Hoover administration.

[719] *NYT*, Friday, November 16, 1928, 27:7.

Walker ordered the New York Police Department to "make good" by November 19 in the Rothstein murder case or to admit failure in the investigation. Meanwhile, rumors surfaced that Rothstein had been a key figure in a nationwide narcotics ring.

Hoover announced that he intended to use the battleship U.S S. *Maryland* during his good will mission to South America.

720 *NYT,* Saturday, November 17, 1928, 21:7. Variant: *NYT* gives "a comedian" in first sentence, but *BDG, LAT,* and *KCT* have it as here.

The British steamship *Vestris,* bound from New York to Buenos Aires, sank 250 miles off the coast of the Virginia Capes on November 12. The gale-buffeted ship had developed leaks which led to a list of 32° and finally to its capsizing. At least 111 persons were drowned. Investigations raised questions about the seaworthiness of the craft and the competence of the captain and crew.

721 *NYT,* Monday, November 19, 1928, 21:7. Variants: *BDG* gives "always tune in on" in second sentence/*LAT* gives "last Friday night" and *KCT* gives "Saturday the old" in sixth sentence.

Coolidge addressed the annual convention of the National Grange on November 16 in Washington, D.C. In his speech he suggested his remedies for farm problems: a federal loan fund, cooperative marketing, and a protective tariff.

722 *NYT,* Tuesday, November 20, 1928, 33:7.

Chevrolet Motor Company recently had announced the development of a six-cylinder automobile. Democratic National Chairman John Raskob's possible return to General Motors remained a rumor three weeks later.

723 *NYT,* Wednesday, November 21, 1928, 31:7.

724 *NYT,* Thursday, November 22, 1928, 31:7. Variant: *BDG* omits third through seventh sentences.

The Coolidges' favorite cause was the Clarke Institute for the Deaf in Northampton, Massachusetts, which had employed the First Lady as teacher before her marriage. She and her husband continued to promote and support the school endowment campaign.

Roosevelt (see DTs 682 and 713) had suffered from the crippling effects of poliomyelitis since August of 1921. In early 1927 he formed the Georgia Warm Springs Foundation, a nonprofit institution which operated a hydrotherapeutic center at Warm Springs for the treatment of polio.

725 *NYT,* Friday, November 23, 1928, 27:7. Variants: *LAT* omits seventh sentence/*LAT* gives "the film weeklies" in eighth sentence/*LAT* begins P. S. "New Yorkers got . . . . "

726 *NYT,* Saturday, November 24, 1928, 19:7. Variant: *BDG* gives first sentence "Tomorrow minds will not be on politics. They will not be on national affairs. They will be on football."

Harvard defeated Yale, 17 to 0.

727 *NYT,* Monday, November 26, 1928, 27:7. Variants: *BDG* gives "is just about" in first sentence/*KCT* gives "of pip courses" in second sentence/*KCT* gives "A Yale man" in close.

728 *NYT,* Tuesday, November 27, 1928, 33:7. Variants: *LAT* gives "introduce you and we will finally" in eleventh sentence/*NYT* gives "need kiddings."

to end eleventh sentence, but *BDG, LAT,* and *KCT* have it as here/*KCT* gives "BILL." as signature.

For Paul Block see DT 668; for General John Pershing see DT 131; and for Bernard Baruch see DT 14.

Herbert B. Swope, journalist, humanitarian, and civic leader of New York; executive editor of the *New York World* from 1920 until his retirement in 1929; winner of a Pultizer Prize for journalism in 1917.

Charles Schwab, industrialist and philanthropist; chairman of the board of Bethlehem Steel Corporation from 1913 until his death in 1939.

729 *LAT,* Wednesday, November 28, 1928, I:1:2; heading from *NYT,* 29:7. Variants: *NYT* gives "Nov. 28." and *KCT* gives "Nov. 25 " in dateline/ *KCT* begins first sentence "Thursday is"/*LAT* gives "Coolidge has asked" in second sentence, but *BDG* and *KCT* have it as here/*BDG* gives "that were we aware" in second sentence/*NYT* omits second, fourth, fifth, and sixth sentences/ *KCT* gives "Democrat, I mean him . . . what's coming" in third sentence.

The Two Black Crows, George Moran and Charles Mack, entertained a generation from the 1910s to the mid-1930s with blackface acts on stage, in motion pictures, and especially through recordings and radio.

730 *NYT,* Thursday, November 29, 1928, 29:7. Variant: *NYT* gives "the result of" in the fourth sentence, but *BDG, LAT,* and *KCT* have it as here.

The *New York World,* a staunchly Democratic journal, supported Smith for the presidency in 1928.

For the *Literary Digest* poll see DTs 677 and 695.

731 *NYT,* Friday, November 30, 1928, 25:7. Variants: *KCT* gives "men-of-war" in first sentence/*KCT* gives "against a bunch . . of Levi overalls." in second sentence/*LAT* begins third sentence "The old"/*KCT* gives "These salmon jiggers from" and *BDG* and *LAT* give "salmon diggers from" in third sentence.

New York University lost to Oregon State University, 25 to 13, in a Thanksgiving Day football contest.

Man o'War won twenty of twenty-one races from 1919 to 1920 and was voted the number one horse in a half-century poll of the Associated Press in 1950. He established five American track records during his brief racing career.

732 *NYT,* Saturday, December 1, 1928, 17:7. Variants: *KCT* ends second sentence "Massachusetts."/*NYT* gives "come one, patriots," in P. S., but *BDG, LAT,* and *KCT* have it as here/*KCT* gives "protect our country." in P. S.

733 *NYT,* Monday, December 3, 1928, 27:7. Variants: *KCT* gives "Stanford, today" in third sentence/*NYT* and *LAT* omit sixth sentence, but *BDG* and *KCT* have it as here.

Stanford University defeated the United States Military Academy, 26 to 0, in a football game in New York City on December 1. In 1927 a disagreement over eligibility requirements led to the discontinuance of the Army-Navy football series for two years The Navy had not won since 1921.

The University of Southern California beat Notre Dame, 27 to 14.

Hoover carried Virginia by more than 13,000 votes in November. Coolidge had little success while hunting quail near Staunton, Virginia, on December 1.

734 *NYT,* Tuesday, December 4, 1928, 31:7. Variants: *BDG* gives "has notified him that" and *KCT* gives "has notified that" in third sentence.

[735] *NYT,* Wednesday, December 5, 1928, 31:7.

Coolidge delivered his annual "State of the Nation" message before a joint session of Congress on December 4.

[736] *NYT,* Thursday, December 6, 1928, 31:7. Variant: *LAT* gives "My December message" in first sentence.

[737] *NYT,* Friday, December 7, 1928, 29:7.

The stock market boomed after Hoover's election, sending prices and trading to all-time highs. A sharp but temporary break in prices began the day of this DT; the *New York Times* averages fell 2.75 points in a week.

[738] *NYT,* Saturday, December 8, 1928, 19:7.

Hoover, in the course of his good will tour of Latin America, had visited Honduras, El Salvador, Nicaragua, Costa Rica, Ecuador, and Peru within his first twelve days abroad.

Investigators from Britain and the United States filed a preliminary report on the sinking of the *Vestris* (see DT 720) on December 6. They placed primary responsibility for the disaster on the captain of the ship, who was one of the 111 persons lost. The report also suggested that the crew delayed in sending a distress signal in order to avoid high salvage claims.

[739] *NYT,* Monday, December 10, 1928, 27:7.

All-American collegiate football teams were being selected as the season ended.

[740] *NYT,* Tuesday, December 11, 1928, 31:7. Variants: *KCT* gives "he asked for another" in second sentence/*NYT* gives "start to" in seventh sentence, but *BDG, LAT,* and *KCT* have it as here/*BDG* gives "start trying to meddle it" in seventh sentence.

Coolidge, at the request of the *St. Louis Post-Dispatch,* contributed an article for the semicentennial edition of the paper, pointing to the need for a "rural White House," easily accessible by automobile from Washington, D.C.

[741] *NYT,* Wednesday, December 12, 1928, 34:5. Variants: *LAT* gives "motors, fitted to light" in first sentence/*LAT* and *KCT* give "They know planes" in third sentence/*NYT* gives "might be wrecked." to end fifth sentence, but *BDG, LAT,* and *KCT* have it as here/*KCT* gives "our fathers." in sixth sentence.

Prince Edward (see DT 165) was on a good will and pleasure tour of Africa when his father, King George V of England, became seriously ill. The prince returned to London by rail and ship. Twice during the 6,425-mile journey he declined offers of air transportation.

[742] *NYT,* Thursday, December 13, 1928, 29:7. Variants: *NYT* gives "offence in selling . . . Michigan may send the mother" in first sentence, but *BDG, LAT,* and *KCT* have it as here/*KCT* gives "ten kids . . . that it is pure." in fourth sentence.

A judge in Michigan sentenced Etta Mae Miller to life imprisonment under the state habitual criminal law. She had been convicted for selling two pints of liquor. Four of her children, the youngest being thirteen years old, were still living at home, and her husband was serving a two-year prison sentence. Similar cases led to modification of the habitual criminal statute.

[743] *NYT,* Friday, December 14, 1928, 36:3. Variants: *LAT* gives "New York is to have a new" in sixth sentence/*NYT* gives "this one," in eighth sentence, but *BDG, LAT,* and *KCT* have it as here/*LAT* gives "he will be just" in eighth sentence.

Hostilities flared on December 7 between Bolivian and Paraguayan troops in the Chaco, a disputed region along the border of the two countries.

Argentine police prepared for the arrival of President-elect Hoover by arresting scores of persons believed active in previous anti-American demonstrations, including protests against the executions of Sacco and Vanzetti. The police also uncovered a plot to bomb Hoover's special train while en route from Chile and arrested two anarchists.

Mayor Walker of New York fired Joseph Warren as Police Commissioner and appointed Grover Whalen, Walker's official greeter, to the position on December 17. Warren had been accused of poor administrative control and failure to act speedily on recent murders in the city, especially in the Rothstein case (see DT 717).

[744] *NYT,* Saturday, December 15, 1928, 17:2. Variants: *KCT* gives "his own doctor" in third sentence/*NYT* omits first, second, third, and fourth sentences, but *BDG, LAT,* and *KCT* have them as here.

Prince Edward's household physician, Sir Hugh Rigby, inserted a tube into King George's chest cavity in order to drain accumulated poisons from the blood stream. The monarch later recovered from his illness.

For Bolivia-Paraguay relations see DT 743.

The United States Supreme Court earlier had decreed that the western border of Oklahoma be redrawn because of a surveying error. A special commission revealed on December 8 that Texas would gain 25,000 acres as a result of the settlement of the dispute.

[745] *NYT,* Monday, December 17, 1928, 27:7. Variants: *BDG* gives "of the line" in second sentence/*KCT* gives "locate it." in fourth sentence/*KCT* gives "filibusters held" in fifth sentence.

A bill authorizing construction of Boulder Dam passed the Senate on December 14, and prospects were considered good for passage by the House.

The Kellogg-Briand Pact (see DT 479), currently before the Senate Foreign Relations committee, faced a possible interpretive resolution by Moses of New Hampshire and Reed of Missouri. The treaty had no irreconcilable opposition, but a few critics feared that it would hinder passage of naval appropriations.

[746] *NYT,* Tuesday, December 18, 1928, 33:7. Variants: *LAT* gives "today but I get . . . it. Brisbane says:" in first and second sentences/*KCT* omits first sentence/*NYT* gives "taking aeroplane." to end third sentence, but *BDG, LAT,* and *KCT* have it as here/*BDG, LAT,* and *KCT* give "and improvement." in eighth sentence.

For Arthur Brisbane see DT 204.

Stanley Baldwin, Conservative prime minister of Britain from 1923 to 1924, 1924 to 1929, and 1935 to 1937.

[747] *NYT,* Wednesday, December 19, 1928, 25:2. Variants: *BDG* and *LAT* end first sentence "armies."/*NYT* omits fifth sentence, but *BDG, LAT,* and *KCT* have it as here/*BDG* gives "Let the winners meet" in sixth sentence

The dispute over the Gran Chaco region heightened as Bolivian troops captured Paraguayan forts along the frontier and both countries mobilized for war.

Rickard recalled that during his career as an international cattle buyer he had encountered hostile Bolivians while driving a herd through Paraguay in 1913. The president of Paraguay offered him an army to lead against the troublemakers, but Rickard reluctantly declined.

748 *NYT,* Thursday, December 20, 1928, 24:3.

King Amanullah and Queen Souriya fled the capital of Afghanistan in the face of a revolt by the army, which the king had neglected to pay. Unrest had been building throughout the country over the monarch's introduction of modern reforms and his wife's announced intention to abolish the traditional seclusion of women. Amanullah was forced to abdicate in January.

749 *NYT,* Friday, December 21, 1928, 30:5. Variants: *NYT* gives "Some nuts have got . . . reached your home town" to begin first sentence, but *BDG, LAT,* and *KCT* have it as here/*LAT* gives "New York to go bareheaded" in first sentence/*NYT* gives "Now, these nuts have worn something on their heads ever since their mothers tied hoods under their chins, but they have never attracted any attention, so they let it rain down their necks to show people that they bathe." as second sentence, but *BDG, LAT,* and *KCT* have it as here.

750 *NYT,* Saturday, December 22, 1928, 17:2. Variant: *LAT* gives origin "WASHINGTON."

A compromise initiated by Senator Borah insured that both the cruiser appropriation bill and the Kellogg-Briand Pact would be considered by the Senate on the first day after the Christmas recess.

751 *NYT,* Monday, December 24, 1928, 10:3. Variants: *KCT* ends second sentence "his book."/*BDG* gives "but its just the 26th of" in sixth sentence.

Although Senate approval of the Kellogg-Briand Pact before the holidays appeared impossible, a delegation of Republican senators assured Coolidge that he could sign the treaty before leaving office.

Bolivia and Paraguay had ceased military action pending attempts at arbitration.

Coolidge signed the Boulder Dam bill despite an appeal from the Arizona state legislature that he veto it. Some Arizonans hinted at court tests of the law.

Hoover's cabinet choices aroused concern among members of the Republican "Old Guard."

752 *NYT,* Tuesday, December 25, 1928, 31:2. Variants: *LAT* gives "to you Mr. and Mrs. Hoover. Herbert, you" in fourth and fifth sentences/*BDG* and *LAT* give "away out on the" in fifth sentence/*KCT* gives "you and Mrs. Charley [and *BDG*] Dawes, Charley. Lots" in seventh and eighth sentences/*LAT* gives "the literary test" in tenth sentence.

753 *NYT,* Wednesday, December 26, 1928, 19:7. Variants: *NYT* gives "disposition." to end second sentence, but *BDG, LAT,* and *KCT* have it as here/*BDG* gives "conscience, we feed 'em" in sixth and seventh sentence.

754 *NYT,* Thursday, December 27, 1928, 25:7. Variants: *NYT* gives "public man's." in third sentence, but *BDG, LAT,* and *KCT* have it as here/*KCT* gives "up here and put" in fifth sentence.

New York Police Commissioner Grover Whalen (see DT 743) initiated a roundup of criminals which netted 183 arrests on December 24. He then staged a three-hour line-up attended by 500 detectives. The whole operation required reserve forces and extra police vehicles to transport the prisoners.

[755] *NYT,* Friday, December 28, 1928, 25:7. Variants: *BDG* ends fourth sentence "your unemployed?"/*KCT* gives "A Californian suggested" in sixth sentence.

The awards were announced on December 26 in the contest for the best plan to make Prohibition more effective (see DT 651). The winner of the first prize of $25,000, Major Chester Mills of New York, suggested that authorities prevent the diversion and criminal use of industrial alcohol. Another prize of $1,000 went to Malcolm Almack, a school boy from Palo Alto, California.

[756] *NYT,* Saturday, December 29, 1928, 19:7. Variants: *LAT* gives "couldn't have hit" in first sentence/*KCT* gives "old Negro fellow," and *BDG* gives "the turkey up" in second sentence/*NYT* gives "It was" to begin third sentence, but *BDG, LAT,* and *KCT* have it as here/*LAT* gives "Washington makes" in fourth sentence.

The Coolidges enjoyed a post-Christmas vacation at the Georgia estate of automobile engineer Howard Coffin. "Old Pete," a black employee of Coffin, conducted the hunt and called the turkeys for the president, who killed two of the birds.

[757] *NYT,* Monday, December 31, 1928, 9:2. Variants: *LAT* gives "New Year statements, please" in first sentence/*LAT* gives "Wildcoats" in ninth sentence/*BDG* gives "who were prosperous." in tenth sentence.

[758] *NYT,* Tuesday, January 1, 1929, 61:3.

[759] *NYT,* Wednesday, January 2, 1929, 29:7.

[760] *NYT,* Thursday, January 3, 1929, 31:7.

Hearst offered a prize of $25,000 for the best plan to replace the Eighteenth Amendment with a fairer measure to enforce Prohibition. His proposal was in answer to William Durant's earlier contest to find a scheme to make the amendment work (see DTs 651 and 755).

[761] *NYT,* Friday, January 4, 1929, 27:7. Variants: *NYT* and *KCT* give "writer I would" in second sentence, but *BDG* and *LAT* have it as here/*LAT* and *KCT* give "boys, even . . . wrong. His" in sixth and seventh sentences.

At the annual Rose Bowl classic on January 1, a crowd of 67,000 and a radio audience of millions witnessed one of the most startling plays in collegiate football history. After recovering a Georgia Tech fumble, Roy Riegels, a center for the University of California, became confused and began to run for his own goal line. He was stopped short of the end zone by a teammate but then was tackled on the one-yard line. On the next play Georgia Tech scored a two-point safety and went on to win the game, 8 to 7.

Bruce Barton, sloganeer, best-selling author, staunch Republican, and founder of one of the most successful advertising agencies in the United States, Batten, Barton, Durstine, and Osborn.

Glenn Frank, editor-in-chief of *Century* magazine from 1921 to 1925, president of the University of Wisconsin from 1925 to 1937, and well-traveled lecturer and prolific writer.

[762] *NYT,* Saturday, January 5, 1929, 21:7. Variants: *BDG, LAT,* and *KCT* give "bigger reception" in third sentence.

Old Point Comfort, located on the north shore of Hampton Roads near Hampton, Virginia, had been the site of a federal military installation since the 1820s. The U.S.S. *Utah,* with Hoover aboard, landed at Old Point Comfort on January 5, following the president-elect's Latin American tour.

President and Mrs. Coolidge spent the holiday season as the guests of Mr. and Mrs. Howard Coffin on Sapelo Island, Georgia (see DT 756).

The British, French, Italian, and Belgian governments had agreed on the appointment of a committee of experts to supervise reparation payments from Germany. American nominees for the committee included Owen Young, lawyer and businessman, and Seymour Gilbert, American agent general for reparation payments.

763 *NYT,* Monday, January 7, 1929, 31:7.

George "Tex" Rickard, sports promoter (see DT 310), died on January 6.

764 *NYT,* Tuesday, January 8, 1929, 33:7. Variants: *BDG, LAT,* and *KCT* give "it began to look" in first sentence/*LAT* gives "and were going" and *BDG* gives "and considered going" and *KCT* gives "They had broken all . . . and were going . . . senator made talking . . . Dam." in second sentence.

A United States Army plane, the *Question Mark,* with a crew of four commanded by Major Carl Spatz, set a world endurance record of 150 hours, forty minutes, and fifteen seconds in the air. The record attempt began on January 1 and ended six days later when a motor of the large Fokker monoplane failed.

Hoover conferred with Coolidge and congressional leaders and interviewed possible cabinet appointees following his return from South America.

765 *NYT,* Wednesday, January 9, 1929, 33:7. Variants: *NYT* gives "one a year" in second sentence, but *BDG, LAT,* and *KCT* have it as here/*BDG* omits tenth and eleventh sentences.

Ratification of the Kellogg-Briand Pact appeared certain, although some Senate Democrats were inclined to minimize the importance of the treaty as a means of preserving peace.

766 *NYT,* Thursday, January 10, 1929, 31:7. Variants: *KCT* gives "big motor show" in first sentence/*LAT* gives "is dozens" in third sentence.

The New York Automobile Show, held annually in either Madison Square Garden or the Grand Central Palace, was one of the greatest industrial expositions in the country. In the current show accessories like vacuum brakes, wire wheels, and directional signals attracted wide attention.

767 *NYT,* Friday, January 11, 1929, 25:7. Variants: *BDG* gives "go as" and *KCT* gives "go to" in fourth sentence/*KCT* gives "that will tell" in fifth sentence.

Harry S. New, postmaster general of the United States from 1923 to 1929. While postmaster general New instituted air mail service.

William J. Donovan, assistant to the United States attorney general from 1925 to 1929. Donovan, a New York Republican, was under consideration for attorney general but did not receive the appointment.

768 *NYT,* Saturday, January 12, 1929, 19:7. Variants: *BDG* gives "up to. Be like" and *LAT* and *KCT* give "up to. It would be like" in second sentence.

A jury in York County, Pennsylvania, returned a verdict of quilty against fourteen-year-old John Curry for his part in the murder of Nelson Rehmeyer, recluse farmer and suspected practitioner of witchcraft. In his trial Curry admitted that he held a strong interest in witchcraft and that he had participated in the crime in order to remove a "hex" inflicted upon a friend. Curry, his friend, and a third accomplice received sentences of life imprisonment.

Defense attorneys claimed that York County officials and citizens were especially harsh on their clients in an effort to lessen the reputation of the region as a center of witchcraft and voodooism.

769 *NYT,* Monday, January 14, 1929, 25:7. Variant: *LAT* gives "but committee" in first sentence.

A delegation of United States officials conferred with Canadian authorities in an attempt to halt the smuggling of liquor across the international border. Little progress was made during the meetings; Canadian officials suggested that the United States strengthen its own laws before seeking aid from other countries.

770 *NYT,* Tuesday, January 15, 1929, 31:7. Variant: *LAT* gives "received much praise" in sixth sentence.

The Senate Appropriations Committee recommended a bill authorizing an additional $25,000,000 for enforcement of Prohibition. Senator William Harris of Georgia, sponsor of the bill, believed that the money was needed to prove to critics that Prohibition could be enforced when sufficient funds were provided.

J(ohn) P(ierpont) Morgan, Jr., chairman of the board of J. P. Morgan & Company, one of the most influential banking houses in the world, and of United States Steel Corporation. Reports circulated on January 14 that Morgan would be appointed to the European War Debts and Reparations Committee (see DT 762). Two days later his appointment and that of Owen Young were approved by the member nations.

771 *NYT,* Wednesday, January 16, 1929, 27:7. Variant: *BDG* gives "relief proposition or birth" in fifth sentence.

The Kellogg-Briand Pact was ratified by the Senate on January 15 with only one dissenting vote and with the vigorous support of Senator Borah. Senators Moses and Reed voted for ratification despite their objections to the possible interference by the treaty with the Monroe Doctrine and the American defense system.

772 *NYT,* Thursday, January 17, 1929, 27:7. Variants: *KCT* gives "now is" in first sentence and "other career." in last sentence.

773 *NYT,* Friday, January 18, 1929, 25:7.

Smith appealed over the radio for contributions from rank-and-file Democrats to liquidate a campaign deficit of $1,500,000.

774 *NYT,* Saturday, January 19, 1929, 19:7.

Smith was elected a director of the County Trust Company of New York on January 17. A few days later Governor and Mrs. Smith, Mr. and Mrs. John Raskob, and other friends left for an extended vacation in Georgia and Florida.

For Augusto Sandino, Nicaraguan guerilla leader, see DT 504; for actress Peggy Hopkins Joyce see DT 613.

Hoover also was bound for a vacation in Florida with family and friends.

For evangelist Aimee McPherson see DT 56; for comedian Ben Turpin see DT 118.

Hoover won pluralities in Florida, Virginia, and North Carolina but ran second in Georgia and South Carolina.

775 *NYT,* Monday, January 21, 1929, 23:7. Variants: *LAT* gives "bureau tomorrow for" in first sentence/*NYT* gives "An applicant" in third sentence, but *BDG* and *LAT* have it as here/*KCT* did not print the DT.

776 *NYT,* Tuesday, January 22, 1929, 31:7. Variants: *LAT* gives "time, in New York, he" and *KCT* gives "like a motor car." in second sentence/*LAT* gives "us. Here . . . York taxicabs" in fifth and sixth sentences.

Whalen, the new police commissioner in New York City (see DT 743 and 754), hoped to remedy traffic snarls in the theater district with new restrictions on parking and jaywalking.

777 *NYT,* Wednesday, January 23, 1929, 27:7.

Ambassador Morrow was favored by several Republican leaders for the position of secretary of state, but Henry Stimson of New York ultimately was appointed to the post.

A number of prominent individuals, including Hoover, Morrow, and Secretary of the Interior Hubert Work (see DT 608), were vacationing in Florida with their families in January.

William "Young" Stribling, a youthful, flashy heavyweight boxer who fought professionally from 1921 until his death in 1933. Stribling was scheduled to fight Jack Sharkey in Miami Beach on February 27. Jack Dempsey had replaced the late Tex Rickard as promoter of the bout.

778 *NYT,* Thursday, January 24, 1929, 29:7.

The Senate passed the Harris bill on January 22, providing an additional fund of $24,000,000 for prohibition enforcement (see DT 770). Secretary of the Treasury Mellon claimed that the administration did not need the extra money, and some observers viewed it as a potential embarrassment for President-elect Hoover. On March 1 a House-Senate conference committee finally agreed on a figure of $3,177,914.

Esther Evans Wilson, a New York socialite, was charged with the near-fatal shooting of her estranged husband, Dallett Wilson, an attorney and a vice chairman of the Republican National Committee. She was convicted of assault and given a three-year prison sentence.

779 *NYT,* Friday, January 25, 1929, 25:7. Variants: *KCT* gives "twenty-four to." in first sentence/*NYT* gives "Don't sick" in fifth sentence, but *BDG, LAT,* and *KCT* have it as here/*KCT* gives "Lehman." in sixth sentence.

For John Raskob see DT 612.

William Kenny, a wealthy New York building contractor and boyhood friend of Governor Smith. Kenny was a principal contributor to Smith's presidential campaign in 1928.

Herbert H. Lehman, a partner in Lehman Brothers, New York investment bankers. Lehman chaired the finance committee of the Democratic party during Smith's campaign. He later served as governor of New York and United States senator.

Bishop James Cannon, Jr., a leading prohibitionist and reformer from Virginia and an official in the Methodist Episcopal Church, South. Cannon broke with the Democratic party to oppose the candidacy of Smith. His campaign efforts in the South were regarded as a chief factor in Hoover's success in the region.

780 *NYT,* Saturday, January 26, 1929, 19:7. Variant: *NYT* omits third sentence, but *BDG, LAT,* and *KCT* have it as here.

The New York Stock Exchange announced on January 25 the creation of 275 additional seats to handle the increased business of the market. It was estimated that the seats would sell for $625,000 each; proceeds were to be distributed among the 1,100 current members.

[781] *NYT*, Monday, January 28, 1929, 25:7. Variants: *LAT* gives "reception tomorrow to" and *BDG* and *KCT* give "reception again tomorrow" in first sentence/*LAT* ends third sentence "amateurs."

George Fried, maritime officer. In January 1926 while commander of the S.S. *President Roosevelt,* Captain Fried saved the entire crew of a sinking British freighter in the stormy North Atlantic. On January 23, 1929, Fried, now commanding officer of the S.S. *America,* directed the rescue of the crew of the Italian freighter *Florida* in the Atlantic. He was given a hero's welcome to New York City.

Harry Manning, chief officer of the *America.* Manning commanded the lifeboat crew which effected the rescue.

[782] *NYT,* Tuesday, January 29, 1929, 31:7. Variants: *BDG, LAT,* and *KCT* give "can be the most" in second sentence.

[783] *NYT,* Wednesday, January 30, 1929, 25:7. Variants: *KCT* gives "along as referee;" in seventh sentence/*LAT* did not print the DT but printed the following for January 30:

*Will Rogers Remarks:*

*New York, Jan. 29.—To the Editor of the Times: Got a fine friendly wire from Alphonzo Bell. He wants to trade cement stock for Fertilizer preferred. I was never afraid of Bell. He is all right. It's the gang a man gets in with that is disastrous. I would hate to see a friend go into the cement business as bad as I would into politics. So let's let the cement lay awhile. It's not what one would call exactly perishable and it will stay in there and in years to come somebody will figure out a way to take it out with a magnet.*

*WILL ROGERS.*

Smith and Hoover met informally and cordially at Hoover's vacation residence in Florida on January 29; it was their first personal contact.

For William Kenny see DT 779; for John Raskob see DT 612.

Alphonzo E. Bell, Southern California farmer, land developer, and oilman; president of Alphonzo E. Bell Company from 1922 until his death in 1947.

[784] *NYT,* Thursday, January 31, 1929, 13:2.

Coolidge agreed to the need for fifteen additional cruisers being considered by Congress but contended that their construction should be delayed indefinitely because of recent naval limitation agreements with other countries. He later dropped his opposition, and Congress passed the necessary appropriations.

Senator Borah called for an international conference on maritime law. He claimed that a recodification was necessary to insure the rights of neutrals and the freedom of the seas in wartime.

[785] *NYT,* Friday, February 1, 1929, 25:7. Variant: *BDG* gives "here. After coming . . . radio, it's" in fifth and sixth sentences.

Albert Einstein, German physicist who developed the theory of relativity in 1905. He recently had published his latest work, a six-page booklet of mathematical formulae.

[786] *NYT,* Saturday, February 2, 1929, 17:7. Variants: *KCT* gives "Mellon tried to use it" in second sentence/*KCT* gives "guaranty" in fourth sentence.

The United States Navy ranked second in the world to Great Britain in total tonnage of naval vessels in 1927.

787 *NYT,* Monday, February 4, 1929, 23:7. Variant: *KCT* gives "fish" in fourth sentence.

Coolidge spoke on February 1 at the dedication of the Edward W. Bok Bird Sanctuary and Singing Tower at Mountain Lake, Florida. The speech marked Coolidge's last extended public address as chief executive.

Hoover landed a forty-five-pound sailfish on January 31 while fishing near Long Key, Florida.

Carter Glass, Democratic United States senator from Virginia from 1920 to 1946.

788 *NYT,* Tuesday, February 5, 1929, 29:7. Variant: *LAT* omits P. S

The likelihood that William Donovan (see DT 767) would be selected as attorney general had risen and fallen repeatedly. The latest rumor held that his selection was uncertain. The appointment ultimately went to James D. Mitchell of Minnesota.

Joseph R. Grundy, woolen manufacturer and president of the Pennsylvania Manufacturers Association from 1909 to 1930. Grundy was an ardent supporter of an upward revision of the tariff.

789 *NYT,* Wednesday, February 6, 1929, 27:7. Variants: *KCT* gives "countries We freed sugar." and *LAT* gives "freed grow" in second sentence/*BDG* gives "untariffed, also hides and the bone steaks" in third sentence/*NYT* omits fifth sentence, but *BDG, LAT,* and *KCT* have it as here/*LAT* omits P. S.

Reed Smoot, Republican United States senator from Utah from 1903 to 1933. Smoot, an expert on tariff, taxation, and public finance, was a proponent of high protective tariffs and a duty on Philippine sugar.

790 *NYT,* Thursday, February 7, 1929, 27:7. Variants: *BDG* gives "has tied the . . . right on" in fifth sentence/*LAT* omits P. S.

The Senate passed a bill on February 5 which authorized construction of fifteen cruisers. The measure was sent to the White House for President Coolidge's signature.

Senator Heflin had offered an amendment to the cruiser bill which provided that the church flag should not be flown above the Stars and Stripes on naval vessels. The church or chaplin's flag usually flew above the American flag at divine services, but Heflin contended that the flag bore a Roman cross and thus was a symbol of papal influence. The amendment failed, 68 to 10.

791 *NYT,* Friday, February 8, 1929, 23:7. Variants: *LAT* omits third sentence/*NYT* omits fourth, fifth, and sixth sentences, but *BDG, LAT,* and *KCT* have it as here/*LAT* omits P. S.

The New York Aviation Show opened at the Grand Central Palace on February 6. Aviators Post 743 of the American Legion sponsored the exposition, the first aeronautical show in New York since 1922

Grundy (see DT 788) was not related to Rockefeller. Rogers probably referred to the comparable economic and social position of the two businessmen.

792 *NYT,* Saturday, February 9, 1929, 17:7. Variants: *NYT* gives "free didn't look good to me." in sixth sentence, but *BDG, LAT,* and *KCT* have it as here/*LAT* omits P. S.

The New York Stock Exchange reported a sharp drop in prices on February 7. A warning from the Federal Reserve Board about the tremendous expansion of speculative loans and an announcement of an increase in the discount rate offered by the Bank of England were thought to have caused the decline. At the same time the exchange closed temporarily as a result of an influenza epidemic among its staff members.

Pope Pius XI announced that a concordat would be signed on February 11 between the Holy See and the government of Italy. The agreement provided for the establishment of an independent Vatican State and formed the basis for all subsequent relations between the two parties.

[793] *NYT,* Monday, February 11, 1929, 21:7.

Hoover visited Fort Myers, Florida, on February 9 to join in a tribute to Thomas Edison on the occasion of the inventor's eighty-second birthday.

[794] *NYT,* Tuesday, February 12, 1929, 25:7. Variants: *LAT* gives "estate talk, with Hoover's influence. Chances" in third and fourth sentences.

Edison, anxious about the declining American supply of natural rubber, had devoted many years researching the subject. He had found more than 1,200 American plants which yielded rubber but only forty worth cultivating on a large scale.

Ford and Firestone (see DT 669) were among the guests at Edison's birthday celebration.

[795] *NYT,* Wednesday, February 13, 1929, 23:7. Variants: *BDG* ends first sentence "today." omitting last threee words/*KCT* gives "schools in . . . boys—lots . . . prominent comebacks—told" in second sentence/*KCT* gives "years here" in fourth sentence/*BDG* gives "would improve every" and *KCT* gives "would aid every" in fifth sentence.

[796] *NYT,* Thursday, February 14, 1929, 29:7.

For J. P. Morgan see DT 770; for Owen Young see DT 762.

Charles Lindbergh and Anne Morrow, daughter of Ambassador and Mrs. Dwight W. Morrow, (see DT 366), announced their engagement on February 12. The couple was married on May 27, 1929, at Englewood, New Jersey.

[797] *NYT,* Friday, February 15, 1929, 23:7. Variants: *BDG* and *KCT* omit second sentence/*KCT* gives "want to" in fourth sentence.

[798] *NYT,* Saturday, February 16, 1929, 19:7. Variant: *KCT* gives "If it's too study . . . behavior, Chicago" in third and fourth sentences.

Officials at Yale University announced on February 14 the establishment of the Institute of Human Relations, a unique interdisciplinary endeavor to study human behavior. The institute was founded with gifts and subsidies totaling $7,500,000.

[799] *NYT,* Monday, February 18, 1929, 25:7. Variants: *NYT* gives "don't want" in fifth sentence, but *BDG, LAT,* and *KCT* have it as here/*NYT* gives "Lake Ochebee" in seventh sentence, but *BDG, LAT,* and *KCT* have it as here.

Coolidge submitted plans on February 16 to delay construction of new cruisers until the beginning of the next fiscal year on July 1. Pro-navy senators denounced the president's proposals and voted $770,000 to begin work on the ships.

The Greece Relief and Refuge Debt Agreement, executed on May 10, 1929, concerned a principal indebtedness of $48,236,629 to be refunded over a period of sixty-two years.

Florida state officials honored Hoover at a dinner in Clewiston, Florida, on February 16. They called for federal funding of the Lake Okeechobee flood prevention and reclamation project.

800 *NYT,* Tuesday, February 19, 1929, 31:7.

Reed, an antiprohibitionist who was ending his career in the Senate on March 4, called Prohibition an "hypocrisy" during Senate debate on February 16. He also mentioned alleged drinking among dry leaders at the national political conventions and threatened to publish a list of men who drank but voted dry.

801 *NYT,* Wednesday, February 20, 1929, 27:7. Variants: *BDG* gives "Lindbergh, the only one" and *LAT* and *KCT* give "the only one" in third sentence.

802 *NYT,* Thursday, February 21, 1929, 29:7. Variant: *KCT* gives "where a Denver paper" in second sentence.

Frederick Bonfils, owner and publisher of the *Denver Post,* offered Coolidge $75,000 a year to become editor of the newspaper. The position would require that Coolidge reside in Colorado.

803 *NYT,* Friday, February 22, 1929, 23:7. Variants: *KCT* gives "No Republicans, no income" in sixth sentence/*LAT* gives "Tom Heflin" in eighth sentence.

804 *NYT,* Saturday, February 23, 1929, 15:7. Variants: *BDG* and *KCT* give "Wichita today." in second sentence.

Lindbergh had been appointed technical adviser to the aeronautics branch of the Department of Commerce, with his appointment so arranged that it would not interfere with his other contracts.

New York City received a seven-inch snowfall during a twenty-four-hour period from February 20 to 22. The storm clogged traffic and public transportation systems and resulted in the deaths of three persons.

805 *NYT,* Monday, February 25, 1929, 25:7.

806 *NYT,* Tuesday, February 26, 1929, 29:7. Variants: *BDG* and *LAT* give "an automobile.' " in fourth sentence.

Lindbergh flew from Abilene, Texas, to Mexico City on February 24 to visit his fianceé, Anne Morrow, and her family.

A prowler entered the Florida vacation residence of Jack Dempsey on the night of February 24 and fired a shot which missed the former heavyweight champion by only a few feet.

807 *NYT,* Wednesday, February 27, 1929, 25:7. Variant: *KCT* omits ninth sentence.

808 *NYT,* Thursday, February 28, 1929, 29:7. Variants: *BDG* and *LAT* give "and came around" in first sentence/*LAT* gives "New is." in second sentence.

For Harry New see DT 767.

William D. Mitchell, United States attorney general from 1929 to 1933. Mitchell was appointed attorney general because of his known constitutional support of Prohibition. Hoover had announced that he intended to transfer the enforcement of Prohibition from the Treasury to the Justice Department.

[809] *NYT,* Friday, March 1, 1929, 27:4-5. Variants: *KCT* gives "just coming down" in first sentence/*KCT* gives "miles, some persons" in fifth sentence/*KCT* gives "else's life—just" in seventh and eighth sentences/*KCT* gives "So, brave Lindy, you're . . . lot. And brave little" in twelfth, thirteenth, and fourteenth sentences.

Lindbergh lost a wheel of his aircraft during a flight from an unknown point in Mexico to Mexico City. He avoided a major catastrophe when he attempted to land his crippled plane on the one remaining wheel but suffered a shoulder dislocation during the maneuver. His fianceé and flight companion, Anne Morrow, was unhurt in the mishap. The next day, February 28, the couple made three short flights in a borrowed plane.

[810] *NYT,* Saturday, March 2, 1929, 19:7.

Mrs. Coolidge received an antique desk from members of the Senate Ladies Luncheon Club.

[811] *LAT,* Monday, March 4, 1929, 1:8. *NYT* and *KCT* did not print the DT.

Photographs of Lindbergh's accident (see DT 809) first appeared in newspapers in New York on March 2 via wirephoto from Mexico City.

[812] *NYT,* Tuesday, March 5, 1929, 33:7.

# INDEX